Charming Beauties and Frightful Beasts

Charming Beauties and Frightful Beasts

Non-Human Animals in South Asian Myth, Ritual and Folklore

Edited by
Fabrizio M. Ferrari and Thomas Dähnhardt

equinox

SHEFFIELD UK BRISTOL CT

Published by Equinox Publishing Ltd.

UK: Kelham House, 3 Lancaster Street, Sheffield, S3 8AF
USA: ISD, 70 Enterprise Drive, Bristol, CT 06010

www.equinoxpub.com

First published in book form in 2013. The chapters in this book were previously published in the journal Religions of South Asia, Volume 7, Number 1, 2013.

British Library Cataloguing-in-Publication Data
A catalogue record for this book is available from the British Library.

Library of Congress Cataloging-in-Publication Data
Charming beauties and frightful beasts : non-human animals in south asian myth, ritual and folklore / edited by Fabrizio M. Ferrari and Thomas Dahnhardt.
pages cm
Includes bibliographical references and index.
ISBN 978-1-908049-58-2 (hb) -- ISBN 978-1-908049-59-9 (pb)
1. South Asia--Religion. 2. South Asia--Religious life and customs. 3. Animals--Religious aspects. 4. Animals--Folklore. 5. Animals--Mythology--South Asia. I. Ferrari, Fabrizio M. II. Dahnhardt, Thomas, 1964-
BL1055.C43 2013
202'.12--dc23

2013014202

ISBN: 978 1 908049 58 2 (hardback)
ISBN: 978 1 908049 59 9 (paperback)

Typeset by CA Typesetting Ltd, www.publisherservices.co.uk
Printed and bound in the UK by Lightning Source UK Ltd., Milton Keynes and Lightning Source Inc., La Vergne, TN

Contents

Fourth Tantra: Devotion, Wisdom, Awe

Fifth Tantra: Awe, Fear, Death

Preface

FABRIZIO M. FERRARI*

THOMAS DÄHNHARDT**

In the complex structure of a universal edifice, each species contributes in its own right to the correct functioning of nature at large and the balance of the environment it inhabits. These, in their turn, articulate themselves in a myriad of micro-natures and micro-environments. If contemplated in such a perspective, the study and understanding of the relation subsisting between human beings and their environment is central for the appreciation of culture and religion. The three volumes in this series explore the wisdom and knowledge acquired by South Asian peoples as a response to their relationship with non-human animals (Volume 1: Fauna), plant life (Volume 2: Flora) and rocks, gems and metals (Volume 3: The Mineral World). The different nar-

* Fabrizio M. Ferrari was educated in Indology at the Ca' Foscari University of Venice (Italy) and received his PhD from SOAS in 2005 for a study on religious folklore in West Bengal. He taught South Asian Religions and Religious Studies at SOAS and is now Professor of Religious Studies at the University of Chester. He is the author of *Oltre il confine, dove la terra è rossa. Canti d'amore e d'estasi dei bāul del Bengala* (Ariele, 2001) and of *Guilty Males and Proud Females: Negotiating Genders in a Bengali Festival* (Seagull, 2010). He wrote the first monograph in English on the Italian anthropologist and historian of religion Ernesto de Martino (*Ernesto de Martino on Religion. The Crisis and the Presence*, Equinox, 2012) and has edited the volume on *Health and Religious Rituals in South Asia: Disease, Possession and Healing* (Routledge, 2011). His research is mainly directed towards the study of religious folklore in the frame of Marxist anthropology. His forthcoming book is *Religion, Devotion and Medicine in North India: The Healing Power of Śītalā* (Bloomsbury, forthcoming 2014).

** Thomas Dähnhardt was educated in modern Indian languages (Hindi and Urdu) at Ca' Foscari University of Venice (Italy) and received his PhD from the Department for Religious Studies at SOAS (University of London) in 1999 for a comparative study on the doctrines and methods taught by a Hindu offspring of the Naqshbandi Sufi order in nineteenth- and early twentieth-century Northern India. After working as a Research Fellow at the Oxford Centre for Islamic Studies (OXCIS) he is currently teaching Hindi and Urdu language and literature in the Department of Asian and North African Studies at Venice University (Italy). His chief areas of interest include the Indo-Islamic culture and the different phenomena of cross-cultural identity resulting from the numerous points of contact between Islam and Hinduism, especially in the field of Sufism, *bhakti* and devotional literature. He is the author of *Change and Continuity in Indian Sufism: A Naqshbandi-Mujaddidi Branch in the Hindu Environment* (New Delhi: DK Publishing, 2002) and of several articles and book chapters on South Asian Sufism and Islamic literature (in Hindi and Urdu).

ratives told and discussed in this and the two following volumes, by drawing on the immensely rich repertoire of beliefs, myths, rituals, folklore, arts and sciences perpetuated all over the social and religious spectrum of the Subcontinent, serve as a canvas on which a wider picture is painted. In so doing, they provide the reader with colorful accounts of the specific theme chosen for the book, and its relation to South Asian civilizations.

The contributions to these volumes seek to invite and stimulate reflections on the multifarious convergences and oppositions of perspectives on the role of the environment in shaping culture across history. In so doing, the volumes offer the necessary tools for a more nuanced and articulate understanding of the active role that animals, plants, minerals and metals, with their presence, behaviour, accessibility, elusiveness and overlaps, continue to exercise on a wide range of issues concerning religion, culture and ethics.

This 'trilogy', we hope, will contribute to fostering the cross-disciplinary study of the enculturation of nature and its manifold and diverse manifestations in South Asia.

Acknowledgments

A number of persons—colleagues, friends, relatives and many informants in India—informed directly and indirectly this work. I am thankful to all of them for their precious inputs, and for their patience in bearing with me and my questions. First of all I wish to express my gratitude to David Clough, head of the department of Theology and Religious Studies at Chester, for being a righteous leader and a very empathetic colleague. His work has been inspirational on so many levels. I learnt a lot from conversations with delegates at the 'Animals as Religious Subjects: A Transdisciplinary Conference' (3rd Biennial Conference of the European Forum for the Study of Religion and the Environment), held at the University of Chester, in association with Gladstone's residential library, Hawarden (Wales), organized by David Clough and my former colleague Celia Deane-Drummond. I am thankful to Louise Child for inviting me to Cardiff University to present my work on animal sacrifice on the occasion of the conference: 'The Power of Sacrifice: Contexts and Representations', and for the feedback I received from many colleagues. I am grateful to Graham Harvey who encouraged me to pursue this project, and to Rachel Fell McDermott, whose recent work on the *Durgā-pūjā* and her analysis of animal sacrifice in Kolkata made me reflect critically on the place of animals in Bengali Hinduism. For his ever so inspiring work and his promptness to share with me his most valuable insights, I feel indebted to Asko Parpola. I am also grateful to Joyce Flueckiger, whose interest in my work made me consider further aspects of the 'donkey/ass' question. A big thank you to Hena Basu, who pointed me to the right Bengali sources on Śītalā's *bāhan*. Finally I wish to express my gratitude to my friends Vijay and Padma Dvivedi for always being so supportive during my sojourns in Varanasi, and for the nice time we had in Adalpura at the Śītalā Dhām.

Fabrizio M. Ferrari

I feel indebted and thankful to many people for providing in one way or the other assistance and guidance through the many difficulties and obstacles I found on my way while working on the present volume. My special thanks go to Professor Gian Giuseppe Filippi (Ca' Foscari University of Venice) who gave me precious advice and shared his profound knowledge of India and traditional thought. Further thoughts of gratitude go to my long-standing friend and former colleague, Maulana Muhammad Akram Nadwi, who over the many happy years I spent at the Oxford Centre for Islamic Studies has always nourished and cultivated my passionate interest for Islam in general and Indo-Islamic civilization in particular. Many thanks to the organizers of and the delegates at the 37th Spalding Symposium on Indian Religions, Merton College, the University of Oxford. Their feedback and interest in this work has been both helpful and encouraging. Last but not least I wish to express my warmest feelings for my family and my daughter Juhi whose presence and serene suggestions both while in India and at home in Europe have accompanied the last year of work and study leading to my contribution to the present volume.

Thomas Dähnhardt

The editors wish to express jointly their gratitude to Janet Joyce, Valerie Hall and Audrey Mann of Equinox Publishing. A word of thanks, and praise, to all the contributors who made the realization of this volume a truly enjoyable task. Last but not least, we are grateful to Fulvio Biancifiori, for the many beautiful photos of Indian animals he made available for this study.

Introduction

THE ANIMAL QUESTION IN SOUTH ASIA: A POST-MODERN *PAÑCATANTRA*

> Now fine and just actions, which political science investigates, admit of much variety and fluctuation of opinion, so that they may be thought to exist only by convention, and not by nature.
>
> (Aristotle, *Nicomachean Ethics* 1.2)

South Asian scriptures bear witness to multiple and contrasting approaches to animals and animal life. Textual injunctions range from abstinence from violence (*ahiṃsā*) and absolute respect for all living beings (e.g. 'All life is bound together by mutual support and interdependence', *Tattvārthasūtra* 5.21) to the liberalization of animal (human and non-human) sacrifice (*Kālikā Purāṇa* 55.3-6). The debate on the 'animal' and its place in the micro- and macro-cosmos has led to countless speculations. Early scriptures in South Asia confirm an enduring dilemma. Are animals 'verily food' (*Taittirīya Brāhmaṇa* 3.9.8)? Were animals created for the sake of sacrifice (*Manu* 5.39)? Should animals be eaten only as medicine (*Suśruta-saṃhitā, sūtrasthāna* 46.53-135)? Or should they be respected as embodied beings in the beginningless *saṃsāra*, like humans? As we learn from Jha's study on *The Myth of the Holy Cow* (2002), several factors (political, social, economic and environmental) have contributed to counter the authority of early Sanskrit sources. The affirmation and consolidation of Buddhism and Jainism as well as that of Hindu devotional movements contributed significantly to challenge previous ideas on the animal body. Further to that, new *ethoi* found their place in the Subcontinent. Islam, Sikhism and Christianity along with other Indic religions all made their contributions to the relation between human and non-human living beings.

Our interest in animals—and therefore the idea behind this work—moves from different premises. Rather than focusing on the scriptural, normative, traditions, this special issue of *Religion of South Asia* intends to discuss folk narratives and the way they have been expressed and transmitted through literature, arts, myth and ritual in South Asia. In folklore—'a reflex of the lifestyle of a people' (Gramsci 2007: 89)—animals provide the most efficacious and long-lasting imagery for the definition and perpetuation of a culturally (localized) informed pedagogy. Animals do what we can't (or should not) do. As such, we found de Martino's analysis of folklore as a way to comment on existential struggle for emancipation extremely useful. And this struggle, in a way or the other, is invariably linked to manage the ecosystem, an arena where creatures interact and inform each other's existence. This is what de Martino called 'progressive folklore' (1951).

From the *Golden Ass* of Apuleius to the annoying—yet wise—Talking Cricket of *Pinocchio*, from the Minotaur of Greek mythology to the wolf of *Little Red Riding Hood*, from the *Planet of the Apes* to Orwell's *Animal Farm*, from the myth of the vampire to the snake of the Bible, folktales in Western culture are rich in parables where animals are the main characters. Sometimes there are hybrid beings, half-animal, half-human. Sometimes there is an emphasis on the human versus the animal. Sometimes there are animals that behave like humans, or humans that act as animals (Doniger 2012: 350). In Western narratives, however, what we often have are not just animals, but humans embodied in an animal (cf. Patton 2006: 34). The 'animality' of the cricket (or the ass, bull, wolf, ape, etc.) manifests itself only when human nature needs a boost, or lacks the skills of the species it is embodied into. With this in mind, we take from Sahlins who noted that 'Western metaphysics...supposes an opposition between nature and culture that is distinctive of our own folklore—and contrastive to the many peoples who consider that beasts are basically human rather than humans basically beasts. These peoples could know no primordial "animal nature", let alone one that must be overcome' (2008: 2; cf. Ingold 2012: 34).

Rather than an encounter, in the Western mind, the human/animal dichotomy seems to be a clash. Agamben recently observed that the human being historically exists only insofar it 'transcends and transforms' the animals that support it (2010: 19). By negating its animal nature, the human is finally able to control and eventually destroy 'animality'. Agamben concludes suggesting that 'man is a fatal disease of the animal' (2010: 19).

Mastering 'the animal' is therefore an ontological necessity in Western (and Westernized) societies. In other words—as suggested by Derrida (2008: 102)—the animal is not just reified, but made into a taboo, an object that is 'at once religiously excluded, kept in silence, reduced to silence, consecrated, and sacrificed, branded a forbidden or just plain branded'. Hence the creation of allegories—and symbols—where the human and the animal meet. Such symbols act as pedagogical tools at the convergence of nature (*physis*) and culture (*nómos*), but at the same time they constantly remind us of the fragility of the human presence. As de Martino informs us: 'since the relationship which constitutes presence is the same relationship that renders culture possible, the threat of not being-here in human history is configured as the risk of losing culture and of receding without compensation into nature' (de Martino in Saunders 1995: 333).

The tension of the Western person is determined by the greatest anxiety of all, that of losing everything and being *regressed* to nature, a dystopia featured by the impossibility of reason. Such is believed to be the territory of the animal—or the animalistic (sub)human that must be dominated—as opposed to the organized culture of which (some) human beings claim to be protagonists (cf. Calarco 2008: 129–30).

It has been observed that the difference between animal and human in Western culture depends on politics and ethics (Waldau 2006: 46), two concepts that are unmistakably anthropocentric (cf. Wiese 2012). Sahlins responds to that by inverting the established paradigm—the *status quo*—and offers an interesting interpretation of what *nómos* actually is. In particular he calls 'realists' those peoples 'who take culture as the original state of human existence and the biological species as secondary and conditional' (2008: 104). This has been captured—though in different ways—by many and diverse contemporary narratives with the intention to criticize modern assumptions or contemporary hegemonic praxis. A good example can be found in one of the many filmic renderings of the 1912 novel *Tarzan of the Apes* by Edgar Rice Burroughs. In *Greystoke: The Legend of Tarzan, Lord of the Apes* (1984, directed by Hugh Hudson), John, the Earl of Greystoke—formerly a feral boy—can be interpreted as a 'realist' when he mourns Kerchak, the chimpanzee that adopted him back in Africa. Unsurprisingly, it is not the expression of grief that strikes the human crowd surrounding him—including the killers of the chimpanzee. What causes outrage is John's desperate cry: 'He was my father!' In so doing, the Earl of Greystoke is publicly advertising a culture that transcends species and therefore offends Victorian values. In that, we agree with Steiner when he suggests that the 'animal question' should be readdressed moving from the Aristotelian notion of *physis* (2006: 126–27).

The only difference is that, perhaps, not all human beings need to reconsider their place in the world in order to distance themselves by the dramatic conclusion that 'human nature endangers our [human] existence' (Sahlins 2008: 112). Besides the colonizing tendency of Western politics and the postcolonial response to it (Krishna 2010: 251), other interpretations exist (rather, they co-exist). While most political and theological discourses reject human-animal symbiosis, folklore is about multiplicity (Deleuze and Guattari 2009: 264, 278; see also Sahlins 1976: 97–98). Indic culture is a good example. In South Asia the individualization of the human being and the otherization of the 'animal other' are less definite. The construction of the body is more flexible. Bodies are porous entities in which the essence of beings moves temporarily into. Transmigration, possession, embodiment, reincarnation, descent are not mystical concepts related to an infantile projection or a secret, supreme, condition of the mind. What in South Asia is ordinary reality, in Western culture has been relegated to fairy tales, is derogatively labelled 'folklore' and explained as allegory. But as Geertz pointed out: '[t]here are some dragons—"tigers in red weather"—that deserve to be looked into' (2000: 63).

So, instead of discussing what animals teach us, we believe that the right question to ask is: What do we *want* animals to tell us? The study of folklore offers a valuable perspective to address such critical matter. In his study on South Asian folklore, Korom (2006: 56–57) has observed that 'wisdom and rationality are valuable commodities not easily acquired' while Stewart noticed that the world that folk narratives address is 'a pragmatic one, where the need to maintain a proper order requires unusual remedies for equally unusual situations' (2004: 7).

The complex mythology that developed in South Asia is an ongoing project aiming at integrating embodied beings and their actions in a wider reality. The presence of animals in folk narratives (but also myths) is not unintentional. We use animals to secure consensus. Animals are *like* humans but do not act as humans. What is problematic is the way their behaviour (i.e. actions) is interpreted, rendered into words and then passed onto history. Two trends can be thus identified. On the one hand, even though 'perfect animals...do not exist in the real world' (White 1991: 16), global consumerism has created the equation that animal is anomaly and therefore its nature must be rectified. On the other, animal actions continue to be part of the law of *karma*, a concept that Olivelle calls a 'theodicy, a legitimization of good and evil' (2009: xxxvii).

In response to that, this special issue seeks to identify those areas where South Asian narratives still perpetuate the original spirit of animal folklore and to appraise what has been lost and what has been domesticated. Like the original *Pañcatantra* (attributed to the Brahmin Viṣṇuśarman, c. 300 CE), the most popular collection of folk tales on animals in South Asia, this collection of articles is not interested in discussing sectarian understandings and representations of animals and animal life. Rather it aims to explore how animality—here intended as other-than-human forms of embodied life—contributed to shaping human paradigms in South Asia and offered alternative worldviews. Non-human animals are discussed as both subjects and objects, as divine messengers and victims of sacrifice, as examples to follow but also as nefarious omens, as wise counsellors as well as portents, as symbols of wealth, pride and courage but also as signifiers of disease and decay.

The structure of this special issue reflects that of the *Pañcatantra*. As in the original text, this is divided into five books (Tantras) whose single stories (our chapters) act as sub-strings inscribed in larger narrative frames. The principal themes of each book are chained to the successive so as to evoke narrative cycles. Such a structural arrangement creates the backbone for the main discussion, that is, a critical exploration of animality as perpetuated in South Asian narratives. Moreover, the thematic subjects chosen for each chapter are meant to describe the underlying state of mind or emotional flavour which, we feel, is conveyed by every contributor. As the ancient Indian concepts of *rasa* (feeling, essence) and *dhvani* (sound, tone), respectively developed in Sanskrit aesthetical theory by the sage Bharata (c. second century BCE—second century CE) and by the Kashmiri scholar Ānandavardhana (ninth century CE), each chapter is thought of as evoking an aesthetic experience which leaves an emotional impact on the reader. The peculiar nature of this impact is determined both by the animal(s) protagonist(s) of each chapter and by the specific way the authors present them through their circumstantial role and functions. The choice of these themes thus revolves around what we have identified as existential modes and attitudes, central to the human quest of life.

The first Tantra (Wonder, Monstrosity and Conflict) explores the portentous nature of animals. The three stories here contained exalt the marvel that animals are and their pedagogical role in humans' life (Olivelle), examine their hidden—perhaps most disturbing—qualities (Smith), and reflect on how they served as a paradigm for another—even more disturbing—domestication enterprise (Torri).

The second Tantra (Conflict, Ethics and Environment) includes tales of human struggle in protecting animal life through balancing ancestral culture with the inevitable clash of tradition and 'modernity', or simply different worldviews. Animals serve here for the purpose of illustrating conflicting ideologies on gendered discourses (Collett), of discussing miracles at the convergence of warrior and saint ethics (Nesbitt) and of claiming territorial kinship with the spirits of the land (Beggiora).

In the third Tantra (Environment, Myth, Devotion) we learn about the presence of animals in foundation myths and in the definition of the environment as social and ancestral territory, an arena that transcends time and space. Non-human animals are holistic healers and controllers of order and disorder (Vargas-O'Bryan), they are the repositories of a secret knowledge which is offered to humans through the gift of their bodies (Chaudhury) and sources of awareness and compassion for all living beings trapped in *saṃsāra* (De Clercq).

The fourth Tantra (Devotion, Wisdom, Awe) mainly focuses on love. Human beings learn from animal behaviour, and stories where animals are protagonists contribute to enrich discourses of piety and loyalty (Pinault), wisdom and passion (Dähnhardt) and moral rectitude and dedication (Dwyer).

In the fifth and last Tantra (Awe, Fear, Death) animality is embodied in ominous presences. Human amazement towards 'the animal' is still there, but other feelings emerge. The animal becomes a tool to offend and harm the enemy (Zeiler), to control anxieties and overcome fears (Allocco) and to tame the tragedy that is disease and its natural consequence, death (Ferrari).

As a natural prosecution of the last theme, we wish here to highlight two important aspects that link the human and the animal dimensions, namely power and fear. Especially in folklore, these aspects—deeply embedded in the environment and embodied in different living receptacles—are central to the definition of culture. Ponniah has explored these themes in his analysis of Tamil folklore (2011: 19–35). His work addresses issues of social mobility at the intersection of function (the effectiveness of ritual power) and performance (the power of ritual actor). Although animals are not mentioned, this model is particularly useful for this study. The animals discussed here are functional to ritual and its outcomes but at the same time they also are the embodiment of power. Within that, animals are located between *doxa* (norms and values unquestionably rooted in society) and *habitus* (cultural disposition) (Bronner 2012: 34, cf. Goody 2010: 93–94). This appears even more clearly when we consider the way we look at animals and the way we represent them in that fluid narrative of human needs, joys, reminiscence, fears, anxieties and expectations that is folklore.

The themes discussed in this special issue of *Religions of South Asia*—wonder, conflict, ethics, environment, devotion, wisdom, awe and death—are looked at through the eyes of different species. We thus concur with Clough when he says that: 'Attending carefully to the differences between animals is both a joy and a responsibility' (2012: 76). Although we may debate about who or what originated such multiplicity of beings (nature, chaos, one or more deities, etc.), what eventually this work has sought to bring is not a convergence of visions but an appreciation of the way incredulity manifests and compels us to tell stories.

REFERENCES

Agamben, G. 2010. *L'aperto. L'uomo e l'animale*. Torino: Bollati Boringhieri.

Bronner, S. J. 2012. 'Practice Theory in Folklore and Folklife Studies.' *Folklore* 123(1): 23–47. http://dx.doi.org/10.1080/0015587X.2012.642985

Calarco, M. 2008. *Zoographies: The Question of the Animal from Heidegger to Derrida*. New York: Columbia University Press.

Clough, D. L. 2012. *On Animals. Volume 1: Systematic Theology*. London and New York: T&T Clark.

de Martino, E. 1951. Il folklore progressive: note lucane. *L'Unità*, 26 June: 3.

Deleuze, G., and F. Guattari. 2009. A Thousand Plateaus: Capitalism and Schizophrenia. London and New York: Continuum.

Derrida, J. 2008. *The Animal that Therefore I am*. New York: Fordham University Press.

Doniger, W. 2012. 'Epilogue.' In Gross and Vallely: 349–53.

Geertz, C. 2000. *Available Lights: Anthropological Reflections on Philosophical Topics*. Princeton, NJ: Princeton University Press.

Goody, J. 2010. *Myth, Ritual and the Oral*. Cambridge: Cambridge University Press. http://dx.doi.org/10.1017/CBO9780511778896

Gramsci, A. 2007. *Quaderni del carcere*. Ed. Valentino Gerratana. 4 vols. Torino: Einaudi.

Gross, A., and A. Vallely (eds). 2012. *Animals and the Human Imagination: A Companion to Animal Studies*. New York: Columbia University Press.

Ingold, T. 2012. 'Hunting and Gathering as Ways of Perceiving the Environment.' In Gross, and Vallely: 31–54.

Jha, D. N. 2004. *The Myth of the Holy Cow*. Reprint of 2002 first edition. London & New York, Verso.

Korom, F. J. 2006. *South Asian Folklore: A Handbook*. Westport, CN and London, Greenwood.

Krishna, N. 2010. *Sacred Animals of India*. New Delhi: Penguin Books.

Olivelle, P. (trans.). 2009. *The Pañcatantra: The Book of India's Folk Wisdom*. Oxford: Oxford University Press.

Patton, K. 2006. '"Caught with Ourselves in the Net of Life and Time." Traditional Views of Animals in Religion.' In Waldau and Patton: 27–39.

Ponniah, K. J. 2011. *The Dynamics of Folk Religion in Society: Pericentralisation as Deconstruction of Sanskritisation*. New Delhi: Serials Publications.

Sahlins, M. 1976. *The Use and Abuse of Biology: An Anthropological Critique of Sociobiology*. Ann Arbor: The University of Michigan Press.

— 2008. *The Western Illusion of Human Nature*. Chicago: Prickly Paradigm Press.

Saunders, G. R. 1995. 'The Crisis of Presence in Italian Pentecostal Conversion.' *American Ethnologist* 22(2): 324–40. http://dx.doi.org/10.1525/ae.1995.22.2.02a00060

Steiner, G. 2006. 'Descartes, Christianity, and Contemporary Speciesism.' In Waldau and Patton: 117–31.

Stewart, T. K. 2004. *Fabulous Females and Peerless Pīrs: Tales of Mad Adventure in Old Bengal.* Oxford and New York: Oxford University Press. http://dx.doi.org/10.1093/0195165292.001.0001

Suśruta-saṁhitā. 2003. Translated by Kaviraj Kunjalal Bhishagratna and edited by Laxmidhar Dwivedi. Varanasi: Chowkhamba Sanskrit Series Office.

Waldau, P. 2006. 'Seeing the Terrain We Walk. Features of the Contemporary Landscape of "Religion and Animals".' In Waldau and Patton: 40–61.

Waldau, P., and K. Patton (eds). 2006. *A Communion of Subjects: Animals in Religion, Science and Ethics.* New York: Columbia University Press.

White, D. G. 1991. *Myths of the Dog-Man.* Chicago and London: The University of Chicago Press.

Wiese, H. 2012. 'Backward Induction in Indian Animal Tales.' *International Journal of Hindu Studies* 16(1): 93–103. http://dx.doi.org/10.1007/s11407-012-9112-4

First Tantra: Wonder, Monstrosity, Conflict

Talking Animals: Explorations in an Indian Literary Genre

PATRICK OLIVELLE*

In our local newspaper here in Austin, Texas, there are two full pages devoted to comics with about 30 comic strips. Discounting the occasional animal appearances, in 30 percent of them animals play the leading role. People in general appear to be fascinated by thinking and talking animals, even if their talk is limited to the bubbles of cartoons. Beyond newspaper cartoons, look at the billions spent on Walt Disney movies and toys and at various Disney Lands. Nor is this a recent fascination.

Animals are certainly good to think, as anthropologists have pointed out, but from the dawn of literature humans have also endowed them with voices so that humans can participate vicariously in an anthropomorphized animal linguistic and social world paralleling the human. This is the birth of the animal fable. There must be something that talking animals achieve that cannot be accomplished by simply human talk or abstract discourse. In this chapter I want to focus on the ways this crossing of species boundaries is represented in a variety of Indian literary genres and look at some of the beliefs and ideologies that may underlie animal fables.[1]

* Patrick Olivelle is Professor of Sanskrit and Indian Religions in the Department of Asian Studies at the University of Texas at Austin and Jacob and Frances Sanger Mossiker Chair in the Humanities. Professor Olivelle served as the Chair of the Department of Asian Studies at the University of Texas at Austin from 1994 to 2007. Prior to coming to Texas, Olivelle taught in the Department of Religious Studies at Indiana University, Bloomington, from 1974 to 1991, where he was the Department Chair 1984–1990. Olivelle's current research focuses on the ancient Indian legal tradition of Dharmaśāstra. He has edited and translated the four early Dharmasūtras. He has also prepared a critical edition and translation of the Law Code of Manu (Mānava Dharmaśāstra). In the mid-1990s Olivelle worked on the late Vedic literature, producing an award-winning translation of the early Upaniṣads, as well as a scholar's edition of them. His early work was focused on the ascetic and monastic traditions of India. He published several editions, translations, and studies of ascetic texts and institutions. His award-winning book on the āśrama system was published in 1993. Olivelle has won several prestigious fellowships, including Guggenheim, NEH, and ACLS. He was elected Vice President of the American Oriental Society in 2004 and President in 2005.

1. Human interactions with animals, of course, go far beyond fables and talking animals. They play crucial roles in human dietary regulations and speculation (Olivelle 2002), in ethics and religion, and in art and music. Animal rights have emerged as a major area of moral

The earliest Indian use of animals in literature was probably as similes. As Stephanie Jamison (2009) has pointed out, such similes abound even in the *Ṛg Veda*, the earliest literary product of India. A god is compared to a bull or a horse; tenderness is like a cow lowing for her calf. We have the metaphors of *narasiṃha*, 'man-lion', *puṃgava*, 'man-bull', *siṃhadaṃṣtra*, 'lion-toothed', *rājasiṃha*, 'king-lion', and the like. What is significant in these metaphors for later animal tales is that a particular characteristic is singled out as defining a particular animal and constituting its very nature (*svabhāva*). Such characterisations are expanded in later times to include a donkey, who is both stupid and over-sexed, a jackal, who is greedy and cunning, and the like (see Olivelle 1997: xxii–xxv). The association of a particular species with a set of physical, moral and intellectual qualities with personality traits plays a central role in animal fables.

The broader classification of the animal kingdom into village or domestic (*grāmya*) and wild (āraṇya), already attested in the rather late hymn of the *Ṛg Veda*, the *Puruṣasūkta* (10.90.8), also plays a significant role in later tales. Associated with this is the division of animals into prey, designated as 'grass eaters', and predators, designated as 'meat eaters'—the former generally with hooves (*śapha*, *khura*) and the latter with five nails (*pañcanakha*), the former being the food and the latter its eaters. These classificatory systems play central roles in storytelling. For example, the moment we see the domesticated bull Saṃjīvaka at the opening of the *Pañcatantra* striking up a friendship with the lion king Piṅgalaka we know that it is not going to end well. The maxim is that there can be no friendship between grass-eaters and meat-eaters, between prey and predator, between food and eater; add to this the mixture of the village and the wilderness, and Saṃjīvaka was bound to end up at the losing end.

But what about talking animals? When do they make their first appearance in the extant corpus of Indian literature? Jamison (2009: 198) has alluded to the monkey Vṛṣākapi (*Ṛg Veda* 10.86) and Saramā, the messenger bitch of Indra (*Ṛg Veda* 10.108), both of whom have speaking roles in the *Ṛg Veda*. There are several talking animals, including fish, in the *Brāhmaṇas*, notably the 'talkative fish' who instructs Manu about building a boat in the story of the great flood. The *Upaniṣad*s too contain several wise animals—a bull, a goose, and a diver bird, who instruct Satyakāma Jābāla (*Chāndogya Upaniṣad* 4.5-8), and a pair of geese whose conversation about the wisdom of Raikva is overheard by Jānaśruti Pautrāyaṇa (*Chāndogya Upaniṣad* 4.1-4). These talking animals set the scene for the discourse in chapter four of this *Upaniṣad*.

Even though these are tantalizing hints, we do not have examples of full-blown animal fables in the Vedic literature. Stephanie Jamison (2009: 217),

discourse. For a comprehensive survey, see Waldau and Patton (2006). For animals in human thought in India, see Balbir and Pinault (2009).

nevertheless, concludes from the hints in the textual tradition, hints that appear to allude to stories well known to the audience, that 'we must assume already for the RVic period not only the existence of a body of story literature, of animal fables, but also (more interestingly) a fairly organized rule for this literature in an instructional setting'. This is a significant point, because many of the later animal fables in India have an explicit or implicit didactic function.

The organization of the Buddhist *Jātakas* supports Jamison's contention. The oldest parts of the *Jātakas* consist of verses, which only allude to an underlying story that the audience was supposed to know already. The *Baka Jātaka* (38) containing the story of the crab, the crane, and the fish, also found in the *Pañcatantra* (I, Story 4.1), for example, has this brief verse:

> Guile profits not your very guileful folk.
> Mark what the guileful crane got from the crab!
>
> (Chalmers 1990: 98)

Without the full story this remark makes little sense, except that if this was all we had, as in some of the *Ṛg Vedic* stories, we can surmise that there may be a tale behind the gnomic verse. The same is true of the verses that begin and end the tales of the *Pañcatantra*. Here is an example:

> When a man wants to meddle in affairs,
> that do not concern him,
> He will surely be struck down dead, like the
> monkey that pulled the wedge.
>
> (*Pañcatantra* I, 6)

This is opaque without the accompanying story of the inquisitive monkey who pulled out the wedge inserted into a half-split piece of timber while his testicles were hanging through the slit—a painful and salutary story about meddling in the affairs of others (*Pañcatantra* I, Story 1).

Besides the *Jātakas*, the oldest extant literature containing animal fables are the Sanskrit epics, especially the *Mahābhārata*, even though the *Rāmāyaṇa* is replete with animals who speak and assume human roles, for example, the monkeys led by Hanumān. The book that made Indian animal fables famous, however, is the *Pañcatantra* and its numerous editions, recasts and offshoots. It is in this genre of literature that the animal fables in India are put to specific literary and ideological use, a genre that I will focus on in this chapter.

At first, however, let me reflect on the religious and cultural backdrop within which the anthropomorphizing habit of Indian animal tales took place. Given the global scope of such anthropomorphism, it is clear that such a backdrop is not a necessary condition for its development. There clearly is an innate propensity for anthropomorphism within the human psyche, as many scholars of culture and religion have pointed out (Guthrie 1993). But the specific contours that such anthropomorphism adopted in India were shaped by its religious and cultural backdrop.

In the early Vedic period, we already find gods, as well as humans, adopting animal forms. Indra becomes a female hyena (*Taittirīya Saṃhitā* 6.2.4.3-4; Jamison 1991: 76), a ram (*Jaiminīya Brāhmaṇa* 3.234-36), and a monkey (*Jaiminīya Brāhmaṇa* 1.363), among others. Prajāpati, the creator god, takes on different animal forms as he copulates with his consort to create the different species of animals (*Bṛhadāraṇyaka Upaniṣad* 1.4.3). The ability to transform oneself into other species, thereby performing tasks specific to the skills of that species, finds its most significant expression in the *avatāras* or incarnations of Viṣṇu. That animals can and do have thoughts and intentions similar to humans is assumed within this worldview. Gods becoming animals interestingly presents a twofold anthropomorphism of gods acting like humans and animals acting like gods, and thus as humans. That animals, within this context, can speak goes without saying.

Parallel to gods becoming animals, we have the tradition of divine animals. I have already referred to Vedic precedents. Kālidāsa's famous epic poem *Raghuvaṃśa* begins with king Dilīpa, Raghu's father and Rāma's great-great-grandfather, who was unable to bear a son because he had unknowingly slighted the heavenly cow Surabhi. Then there is the divine eagle Garuḍa, and the divine talking monkeys of the *Rāmāyaṇa*. In classical Hinduism all the gods have their animal mounts, who share divine characteristics. Even extraordinary humans can assume animal guises, such as the seer in the *Mahābhārata* (1.109) who mated with his wife in the guise of a deer and doe and was shot by king Pāṇḍu, thus drawing the seer's wrath and curse. There is, then, no unbridgeable gulf between gods, humans and animals within the Indian imagination.

The most significant religio-cultural belief that is connected to animal anthropomorphism, however, is rebirth. Taking an animal rebirth as part of karmic retribution was a well-established belief at least by the early centuries prior to the Common Era. It was also believed that, just as residence in various hells, so birth as animals was a punishment for sins committed in previous lives. The *Viṣṇu Dharmasūtra*, a seventh-century Kashmiri text, provides a clear statement (44.1-9):

> Now, sinners who have experienced suffering in various hells take birth in animal wombs. Those guilty of the most grievous sins causing loss of caste become successively all the immobile beings. Those guilty of grievous sins causing loss of caste enter the wombs of worms; those guilty of secondary sins causing loss of caste, the wombs of birds; those guilty of lesser sins causing loss of caste, the wombs of animals born in water; those guilty of sins causing exclusion from caste, the wombs of animals living in water; those guilty of sins causing them to be of mixed caste, the wombs of wild animals (*mṛga*); those guilty of sins making them unworthy of receiving gifts, the wombs of farm animals (*paśu*); and those guilty of sins causing them to be impure, the wombs of untouchable people among humans.

Besides the general theme of being born as animals due to past sins, this text also provides two significant bits of information. Particular sins cause a person to be born in the wombs of particular animals; so the choice of animals is not random but causally determined. Second, more serious sins cause a person to be born as worse animals, thus creating a hierarchy of more desirable and less desirable animals. Clearly, anthropomorphism is again at work in this classification of animals, farm animals (*paśu*) being at the very top of this hierarchy, just below untouchable humans,[2] and worms at the very bottom.

Within this religio-cultural background, it is easy to make the transition from human to animal; the crossing of these classificatory boundaries between species is facilitated by their lack of permanence. If humans can become animals, then animals may assume human roles and even human speech. Rebirth as the ideological backdrop for animal tales is explicitly stated in the *Jātaka* tales whose very purpose is to narrate the previous life stories of the Buddha.

I turn now to the *Pañcatantra*, the most famous of the Indian collections of animal fables. In this text we have, I think for the first time, the question of the linguistic abilities of animals asked explicitly. A young deer named Citrāṅga has been trapped, and the beauty of the little one prompts the trapper to take it to the young prince of the kingdom, who keeps the animal as a pet in his own bedroom. The rainy season comes along, when traditionally lovers pine for their absent partners, and the young deer pines for its herd. In the middle of the night, his longing unbearable, the deer utters this couplet:

> When, O when will I ever get to run
> after my herd of deer,
> As they romp and revel, and tear about,
> spurred by the wind and rain?
>
> (*Pañcatantra* II, 80)

The prince is startled when he discovers that the words came from the deer. The fright causes him to run a high fever, and he is on the point of death. As the people, fearing it is demonic, are about to beat the poor deer to death, one wise man interprets the deer's speech and says: 'All species of animals, my friend, do indeed speak, but not in front of people. This animal probably did not notice you when he gave vent to his longings. The rainy season stirred his longings, and his thoughts went back to his herd' (Olivelle 1997: 99). So speech by animals is nothing extraordinary; they just do not speak in front of humans. The issue of the deer speaking in perfect Sanskrit verse, however, is not addressed!

But why use animals as dummies for human ventriloquists in the first place? Stephanie Jamison (2009) has expressed the view—as an answer to why the Vedic literature does not contain animal stories—that animal tales are used in education when it is directed at children and the uneducated rather

2. This is a good example of how innocent looking lists were used to impart strong social messages. Placing the outcaste within a list containing animals clearly places him on the same plane.

than at the learned. Clearly, the very setting of the story collections such as the *Pañcatantra* and its later offspring, the *Hitopadeśa*, indicates that they were directed at children, in their case the stupid children of a king. Likewise, Jamison argues that the *Jātataks* were intended for ordinary folks.

Although this is an insightful observation, I think there are also other reasons for using animal fables in Indian literature. The snippets of talking animals in the *Upaniṣads*, for example, probably fall into the general *Upaniṣadic* pattern of wisdom and knowledge coming from unexpected and extraordinary sources: non-Brahmins, poor and low-caste men, women, Gandharvas, and animals. Clearly, children like animals and animal stories, and using them is a fine pedagogical tool in instructing children. But, even adults—even intelligent and educated adults—are fascinated by episodes where the main characters are animals and which carry significant messages, sometimes explicit but more often implicit and below the surface, messages that may be religious, philosophical, or scientific. Walt Disney enterprises prove this point.

Just as animal prohibitions and prescriptions within the dietary rules of various cultures, including the Indian (Olivelle 2002), are an effective and almost universal tool for guarding social boundaries, as Mary Douglas (1966) has painstakingly pointed out, so animal stories may be more effective tools of social control and instruction than learned discourses and śāstric writings. What is clear is that most, if not all, the collections of animals fables in India promote a particular ideology and are not just for 'fun', not simply fairy tales for the entertainment of children.

I want to highlight a few aspects of these ideologically driven didactic functions of animal fables. Animals, divided as they are into distinct species, provide a wonderful canvas to paint the picture of a society divided into distinct groups. We see already in the Puruṣa Hymn of the *Ṛg Veda* (10.90) that the four social classes (*varṇa*) of ancient Indian society were viewed as originating from different bodily parts of the primordial person, much like the sun and the moon, and animals and birds. Such social classes are not contingent social formations but essentially different species. From an early period, as I have noted, Indians projected distinct characters and characteristics onto different animals; they created distinct natures—*svabhāvas*—for each species. Such *svabhāvas* are, of course, culturally created and projected, although these creations are based on certain observed behaviour patterns of animals. And we know that *svabhāva* (inherent nature) is closely related to and drives *svadharma* (innate duties and propensities); nature drives behaviour and action. The debate between nature and nurture, between one's birth and one's character—whether one's nature or the way one is brought up is superior—has been an ongoing controversy reflected explicitly even in the *Pañcatantra*. Arguments embedded in stories are advanced for both sides. For the priority of character, several gnomic verses are cited, and I give but two:

A man's nobility comes not
from the quality of his birth;
The eminence of mortal men
rests on how they conduct themselves.
Disgrace and in its train a web
of disasters, hundreds of them,
Hound a man who is an ingrate,
both in this world and in the next.

(*Pañcatantra* I, 166)

Knowledge is the true eye, not mere eyesight;
Conduct makes one noble, not noble birth;
To be content is true prosperity;
To refrain from wrong is erudition.

(*Pañcatantra* II, 46)

The story of the crow Laghupatanaka and the mouse Hiraṇyaka illustrates this view (*Pañcatantra* II, Story 1). Seeing that Hiraṇyaka, because of his friendship with the dove king Citragrīva, had freed a flock of doves from a fowler's net in which they were trapped, Laghupatanaka wanted to befriend Hiraṇyaka. Here is their encounter and arguments that led to their lasting friendship. When Laghupatanaka calls out at Hiraṇyaka's hole, he asks:

'Hello! Who are you?'
The crow: 'I am a crow named Laghupatanaka'.
When Hiraṇyaka heard that and from inside saw the crow standing in front of the entrance to his hole, he told the crow: 'Get away from this place!'
The crow: 'I saw how you freed Citragrīva and I want to become friends with you. So, if one day I happen to get into a similar trouble, I can get you to free me. Please, sir, you must do me this favor. You must become my friend.'
Hiraṇyaka laughed and told him: 'How can there be any friendship between you and me?

The impossible is impossible;
Only what's possible can a man do;
carts don't go in water,
or boats on dry terrain. (8)
The things that are found to join in the world,
Only those things should the wise seek to join;
You are the eater, and I am the food;
what friendship can there be,
between the two of us?' (9)

The crow replied:

'Even if I were to eat you, good sir,
It would not amount to much food for me;
But if you live, my life would be assured,
Just as Citragrīva's, my flawless friend. (10)

Surely it is not right for you to dismiss my request out of hand.

For people place their trust even in beasts,
And make treaties with them, when they're upright,
Solely because their character is good—
You and Citragrīva illustrate this. (11)

> A good man, even when he is enraged,
> Does not change his mind and become hostile;
> a straw torch cannot heat
> the water of the sea. (12)
> Your virtues, even though they're not broadcast,
> Have attained great renown all by themselves;
> a jasmine spreads its scent,
> e'en when its covered up.' (13)
>
> When he heard this, Hiranıyaka said to the crow: 'Look, you are fickle by nature. And it is said:
>
> The fickle are not faithful to themselves;
> How can they be faithful to other men?
> every venture, therefore,
> the fickle always spoil. (14)
>
> So, get away from this place; you are blocking the entrance to my fortress.'
>
> The crow: 'Fickle! Not fickle!—Friend, why such harsh words? I have made up my mind once and for all. I am attracted by your virtues. So, come what may, I am going to become friends with you.'
>
> Hiraṇyaka: 'Look, my man. You are my enemy. So how can you expect me to be friends with you? As it is said:
>
> Never form an alliance with a foe,
> Even though he is closely tied to you.
> water, though very hot,
> will still put a fire out." (15)
>
> The crow: 'Come, my friend. How can we be enemies? We haven't even seen each other! Why do you utter such nonsense?'

After a lengthy argument, Hiraṇyaka relents:

> After listening to that, Hiraıyaka said to the crow: 'All right, you have convinced me. I'll go along with your wish. I said what I did only to test your intentions, so that, in the event you did kill me, you would not think that I was a fool and you beat me by the power of your wit. Now that I have spelled this out to you, I place my head in your bosom.'
>
> (Olivelle 1997: 78)

Although Laghupatanaka wins the argument here, the proponents of nature over nurture won the debate. As the *Pañcatantra* (I, 78) saying goes, a dog's tail will never become straight however much oil or heat you may apply. This is the principle on which the theory of 'natural enmity' between species is enunciated in the *Pañcatantra*: the well-known enmity between the cobra and the mongoose, and the lesser-known enmity between owls and crows, are all based on the very natures of these species.

The principle that nature (birth, pedigree) rather than upbringing determines behaviour is illustrated in the oft-repeated proverb: there can be no friendship between grass-eaters and meat-eaters, between a food and its eater (II, 9). Several stories illustrate the end result of such friendships; the ox and the camel who befriended lions, the frogs who went for a joyride on a snake's back, all ended up dead (I, frame story, Story 7; III, Story 8). That every creature sinks back to its own nature is illustrated by the mouse transformed into a girl (III, Story 7). Indeed, in this story the girl does not voluntarily return to her native state as a mouse; the cosmos itself, represented by the divine beings who rejected her as a bride, determined her ultimate fate. As I have noted, the proverbial enmity between the snake and the mongoose (V, frame story) illustrates the primacy of nature. The story of the owls and crows (III, frame story) is based on the natural and inborn enmity between the two species, which is traced in one story to an incident in the mythical past (III, Story 2). The big mistake that the owl king Arimardana made was to give shelter to a crow, his natural enemy. The mouse Hiraṇyaka expounds this theory of enemies. If someone becomes your enemy for some reason, you can always make amends and restore the friendship. But when the enmity is inborn and natural, it can never be eliminated.

I will cite but a single story that nicely illustrates the danger of trusting outward appearances of virtue and holiness. This is the story of a partridge and a hare who go to a holy cat to settle their dispute (*Pañcatantra* III, Story 2.2):

> Once upon a time I[3] lived in a certain tree. In a hole under that same tree lived a bird named Kapiñjala, the Partridge. As time passed and since we lived so close by, we became thick friends. Every day early in the evening, after we had taken our meals and finished our excursions, we used to spend the time together reciting proverbs and posing questions and counter-questions.
>
> One day Kapiñjala failed to turn up at our normal time of conversation, even though it was evening. That made my heart extremely anxious and I wondered: 'Now, why has he not come back? Is it because he has been killed or captured? Or has he found some other residence more to his liking?' As I was thinking in this manner, many days passed by.
>
> Soon thereafter a hare named Dīrghakarṇa, the Long-eared, came there and occupied the hole in which Kapiñjala used to live. Seeing the hare, I thought to myself: 'My friend is nowhere to be found. So why should I bother about his residence?'
>
> The hare hadn't been there too long before Kapiñjala returned. Seeing the hare occupying his hole, he said: 'Hey, this is my place! Get out of here at once.'
>
> The hare: 'You fool! Don't you know the rule: the one who is there has the right to enjoy both house and food.'
>
> Kapiñjala: 'There are people who can arbitrate such issues. Let us ask them what is proper. For it is stated in the Codes of Law:
>
> In cases relating to reservoirs,
> Wells and ponds, houses and lodges as well,
> The outcome rests on what the neighbors say—
> that's the view of Manu.' (47)
>
> 'By all means', agreed the hare. And the two of them set out to file their lawsuit. I was curious as to how the case would be settled and followed them close behind. They hadn't gone too far before Kapiñjala asked the hare: 'But who will hear our case?'

3. The narrator of the story is the crow in the story of the owl being crowned king of birds (*Pañcatantra* III, Story 2).

The hare replied: 'What about that old cat named Dadhikarṇa, the Curd-ears, who lives on the bank of the river devoted to austerities? He shows compassion to all animals and knows the Codes of Law well. He will be able to settle our case.'
When he heard that, Kapiñjala said: 'I don't want anything to do with that vile fellow. For it is said:

In one who puts on a hermit's disguise,
never place your trust;
We see many hermits at holy sites,
baring throats and teeth.' (48)

Now the cat, Dadhikarṇa, had assumed that fake appearance to gain an easy living. When he heard Kapiñjala's words, he wanted to win the bird's confidence. So with renewed vigor he began to gaze at the sun standing on two feet with his arms raised above his head.[4] With one eye closed, he remained like this reciting silent prayers. Seeing him praying like that kindled their trust in him. They crept towards him softly and told him of their dispute regarding the dwelling place: 'O hermit! O teacher of the law! We have a dispute. Please settle this dispute of ours in accordance with the Codes of Law.'
The cat replied: 'I am old and my hearing is weak. I cannot hear too well from afar. Please come near and speak aloud.'
So the two came nearer and spoke to him. Dadhikarṇa then, wanting to inspire confidence in them so as to draw them closer, recited these verses from the Law Codes:

Break the Law, and it will break you apart;
Keep the Law, and the Law will keep you safe.
Therefore, a man should never break the Law,
Lest the Law, broken, will break him apart. (49)
The Law is the one friend who follows you,
even after you die;
Along with your body everything else,
is completely destroyed. (50)
When we offer animal oblations,
into blind darkness we sink;
There has been no Law, there shall never be,
higher than non-injury. (51)
The wives of others like his own mother,
What belongs to others like clods of earth,
And all the creatures on earth like himself—
The man who sees this way, he truly sees. (52)

To make a long story short, through this sort of false piety he won their confidence to such a degree that they came right up to him. Then in one fell swoop that vile cat got hold of them both and killed them.

(Olivelle 1997: 118–20)

A particular species of animal represents a particular anthromorphized nature. Alan Dundes (1997) has shown how the tale of the sparrow and the crow, a story told to children across much of India, carries the message of the inherent danger in associating with someone of a low caste or an outcaste.

4. It was a common ascetic practice to gaze at the sun with upraised arms while standing on one foot. Standing on two feet seems to be an allowance made to the four-footed animal.

Sparrow is the Brahmin and crow is the outcaste. When the foolish sparrow mother permits her friend Crow to stay overnight in her house on a particularly rainy day, disaster strikes that house. Crow eats all her food and leaves only her excrement behind. And Sparrow's children, trying to get some food, only get their hands soiled in Crow's muck.

Whether it is a grass-eater consorting with a meat-eater, a mouse with a crow, owls with crows, frogs with a cobra, fish with a heron, or a camel with a lion, the outcome is always the same. As the *Pañcatantra* (I, Story 7) says: 'Association between grass-eaters and meat-eaters is incompatible'. Animal society functions naturally and appropriately when the species are kept separate and in their distinct roles. Human society, likewise, made up of different species of humans functions best when these species are kept separate and social boundaries safeguarded.

There are other pedagogical ends served by animal fables, and it is the very richness of the possibilities offered by these tales that make them ever popular with the invitation to various and often contradictory reader responses. One of these pedagogical goals pertains to another controversy in ancient India between fate and human effort: which has the priority. The *Pañcatantra* comes down squarely on the side of human effort and the need to be active and proactive in order to succeed. A good example of this is the story of the three fish (I, Story 8.2) that lived in a lake:

> In a certain large lake there once lived three big fish. They were named Farsighted, Quick-witted, and Inevitable. One day as he was swimming in the water, Farsighted heard a conversation between some fishermen who were passing nearby: 'This lake has a lot of fish. Let us do some fishing here tomorrow.'
>
> When he heard this, Farsighted thought to himself: 'They are sure to come back. So, I will get hold of Quick-witted and Inevitable and go with them to another lake with open channels.' He called his two friends together and asked them to come along.
>
> Quick-witted replied: 'If in fact the fisher folk come back here, I will save myself by some strategy that fits the circumstances'.
>
> Inevitable, whose end was near, paid no heed to Farsighted's plea and remained idly by making no preparation for the journey. Seeing that the two were determined to remain there, Farsighted made his way into a stream of the river and proceeded to another lake.
>
> The day after he left, the fishermen together with their helpers blocked off the outlet, spread a dragnet, and caught every single fish. When this happened, Quick-witted lay in the net and made himself appear as if he were already dead. The fishermen, thinking, 'This big fish has died on his own', drew him out of the net and threw him near the water. He then jumped in and fled quickly to another lake. Inevitable darted here and there, totally at a loss and not knowing what to do. The fishermen bound him with the net and beat him to death with clubs.
>
> The lady sandpiper continued: 'Therefore I say:
>
> Farsighted and Quick-witted,
> Happily did these two thrive;
> While Inevitable died.'
>
> (Olivelle 1997: 52–53).

The *Pañcatantra* presents itself as a *Nītiśāstra*, a scientific composition on politics and government, given that the setting is the teaching of this science by a Brahmin expert on pedagogy to a king's stupid and ill-behaved sons. The *Pañcatantra* ends with a moral discourse on Hasty Actions: think before you act! One story is about a Brahmin boy who had a little bag of flour—he daydreams of selling it and buying a goat, then a cow and so on, until he becomes very rich, marries, and has a son. When his wife scolds the son, he raises the stick to beat his wife but hits the pot containing the flour; the flour comes down on his head and paints his body white. Or the more famous story of the Brahmin who left his pet mongoose to look after his only son. The mongoose comes running out to greet his returning master. Seeing his bloody mouth and paws, the Brahmin thinks the mongoose has eaten his son and beats it to death, only to discover that the mongoose had killed a vicious snake that had come to attack his son.

The moral of each story, the teachings of story collections, may be different. Yet, I think that the organization of animal society according to the human, and thus presenting animal interaction as a mirror of the human is at the heart of the Indian animal tales and the phenomenon of talking animals.

REFERENCES

Balbir, N., and G. J. Pinault (eds). 2009. *Penser, dire et représenter l'animal dans le monde indien.* Paris: Honoré Champion.

Chalmers, R. 1990. *The Jātakas or Stories of the Buddha's Former Births.* 1st edn, 1895. Reprint. 3 Volumes. Delhi: Motilal Banarsidass.

Douglas, M. 1966. *Purity and Danger: An Analysis of the Concepts of Pollution and Taboo.* London: Routledge. http://dx.doi.org/10.4324/9780203361832

Dundes, A. 1997. *Two Tales of Crow and Sparrow.* London: Rowman & Littlefield.

Guthrie, S. 1993. *Faces in the Clouds: A New Theory of Religion.* New York: Oxford University Press.

Jamison, S. 1991. *The Ravenous Hyenas and the Wounded Sun: Myth and Ritual in Ancient India.* Ithaca, NY: Cornell University Press.

Jamison, S. 2009. 'The Function of Animals in the Rig Veda, RV X.28, and the Origins of Story Literature in India.' In N. Balbir and G. J. Pinault (eds), *Penser, dire et représenter l'animal dans le monde indien*: 197–218. Paris: Honoré Champion.

Olivelle, P. (trans.). 1997. *The Pañcatantra: The Book of India's Folk Wisdom.* Oxford: Oxford University Press.

— 2002. 'Food for Thought: Dietary Regulations and Social Organization in Ancient India.' 2001 Gonda Lecture. Amsterdam: Royal Netherlands Academy of Arts and Sciences. Reprinted in Olivelle, 2008: 367–92.

— 2008. *Collected Essays I: Language, Texts, and Society*. Florence: University of Florence Press.

— (trans.) 2009. *Viṣṇu Dharmasūtra: Viṣṇu's Code of Law: A Critical Edition and Translation of the Vaiṣṇava-Dharmaśāstra.* Harvard Oriental Series, No. 73. Cambridge, MA: Harvard University Press.

Waldau, P., and K. Patton (eds). 2006. *A Communion of Subjects: Animals in Religion, Science, and Ethics.* New York: Columbia University Press.

Monstrous Animals on Hindu Temples, with Special Reference to Khajuraho

DAVID SMITH*

A variety of monstrous animals features in the temple art of South Asia. Leaving aside the *kīrtimukha* and the *makara*,[1] whose symbolic roles are clear cut (Kramrisch 1976: II, 322–31), my concern is with *vyālas*, hybrids of lion, horse and other animals, which are visible in large numbers on medieval temples; and in particular with the *vyālas* on the walls of the temples at Khajuraho, in Madhya Pradesh, dating from the middle of the tenth century to the second half of the eleventh. Unlike south India, where the *vyāla* equivalent faces outward towards the onlooker, the Khajuraho-type *vyāla* faces sideways, on the same plane as its wall.[2] *Vyālas* commonly rear up over an attacking warrior or over a defeated elephant, but the Khajuraho-type, as it rears up, turns backwards towards its diminutive rider (Fig. 1).[3] This chapter discusses possible meanings for these monsters; and in particular addresses the most specific problem posed by the *vyālas* at Khajuraho, as: What might be the significance of their constant propinquity to *apasarases*, the dancing girls of the gods?

* David Smith was Reader in South Asian Religions at Lancaster University from 1997 to 2011, when he took early retirement. He has written extensively on Sanskrit court culture (from *Ratnakara's Haravijaya: An Introduction to the Sanskrit Court Epic*, Oxford University Press, 1985 to a translation of Bana's *Princess Kadambari vol. 1*, New York University Press, 2010). He is the author of *Hinduism and Modernity* (Blackwell, 2003) and *The Dance of Siva: religion, art and poetry in South India* (Cambridge University Press, 1996). He is currently writing a book on Hindu Eroticism for I. B. Tauris; and preparing a study of the sculpture of Khajuraho.

1. Kīrtimukha (lit. 'glorious face') indicates a monster with huge fangs and a swallowing mouth. The *makara* is an aquatic animal and the vehicle of the goddess Gaṅgā. Usually the *makara* has the frontal part in animal form (stag, elephant or crocodile) and the hind part as a fish tail.
2. There are rare exceptions, e.g. at the top of the columns inside the closed hall of the Lakṣmaṇa temple.
3. The complex angling of surfaces makes it impossible for all faces, of wall and of sculptures, to be seen at once.

Figure 1. South wall, Jagadamba temple, Khajuraho, with eight columns of vyālas visible. (All figures ©David Smith.)

Prescriptive texts in Sanskrit on temple building, more or less contemporary to the temples under consideration, briefly list the various forms that *vyālas* can take.[4] The only two detailed studies of the *vyāla* to date, by Dhaky (1965) and by Zhu (1997), restrict themselves almost entirely to the description of the varying physical forms of the *vyāla*. But the present study is sympathetic to Hiram Woodward's claim that 'The study of a "text" as rich as the Lakshmana [temple at Khajuraho], like Shakespeare's plays or Beethoven's symphonies, should be an inexhaustible enterprise' (1989: 27). The art of Khajuraho is high art, the product surely of royal ateliers and manifestly complex aesthetic concerns. There can be no doubt that these temples set out to be an expression of religion at the highest level of artistic achievement. But only the occasional inscriptions connect the temples with their builders; in north Indian temples there are seldom representations of historical people among the many sculptures. The temples are representations of the world of the gods through imaginative reconstruction of human beings and animals. There is no direct explanation of the specific architecture and iconography at Khajuraho; there are no contemporary accounts of these temples. Furthest from any textual explanation is the *vyāla*.

A notable feature of the Khajuraho temples is the way much of the walls, instead of having just the occasional relievo shrine of a deity bounded by a pillar on each side, is in addition to such shrines covered by registers of free-standing statues, with gods, *apsaras*es and *vyāla*s standing in line, equal in height. They each stand in their own space, without any framing. Usually the *vyālas* are set back in a recess, but viewed from a slight distance they look

4. Rather more is said in two anomalous texts *Śilparatnakośa* and *Śilpaprakāśa*, but they are 'preserved' only in MSS 'discovered' by Pandit Rath Sharma, a notorious forger; and the added details in these texts reflect, I believe, the fact that the *vyāla* sparks curiosity today, rather than giving any historically valid information.

level with gods and *apsarases*. By this constant repetition the freestanding gods, outside the shrines, may be said to be demeaned, and the *apsarases* and *vyālas* elevated in status. Moreover, because the gods have elaborate headdresses and they all three have the same space within the register, the gods have to be slightly shorter beneath their headdress than their neighbours. There are fewer *vyālas* than deities and *apsarases*, but there are many more than there were in earlier north Indian temples, where *vyālas* were positioned only on either side of a shrine or door, looking away from it and manifestly acting as guardian. Small *vyālas* continue in that role at Khajuraho, but the overall presence of *vyālas* has been greatly magnified. Out of a total of 646 exterior statues counted by Cunningham (1994: 420) on the largest and one of the latest temples, the Kandariya, 120 are *vyālas*, as counted by Zhu (1997: 182).

Kramrisch's work on the Hindu temple is justly famous, for she 'provid[es] the conceptual basis for virtually all subsequent studies of Indian temples' (Smith 1994: 95). She finds the meaning of the temple not only in the numerous prescriptive Sanskrit texts on temple building, but in the light of Hindu spirituality as evidenced in the *Veda* and the *Upaniṣad*, texts composed long before any extant temple had come into existence; and also, with more justification, she frequently refers to later yogic and tantric texts. She is at her most ingenious and creative in explaining the *vyāla*, using for it the term *śārdūla* (tiger): She begins by going back to the Vedic *Brāhmaṇas*: 'Vāk, the uttered word, is a lioness [*siṃhī*]', (1976: II, 332) then adopts the word *śārdūla*, 'tiger', for the *vyāla*.

> On the walls of the temple and the pillars of its halls, man rides the monster, Śārdūla, whose prancing gallop has the rhythm of Nature and inspiration. Hers [the śārdūla's] is the fiery splendour of creative thought; her shape is rhythm itself. This noble beast embodies at the same time the lordly power of the wild animals; and represents the Lordly power (*rājanya*) in general; man, who rides it, copes with it, is particularly the Kṣatriya, the warrior, the royal knight; it [the śārdūla/*vyāla*] is his body of Fame (*yaśaśśarīram*), his royal Splendour.
>
> (1976: II, 336)

Noting in passing that on the Khajuraho temples 'images of the Śārdūla alternate with images of the Apsarās', she continues:

> The Śārdūla, an animal of perfervid ingenuity, composed of rhythm, is an embodiment per artem of the Lion, the Lordly Power of the wild beasts, who is Prakṛti, Śakti, Māyā. This image, composed of Rhythm, is Vāk ['Speech']. Vāk is Life (*Aitareya Brāhmaṇa*, X. 6. 38). The pilgrim who circumambulates the temple and whose eyes dwell on its images 'wanders in the trek of the Apsarās and the Gandharvas and the wild beasts' (*Ṛg Veda* X. 136. 6). He is cognizant of all that is knowable in this universe, says the commentator, he is qualified to confront and to ride the Śārdūla.
>
> (1976: II, 337)[5]

5. The commentator, Sāyaṇa, does not refer to the Śārdūla.

Kramrisch's spiritual reading is equally applied to the *surasundarīs*, the *apsarases*:

> the Celestial Beauties on the walls of the temple, serve man, the devotee; they satisfy his response to them so that, increased in power, released from their attractions and transformed, he proceeds in his devotion towards God in the innermost sanctuary of his heart and in the temple. They help man towards reintegration, akin to those celestial damsels (apsarās) who appear at the time when he, a knower of Brahman departs from this world: 'Him approach 500 celestial damsels, 100 carrying scented powders, saffron, turmeric and the like, in their hands, 100 carrying fruits, 100 carrying various ornaments and 100 carrying garlands. They adorn him with ornaments befitting Brahmā himself. Thus adorned with Brahmā ornaments and knowing Brahman he goes to Brahman.'
>
> (1976: II, 339)[6]

But this is a unique passage in the *Upaniṣads*: nowhere else do the *Upaniṣads* mention 'celestial damsels' (*apsarases*). They are frequent in the epics and in later literature, both as dancing in Indra's heaven and as welcoming dead heroes to heavenly delights. Medieval hero stones in several parts of India commemorate the deaths of warriors on the battlefield by showing them in heaven with *apsarases* while looking down at their own corpses. The connection between *apsarases* and war far outweighs any supposition of spiritual significance. It is true that Kramrisch also later in the same discussion brings in *yoginīs*, who very definitely have to do with both the spiritual and bloodshed. *Yoginīs* bring us closer to the *vyāla* in that they often have animal heads or animal mounts. But *yoginīs* are not usually on mainstream temples. They have their own temple, as at Khajuraho; perhaps the earliest extant *yoginī* temple. But *yoginīs* would disrupt the aesthetic concerns of the royal temple.

It is important to note that Kramrisch does connect the *apsaras* and the *vyāla*:

> Surasundarī, which means Celestial Beauty, is but one of the names and types in which the image of Śakti is carved on the walls of the temple... While every man is not equipped for riding the Śārdūla, he may be led by Śakti and grasp the meaning of her hands (hasta), postures and actions. While the Śārdūla is the 'angel' of active man, the various images of Śakti assist his contemplative and passive nature. The images of Śārdūla (Vyāla), and Śakti are collateral; they alternate on the walls of the temples of Khajuraho and on the capitals of the pillars... The rearing body of the animal and the shape of the woman are seen to sway in similar curves; they are one in nature and form though different in functions and appearance, for Śakti is Vāk, the 'active power of Brahman proceeding from him' (ṚV. X. 125) and the Śārdūla is Vāk.
>
> (1976: II, 338)

Particularly important in this passage is its close, with the discernment of similar curves in animal and woman, and the claim that 'they are one in nature and form'; and we shall return to these points later. I am not sure what

6. Quoting *Kauśītakī Brāhmaṇa Upaniṣad* I. 4.

Kramrisch means by the images of Śakti assisting man's 'contemplative and passive nature'. It is true that on the Khajuraho temples, sculptures representing human women are bold and urgent in their approaches to men, gazing ardently at them while the men look aside (Smith 2011). Thus far, Kramrisch is confirmed by the sculpture—human males are somewhat passive; so too the freestanding gods, who do nothing but stand about. But the *apsarases* themselves show no inclination to serve. They have their own diminutive servants at their feet; and stand just as calm and selfpossessed as the gods.

Madhusan Dhaky, taking as his starting point the brief list of sixteen forms of the *vyāla* given in Sanskrit temple texts (*vāstuśāstra*), surveyed the whole range of the shapes it takes on temples. 'The basic face is...that of a lion with a forehead of an antelope, ears of a boar and horns of a ram. The shoulders should resemble those of a horse with leonine curve and feline feet' (Dhaky 1965: 15–16). 'In these hyper-hybrid beasts the Indian sculptor has...succeeded in communicating the subtle, specific likeness of a particular animal for its *vyāla* form.' However, Dhaky notes, 'Several forms encountered actually on the temples are altogether baffling, indefinable in their variations' (p. 18). He points out that the *vyālas* are placed in 'the deep *salilāntaras* (recesses [for the descent of rain] water)' on the walls of the shrine and hall. 'With their full stature and entourage they hide in and haunt these semiobscure corners' (p. 13). Although the *vyālas* sometimes have a rider, '[n]ormally, they are unbridled, autonomous, delimited only by the space they occupy' (p. 19). Eventually in the seventeenth century 'atrophied and abject, they are seen swaying, staggering and trying hard to adapt to the changing conditions. They remind us of the last days of the dinosaurs.' Dhaky goes on to remark that: 'Their original significance, as well as purpose were by now forgotten' (p. 30). But he makes no attempt to suggest what that significance might have been.

Zhu gives an exact account of the variety of hybrid forms of the *vyāla* on 20 temples, including seven temples at Khajuraho. Her view of the symbolism of the *vyāla* is as follows:

> The *vyāla* is the symbol of the supernatural—the invisible or unseen forces: rain, storms, drought, flood, disasters whether natural or manmade. The *vyāla* trampling on an elephant expresses the power of the supernatural over the kingdom (and by extension, the world). The riders of the *vyāla* or the warriors fighting it show man's struggle to control nature. He is obliged to unwillingly submit to it, but sometimes he is the victor. His position of rider on the *vyāla* and his expression show it clearly.
>
> (Zhu 1997: 192)[7]

'We see that the artists took more liberty in the creation of the *vyālas* than in that of the divinities...sometimes they are placid, subjugated...sometimes they are virile or powerful...sometimes they are playful or malicious...sympathetic or amusing... they contort their bodies which have at the same time an animal force and a nymph-like beauty (*une force d'animal, et une beauté de nymphe*)' (Zhu 1997: 194). Here we have

7. My translation from the French for all quotations from Zhu.

a brief connection between the *vyāla* and *apsaras* that perhaps echoes Kramrisch's 'one in nature and form'.

Although Zhu sees the *vyāla* as principally 'protector of the temple', 'their function is only to frighten invaders or enemies who wish harm to the temple... But for those who construct the temple or venerate the deities, they are protectors. Even if sometimes they show their force or their ferocity, they are all the same friends, and their "sport" can be considered as a game' (Zhu 1997: 195). Key to this interpretation, which echoes Kramrisch, is the fact that the *vyāla* nearly always has a dual relationship: with the rider on its back, and with the warrior attacking at its feet. Zhu concludes her assessment at the end of her Khajuraho section, by saying that she had tried to discover if the *vyāla*s had a particular relation with the divinities or the guardians of the quarters (*dikpāla*s) or if each type of *vyāla* had a fixed place, but admits that she had found nothing that answered those questions (p. 196).

I begin my own explanation of the *vyāla* by emphasizing the contrast between the big *vyāla* who neighbour the freestanding gods and *apsaras*es, and the small *vyāla* who continue their regular duties, facing away from the pillars of the relievo shrines of the gods on the walls, and from doorjambs to the shrine proper. Thus on the south wall of the southeast subsidiary shrine of the Lakṣmaṇa temple, the relievo shrine of Narasiṃha, Manlion Viṣṇu, is flanked by the usual pattern of alternating *apsara* and *vyāla*; and its pillars are flanked by small *vyāla*, looking away from the shrine, and clearly functioning as protectors (Fig. 2). These small *vyāla* do not curve back over themselves to look behind. The large *vyāla* at Khajuraho, the specifically Khajuraho-style *vyāla*, do not face outwards to potential dangers; they are lined up to express their own being, rather than to protect.

Figure 2. South wall of south-east shrine of Lakṣmaṇa temple, Khajuraho.

The *vyāla*'s form was originally conceived, no doubt, to express protection, to frighten. Christa Sütterlin shows that apotropaic monsters around the world make gestures based on animal qualities belonging to an earlier stage of human evolution. With regard to the mouth:

> the mouth pulled apart is a relic found in children's culture all over the world, and its meaning is the same...anger and threat. This gesture consists in uncovering the lower row of teeth by opening and pulling down the corners of the mouth. What should be exposed can be seen primarily today in primates that still have the elongated upper canine teeth that are seen to their full extent when the animal is pulling down the lower lip while threatening. The teeth might have evolved as show organs as well as weapons. The expression, which is still performed in humans even though their upper canines are not threatening, is cross-cultural, and the rate of recognition by members of different cultures is very high. Apparently the expression survived the organ for which it was evolved.
>
> (Sütterlin 1989: 72)

Sculptural forms 'that are referred to as grotesque, humoresque, vicious and wicked in Western Christian tradition reveal a powerful meaning that is independent from an ecclesiastical or even a cultural context' (Sütterlin 1989: 69). 'Evidently when humans communicate with danger, illness or evil forces, they behave as they would in conflicts with their fellow humans: they threaten and appease, they bluff and display themselves—putting on horns and teeth, showing the beard—to make themselves strong and dominant' (p. 74). Very relevant also is her further point concerning these distortions of the face: 'they also may be a means by which humans show themselves unpredictable, by which they break the rules of communication altogether' (p. 72). The *vyāla*s are unpredictable in their hybridity, and in their varying relationship with the rider on their backs. Contrast this breaking of the 'rules of communication' with Kramrisch's assertion, noted above, that the *vyāla* 'is Vāk [speech]'. Very much to the point is Dhaky's comment on the hybridity of the *vyāla* as 'baffling'.

So, in some sense, the *vyāla*'s monstrous face parallels, magnifies, a human face expressing aggression. Its horns and bulging eyes add to the effect, but it curves back to look at its rider rather than outward to the onlooker. Another key point is that its irises, clearly incised, look upwards, away from both men. In fact, most eyes at Khajuraho with irises marked outlook slightly upward, but in the huge eye of the *vyāla* the upwardness is much more marked.

I want now to consider the three principal components of the *vyāla*'s hybridity: lion, horse and elephant. The *vyāla* is always based on the lion, and when its head is mainly lionlike it is called a lion *vyāla* (*siṃhavyāla*). Horseheaded *vyāla*s are rare. Zhu (1997: 143) mentions them as listed by the *Samarāṅgaṇasūtradhāra* and *Aparājitapṛcchā* but gives no examples from Khajuraho. Nevertheless, the horse underlies the *vyāla*: the *vyāla* is a lion acting as a horse. When the *vyāla* has an elephant trunk, it is called an elephant *vyāla* (*gajavyāla*). On the Kandariya's outer walls, of the 120 *vyāla*s, 19 are *gajavyāla*s, and 94 are *siṃhavyāla*s, as ennumerated by Zhu (1997: 182). But the elephant has a dual presence, in that it is often shown beneath the *vyāla*'s feet, as its defeated opponent. That the lion defeats the elephant is a commonplace of Sanskrit poetry. But the elephant is a highly important figure. It is the largest animal as well as the largest tamed animal; it is the most powerful weapon of war; and it also has a cosmic function, in that the elephants of the four or eight divisions of the horizon support the world. While the east facing lion on the *śukanāsa* ledge high on the spire stands guard over the entrance to the shrine of the temple, four elephants radiate out from the spire as the elephants who support the world. One of the Khajuraho temple inscriptions refers to these elephants falling from the sky when Śiva dances his dance of destruction. At Khajuraho, as elsewhere, some of these elephants and lions who were on high are now to be seen on the ground, sometimes placed above steps by temple renovators. Figure 3 shows two lions and elephant on the ground beside the north side of the Lakṣmaṇa temple. As with the lion on the right, such lions often have a human warrior before them, contending with them.

Figure 3. Two lions, one with warrior, and an elephant, all displaced, to north of Lakṣmaṇa temple, Khajuraho.

Kramrisch gives a detailed analysis of the most famous lion and warrior sculpture at Khajuraho, in the porch of the Mahādeo Temple, a small shrine between the Kandarīya and the Devī Jagadambā Temple.

> By the response of their physiognomies and heroic bodies, the animal and the man are confronted in similar arcs of breathing chests; while the frame of man yields it by an extreme effort in which is power, defiance and submissiveness, agony, in its literal sense—it holds the outlines of his back in its grip—the curve of the animal's front has quiet power and the deep saddle of its back curve, dignity. The Lion but raises its paw while man throws forth his whole weight in the fight by which he wins the monster's protection.
>
> (Kramrisch 1976: II, 368)

Here in the relatively straightforward combat of man and lion is *in nuce* the complexity of the *vyāla*: the man is both defiant and submissive, and his effort 'wins the monster's protection'. And further, she gives a spiritual interpretation: 'It shows man as he approaches the Centre, under the threat of the Lion; man draws the sword of Knowledge and protects himself from Māyā with the shield of dispassion' (Kramrisch 1976: II, 336).

The *vyāla* is Māyā for Kramrisch, but we must not forget that all three animals that underlie the *vyāla* are most obviously animals of war; and the temple itself is very often the product of the spoils of war. The *apsaras*es also relate to war. Warriors go to Indra's heaven. The *apsaras*es, who are his dancing girls, entertain and are at the disposal of the dead warriors. Herostones in various parts of India, commemorating a heroic warrior's death, show him welcomed by *apsaras*es and enjoying their company in heaven while his dead body lies on the battlefield. But other than occasionally surviving inscriptions which refer to a royal founder's military successes, temples at Khajuraho make little reference to the battlefield other than small friezes showing marching armies and hunting scenes: the uncertainties of human conflict have little place in the certainties the temple seeks to establish. Above all, the *apsaras*es are shown in a pure idealized world, with actual lovemaking relegated to the lesser, human world, sculpted on a smaller scale.[8]

I now turn to connections between *vyāla* and *apsaras*, and first consider the possibility that the *vyāla* is female. We saw earlier that Kramrisch's concern with a theological understanding of the *vyāla* led her to take it as feminine in order to tap into Vedic references to speech (Vāk). The *vyāla*'s background proximity to the *apsaras* suggests that it might relate to the sexuality of the *apsaras*, to the power and danger of sexuality. Figure 4 shows the intensity of the voluptuousness of the *apsaras*es right beside the intensity of action in the *vyāla*, inside the Lakṣmaṇa temple. If feminine, the *vyāla* would be one step nearer to the *apsaras*. Woman is commonly seen by men as more animal than man. In the *Nāṭyaśāstra*, the early text on dance and theatre, a whole range of animals are said to represent different types of women, rather parallel to the way that 16 types of animal go to make up the *vyāla*. For the *Nāṭyaśāstra*, 14 different animals plus gods and other supernatural beings exemplify the different types of women (*Nāṭyaśāstra* 22.100-101). Among these:

> The woman for whom honour and dishonour are the same,
> who has a rough skin and a harsh voice,
> who is wily, a bold liar, and yelloweyed, is a tiger/a *vyāla*.
>
> (*Nāṭyaśāstra* 22.118)

The preceding type of woman is one who takes after a *yakṣa*, so it is not impossible that a mythological *vyāla* is referred to here, rather than a tiger. We might say with the *Nāṭyaśāstra* that the temple *vyāja* is a bold liar, a haughty teller of untruths (*anṛtoddhatakatha*), because the *vyālas* we are looking at are untrue forms, and we cannot tell what they mean. Furthermore, with regard to the possible femininity of the *vyāla*, one might argue that the multiplicity

8. With the exception of the famous erotic panels between the spire and closed hall of the Lakṣmaṇa, Viśvanātha and Kandariyā temples, where the humans taking part are the same height as *apsarases*, gods, and *vyālas*.

of components of the monster is the multiple fecundity of the mother gone haywire; that monstrosity is essentially feminine. But that would lead into the burgeoning field of feminist monster studies, for which there is no space here.

Figure 4. *Vyālas* beside *apsarases*, interior of Lakṣmaṇa temple, Khajuraho.

An important factor is that the sex of the north Indian *vyāla* is not shown. In the south of India, the sheathed penis of the *vyāla* (Tamil, *yāḷi*), modelled on that of a horse or bull, is commonly shown, and all the more visible because the monster manifests face on, leaping down onto the onlooker, whereas in the north the sex of the *vyāla* is hidden. Partly because the *vyāla* is turned sideways and half the time one uplifted hind leg hides the penis, if penis it does have. And when it is the hind leg nearest the wall that is raised, the penis area is still hidden because the tail wraps round between the legs. It is hard not to get the impression that the sculptor intends the sexuality to be hidden. Geer (2008: 335–36) says of the lion that in reality 'in lions as well as in the other cats, the penis is small and situated just below the anus', and that in some Buddhist sculpture in Sri Lanka the lion is given the penis of a bull instead. Zhu says nothing about sex organs in relation to the *vyāla* she studies, but in the South-western subsidiary chapel of the Lakṣmaṇa temple, on its northern side to the left of Varāha, her photograph shows a dog *vyāla*, *śvānavyāla*, and the penis is clearly visible. This is the only dog *vyāla* she finds in Khajuraho. So at Khajuraho the *vyāla*'s penis generally is not shown. Three reasons why it is not visible would be because lions' penises are not very obvious; or because the sculptor chooses to hide it; or because the *vyāla* is female. Most likely, in my view, is that the sculptor sought to keep us guessing, to make the *vyāla* 'baffling'.

There is an aspect of the symbolism of a lion's, or tiger's, head that is not usually mentioned in an Indian context, namely that it may, as in European fin-de-siècle art, represent a woman's vagina (Dijkstra 1986). Such a reading may be given of full-frontal representations of Durgā astride her tiger. More conclusively, Mūkāmbikā Bhagavatī in south Karnataka is 'a naked, forest-dwelling goddess with a tiger's head in the place of her vagina' (Caldwell 1999: 148). For this symbolism to apply, it does not matter whether the animal head is male or female, except the male lion's head with its mane would be more impressive.

Attribution of animality to women can, however, move women to a higher plane, for animality can denote superhuman qualities, just as forms of Viṣṇu have animal heads, not to speak of Gaṇeśa, most popular of gods. This is especially true of *yoginī*s, spiritually advanced semi-divine creatures who are a kind of cross between witches and goddesses. Moreover it might well be that the earliest of the few extant *yoginī* temples is to be found precisely in Khajuraho. What is particularly significant is that the temple is rectangular, rather than circular like other *yoginī* temples. The circular form of those temples, with a single opening, directly corresponds to the form of the womb. Once the form of a womblike circle had been adopted it seems to me inconceivable that builders would have returned to a rectangular plan. In that case Khajuraho would have the earliest extant *yoginī* temple. None of the three surviving statues have animal heads, but it is likely that some of the inhabitants of the 64 shrines (plus one larger one) had animal heads. A few hundred metres to the south west of the Lakṣmaṇa temple was this old temple of fierce and dangerous *yoginī*s. The worshipper seeing the massed semidivine femininity, the *apsaras*es, on the Lakṣmaṇa temple, and the other nearby structures, may well have felt in them resonances with the sixty-four *yoginī*s. And likewise the hybridity of the *vyāla*s may have resonated with the hybridity of the *yoginī*s, if some of the latter did indeed have animal heads.

Nor were the *apsaras*es entirely lacking in manifestly dangerous qualities on their own account. There are a number of cases where an *apsaras* has on her body, on her thigh, a scorpion—an item of heavy symbolism, small though in size. Figure 5 shows an *apsaras* with a scorpion on her thigh and her *mons veneris* revealed. In an illuminating paper, Simona Cohen, a historian of western art, directs her attention to the scorpion at Khajuraho. She carefully enumerates the occurrence of the scorpion on *apsaras*es:

> While the Lakshmana and the Parsvanatha temples, both dating to the second half of the 10th century, lack this theme, it seems to have made its first appearance inside the mahamandapa of the Visvanatha temple, dated by an inscription to 999 AD. This was followed in the early 11th century by the Citragupta temple with two scorpion

> apsarases on the exterior, the Devi Jagadambi with two on the exterior and one in the mahamandapa, and the Kandariya Mahadeva (ca. 1030) with ten on the exterior and two in the pradaksinapatha. The Vamana, Javari, Adinatha (Jain) temples of the second half of the 11th century and the Chaturbhuja of the early 12th century each have one scorpion apsaras on the exterior. On the later Duladeo temple, probably built towards the mid twelfth century, the theme no longer appears. Thus we have a total of 22 extant figures integrated into the sculptural programs of eight temples. It is possible that additional scorpion apsarases belonging to the 11th century temples at Khajuraho have been destroyed or dislocated.
>
> (Cohen 2000: 19)[9]

Figure 5. *Apsaras* with scorpion on her thigh, interior of Kandariya temple, Khajuraho.

To these can be added from Krishna Deva's study of the temples, one instance in the interior of the Parsvanatha, and one in the interior of the Citragupta

9. My source is the author's manuscript, p. 1; she informs me that the printed text introduced errors.

(1990: 264 and 269). Krishna Deva regularly refers to an *apsaras* as 'disrobing with or without a scorpion', and he takes the common Indian view that the scorpion is merely the reason for the woman undressing rather than finding any symbolic charge. Cohen, for her part, draws on a wide range of material, including Indian astrological texts, to demonstrate the impressively ancient and extensive symbolisms of the scorpion in India and beyond. In summary,

> the scorpion was a uniquely ambivalent symbol associated, on the one hand, with poison and death and, on the other, with fertility and procreation. These conflicting connotations were mutually supportive in establishing the scorpion image as an apotropaic symbol. Its potency as a magical protective image accrued from its inherent malevolence.

Cohen proceeds to argue,

> A similar ambivalence was conveyed by the *apsarā*, who functioned as a classic symbol of fertility, beauty and benevolence, in a concrete as well as a spiritual and more abstract sense, and at the same time could personify the temptations of the flesh and its perils in the broader context of man's spiritual striving for *mokṣa*.[10]

We should note that the dangerous power of the scorpion at Khajuraho is shown by its presence on the concave stomach of an eightarmed Cāmuṇḍā in the Archaeological Museum at Khajuraho and of a twelvearmed Cāmuṇḍā on the Kandariya (Lorenzetti 2000: 70; Krishna Deva 1990: 154).

What of the *vyāla* in this? It is possible to find parallels between the *vyāla* and the scorpion, between the constant companion of the *apsaras* and the occasional guest on her thigh. The *vyāla* lurks in recesses, the scorpion lurks in dark places. The scorpion startles one when discovered. It attacks instinctively, and is instinctively attacked by people. The same might be said of the *vyāla*. The curve of the scorpion parallels the curve of the *vyāla*'s back, and most notably the *vyāla* is swung round upon itself in way that makes the most analogous movement to the scorpion that is possible for it.

Perhaps the scorpion's claws mirror the embrace of a woman, and the sting in the tail the danger of her sexuality. Then again the curving sweep of the scorpion's tail parallels the involuntary nature of the male erection, the autonomous nature of sexuality as something outside, or lower than, the human. The scorpion expresses both the danger and the intensity of sexual experience. And perhaps the *vyāla* mirrors all that. One thing is highly plausible, I suggest. The warrior on the ground who fights against the *vyāla* usually directs his sword or spear towards his opponent's groin: that the *vyāla* is often attacked in its sexual parts, or where its sexual parts ought to be, is a mirror inversion of an important part of the inherent symbolism of the scorpion.

It now remains to look more carefully at the *vyāla*'s relationship with the two men who usually accompany it at Khajuraho. Like the *apsaras*, the *vyāla*

10. Author's own manuscript, p. 9.

has a close encounter with men, violent, arduous, and ardent; but in the case of the *apsarases*, the men are not displayed on the temple, nor does she dance at Khajuraho for gods or men. Both men, the rider and the opposing warrior, are already present in Gupta versions of the monster as leogryph, as in the frontispiece of Dhaky's book. There both rider and warrior are of equal size. Indeed usually the rider is of normal human size on later *vyāla* in Orissa and Tamil Nadu. But in the Khajuraho type of *vyāla* there is a remarkable disparity in size between the man on the ground and the man on the *vyāla*'s back; the latter is tiny. Figure 6 shows the typical Khajuraho-type *vyāla* face to face with his little rider.[11] Not only is the rider tiny, but it is often difficult to make out what he is actually doing: his interaction with the *vyāla* is ambiguous and mysterious. Sometimes peering like a miniature dentist into the monster's mouth, sometimes seeming to supplicate the monster; seldom simply a rider. Why is the 'rider' so small? It is the case that horse riders on the friezes, as in the case of the frieze around the base of the Lakṣmaṇa temple, are often shown as tiny alongside full-height infantry, because the frame of the register is mainly taken up by the horses they ride. But it seems to me more likely in the case of the *vyāla* that it is not the restricted space in itself that makes the rider small, but rather the emphatic reduction of his status vis-à-vis the beast that is the *vyāla*. It worth noting that the earliest of the main Khajuraho temples, the Lakṣmaṇa temple has in the inner ambulatory two *vyāla*s who have full-size riders, and do not turn back on themselves, facing forwards like ordinary steeds. One is on the south wall of the shrine, to the right of Varāha, and the other on the north wall, to the left of Hayagrīva. These two are old forms that the sculptors of Khajuraho deliberately distanced themselves from.

Far from being the competent bridler of desires discerned by Kramrisch in her highly theological and text based interpretation, the rider at Khajuraho is on the contrary not much more than a gnat in relation to the *vyāla*. The back, neck, and mouth of the *vyāla* are his sphere of operations, but he operates in a whimsical and ineffectual manner. In his size and demeanour he is the emphatic opposite to the strenuous determination of his much larger fellow human below. Whereas the figure below is absolutely a warrior in contention with the *vyāla*, his back straining as he prepares a mighty blow and curving like that of his mighty opponent; and he points or lunges his weapon at the exposed groin of the monster, the small figure, in total contrast, fusses about the open mouth of the monster, possible symbol of the vagina, the *vagina dentata*.

11. In Fig. 6 note how precisely the curving back of the *apsaras* to the right copies the curve of the *vyāla*'s back. The only atypical thing in this is that the warrior on the ground swings back a sword, rather than directly thrusting at the *vyāla*'s groin. But the sword does have a curved blade to match the other curves, including that of the warrior's own back.

Figure 6. *Vyāla* with rider and attacking warrior, south wall of Lakṣmaṇa temple, Khajuraho.

Monsters normally mean conflict, a conflict already asserted in their mixture of forms. But the conflict that these monsters are involved in is trivial—their human foes, for the most part, do not seriously trouble them, though we must make the major proviso here that where their sexual parts are being attacked, they may be about to be seriously troubled. And they certainly would appear to have no time for anything outside their own frame—ignoring the attack on their vulnerable underbelly, seemingly obsessed with the tiny figure on their back whom they wheel round to face. At Khajuraho they stand beside gods and *apsaras*es who are not visibly interacting with anyone else. The monsters turn away from the heroic men who beset them, in order to play with their riders. The most noticeable interactions on the walls are the human sexual activities, often with onlookers incorporated. The repeated, limited and stereotyped interactions of the monsters have some sort of counterpart with the human eroticism. The man on foot confronted by the more powerful animal force, is in some sense a version of male versus female (Smith 1994: 95); and the tiny rider peering into the monster's mouth is in some sense the curious male examining the origin of the world, the *yoni*. Finally, in Figure 7 we see a womanfaced *vyāla* on the north wall of the Viśvanātha, whose lips seem ready to kiss the tiny rider who looks at her undismayed. Such *vyāla*s are rare, but she suggests the possibility of the *vyāla* in general being feminine, or of alternating sexuality. Contrast the *vyāla*'s interest in its rider with the self-absorption of the *apsaras* to the left.

Figure 7. A woman-faced *vyāla* on north wall of Viśvanātha temple, Khajuraho.

The monsters are emphatically present in the temple. They were originally protecting forces, but they don't face outwards to possible new opponents. They are now a self-contained force that circles back upon itself like a scorpion's tail. As the manifest force that accompanies the *apsarases*, they are symbols of the force of sexuality. The repetition of the gods demeans the gods, the repetition of the *apsarases* empowers them, the repetition of the monsters emphasizes a free floating power, perhaps a power that ought to belong to the gods, but that is most inherent in the *apsarases*, and most apparent in the *vyāla*.

The monster is first and foremost a statement of physical power and prowess. A combination of two or more life forms, plus its rider and its attacker, it is necessarily much more than an ordinary animal. Its eye shows its intelligence. It tramples the foe who attacks, but often it receives a blow in its vital parts, its sexual parts even, and there is reason sometimes to suspect that its life may soon be over, not unlike a scorpion that stings itself, since the attacking warrior is a more less inseparable part of the *vyāla* entity. On that account its still remaining might is all the more impressive. Its twisting writhing back, visible to itself as it looks over its shoulder, is its most striking characteristic. This beautifully curving back mirrors the often curving twisted backs of the *apsarases* who stand beside it as well as the curve of the scorpion's tail. Held back in the niche of the *salilāntara* water chute, it is not unreasonable to take the *vyāla* as representative of the subterranean, the hidden side of human nature as well as the alter ego of the *apsarases*.

REFERENCES

Caldwell, S. 1999. *Oh Terrifying Mother: Sexuality, Violence and Worship of the Goddess Kali*. New Delhi: Oxford University Press.

Cohen, S. 2000. 'The Scorpion Apsaras at Khajuraho: Migrations of a Symbol.' *Journal of the Asiatic Society of Bombay* 74: 19–38.

Cunningham, A. 1994. *Four Reports Made During the Years 1862-636465*. Archaeological Survey of India, Delhi: Rahul Publishing House (reprint).

Dhaky, M. A. 1965. *The Vyala Figures on the Mediaeval Temples of India*. Varanasi: Prithivi Prakashan.

Dijkstra, B. 1986. *Idols of Perversity: Fantasies of Feminine Evil in Fin-de-Siècle Culture*. New York: Oxford University Press.

Geer, A. E. van der. 2008. *Animals in Stone: Indian Mammals Sculptured through Time*. Leiden: E. J. Brill. http://dx.doi.org/10.1163/ej.9789004168190.i-462

Ghosh, M. (ed.). 1967. *Nāṭyaśāstra*. Calcutta: Manisha.

Kramrisch, S. 1976. *The Hindu Temple*. 2 vols, Delhi: Motilal Banarsidass (reprint).

Krishna Deva. 1990. *Temples of Khajuraho*. 2 vols. New Delhi: Archaeological Survey of India.

Lorenzetti, T. 2000. *A Guide to the Appreciation of Indian Sculptures in the Archaeological Museum of Khajuraho*. Varanasi: Indica Books.

Smith, D. 2011. 'Facial Expression in the Erotic Art of Khajuraho. A Preliminary Investigation.' *Warsaw Indological Studies* 4: 115–33.

Smith, W. 1994. Review of Vishaka N. Desai and Darielle Mason (eds), *Gods, Guardians, and Lovers: Temple Sculptures from North India A.D. 700–1200*. *Art Journal* 53(2): 94–97.

Sütterlin, C. 1989. 'Universals in Apotropaic Symbolism: A Behavioral and Comparative Approach to Some Medieval Sculptures.' *Leonardo* 22(1): 65–74. http://dx.doi.org/10.2307/1575143

Woodward, H. W. Jr. 1989. 'The Lakṣmaṇa Temple, Khajuraho, and Its Meanings.' *Ars Orientalis* 19: 27–48.

Zhu, X. 1997. 'Les Vyāla dans l'art de l'inde.' 2 vols, Unpublished PhD dissertation. Paris: Université de Paris Sorbonne.

Her Majesty's Servants: The Tame and the Wild under the British Raj

DAVIDE TORRI*

INTRODUCTION: WHERE WILD THINGS ARE

Let the robber retreat—let the tiger turn tail
In the name of the Empress, the Overland Mail!

(Kipling 1960: 33)

Under the lens of British colonialism, South Asian fauna came to epitomize a system of social relations that can be divided into three groups: the ruler, the ruled and the unruly. The complete apparatus of dominance and repression, as well as the enforcing of a discourse on the necessity of a superior order, clearly surfaces in many of the texts produced by the literates working in, or simply travelling through, the 'Jewel of the Crown', the British Indian Empire. The Victorian worldview was strongly affected by South Asian real and imaginary landscapes, and for almost two centuries it contributed—for better or worse, directly or indirectly—to the intellectual life of South Asia (Saïd 1994: 40–41). Animal motifs assumed a central position in the colonial imaginary landscape. Along with other natural indigenous features (plants, rivers, mountains, etc.) they contributed to shape a fictional idea—an India of the mind—that served for the purpose of legitimizing colonialism. If Europeans were to bring the bright light of Civilization, the colonized place should be exotic to the verge of barbarianism, the wildlife dangerously wild and geographical features mysterious and extreme in their essence.

* Davide Torri received his PhD from the University of Naples 'L'Orientale' and is currently Researcher at the Asia-Europe Cluster of Excellence in the Karl Jaspers Centre for Advanced Transcultural Studies at the University of Heidelburg, Germany. He specializes in the study of Himalayan and sub-Himalayan shamanism. His publications—both journal articles and book chapters—explore ritual possession among Indian and Nepali indigenous ethnic minorities such as Lepchas, Hyolmos, Tamang and Tharus. He is the author of *Il lama e il Pombo. Gli Hyolmo del Nepal tra sciamanismo e Buddhismo* (Roma: Edizioni Nuova Culture, 2012) and is currently co-editing with Diana Riboli *Shamanism and Violence: Power, Repression and Suffering in Indigenous Religious Conflicts* for Ashgate (forthcoming, 2013).

The complex relationships linking British rulers with their subaltern subjects and possessions *d'outremer* took place within the domain of ideas. Literature played a major role in shaping politics and policies, ideas and prejudices (Greenberger 1969: 1). As stated by Saïd, European writings and discourses on Africa, India and other colonized countries were 'part of the general European effort to rule distant lands and peoples' (1994: xi). The British worldview was built along straight evolutionary lines based on the assumption of a moral and racial superiority, thus thwarting every serious effort at real comprehension of the (colonial) Other.

Such a *Weltanschauung* was based on the myth of the 'national character' of the British stock: a people born to dominate and conquer, brave and honest, active and masculine. Empire was thus a 'manly' endeavour, as masterfully expressed by the female heroine of Bithia Mary Croker's novel, *Diana Barrington*: 'I like to know that my husband is a man, and not an old woman. He shoots tigers, plays polo, and ride races, with my full approval' (Croker 1896: 273).

India was to England a land of mystery and adventure, the equivalent of the Wild West of the American frontier: a land in which to express manliness and muscular Christianity (Greenberger 1969: 25). Adventure was the 'energizing myth of empire' (Green 1979: xi) and a prerequisite for *jingoism*, the British version for that virulent and aggressive form of patriotism which is better known as chauvinism.

The Indian landscape was something dangerous but passive, the exuberance of natural manifestations, an unruly domain to be ordered, the people—the natives—childish and half-civilized: 'half-demons and half child' (Kipling 1960: 323), 'lesser breeds without a law' (p. 328) as in Kipling's notorious verses.[1] British colonialism was a mission and a duty.[2] It was 'a fateful superiority' (Saïd 1989: 215). The narratives of the Empire are, in fact, always teleological in their essence.

In this chapter I will discuss how human and non-human indigenous animals, or even the hybrid system they form, are discussed within the colonial system as a vast, uncharted and uncanny new territory to conquer with sword and pen alike. Moving from Rudyard Kipling as my main source—since 'his fiction represents the empire and its conscious legitimization' (Saïd 1994: xi) and 'his writings consciously dealt with anxieties and ambiguities of Empire' (Kutzer 2000: 13)—this chapter eventually argues that the colonialism of the mind exerted by the British Empire did not spare non-human animals and such perdurable effects still linger and affect uncritical policies of exploitation of South Asia.

1. 'The White Man's Burden', originally published in *The Times*, February 4, 1899 as a comment to the US intervention in the Philippines.
2. See Edwards (1953). In a similar way, the US proclaimed their version of this concept with the *Manifest Destiny* of the nation (Greenberg 2005).

MASTERS AND SERVANTS: OTHER-THAN-HUMAN ANIMALS AS RACIALIZED OTHERS

> In the deep shade, at the farther end of the room, a figure ran backwards and forward. What it was, whether beast or human, one could not, at first sight, tell: it grovelled, seemingly, on all fours, it snatched and growled like some strange wild animal: but it was covered with clothing, and a quantity of dark, grizzled hair, wild as a mane, hid its head and face.
>
> (Brontë 1847: 321)

Edward Saïd, in *Representing the Colonized*, wrote that the colonial subjects are 'fixed in zones of dependency and peripherality, stigmatised in the designation of underdeveloped, developing states, ruled by a superior, developed of metropolitan colonizer who was posited as a categorically antithetical overlord' (Saïd 1989: 207). This antithetical overlord possesses an inherent and intrinsic attitude to lead clearly expressed in terms of race: 'In the first place, I believe in the British Empire and, in the second place, I believe in the British race. I believe that the British race is the greatest of governing races that the world has ever seen' (Chamberlain 1897: 89). Hence the necessity to keep the blood pure, to avoid intermarriage and the adoption of native customs. The fear of hybridity and the risk of going native could undermine the racist division separating the conqueror from the conquered once. Representing indigenous populations as beasts was therefore a stratagem. 'Kipling constructs animals as racialized others' (Nyman 2003: 38), but neither was he the first nor the last: 'In text ranging for the mid-Victorian *Wuthering Heights* (1847) through the high-Victorian *Black Beauty* (1877) to the early Edwardian *Green Mansions* (1904) the imperialist encounter between English male aggressor and colonized people is figured in animal metaphor' (Denenholz-Morse 2007: 181).

The animalization of subaltern subjects was not limited to the colonial Other. There was also an internal Other to be subdued and thus considered ontologically inferior: members of the working class, Irish people, women, Gypsies and Travellers, and so on. Brontë's Heathcliff is more than once described as a wolfish being, alternatively resembling a wild animal, an Indian prince or a gypsy (Denenholz-Morse 2007: 182), while the insane Bertha from *Jane Eyre*, whose madness is linking her non-human behaviour, is overtly paired with the condition of animals and savages.[3]

3. Madness is depicted as a process of going native or going animalistic. The same topic is to be found in one of the most famous of Conan Doyle's Sherlock Holmes' novels, *The Speckled Band*, where a British Doctor, back from the Indies, shows a strange behaviour. He keeps wild animals inside his home and is on friendly terms with a group of gypsies. Another clue is to be found in R. L. Stevenson's *The Strange Case of Dr Jekyll and Mr Hyde*, the latter being described as something less than human, driven by the worst instincts and far from the domain of reason: 'the apelike, murderous Hyde, moreover, is the stereotype of the shillelagh-wielding Irish hooligan, conjuring up fears of Fenianism' (Brantlinger 2009: 48).

Partially because of the growing influence of Darwin's theories, 'the animal was often envisioned as a devolved human being' (Denenholz-Morse 2007: 186). The popularization of Darwin's thought—a controversial topic as far as faith and religion are concerned—was used to explain phenomena of social adaptation and aggressive expansion. As among other species, the weaker must be, and surely will be, subdued by the fittest. The 'savage' soon became the epitome of the missing link between the human and the animal. To the eyes of the Colonizer, 'savagery' was conceived just as a prelude to annihilation.

In most colonial literature, 'natives' have been depicted by European observers as animal-like or child-like beings (Jahoda 1999: 51, 129). These two groups were employed to denote lack of reason. In particular, to be likened to animals was to be lower than Europeans. Indigenous populations were thought to be governed by the lowest instincts and appetites, cruel and amoral. Conversely, being equated to children was meant to point out at a lack in discipline and self-regulation, a naïveté and a social status lower than those of adult people (Saminaden, Loughnan and Haslam 2010: 91). Both models became ways to dehumanize the colonized Other. By postulating a phylogenetically lower position as in the case of animals, one invites punishment, while by postulating an ontogenetically lower position one invites paternalistic control (Saminaden, Loughnan and Haslam 2010: 91). Animalization or infantilization contributed to the enactment and legitimization of a practice of domination (Cosslett 2006: 126). At the same time, 'by its mere existence, the animal trope, as it is used in the colonial context, poses a threat to the maintenance of order and hierarchy' (Nyman 2003: 39) since the animal, like the child, being governed not by reason but by instinct and desire, is constantly attracted by the lure of disobedience.

Anthropology played a key role in the study of the colonial subject and thus in the representation of non-Western societies. The simple fact of an 'ethnographic encounter between a sovereign European observer and a non-European native occupying, so to speak, a lesser status and a distant place' (Saïd 1989: 207) helped and made possible patterns of exploitation, oppression and control of native cultures and societies under the *aegis* of the Empire (Asad 1973: 11-12). Colonization was commonly thought of as process enabling the primitive subjects of European imperial powers to move from the lowest stage (primitive animal-like) to that of primitive child-like subjects. The current positivist notion of progress was used to give legitimacy to dominion and genocidal practices aimed at a whole world of human and non-human animals waiting to be punished, disciplined and harnessed in order to serve the Empire.

THE TAME: ALL THE QUEEN'S ANIMALS

During the Victorian Age the world under the Union Jack was a 'world of unstated assumptions' (Greenberger 1969: 3) built upon a common and shared faith in the values of European Civilization, with the Empire as its spear point. India was the Queen's brightest jewel with only few minor shady areas: criminal 'tribes' wandering in the countryside, outlaws hiding in the still large jungles stretching through the Indian subcontinent, unrest along the Northwestern border (Benson and Esher 1908: 401) and in Upper Burma and superstition still lingering in the minds of her subjects. But for the main part it was assumed that the British rule in the Subcontinent was a stable presence lying on a reliable (domesticated) part of the population. The land was rich and productive, the people cooperating.

A similar assumption is found in Kipling's *The Jungle Book*: there is a law to be respected even in the jungle. In particular, the jungle serves the purpose of describing the colonial periphery as opposed to the imperial metropolis. As clearly demonstrated by Don Randall, the jungle is neither an environment in the proper sense of the term, nor a 'culturally unmarked "world"; it is India as jungle' (Randall 1998: 107). More accurately, it is *native* India, a 'confusing and confused space which has an internal code that Mowgli masters and he has the power to shape' (Kutzer 2000: 24). The internal code of the jungle, the Law, is 'detailed and pervasive, but morally neutral' (Murray 1992: 1).

When Mowgli, the man-cub, gets lost in the jungle, he does not find his place among monkeys, as it happens to the young Tarzan in H. R. Haggard's novel. They are similar to Man, perhaps too much, and therefore they are sinister in nature. Mowgli's place is among the wolves, the free animals who abide the Law and live in an ordered and hierarchical society among other jungle animals. They are on good term with Baloo, the Bear, teacher of the Law, and even when they have to kill other animals, they do it according to the rules. In this way each one has a place to stay and a role to play thus ensuring long-lasting equilibrium and control of useless violence.

It is not by chance that 'the animals Mowgli's define himself with are powerful carnivores: wolves, bears, panthers, pythons' (Cosslett 2006: 140). As McLure puts it: 'had he [Mowgli] been adopted by the antelopes, for instance, it would have been harder for Kipling to ignore the degree of anxiety and amount of carnage licensed by his Social Darwinian Jungle Law' (McLure 1981: 59). Mowgli, the man-cub who is bound to become the Master of the Jungle, has to be a predator, one who can exert violence, and therefore he should be able to claim a key role among carnivores. The Law needs to be enforced.

The introduction of Law in the jungle is a requirement because—as confirmed in Kipling's *How Fear Came* (1895)—the tiger's brutality and the ape's fecklessness have brought fear and shame to the Jungle (Murray 1992: 6). The Law has to be respected because, if broken, it may lead to the intervention of external authorities: white men, armed with guns, on elephants.

Generally, the jungle (as the forest in European folklore) is the ideal space for chaotic forces, well beyond the boundary of human control. But in the British colonial imagery, the Jungle is of a very different nature. It is the

Jungle of Indology, 'disorderly, but for the duly informed, analytically adept, Western specialist, not beyond reasoned comprehension' (Randall 1998: 108). Savage non-human animals are thus depicted as living a life regulated by the Law, each one occupying a niche in a social taxonomy entailing rights and duties upon each one of them. Among the most prominent of the Law-abiding beings we find wolves, which Kipling terms as *The Free People*. They are strong and courageous, natural-born fighters and warriors, members of a knit-closed group—the wolf-pack—hierarchically focused on a single chief. They accept the man-cub, Mowgli the Frog, but as he grows to be a man they start conspiring against him. They are inspired by Shere Khan, the Tiger who observes that Mowgli is a man, a 'natural' master to them all, as expressed by the simple fact that no one is able to stare into his eyes. The man's gaze is the master's gaze. This truth is revealed to the man-cub by Bagheera, the black panther, a renegade born in captivity at Udaipur and then fled to the Jungle, but still carrying the collar mark on his neck.

Imperial hierarchies and orientalist assumptions are also clearly expressed in *Her Majesty's Servants*,[4] one of the finest pieces of literature addressing the topic of subjugation of natives, although in an allegorical form. The Viceroy of India is at Rawalpindi to review the troops and to receive the Amir of Afghanistan. He and his attendants, we are told, are proud and savages. Their horses too possess a fierce nature and they are wild and unruly: 'the Amir had brought with him for a bodyguard eight hundred men and horses who had never seen a camp or a locomotive before in their lives—savage men and savage horses from somewhere at the back of Central Asia' (Kipling 1994: 131).

There is a total similarity of qualities in the men and horses of the North-West Frontier. What appears as a children story is in fact a tool to convey a specific meaning. In the *The Jungle Book* the animals are endowed with the gift of speech. So, the night before the army parade is scheduled we are taken by the author between the tents, where the animals serving the British Army are left to comment and speculate on their conditions.[5] There is a troop-horse from the Ninth Lancers, a baggage camel of the thirty-ninth Native Infantry, two white gun-bullocks, a couple of mules from the screw-gun battery, an elephant and a fox-terrier.

At the lowest level we find the camels of the Native Infantry: they are not brave, quite dull, and scared by nightmares. They represent, obviously, the bulk of the Native Infantry. Then there are the gun-bullocks: they are Hindus ('We are brothers from Hapur. Our father was a sacred bull of Shiva'), they do their work without questioning it and fatalistically graze amidst the shell-

4. Also titled, in certain editions, 'Servants of the Queen'.
5. At some point the camels break loose and run among the tents bringing chaos all over the camp. One British officer finds himself close to a group of animals and listens to their talks. He learned 'enough of the beast language—not wild-beast language, but camp-beast language of course—from the natives.' As Cosslett notes, 'Kipling is treating the animal language as if it were a "native" dialect' (2006: 130).

ing and the killing (Kipling 1994: 138). There is only one thing scaring them: Englishmen, because of their beef-eating habit. Then there is an elephant. He is powerful but easily scared. He is able to see into his mind while others are unable. Because of that he has to be picketed at night: 'I should never be here. I should be a king in the forest, as I used to be, sleeping half the day and bathing when I liked' (p. 141). The elephant has a quasi-royal, although dismissed, status among indigenous beings. The mules are halfway between indigenous and European non-human animals: they are smart and courageous, despite the fact the horses look upon them because they are half-breed ('for every mule hates to be reminded that his father was a donkey', p. 139). Finally the horse is the aristocracy among all animal-soldiers, as all the horses of the English cavalry are brought to India from Australia and they are trained to 'obey the man at our head' and charge courageously 'among a lot of yelling, hairy men with knives' (pp. 135–36).

'Why do they have to fight at all?' asks the mule at some point. The horse is the one to answer: 'Because we are told to'. 'Orders' said Billy the mule; and his teeth snapped. '*Hukm hai!*' (It is an order), said the camel with a gurgle, and Two Tails and the bullocks repeated, '*Hukm Hai!*' (Kipling 1994: 142). 'Who gives the orders?' the horse is then asked by the younger mule. 'The man', is the answer. The fox-terrier, Vixen, at this point enters the chat and all the others become suddenly aware that a white man must be somewhere near, since pets are prerogative of the Europeans: 'Of Course he is', said Vixen. 'do you suppose I'm looked after by a black bullock-driver?' (p. 143). All the animals go away, and only the Horse and the Dog continue talking for a while.

The day after, they all parade proudly among the ranks and files of Her Majesty's mighty army in order to impress the wild bunch of men and horses from beyond the Khyber Pass. And the simple vision of such an ordered array of marching troops, both human and non-human, impresses the potentially hostile neighbours and inspires an overwhelming sense of awe and respect, ultimately leading to accept the presumed superiority of the British Raj. Staring at the parade, an amazed 'old grizzled, long-haired Central Asian Chief' (Kipling 1994: 145) asks a native officer how is it possible that thousands and thousands of men and animals march together perfectly arrayed. Obeying an order, says the native officer. Still amazed, the chief asks again: 'Are the beast as wise as the men?' And in the following answer lays what Edward Saïd would describe 'an order of sovereignty...set up from East to West, a mock chain of being whose clearest form was given once by Kipling ' (Saïd 1994: 45):

> They obey as the men do. Mule, horse, elephant, or bullock, he obeys his driver, and the driver his sergeant, and the sergeant his lieutenant, and the lieutenant his captain, and the captain his major, and the major his colonel, and the colonel his brigadier commanding three regiments, and the brigadier his general, who obeys the Viceroy, who is the servant of the Empress. Thus is done.
>
> (Kipling 1994: 146)

Between the Jungle and the Military Camp there is another ideological space which is worth considering. In Kipling's short story *Rikki Tikki Tavi* (Kipling 1994: 95–109), the politics of contended spaces between Colonizers and Colonized, with the latter's field dramatically split in two, is dramatically acknowledged. Rikki Tikki Tavi, the mongoose, embodies the quality of the loyal and faithful subaltern willing to give up his life to protect his new master and to fight on behalf of him. A twofold hybridity is at work here: a spatial and a social one, since the mongoose:

> finds himself between the worlds of the domesticated and the wild in the family garden, which is only 'half-cultivated', and contains hybrid roses as well as bamboo, a garden containing poisonous snakes that threaten the idyllic life of the colonizers. The 'half-wild' garden the British family has invaded and colonized is a metaphor for India itself, a garden-paradise harboring dangerous 'natives' in the form of snakes who resent the intrusion of humans into their kingdom. The colonizers—the British family—are incapable of fully taming the garden of India without help from cooperative natives. Rikki-tikki, in fact, can be seen as one of these helpful natives. The bungalow is conspicuously free of native servants—there is not a cook, nurse, butler, gardener, or housemaid to be seen—leaving the role of servant to the mongoose. Rikki exists, in the context of the tale, in order to make life safe and tidy for the European settlers.
>
> (Kutzer 2000: 26)

The mere existence of a contended space between colonial masters and colonized subjects determine a politically polarized environment. At the same time, on a social level, it calls for the creation of a social class of betwixt and between individuals to act as intermediates between the two radically different realities. It is the socially hybrid nature of the collaborationist or the faithful and loyal servant, whose allegiances lie in a blurred dimension of overlapping boundaries, tragically trusted by no one, not even the master he serves.

THE WILD: CAN THE SUBALTERN GROWL?

> Smell of Negro—a skulking negro may sometimes be smelt out like a fox
>
> (Galton 1872: 314)

The use of the animal trope in colonial India points up to either the essentially ambiguous character of the 'native' Other (even when this seems to act as loyal servant) or its innate subalternity and inferiority. The chance of refusal, disobedience or rebellion is always beyond the corner. Elephants, for instance, are portrayed as subordinate subjects but at the same time they have an ability to refuse and revolt. The persistent call of the jungle echoes in their thoughts, and this is the reason why they got to be chained every night. Night is also a time for sedition and magic, a secluded fraction of time where colonial control fades, or seems to be fading. Being dark, night is made of the same nature that 'natives' are made of. This is well expressed by the elephant talking to the other animals in *Her Majesty's Servants*. When cannon-balls fly the pachyderm understands deeply what is going on and what may happen. And so he refuses to step out towards the enemy lines. Moreover, he has memory of a precedent life when he was not in the army (i.e. the imperial order) but he was enjoying the jungle. Such memory precludes obedience (Kipling 1994: 141). As a matter of fact, elephants often flee the camp during the night to perform their secret dances in the midst of the jungle, away from human eyes, as in the novel *Toomai of the Elephants* (pp. 111–28), where the old elephant Kala Naag returns, if briefly, to the jungle. It is a rebellion *in posse*, and thus a significant threat to colonial order.

Monkeys, unlike elephants, represent the other end of the rope. When Mowgli is lost in the jungle, he finds his place among the wolf-pack. However a strange encountering takes place when the man-cub is kidnapped by the *bandar log*, the monkey people, and brought to a secluded decaying palace hidden in the jungle among the lost ruins of an ancient city. Mowgli fantasizes briefly of a life among monkeys, a sweet life full of fun, pleasant food and where time is spent playing all day. Moreover, the monkeys recognize a blood-affinity: Mowgli has no tail, but they share the ability to stand on two feet. But Baloo, the bear teacher of the Law and Mowgli's mentor, explains how things really are:

> They [the monkeys] have no law. They are outcasts. They have no speech of their own, but use the stolen words which they overhear when they listen, and peep, and wait up above in the branches. Their way is not our way. They are without leaders. They have no remembrance. They boast and chatter and pretend that they are a great people about to do great affairs in the jungle, but the falling of a nut turns their minds to laughter and all is forgotten. We of the jungle have no dealings with them. We do not drink where the monkeys drink; we do not go where the monkeys go; we do not hunt where they hunt; we do not die where they die.
>
> (Kipling 1994: 35)

A life beyond the Law is a disruptive challenge to authority (Brantlinger 2009: 82). The monkeys—who have neither Law nor leadership—are outcastes, Kipling explains. Theirs is just mockery of an ordained society. They mimic human language and laughing and, most of all, human life by residing among human ruins. Yet their mimicry, though not open resistance, is to a certain extent 'resemblance and menace' (Bhabha 1994: 86). The monkey people are the undecipherable mob, having neither discipline nor being capable of it. They represent 'degenerate Indian natives' (Cosslett 2006: 138), 'half civilized savages' (Nyman 2003: 48) since 'the English speaking "baboos" were never expected to be more than "mimic" man' (Brantlinger 2009: 8). Such equation will be repeated by Mowgli himself on occasion of his first meeting with the men from the native village: 'They have no manners, these Men Folk... Only the grey ape would behave as they do' (Kipling 1994: 57). In other words, the monkeys have a language which is a senseless chattering, an imitation of language, made up of conjuring stolen words. The lack of 'true' language is itself the epitome of barbarism, just as the lack of memory which identifies the natives as beings with no historical awareness. Like the destitute shelters of the Indians, the monkeys live in an ancient urban complex turned into a heap of ruins.

A further example of the ambiguity defining the border between the tamed and the wild can be found in the episode when Baloo and Bagheera ally with Kaa, the enchanting snake, in order to confront the monkey people and rescue Mowgli. The serpent's hypnotic power will condemn the superstitious monkeys to die according to the snake's will but the bear and the panther too are drawn towards the spires of the deadly snake. The only one unaffected is the man-cub: 'It is only old Kaa making circles on the dust' (Kipling 1994: 52), says Mowgli, and few lines later, he adds: 'I saw no more than a big snake making foolish circles till the dark came' (p. 53). Mowgli here may well represent the rationality of the Colonial Master but at the same time he is neither fully human nor non-human. He is the feral boy running with the wolf-pack bound to become the Master of the Jungle. From Kipling's viewpoint, Mowgli represents the persisting risk of going native, a social threat that is expressed through the fear of hybridity.[6]

Coming back to snakes, these are perhaps the most ambiguous non-human animals. Lurking in the shadows or protecting their secret abodes, in both reality and fiction they appear to possess the equally deadly powers of assassination (cobras are known in the jungle as the Poison People) and magic. Kaa, the python, is described as dangerous and lives alone in the jungle like a powerful Tantric practitioner. In *The King's Ankus* (Kipling 1994: 238–54), Kaa introduces Mowgli to White Hood, a timeless white cobra protecting a treasure in a cave under the Monkeys' city in ruins. The cobra protects the treasure of a king of the ancient times, even though the city is now in ruins and nobody has memories of a Kingdom of Man. Mowgli overtly challenges White Hood over the right to take the King's Ankus (a jewelled goad). White Hood prepares to kill him but Mowgli pins him down with the Ankus and with his knife and reveals that he no longer has poison in his fangs. The dreadful warden of the past, feared by everyone, is powerless. Just as Kaa's hypnotic power bears no consequences upon Mowgli.

Another example of the ambiguity of snakes is found in *Rikki-Tikki-Tavi*. Here, however, the denigration of the natives is not symbolic. The serpents

6. The dangers of hybridity are well expressed in Kipling's short novel *The Mark of the Beast* (1890), where an Englishman defies a statue of Hanuman, the monkey god, only to find himself all of a sudden in the morbid embrace of a leprous figure. The leper literally marks him and condemns him to a slow descent toward an increasingly strange behaviour, which ultimately coincides with that of a beast, i.e. a werewolf. The leper himself is described like a 'silver man', mewing like an otter and without a human face. Leaning onto the blasphemous soldier, he inscribes with his teeth a mark resembling a leopard spot on his chest. Paraphrasing Nietzsche, the more you look into India, the more India will look into you.

Nag and Nagaini form the antagonistic couple of Hindu 'natives' who fight against Rikki-Tikki-Tavi, the mongoose incarnating the trope of the loyal servant.[7] 'Nag is everywhere' (Kipling 1994: 101) says alarmed Chuchundra the muskrat to Rikki-Tikki-Tavi after he has killed another poisonous snake, Karait. The Snakes—that is, rebellious Hindus—incarnate conspiracy power and intelligence but in the end they are both killed by the combined efforts of Rikki-Tikki-Tavi and his master. The savagery and obscurity of the natives must be extirpated. So when Nagaini surrenders and asks to be spared with just one of her eggs, she is denied the grace and is slain shortly after. This is reminiscent of her attack on Teddy and his mother while they are having breakfast on the veranda, an event that can be linked to the several accounts of violence against British women and children during the 'Mutiny' (India's First War of Independence, 1857). It must be noted here that the objects of such violence which were to reverberate through the British press were always women and children, while the White Male was always depicted fighting back like a lion. In history as in fiction the forces menacing British supremacy are annihilated without remorse.

In cases of rebellious attacks on the colonizing master, deadly punishments are inflicted to the culprits even after several years. It is the case of the Crocodile in the *Jungle Books* chapter titled 'The Undertakers' (cf. Leighton and Surridge 2007: 249–70). Here, a crocodile, the Mugger of Mugger-Ghaut, engages in a dialogue with a jackal and an adjutant-crane under a bridge. He remembers the days of the past, well before the building of the bridge crossing his river, when he was revered as a river-deity by the villagers. In the only direct reference to the Mutiny in Kipling's novels, the crocodile remembers how the corpses of the British used to float down, side by side, and he was feeding on them, the white-faces, killed by the 'natives'. There is a reference to the violence on women and children as well, as the Mugger evokes old memories: while he was floating in the river a boat with the survivors was passing by. On the boat, a child was playing, his hand stretched out into the water. Out of sport, because he was already well-fed, the crocodile tried to bite it, but the hand being so small passed between his teeth unscathed. As the three are talking, the engineer who built the bridge passes by and spots the crocodile. He decides to have a shot at it with a heavy gun. The crocodile is immediately killed, and the engineer remembers how he was menaced, while still a child—a Mutiny's child—by a crocodile, ignoring he has just got his revenge. The Empire has its reckoning, sooner or later, just like old riverine gods were dismissed by British technology.[8]

7. The snakes are overtly Hindus: 'I am Nag. The great god Brahm put his mark upon all our people when the first cobra spread his hood to keep the sun off Brahm as he slept Look, and be afraid!' (Kipling 1994: 98).
8. See Worth (2008) on the role of telegraph and telegraphers during the 1857–1858 Rebellion. In particular, telegraph lines are described running through a 'howling wildernesses' and 'menaced by savage beasts of more savage men' (p. 7).

Yet another reference to India's First War of Independence is probably hinted at in the battle between the wolf-pack guided by Mowgli and the marauding bunch—the much despised barbarian horde—of the wild red dogs of India. The epic theme of the raging battle between the few and proud against the reckless multitude was a very popular topic celebrating the virtues of the British heroes and martyrs fighting under the Imperial flag while being largely outnumbered by their enemies. A topic, in fact, not limited to India, but exploited also for the Imperial wars in Sudan against the Mahdi Army or the fight for the Zululand in South Africa.

> 'Red Dog' returns to the theme of the aristocratic few standing out against the mob. One cannot miss the resemblance between the battle of the wolves against the red dogs and Kipling's other great set-piece description of battle, the stand of the British square against the dervishes in *The Light That Failed*.
>
> (Paffard 1989: 94)

But the most obvious symbol of resistance is with all probability the tiger. Indeed, the prominence of the tiger at the top of the food-chain in South Asia was surely striking the imagination of the West and 'many young, middle-class British men who come to India to forge new careers, saw bagging a tiger as a rite of passage' (Schell 2007: 229). They developed a 'British mystique, almost a philosophy of tiger-hunting in India' (Mukherjee 1993: 212). Big game hunting in India and Africa 'clearly alluded to the violent, heroic underside of Imperialism' (Ritvo 1987: 248) subduing both dangerous wildlife and, as the two sides of the same coin, unpredictable natives.

> No matter how many successful campaigns the British had waged, how many decisive battles they have won, how many cantonments they had founded to guard settlements, some basic fear of India continued to haunt British Indian life and imagination. Therefore the tiger had to be shot again and again.
>
> (Mukherjee 1987: 12)

In Kipling's narrative, Mowgli has to kill Shere Khan (Kipling 1994: 66–67) in order to become the Master of the Jungle. And Shere Khan is one of the few animals refractory to the authority of the Jungle Law (Mukherjee 1993: 204). The tiger has a long history as a symbol of India or her ruling class. The name itself chosen by Kipling for the *Jungle Books* villain, Shere Khan, is taken from history. Sher Shah Suri, better known as Sher Khan (an Afghan Pathan), was in fact an unruly commander of the army of Babur (a 'tiger' himself). He became governor of Bihar under the reign of Babur and later he founded his own dynasty against the will of his previous masters.

The tiger's prominence as a symbolic enemy, representing at once indigenous resistance on human and non-human level in a colonial discourse on domination and conquest, is thus a metaphoric expression of an irreducible alterity that the Empire needs to tame, harness or annihilate in order to exert the degree of control it requires. In Victorian narratives, the subaltern can definitely growl. Resistance to the Empire is widespread and threatening. But, being voiced through Imperial literature, roars of rebellion are emptied of their most critical contents. What is left is just the voice of those doomed to be defeated when confronting the most dangerous Other of all, the Other-with-the-Whip.

CONCLUSION

The British fascination for the wildest creatures of the jungle in contraposition to the domesticated flocks as metaphors of the savage and the tamed contributed to further reflections and a general reshaping of discourses on Western dominance as well as colonial perceptions of South Asia. Since the beginning of the colonial experience in India, the boundaries between the human and non-human subjects became so thin and blurred that they were rapidly assimilated as integral part of the Empire's expansionist agenda. The imperialist discourse, a mythology in the making, was made up of a series of performative utterances used to describe and to shape the surrounding world. A world that was to be subjugated, tamed and ruled upon by a self-appointed superior authority.

The living landscape of South Asia—environment, flora, fauna, people—could not escape the literary cage of the Empire: an exercise in power and dominance in which the 'animal tales' or descriptions are just an allegorical description. Human and non-human indigenous animals or even the hybrid system they form vis-à-vis the Empire are in fact a vast, mysterious new territory to dominate with both the sword and the pen for a colonialism of the mind whose perdurable effects still linger and continue to produce a good many uncritical descriptions.

REFERENCES

Asad, T. (ed.). 1973. *Anthropology and the Colonial Encounter*. New York: Humanities Press.

Benson, A. C., and R. Baliol Brett Esher (eds). 1908. *The Letters of Queen Victoria. A Selection from Her Majesty's Correspondence between the Years 1837 and 1861* (3 vols.). London: John Murray.

Bhabha, H. 1994. *The Location of Culture*. New York: Routledge.

Brantlinger, P. 1988. *The Rule of Darkness. British Literature and Imperialism, 1830–1914*. Ithaca, NY: Cornell University Press.

— 2009. *Victorian Literature and Postcolonial Studies*. Edinburgh: Edinburgh University Press.

Brontë, C. 1847. *Jane Eyre*. London: Smith, Elder & Co.

Chamberlain, J. 1897. 'A Young Nation.' In J. Chamberlain, *Foreign and Colonial Speeches*: 89. London: Routledge.

Cosslett, T. 2006. *Talking Animals in British Children's Fiction 1786–1914*. Aldershot: Ashgate.

Croker, B. M. 1896. *Diana Barrington: A Romance of Central India*. London: Chatto & Windus.

Denenholz-Morse, D. 2007. '"The Mark of the Beast": Animals as Sites of Imperial Encounter from *Wuthering Heights* to *Green Mansions*.' In Denenholz-Morse and Danahay: 181–200.

Denenholz-Morse, D., and M. A. Danahay (eds). 2007. *Animal Victorian Dreams. Representations of Animals in Victorian Literature and Culture*. Farnham: Ashgate.

Edwards, M. 1953. 'Rudyard Kipling and the Imperial Imagination.' *The 20th Century* 153: 443–54.
Galton, F. 1872. *The Art of Travel*. London: John Murray.
Green, M. 1979. *Dreams of Adventure, Deeds of Empire*. New York: Basic Books.
Greenberg, A. S. 2005. *Manifest Manhood and the Antebellum American Empire*. New York: Cambridge University Press.
Greenberger, A. 1969. *The British Image of India. A Study in the Literature of Imperialism 1880–1960*. London: Oxford University Press.
Jahoda, G. 1999. *Images of Savages: Ancients Roots of Modern Prejudice in Western Culture*. London and New York: Routledge.
Kipling , R. 1894. *The Jungle Book*. London: Macmillan.
— 1895. *The Second Jungle Book*. London: Macmillan.
— 1960. *Rudyard Kipling's Verse Definitive Edition*. London: Hodder & Stoughton.
— 1994. *The Jungle Books*. London: Penguin.
Kutzer, M. D. 2000. *Empire's Children: Empire and Imperialism in Classic British Children's Book*. New York: Garland Publishing.
Leighton, M. E., and L. Surridge. 2007. 'The Empire Bites Back: The Racialized Crocodile of the Nineteenth Century.' In Denenholz-Morse and Danahay: 249–70.
Mclure, J. A. 1981. *Kipling and Conrad. The Colonial Fiction*. Cambridge: Harvard University Press.
Mukherjee, S. 1987. 'Tigers in Fiction: An Aspect of the Colonial Encounter.' *Kunapipi* 9(3): 1–13.
— 1993. *Forster and Further: the Tradition of Anglo-Indian Fiction*. Mumbai: Orient Longman.
Murray, J. 1992. 'The Law of the Jungle Books.' *Children's Literature* 20: 1–14. http://dx.doi.org/10.1353/chl.0.0579
Nyman, J. 2003. *Postcolonial Animal Tale from Kipling to Coetzee*. New Delhi: Atlantic.
Paffard, M. 1989. *Kipling's Indian Fiction*. London: Macmillan & Co.
Randall, D. 1998. 'Post-Mutiny Allegories of Empire in Rudyard Kipling's Jungle Books.' *Texas Studies in Literature and Language* 40(1): 97–120.
Ritvo, H. 1987. *The Animal Estate: The English and Other Creatures in the Victorian Age*. Cambridge: Harvard University Press.
Saïd, E. 1989. 'Representing the Colonized: Anthropology's Interlocutors.' *Critical Inquiry* 15(2): 205–25. http://dx.doi.org/10.1086/448481
— 1994 (1993). *Culture and Imperialism*. Reprint. New York: Knopf.
Saminaden, A., S. Loughnan and N. Haslam. 2010. 'Afterimages of Savages: Implicit Associations between Primitives, Animals and Children.' *British Journal of Social Psychology* 49(1): 91–105. http://dx.doi.org/10.1348/014466609X415293
Schell, H. 2007. 'Tiger Tales.' In Denenholz-Morse and Danahay: 231–48. Farnham: Ashgate.
Worth, A. 2008. 'All India Becoming Tranquil: Wiring the Raj.' *Journal of Colonialism and Colonial History* 9(1): 1–44. http://dx.doi.org/10.1353/cch.2008.0013

Second Tantra: Conflict, Ethics, Environment

Beware the Crocodile: Female and Male Nature in Aśvaghoṣa's *Saundarananda*

ALICE COLLETT*

In this chapter, I want to look at anxieties of masculinity as expressed through the figurative language which likens women and men to animals in Aśvaghoṣa's *Saundarananda.* Aśvaghoṣa was a Brahmin convert to Buddhism and his views on women in his more popular poem—the *Buddhacarita*—have been in the past taken to be representative of universal views about women in early Indian Buddhism. In this contribution, instead of accepting that Aśvaghoṣa's views are hegemonic, I want to situate them within a particular socio-historical milieu in which social/male anxieties about women are evidenced more widely. Within this historical content of a developing, broader social anxiety about women, I seek to identify Aśvaghoṣa's poetry as a personal expression of this phenomenon and situate it less within Buddhism than on the boundary between the two dominating traditions, namely Brahmanism and Buddhism.

In chapter eight of the *Saundarananda*, entitled 'the attack on women' (*strīvighāta*), Aśvaghoṣa employs animal, bird and reptile similes and metaphors through which he illuminates this anxiety. As noted by Gerow (1971: 35), figures of speech, especially simile and its related form metaphor (*rūpaka*, metaphor or 'characterization') are the foundation of any forms of poetry. This is especially true of poetry in the Indian classical period. Thus, I want to assess Aśvaghoṣa's use of figurative language in the *Saundarananda* to illustrate my point.

Aśvaghoṣa lived during the Kuṣāna period, between the first and second century CE. Recently, in looking at women within this time period and more

* Alice Collett is currently a Fellow of the Arts and Humanities Council of Great Britain (AHRC) and Lecturer at York St John University. She received her MA from the University of Bristol in 1999 and her PhD from Cardiff University in 2004. Since then she has worked in different universities in North America and the UK, and published several articles on women in early Indian Buddhism, including two which look at reception history and review the modern scholarly debate on the subject. Her recent books include *Women in Early Indian Buddhism: Comparative Textual Studies* (in press), an edited volume which includes study of Buddhist texts in five different languages. She is currently working on a monograph entitled *Women in the Pāli Canon and Commentaries*, for which she is in receipt of an AHRC research award.

broadly 'between the empires',[1] Stephanie Jamison (2006: 213) has speculatively noted that:

> The notion of women's autonomy seems to have grown in the period we are discussing, the notion of a kind of subversive mental independence. It indeed was not just a notion, but embodied in the threatening figure of the heterodox female ascetic, for us most clear in the Buddhist bhikkhunī. And the later texts like Manu react to this independence with a crackdown (at least conceptually) on women's autonomous action and an almost startling misogyny, in contrast to the earlier texts.

In this chapter, I want to take Jamison's conclusion as a starting point and use it as a basis to assess Aśvaghoṣa's attack on women. Jamison's assessment is based upon her reading of Brahmanical rather than Buddhist texts. This trend, however, seems to exist within and between both traditions, although it appears not wholly pervasive in either. Aśvaghoṣa was himself brought up a Brahmin and clearly shows himself to be highly knowledgeable in many aspects of Brahmanical lore (cf. Johnson 1998: xiii; Olivelle 2009: xvii; Patton 2008). A strong relationship has already been established between Aśvaghoṣa's work and Brahmanical texts, most especially the Sanskrit epics. During this period of history, with the ensuing changes of dynasty between the empires, the fortunes of Buddhism and Brahmanism waxed and waned to some extent, some rulers patronizing Buddhism whilst others favoured Brahmanism. However, the rise of Buddhism throughout the period was significant, such that, as noted by Hiltebeitel (2001: 6–7) and Fitzgerald (2004: 120–21) and reiterated by Olivelle (2005: 37–38), the composition of the Sanskrit epics may well have been a reaction to the rise of Buddhism. Olivelle, concurring with this, added that perhaps the *Mānava-Dharmaśāstra* was also of this order—a response and attempt to reinstate Brahmans as the most powerful class within the communities living along the North Indian plains and forests (Olivelle 2005: 37–39). Within this broader discourse of reactions and responses between the two traditions is where we can situate Jamison's speculation. Further, Olivelle, in his recently published translation of Aśvaghoṣa's other main work, the *Buddhacarita*, situates Aśvaghoṣa's work as something of a reply to the epics, enacting, for example, the positing of the Buddha as the new Rāma (Olivelle 2009: xx). Taking all this into consideration, I want to argue that Aśvaghoṣa's 'almost startling misogyny' in the *Saundarananda* is a personal example of this broader social context and growing social anxiety about independent women.

Although, during the time of Aśvaghoṣa's writing Buddhist nuns had a significant presence within north Indian Buddhist communities, when reading Aśvaghoṣa one could easily come to the conclusion that the path of discipleship following the Buddha was a path only available to men, and that women

1. This refers to the period after the end of the Mauryan empire (end of second century BCE) and the rise of the Gupta empire (beginning of fourth century CE).

were excluded from practising.[2] This was far from the situation, however. In an article from the 1990s, Schopen notes that the compliers of various Buddhist monastic codes were 'very anxious men' (1996: 563). According to Schopen, they were anxious about a variety of things, including women, and especially nuns, whom they took measures to contain, restrain and control. If we place Schopen's comments alongside those of Jamison, and Olivelle's conjecture that the *Mānava-Dharmaśāstra* was a response to the rise in popularity of Buddhism, situating Aśvaghoṣa's work within this context we can begin to read into his texts this same male anxiety about women. In sum, these scholars demonstrate that this concern was not confined to one tradition or another, but perhaps there was some parity between the two. Whether then one seeks to situate Aśvaghoṣa's misogyny on one side or the other is perhaps a mute point. However, as Aśvaghoṣa's work appears to demonstrate a certain degree of fear and disgust of women rather than a desire to contain and control them, perhaps in this regard one might be inclined to argue that his conversion was complete, as this sense of jeopardy is more visible in early Buddhism than Brahmanism.

However, misogyny such as that displayed in Aśvaghoṣa's *Saundarananda* is not the sole or even primary attitude to women discernible in each group of texts from the period. In my other works I have shown that the notion that women were viewed negatively within early Indian Buddhism has been overstated and that contrary to this there is a great deal that is positive in the extant textual record (Collett 2006, 2009a, 2009b and 2011). Also, one simply needs to bring to mind the main heroines of the epics—Draupadī and Valmikī's Sītā—to realize that there were representations of strong female role models from the period within Brahmanical literature as well.

Despite these many positive representations of women from contemporaneous literature, Aśvaghoṣa's fear and disgust of women features in both of his major works, although to varying degrees. With regards to both the *Buddhacarita* and the *Saundarananda*, Aśvaghoṣa took stories already known within the Buddhist tradition in which women are much less vilified and re-worked them into long (epic) poems. The *Buddhacarita* retells the legendary account of the life of Gautama Buddha, while the *Saundarananda* is a reproduction of the biography of the half-brother of Gautama, Nanda. The only version of Nanda's biography that pre-dates Aśvaghoṣa is the version in the *Udāna*, although there are verses attributed to Nanda in the *Theragāthā* as well.[3] The story in the *Udāna* begins with Nanda declaring to

2. Schopen's archaeological evidence demonstrates that among the extant donor inscriptions at *stūpa* sites—dating from the Kuṣāna period—that can be identified with an individual or individuals, a high percentage were donated by Buddhist nuns (1997: 238ff.).

3. *Theragāthā* verses 157-58. Other versions of Nanda's biography appear in the *Jātakaṭṭhakathā* (182), which in its extant form is later, although based upon stories in circulation prior to its completion. The later Buddhist commentarial tradition produces other versions of the narrative in the *Udāna*, *Theragāthā* and *Dhammapada* commentaries (*Udāna-aṭṭhakathā* 3.2, *Theragāthā-aṭṭhakathā* 2.31-34, *Dhammpada-aṭṭhakathā* 1.9).

the monks that he cannot endure to follow the path of training any longer. The monks tell this to the Buddha who asked Nanda why this is so. Nanda informs him that, when he was leaving to go forth, a young girl, the beauty of the region, said to him, 'Come back soon!' As he is constantly thinking of that, Nanda cannot endure the monastic life. The Buddha then, by means of his magical powers, transports Nanda to a heavenly world inhabited by beautiful nymphs, in comparison to whom any human woman appears ugly. The Buddha asks Nanda which of the two are more beautiful, to which Nanda replies:

> Just as if, Venerable One, she were a mutilated monkey with ears and nose cut off, even so, Venerable One, this Sakyan girl, the beauty of the district, if set beside these five hundred water nymphs, does not compare to even a small fraction of them...
>
> (*Udāna* 3.2, in Steinthal 1982)

The Buddha tells Nanda that if he commits himself to his practice he will have access to the heavenly world and its beauties. Nanda thus focuses on his practice, but as he does, develops non-attachment and decreases his interest in sensual pleasures. It is this basic plot that Aśvaghoṣa follows in his poetic rendering of the story. However, there is one important change: the re-conceptualization of the young girl as Nanda's wife. The later versions that post-date Aśvaghoṣa, in the commentaries, follow this same basic plot, with most of them rendering the woman as Nanda's wife.[4]

Although, in the *Udāna* story, the human girl is likened to a mutilated monkey in terms of her appearance, a distinct difference between this narrative, along with Nanda's verses in the *Theragāthā*, and Aśvaghoṣa can be discerned with regards views on women. In both earlier works, women are not blamed for sexually manipulating men, but rather the problem is apportioned as psychopathology; that is, it is Nanda's own predicament that he must work to overcome. As noted above, the *Udāna* narrative commences with Nanda lamenting that he is not fit for the life of celibacy, and when the other monks learn about his obsession with sensual pleasures, they tease him. The first of the two verses in the *Theragāthā* indicate the same, that Nanda owns the problem:

> Distracted by my addiction to ornamentation, I was conceited, vain and afflicted by desire for pleasures.
>
> (*Theragāthā*, verse 157)

In contrast to this, Aśvaghoṣa tends to blame women:

4. The wife may have been Aśvaghoṣa's invention, as his is the first reference to her. A wife is not mentioned *per se* in the *Jātakaṭṭhakathā* version, but the woman is called Janapadakalyāṇī, which is the compound in the *Udāna* version meaning 'the beauty of the district' but comes to be the name of Nanda's wife in at least one later commentarial account, and of his half-sister in others.

> Like creepers poisonous to the touch, like scoured caves still harboring snakes, like unsheathed swords held in the hand, women are ruinous in the end. When women want sex they arouse lust; when women don't want sex they bring danger... Women behave ignobly, maliciously spying out the weakness of others... When nobly-born men become destitute...it is because of women.
>
> (Sau. 8.31-34, in Covill 2007: 161)

Alongside this attributing a pernicious nature to women, most evident in the *Saundarananda*, goes an emasculation of men, who rather than being represented by the more usual, very male, bull or leonine figures of speech of the period are likened to docile, helpless creatures in the face of these injurious 'hordes of crocodiles'; that is, women. Although Aśvaghoṣa's is a Buddhist text, the way men and women are portrayed, especially with regards to figurative language, bears a stronger resemblance to the Sanskrit epics in style.

With regards to the figurative language invoking animals to illuminate male and female traits, a close symmetry can be identified between Aśvaghoṣa's poems and the epics. In all three texts, the use of animal similes and metaphor to illuminate human characteristics is a constant though not overwhelming feature, subsidiary to the main plots. Typical for this period, all three texts liken men to lions, tigers and bulls, that is animals that symbolize strength, prowess and courage. Rāma, the hero of the *Rāmāyaṇa*, is often said to be a tiger amongst men (*manjuvyāghra*) or a bull amongst men (*puruṣarṣabha*) or, less often, a tiger amongst kings (*nṛpaśārdūla*).[5] Similarly, in the *Mahābhārata*, the righteous Yudhiṣṭhira, along with his brothers and other significant male figures, is typically called a tiger amongst men (*puruṣavyāghra*), bull among men (*puruṣarṣabha*), and also, with the foci on lineage in the *Mahābhārata*, bull among Bhāratas (*bhāratarṣabha*).[6]

Although Nanda, the protagonist in the *Saundarananda*, is not himself awarded such esteem in a replete manner as the epic heroes, we only need compare the birth of Nanda with a description of the righteous cousins from the *Mahābhārata* to evidence the similarity between their masculine stature. At birth, it is said of Nanda that:

> He was long-armed and wide-chested, with the shoulders of a lion and the eyes of a bull—and he bore the epithet 'handsome' due to his superlative looks.
>
> (Sau. 2.58, in Covill 2007: 59)

Similarly, in the *Mahābhārata*, when Arjuna and Bhīma along with Kṛṣṇa entered Jarāsaṃdha's palace, 'as Himālayan lions enter a cowpen':

5. Bulls and tigers were also important in the Indus Valley civilization, which is evident from their presence on some of the steatite seals and other remains from the period.
6. For such references to Rāma, see for example, Rām. 2.10.17, 2.13.18, 2.21.7, 3.4.25, 3.4.27, 3.4.31, 7, for Yudhiṣṭhira, see for example Mbh. 2.2.31, 2.5.105, 2.9.30 2.12.18, 2.14.5, 2.17.39.

> The people of Māgadha fell dumb with astonishment at the sight of them, broad-chested and imposing like elephants, tall as great columns. Those bulls among men passed through the crowds of people milling around the palace's three outer enclosures and strode proudly and fearlessly up to the king.
>
> (Mbh. 2.21: 30, in Wilmott 2006: 177)

Compare this with the young men who, in the *Saundarananda*, come to the hermitage of the Buddha seeking to become followers:

> They are tall like golden columns, lion-chested and strong armed, potential vessels of wide fame, majesty and self-regulation.
>
> (Sau. 1.19, in Covill 2007: 37)

Masculinity between the texts can be seen to be fairly established: men are tall, broad-chested, with easy leonine prowess and stoic, bull-like majesty.[7]

Although men are frequently symbolized through animal representation in terms of their qualities and characteristics, this is less so the case for women. The reason for this is because the social constructs for womanhood and femininity revolved around aspects not easily illustrated through animal imagery. The social construct for the period was circumscribed around female beauty on the one hand and domesticity on the other. Domesticity, or the roles of wife and mother, cannot easily be represented by invoking animal imagery. Although animals are parents, or more particularly mothers, the ways in which animals rear their young is not usually evocative enough of human parenting to produce such representations and portrayals. However, this does happen occasionally, such as when Rāma tells his mother he is exiled to the forest, and she replies she will be like a cow without its calf (Rām. 2.17.32), likening herself to a maternal bovine several times (Rām. 2.17.33 and 2.21.5).[8]

Secondly, female beauty in this period was very much tied up with notions of ornamentation: it was the ornamented and decorated female (or male, for that matter) body that was considered more becoming, 'the body adorned' as Dehejia (2009) puts it. It is therefore difficult to use comparisons with animals as they are not ornamented themselves. Nevertheless, two different animals are frequently used to symbolize female beauty: the graceful and shy gazelle and the elephant. This is again to do with notions of female beauty. The most becoming female form, as evidenced by Dehejia in early sculpture, is the quintessential hourglass shape- large rounded hips and breasts with an accompanying inhumanly tiny waist. The full thighs, part of the comely hips, seen on this form of a woman in early Indian sculpture are likened to the

7. Powers (2009) provides an investigation of the representation of the Buddha as the bull among men in early Indian Buddhism. Aśvaghoṣa does not draw on this epithet as much as does other early Buddhist literature, as suggested by Powers.
8. The cow is important in Vedic mythology, as is the bull, and these figurative allusions are suggestive of the viral bull and maternal cow of the Veda. See Doniger O'Flaherty (1980) for a discussion of the bull and cow in Vedic myth. According to Doniger, in the Veda, '[t]he good or evil cow is...assimilated to the figure of the good or evil woman' (1980: 251).

trunk of an elephant, as is said of Sītā's rounded and charming thighs (Rām. 3.46).[9] Moreover, there are the occasional animalistic references to women displaying strength, such as Sītā calling herself a lioness to Ravana's jackal, as he attempts to abduct her.[10]

Looking more closely at the *Saundarananda*, many of the above uses of animal simile are evident. In Sanskrit poetry, a popular trope came to be the detailed evocation of the passion and emotionally charged attachment of lovers. Such lovers are often liked to *chakravāka* birds, a species which is said to go about in pairs and to exhibit distress if parted from one another. Aśvaghoṣa's *Saundarananda* is perhaps one of the first examples of this avifaunal representation. In the *Saundarananda*, when the Buddha-to-be and Nanda had grown into men and Gautama left for the forest, Nanda remained in his palace with his wife, 'making love his only concern' (*madanaikakāryaḥ*), as, 'Nanda was fitted for love, and so lived united with his beloved like a *cakravāka* bird with its mate' (Sau. 4.1 and 2, in Covill 2007: 81). At this point Aśvaghoṣa describes his delectable wife, the exquisite Sundarī:

> She seemed a lotus-pool in womanly form, with her laughter for swans, her eyes for bees and her swelling breasts as budding lotus calyxes... With her captivating beauty and manner to match, in the world of humankind she, Sundarī, was the loveliest of women.
>
> (Sau. 4.4-5, in Covill 2007: 81)

Once the narrative progresses and Nanda finds himself accompanying the Buddha to the forest for his unwanted life of discipleship, he laments his separation from his wife drawing upon, once more, the simile of the lovers as *cakravāka* birds. He despairs, 'I find no peace, like a *cakravāka* bird separated from its mate' (Sau. 7.17, in Covill 2007: 137).

Following the chapters on Nanda's enforced ordination, his wife's lament at the separation and his own, is the chapter which contains the attack on women. Here an ascetic comes upon Nanda in his yearning and imparts upon him his considered knowledge of womankind. The ascetic portrays women as pernicious and duplicitous, thoroughly lacking in morality and solely self-serving, concerned only with manipulating others to satisfy her own needs. This is typified in the following quote, in which the ascetic asks Nanda a rhetorical question as to why women deserve his attention, and then continues:

9. Also see, as one other example of many, Ambapāli, the ex-courtesan in the *Therīgāthā* (verse 267), who reflecting upon the ravages of old age says, 'Formerly, both my thighs were beautiful like an elephant's trunk, but in old age they are like stalks of bamboo...'

10. Women have also occasionally been likened to lions in early Mahāyāna Buddhism. See for example, the *Śrimālādevīsiṃhanādasūtra*, on the women who roared like a lion (as does the Buddha), and the nun with a name likening her to a lion on the *Gaṇḍhavyūhasūtra*, both in Paul (1979: 94–105 and 289–302).

> Women have no regard for handsome looks, wealth, intelligence, lineage or valor; like hordes of crocodiles in a river, they attack without discrimination. A woman never remembers sweet words, caresses or affection. Even when coaxed, a woman is flighty, so depend on her no more than you would on your enemies.
>
> (Sau. 8.37, in Covill 2007: 163)

In this representation of women, long gone is the 'captivating beauty and manner to match' of the exquisite Sundarī, and although women can be described as appealing, the ascetic warns Nanda that they are indeed always duplicitous, 'women's speech is honeyed but there is the deadliest poison in their hearts' (Sau. 8.35, in Covill 2007: 161). The ascetic, it seems, although despising women, feels sympathy for Nanda in his longing and ruminates with a list of metaphors which liken Nanda to an animal that has escaped great danger but seeks to be returned to its peril:

> How pitiful that the wayward deer has escaped from the great danger posed by the hunter, but now in his longing for the herd is about to leap into the net, fooled by the sound of singing! Here is a bird that was enmeshed in a net, freed by a well-wisher to glide through the forest of fruit and flowers, now voluntarily trying to get into a cage! Here is a young elephant pulled out of the thick mud at a treacherous riverbank by another elephant, that wants to once more descend into the crocodile infested river, impelled by its thirst for water! Here is a lad sleeping in a shelter with a snake, who, when woken by a mindful elder, is filled with confusion and tries to grab the fierce snake himself! Here is a bird flown away from a forest tree ablaze with a raging fire, that wishes to fly back there, its qualms forgotten in its longing for its nest! Here is a pheasant in a helpless swoon of lust when separated from its mate through fear of a hawk, living in wretchedness and attaining neither resolution nor modesty! Here is a wretched, undisciplined dog, full of greed but lacking decency and wisdom, who wants to feed once more on the food he has vomited!
>
> (Sau. 8.15-21, in Covill 2007: 155–57)

This passage represents the most interesting animal characterization in the *Saundarananda*, situated as it is within a thoroughgoing display of misogyny, but also in its displacing of robust masculinity with male feebleness and foolhardiness. As this passage is so interesting, I will take some of the images in turn and assess how female and male nature is being characterized. Firstly, man is represented as a wayward deer (*mṛga*). The word used adjectivally to describe the deer is *capala*, meaning 'fickle' or 'wanton'. These characteristics are much more often associated with women than men in the literature of the period. Later on in the *Saundarananda*, Aśvaghoṣa himself maligns women's incandescently fickle sexual fidelity, when he has the ascetic say '[j]ust as a cow, even when herded, goes grazing from one field to the another, so will a woman move on to take her pleasure' (Sau. 8.41, in Covill 2007: 165). Righteous men, however, should not be fickle (*capala*), as notes the *Mānava-Dharmaśāstra* (4.177). Good monks as well, according to the Pāli Canon, should not have this characteristic.[11] In Sanskrit poetry and narrative, women's beauty and demeanour are often likened to those of a graceful gazelle. A woman can also be an unnerved doe, such as the frightened Sītā surrounded by demonesses (*rākṣasī*) while in captivity (Rām. 53.5 and 54.30). Olivelle notes of deer that they evoke charm and innocence, something often said of women.[12] He also notes that in the *Pañcatantra* deer only ever appear with a hunter nearby, as in Indic literature they are represented as the ultimate prey (Olivelle 1997: xxiii). Here then, men are cast as fickle, effeminate creatures, easily frightened and easy prey.[13] Such a depiction is a far cry from the broad-chested, leonine epic heroes described above.

Next, men are likened to birds. Birds have a significant place in Sanskrit literary tradition and different types of birds have differing characteristics. In the above passage men are likened to birds three times, twice to what appears to be a generic bird, and once to a pheasant. In the first instance, the word used is a generic one—*vihaga*, which literally means 'sky-goer'. This bird, however, is enmeshed in a net (*jālasaṃvṛtaḥ*), thus evoking an image of a small, frail creature that is helpless in its captivity. The poor creature cannot free itself, powerless as it is, trapped and entangled. The third avifauna reference is to a pheasant, who displays fear of hawks. The pheasant appears to be representative of fowl in mating, so obsessed with chasing and attracting the female that any encroaching danger barely distils their amour. Thus, the bird, in its 'helpless swoon of lust' (Sau. 8.15-21) loses all sense of dignity.

Next, men are compared to young elephants. In early Indian literature, elephants are used to represent and symbolize a variety of human traits and characteristics. Olivelle (1997: xxiii) says of the elephant that, in the world of the *Pañcatantra*, it 'has a split personality, being both domestic (docile, a good worker, intelligent) and wild (ferocious, unpredictable)'. As well as these two sets of characteristics, a rutting elephant represents a third type.[14] I have

11. See for example, the *Gulissāni Sutta* in the *Majjhima Nikāya* (69) and *Saṃyutta Nikāya*, Book 1.13. In Nanda's *Theragāthā* verse, above, Nanda calls himself fickle (*capala*).
12. Olivelle (1997: xxiii). The extant *Pañcatantra* is later than Aśvaghoṣa, although many of the characteristics of the folkloric anthropomorphized animals noted by Olivelle in his introduction to his translation are similar to the characteristics inferred by Aśvaghoṣa. Although the extant *Pañcatantra* is later, many of the stories, of course, come from a common stock of folkloric stories, some of which can be identified on stone reliefs and sculpture dating from the Kuṣāna period and earlier. Likewise, the *Jātakaṭṭhakathā*, dated later in its extant form, sharing some stories with the *Pañcatantra* and retelling stories identified on earlier sculpture, represents animals similarly.
13. The art and literature of the period is not without a few references to the male deer, or stag. There is the well-known *jātaka* story of the golden stag (12), who offers his life for another (referred to in the *Milindapañha*, and depicted on the railings of the Bharhut *stūpa*). Also, although in the sculpture of the period deer are usually depicted in peaceful scenes, I have found one image in which two large deer are carrying riders upon their backs (Snead 1989: 102 Pl. 69). However, the combination with the word *capala*, and within the context of the overall passages, the stag does not appear to be the frame of reference here.
14. Covill (2009) includes a chapter on elephant figures of speech in the *Saundarananda*. As Covill notes, elephant imagery is used substantially during this historical period. She highlights

quoted two examples of elephant similes above, with women's thighs being likened to the trunk of an elephant and the heroes of the *Mahābhārata* being represented as 'broad-chested and imposing like elephants' (Mbh. 2.21.30). Other symbolic aspects of the elephant are related to the taming of elephants. The *Saundarananda* itself provides two examples, such as when the princes mentioned earlier are said to have 'wandered with youthful unrestraint, like elephants without guiding hooks' (Sau. 1.34, in Covill 2007: 39). Also, in Nanda's lament, when he thinks of his beautiful wife he has left behind he 'gave a heavy sigh, like a newly caught elephant in confinement' (Sau. 7.4, in Covill 2007: 133). The picture painted of the young elephant above is of a semi-wild beast with the potential to be tamed, but which in its youth is foolhardy and ignorant of dangers. In the *Saundarananda*, Nanda is said to have been 17 years old when he leaves home with the Buddha. It is unclear how much time has elapsed between this event and his conversation with the ascetic, but one is led to believe Nanda to be still a fairly young man. However, as the notion of 'coming of age' during this historical period often involved children of seven or eight taking on adult responsibilities, it may well be that the young elephant does not represent a youth possessive of a foolhardy nature that can be ironed out with the advent of maturity, but rather an adult man who has somehow remained foolhardy and ignorant of the perils of a dangerous foe.[15]

Lastly, men are compared to dogs. Mythology aside, dogs were generally not favoured in ancient India and not kept as pets, but considered lowly and polluting creatures.[16] They are associated with death and often depicted as scavengers tearing up and devouring corpses. Dogs seldom appear on sculptures from the period, but when they occasionally do, they are represented as scavengers, devouring a boar, for example. In contemporaneous *dharmaśāstr*ic literature, the polluting nature of dogs is evident in that the sound of dogs barking renders recitation of the Veda impure (*Dharmasūtra* of *Apastamba* 1.10.19). However, in this kind of literature many different animals are said at various times to be in some way polluting. In the *Mahābhārata* the nature of men is likened to the tarnished nature of dogs when Yudhiṣṭhira says of men in war that 'we are not dogs but we are like dogs greedy for a piece of meat'.[17] However, in the *Mahābhārata* dogs do seem to be raised in status on occasion

---

that elephants are 'caught in the wild at an appropriate age...kept in captivity and subjected to a long and difficult training period' (p. 72). With regards to the above reference, Covill situates this as part of the overall 'training' of Nanda, likened to an elephant by Aśvaghoṣa with recourse to 15 different figures of speech.

15. For a discussion of the notion of 'coming of age' in early Buddhism and Brahmanism, see Collett (forthcoming), chapter on Paṭācārā.

16. Dogs, along with snakes and crocodiles discussed below, all feature in myth from the period. For example, the god Yama has two dogs in the Vedic myths, and dogs are inferred in a lineal descent line in the *Mahābhārata*. Also, snakes or serpents are associated with both Viṣṇu and the Buddha. However, these more positive representations in the world of mythology do not appear directly relevant to Aśvaghoṣa's figurative expressions.

17. Mbh 12.7.10 (trans. Fitzgerald) as cited in Hiltebeitel (2001: 171).

to that of benign village animal, in that Yudhiṣṭhira is sometimes accompanied by a dog, and cruelty towards dogs is considered an undharmic act.[18]

In a *sutta* in the Pāli Canon, Brahmins are said to be worse than dogs. Here the dog is again the most polluting of creatures.[19] In the later folkloric tales, Olivelle (1997: xxiii) notes that although dogs are not main characters in any of the stories in the *Pañcatantra*, they do appear in several, but are always 'despised as unclean and greedy, an animal without an ounce of self-respect'. In the passage mentioned above, men are not only likened to dogs but are depicted as the worse kind of vile dog that wants to eat its own vomit. If this metaphor is taken to its full conclusion, it could be presumed that women are the dog's vomit. However, there is at least one reference in the Pāli Canon where sensual desires are likened to vomit, glossed as dog's vomit. This is a possible interpretation of the metaphor—men are lowly dogs desiring the most base and vile of experiences; sensual pleasure.[20]

Turning now to the ways in which women are represented in the same passage, the females' duplicitous nature is illuminated by them being both dangerous and enticing. Thus, the deer has escaped the hunter (woman) but is still 'longing for the herd' (his love). The elephant wants to descend into the crocodile-infested river (women) because of its thirst for water (the love of women). Each metaphor except for the last evokes both a danger and a thing desired.

Danger	Attraction
hunter	herd
entanglement	cage[22]
crocodile-infested river	water
snake	shelter
hawk	mate

In terms of the 'woman as danger' aspect of the female, women are the hunters, pursuing the fickle deer. There are some instances of women being represented in this way in other literature from the period, as it is part of what appears to have been a social construct of female sexuality to depict women as sexual aggressors and men as hapless victims of the voracious female sexual appetite. The extent to which this has been depicted in early Buddhist texts has been overstated, but as the above passage demonstrates,

18. See various discussions in Hiltebeitel (2001), such as pages 170–72 and 195–98. Hiltebeitel also notes that Yudhiṣṭhira's *dharma* is exemplified by his non-cruelty to a dog, p. 209.
19. *Aṅguttara Nikāya*, 5.19, see Freiberger (2009).
20. See Sumedhā's verse 478 in the *Therīgāthā*, and the commentary which glosses this as dog's vomit.
21. Here the cage represents the home comfort of the bird, but carried the same association as the English metaphor of the 'gilded cage'.

such depictions do exist. I have shown elsewhere the problems with the idea of this as part of a pervasive social construct (Collett 2013). The general parameters of this type of gendered portrayal are of women as temptresses and seductresses, seeking to entice and ensnare men. To quote just one other example, in *Therīgāthā* 72, the nun Vimalā speaks of her former life as a prostitute in which she sought to entice men into her lair: 'Having decorated this body, well painted, enticing fools, I stood at the brothel door as a hunter having laid out a snare'.

Women are also likened to crocodiles, a dangerous wild predatory creature. There is a folklore tale of an anthropomorphized crocodile that can be dated prior to Aśvaghoṣa and crocodiles do appear in sculptures of the time as well as being evidenced in mythology morphed into the *makara*. In art, they generally appear to represent water or a particular river, but are also occasionally depicted as being ridden (Bautze 1995: 27–28). The folkloric story of the crocodile is initially found in the *Cariyapiṭaka*, a Buddhist text that can be dated to the second century BCE.[22] This is the well-known story of the monkey and the crocodile, which later appears in the *Jātakaṭṭhakathā* and the *Pañcatantra*.[23] Olivelle's description of crocodiles in the *Pañcatantra* equates with Aśvaghoṣa's usage; they are the 'hidden danger lurking beneath the water of the lotus-pond' (1997: xxiii). Aśvaghoṣa twice likens women to crocodiles in the context of his attack on women. In both occasions he uses the simile or metaphor to evoke the feeling of a hidden danger lurking beneath the surface. This relates back to the ascetic's tirade on women when he warns Nanda that although on superficial appearance they are sweet and honey-tongued, beneath the veneer women are cruel and vicious. The ascetic says, 'they enthral with their charming talk and attack with their sharp minds'.

In the metaphor of the lad who grasps at a snake in the shelter, both aspects of women as danger/comfort are engendered once again. The snake is the lurking danger, just visible in one's peripheral vision, in the otherwise secure refuge/shelter. The snake in this historical period is represented in different ways. Aśvaghoṣa's metaphorical expression is closest to how Olivelle identifies the folkloric anthropomorphized snake in the *Pañcatantra*. Here, a snake epitomizes peril: 'A common image of danger lurking in the most unexpected of places is that of a snake hidden in one's house' (Olivelle 1997: xxiv). However, he also characterizes snakes as 'double-tongued and double-crossing' and notes there can be no friendship with a snake. This is a further reading than Aśvaghoṣa's usage dictates. Underlying the metaphor here, appears to be the more visceral and onomatopoeic qualities of a snake as seen in other places in Aśvaghoṣa's work and in the epics. In these texts, used as a simile for human characteristics, the snake-like quali-

22. *Cariyapiṭaka* 3.7. See Horner's translation (2007: 39).
23. *Jātakaṭṭhakathā* (57) and *Pañcatantra*, in Olivelle (1997: 146–54).

ties of humans can represent an otherwise healthy/righteous/good human momentarily turned. Both women and men can be said to resemble a snake at times of anger or distress when they hiss like snakes when angry or are viperous in deceit. For instance, Lakṣmaṇa when made angry 'hisses like a snake' (Rām. 20.20.3), or when Rāma's father calls his young wife a deadly poisonous viper when she turns on him and tries to manipulate him (Rām. 10.35). Demons too can be likened to snakes, such as the demoness who tries to trick Rāma. In this case the snake simply represents a writhing form of an otherwise noxious epic character. In the above quote from the *Saundarananda*, in which women are honey-tongued but poisonous, this is a more subtle manifestation of these varying usages; women appear to be enthralling and charming, but underneath are viperous.

From this assessment of figures of speech in Aśvaghoṣa's *Saundarananda*, in which women and men are likened to animals, and animal behaviour is evoked to represent gendered traits, some general conclusions can be drawn. Aśvaghoṣa's poem illustrates that a man faced with a beautiful woman whom he desires loses his easy leonine prowess and bull-like majesty. He is turned into an effeminate and easily frightened deer, a poor hapless bird, a dumb pheasant, a foolhardy young elephant, and a vile, salivating dog. A woman, on the other hand, when she spies a potential mate, becomes a predatory and deadly hunter, resembling a snapping crocodile or a swooping hawk. But this is not obvious, it is hidden behind honeyed words and an enticing allure. The viperous danger of women is almost wholly occluded from view, just as a crocodile lurks beneath the murky river's surface, ready to pounce, just as the snake slithers silently in the long grass. And this does seem to reflect an anxiety, perhaps an anxiety of emasculation, if that is not stretching the point too far. Nanda is the poor, hapless besotted fool, but rather than, as in the *Udāna* and *Theragāthā*, this being recognized as Nanda's own sad predicament, here it is articulated as malediction against women. Johnson and Covill, in spending much time working on translations of Aśvaghoṣa's poems both raise the question as to whether the struggle identified in the poems—to relinquish erotic love and the sensual pleasures of love-making—was a personal struggle for the poet.[24] Taking this one step further, I want to raise the question: is the fear and anxiety expressed about women in the *Saundarananda* also personal to Aśvaghoṣa? It is not conceptualized as such, quite the opposite actually, here it is a prefigured, universal dynamic between the sexes. However, somewhat ironically given the prejudicial nature of the writer, this dynamic appears to be a scenario in which women are the more powerful and very much have the upper hand.

24. '...for the passion with which he denounces the ordinary joys of life draw its force not merely from a revulsion of feeling, but also from the necessity of convincing himself' (Johnson 1998: xcvi–xcvii). Also see Covill (2007: 18).

REFERENCES

Bautze, J. K. 1995. *Early Indian Terracottas*. Leiden: E. J. Brill.

Collett, A. 2006. 'Buddhism and Gender: Reframing and Refocusing the Debate.' *Journal of Feminist Studies in Religion* 22(2): 55–84. http://dx.doi.org/10.2979/FSR.2006.22.2.55

— 2009a. 'Historico-Critical Hermeneutics in the Study of Women in Early Indian Buddhism.' *Numen* 56: 91–117. http://dx.doi.org/10.1163/156852708X373276

— 2009b. 'Somā, the Learned Brahmin.' *Religions of South Asia* 3(1): 93–109.

— 2011. 'The Female Past in Early Indian Buddhism: The Shared Narrative of the Seven Sisters in the *Therī-Apadāna*.' *Religions of South Asia* 5(1/2): 209–26.

— (ed.). 2013. *Women in Early Indian Buddhism: Comparative Textual Studies*. Oxford: Oxford University Press.

— Forthcoming. *Pāli Biographies of Buddhist Nuns*.

Covill, L. 2007. *Handsome Nanda (Saundarananda)*. New York: New York University Press and JJC Foundation.

— 2009. *A Metaphorical Study of Saundarananda*. Delhi: Motilal Banarsidass.

Dehejia, V. 2009. *The Body Adorned: Dissolving Boundaries between the Sacred and Profane in India's Art*. New York: Columbia University Press.

Doniger O'Flaherty, W. 1980. *Women, Androgens, and Other Mythical Beasts*. Chicago: University of Chicago Press.

Fitzgerald, James L., (ed.). 2004 *The Mahābhārata, Volume 7: Book 11: The Book of the Women Book 12: The Book of Peace. Vol. 7*. Chicago: University of Chicago Press,

Freiberger, O. 2009. 'Negative Campaigning: Polemics against Brahmins in a Buddhist Sutta.' *Religions of South Asia* 3(1): 61–76.

Gerow, E. 1971. *A Glossary of Indian Figures of Speech*. The Hague: Mouton & Co. http://dx.doi.org/10.1515/9783110905250

Goldman, R. (trans.). 2005. *Ramayana, Book One, Boyhood, by Valmiki*. New York: New York University Press and JJC Foundation.

Hiltebeitel, A. 2001. *Rethinking the Mahābhārata: A Reader's Guide to the Education of the Dharma King*. Chicago and London: University of Chicago Press.

Horner, I. B. (trans.). 2007. *Cariyapiṭaka. The Minor Anthologies of the Pali Canon, Part III*. Reprint 1975. Lancaster: The Pali Text Society.

Jamison, S. 2006. 'Women "Between the Empires" and "Between the Lines".' In P. Olivelle (ed.), *Between the Empires: Society in India 300 BCE to 400 CE*: 191–214. New York: Oxford University Press.

Johnson. E. H. 1975. *The Saundarananda of Aśvaghoṣa*. Reprint 1928. Delhi: Motilal Banarsidass.

— (trans.). 1998. *The Buddhacarita or Acts of the Buddha*. Reprint 1936. Delhi: Motilal Banarsidass.

Oldenburg, H., and R. Pischel (eds). 1999. *The Thera- and Therīgāthā: Stanzas Ascribed to Elders of the Buddhist Order of Recluses*. Reprint 1883. Oxford: The Pali Text Society.

Olivelle, P. (trans.). 1996. *Dharmasūtras: The Law Codes of Ancient India*. Oxford: Oxford University Press.

— (trans.). 1997. *The Pañcatantra: The Book of India's Folk Wisdom*. Oxford: Oxford University Press.

— (ed.). 2005. *Manu's Code of Law: A Critical Edition and Translation of the Mānava-Dharmaśāstra*. New York: Oxford University Press.

— 2009. *Life of the Buddha by Aśvaghoṣa*. New York: New York University Press and JJC Foundation.

Patton, L. 2008. 'Ṛṣis Imagined across Difference: Some Possibilities for the Study of Conceptual Metaphor in Early India.' *Journal of Hindu Studies* 1(1/2): 49–76. http://dx.doi.org/10.1093/jhs/hin004

Pollock, S. (trans.). 2006. *Ramayana, Book Three, The Forest, by Valmiki*. New York: New York University Press and JJC Foundation.

— (trans.). 2008. *Ramayana, Book Two: Ayodhya, by Valmiki*. New York: New York University Press & JJC Foundation.

Powers, J. 2009. *A Bull of a Man: Images of Masculinity, Sex, and the Body in Indian Buddhism*. Cambridge, MA: Harvard University Press.

Schopen, G. 1996. 'The Suppression of Nuns and the Ritual Murder of their Special Dead in Two Buddhist Monastic Texts.' *Journal of Indian Philosophy* 24(6): 563–92. http://dx.doi.org/10.1007/BF00165539

— 1997. *Bones, Stones, and Buddhist Monks: Collected Papers on the Archaeology, Epigraphy, and Texts of Monastic Buddhism in India.* Hawai'i: University of Hawai'i Press.

Snead, S. 1989. *Animals in the Four Worlds: Sculptures from India.* Chicago: University of Chicago Press.

Steinthal, P. (ed.). 1982. *Udāna.* Reprint 1885. Oxford: The Pali Text Society.

Wilmott, P. (trans.). 2006. *Mahābhārata, Book Two: The Great Hall.* New York: New York University Press.

Sparrows and Lions: Fauna in Sikh Imagery, Symbolism and Ethics

ELEANOR NESBITT*

Central to Sikh tradition is an event in 1699 which is usually referred to as the founding of the Khālsā.[1] On the day of the annual Vaisākhī (Spring harvest) festival, Guru Gobind Singh, the tenth Guru, rallied his followers in Anandpur (in the state of Punjab) and loudly called for the head of a Sikh. (The Punjabi word *sikh* means 'disciple', 'learner'.) When five volunteers had in turn come forward—and had apparently each been beheaded in his tent—the Guru brought them out intact for ritual initiation with *amṛt*, water that his wife had sweetened by adding some *patāse* (sugar sweets). The assembled crowd then saw two sparrows swallow some of this water and immediately attack the Guru's falcon and put it to flight. Clearly, people realized, the *amṛt* could turn initiates into fearless warriors. The Guru renamed the five initiates with the surname Singh (lion), and since that day this has been the second name of male Sikhs, whether or not they have been initiated.

While accounts of the Khālsā's inauguration figure prominently in the writing of both devotees and scholars, and although sparrows, lions and many other non-human animals also feature elsewhere in the Sikh tradition, little if any scholarly attention has been paid to fauna in Sikh narrative, symbol and imagery.[2] Also, Sikh formulation of ethical concern regarding

* Eleanor Nesbitt is Professor Emerita at the Institute of Education, University of Warwick. She is a specialist in Sikh studies and is one of the founders of the Punjab Research Group. Her academic interests include the religious socialization of young people of Christian, Hindu and Sikh background, qualitative research methods and the study of religion. She co-directed the AHRC-funded project 'Investigating the Religious Identity Formation of Young People in Mixed Faith Families'. Professor Nesbitt is reviews editor of the *Journal of Punjab Studies* and is on the editorial board of *The British Journal of Religious Education*, *Fieldwork in Religion* and *Religions of South Asia*. Her books include *Sikhism. A Very Short Introduction* (Oxford University Press, 2005).

1. 'Khālsā' refers to Sikhs who have been initiated ceremonially into a strict discipline of obedience to the Guru that includes five tangible indicators of identity.
2. On animals in Indian religious traditions more generally see Julia Leslie's exceptional work as a Sanskritist and ornithologist on the identity and significance of the *krauñca* bird in Vālmīki's *Rāmāyana* (Leslie 1998). Among other scholarly examples, K. N. Dave had earlier produced a book on birds in Sanskrit literature (1985) while the correct classification of

animals has been minimal, and has focused almost solely on the subject of vegetarianism.

The present chapter intends to map the territory in the hope that others may explore such issues in more detail. The territory concerned includes art work (whether reliefs in Sikh historic *gurdwārās*, the religious iconography of 'calendar' art, or the work of contemporary artists). It comprises, as well, traditional Sikh narratives, including *janam sākhī* (lit. 'birth witness') accounts of the life of Guru Nānak and other tales of miraculous occurrences. It is such stories which provide the subject matter for Sikh religious art. Sikh ethics and practices, mainly regarding the slaughter of animals, will also be discussed, as too will the abundant animal imagery of the Sikh scriptures.

The historical framework for this contribution is simply as follows: Sikhism's origins lie in a pre-industrial, predominantly rural, indeed agrarian, society whereas the contemporary Sikh community is an increasingly far-flung, and urban community. In fact, the 2001 census showed that Punjab is now one of India's three most urban states, with over 35 per cent of its population currently living in urban areas. At least in the diaspora, Sikhs are out of touch with the countryside of Punjab and, on top of this, for many Sikhs (whose grasp of spoken Punjabi, let alone of earlier Indian literary expression, is impoverished), the richly evocative language of scripture is all but impenetrable. Moreover, for twenty-first century Sikhs the 'enchanted universe' (Oberoi 1994: 139–203) of previous centuries has been discredited by a more 'scientific' unease with miracles. Sikhs, however, belong to a global society in which contemporary agendas encourage some ecological awareness, inclusive of all creation, and belong to an ethnically and religiously diverse society in which symbols and words (often with animal associations) gain new life as signifiers of identity. My contention is that an examination of the roles of non-human animals in the Sikh universe, including warfare, hunting, agriculture, religious poetry and identity formation, illuminates the community's history and sociology, and suggests the value for Sikhs of pondering this aspect of their tradition.

The discussion is also framed by a particular interactive model of Sikh society, namely the interaction between, firstly, Punjabi culture, secondly, *sikhī* (by which I mean principally the earlier Gurus' insights as expressed in the *Ādi Granth* together with the successive disciplinary codes associated with the tenth Guru, Guru Gobind Singh) and, thirdly, in the contemporary period, the catalyst of modernity (Dusenbery 2008; Nayar 2011; Nesbitt 2005). When applying this analytical model, it needs to be borne in mind that the Gurus themselves shared a Punjabi heritage and also that their own behaviour differed from one to another, at least insofar as only some (and most famously Guru Hargobind and Guru Gobind Singh) were hunters and warriors. Also,

---

Guru Gobind Singh's *chittā bāj* (white falcon) is discussed in a more popular fashion in the *Sikh Information Portal*. See Anonymous n.d.(a).

while the impact of the media, travel and other aspects of globalization is more rapid and far-reaching than ever before, some Sikhs have had contact with Europeans (and so with 'modernity') since the early nineteenth century.[3] Finally, intrinsic to Sikh tradition is emphasis on maintaining a fine balance, one that is encapsulated in such word-pairs as *mīrī pīrī* (temporal and spiritual), *simran* and *sevā* (meditation and service) and *sant sipāhī* (saint soldier). It is instructive to keep this balance (or tension) in mind when surveying animal-related Sikh narratives, ethics and imagery—elements of Sikh tradition which converge distinctively at historic Sikh shrines.

ANIMAL PRESENCES IN SIKHISM: FROM PILGRIMAGE PLACES TO POPULAR ART

Every year many thousands of Sikhs visit historic shrines, and animals—and trees (Dogra 2011)—are at the heart of the episodes which many such shrines commemorate. For example, several *gurdwārās* mark the place where a Guru tethered his horse.[4] At Nanded in Maharashtra pilgrims see horses that are revered as descendants of Guru Gobind Singh's stallion, Nīlā (Neela) ('blue', a name referring to its reputedly blue colour).[5] At Hemkund, in Uttarānchal, high in the mountains, where Guru Gobind Singh is believed to have meditated in a previous life, pilgrims look out for his legendary white falcon.[6]

Pictures of pilgrim places sometimes feature associated creatures. The Golden Temple in Amṛtsar rises from a pool in which huge fishes are depicted (see, for example, a 'woodcut of the Harmandir Sāhib, circa 1870' reproduced in P. Singh 1989: 79). These fishes thrive on the *karāh prashād* (the sweet—made of semolina, sugar, ghee and water—that is distributed to those who come to worship) on which devotees feed them. Disquietingly for Sikhs of today's mainstream, influenced as it is by the Tat Khālsā reformers of a century ago, the skilfulness of eighteenth-century artists employed by Mahārājā Ranjīt Singh to decorate Sikh shrines is replete with non-human images, divine as well as animal. Nihang and Singh (2008: 125) reproduce a detail of raised relief

3. The British rule of Punjab (from 1849 to 1947) helped shape the historical development of 'Sikhism' (Nesbitt 2005). For example, the ideas of the Tat Khālsā ('true Khālsā') intellectuals were infused in the colonial period by the principled monotheism of the Protestant missionaries to whom they owed such influential institutions as the *Gurmukhī* printing press and modern schooling.
4. These include Gurdwārā Gau Ghāt (Patna) where Guru Tegh Bahādar tied his horse. Guru Gobind Singh tied his horse at the following sites: Gurdwārā Jandsar Sāhib (close to the Punjabi city of Bhatinda), Gurdwārā Manjī Sāhib (Alamgir, Ludhiana District) and Gurdwārā Mehdiānā Sāhib (Mehdiānā, Tehsil Jagraon, District Ludhiana).
5. Neela appears prominently in devotional and historical Sikh media, including the Internet. See Anonymous n.d.(b).
6. Oral communication, Jasjit Singh, July 2011.

from the interior of Srī Abchal Nagar *gurdwārā* at Nanded in Maharashtra, the place where the tenth Guru's human life ended:

> When the takht [historic shrine] was built anew, the interior walls were lavishly decorated with designs and motifs emblematic of the militant side of the tenth Guru's character as well as the pluralistic outlook of the Sikhs of that time. Akali Nihangs engaging lions with katars [punch daggers], Udasis sitting amidst wild jungle beasts as *Pasupati* (masters of the beasts), Chandi [the goddess Durga] riding a tiger and engaging the demon hordes...were depicted by the artists sent by Ranjit Singh to carry out the work.

Surprisingly but possibly showing the effect of the Tat Khālsā perspective, a recent chapter on Sikh art commences with the assertion that 'Sikh art is aniconic' (N. G. K. Singh 2011: 157). In fact, most popular devotional pictures, of the type to be found in calendars (on display in almost every Sikh home), show the Gurus, and in many of these the Gurus appear in close association with animals. Some of these pictures show episodes from the Sikhs' heroic past in which animals are integral. Thus, the youthful Guru Nānak with a hooded cobra (McLeod 1991: 88, 128) illustrates a story from the *janam sākhī* tradition (McLeod 1980a: 90): Rāi Bulār, the headman of Talwandī village, had observed a cobra with its hood distended to shield the sleeping young man from the noon sun. Such stories and visual images illustrate continuity with older Indic traditions in which the superhuman status of a divine figure (notably the gods Śiva and Viṣṇu but also the Buddha or Jain *tīrthankaras*, i.e. spiritual masters)—is signalled by the proximity of a potentially deadly snake. Such cobra images and stories are unproblematic in an enchanted universe in which gods, humans and (other) animals converse as personae in a cosmic and microcosmic drama.

In some popular iconography, animals are more incidental. For example, in a picture showing Guru Nānak as ploughman (McLeod 1991: 94; Nesbitt and Kaur 1999: 34), the two white oxen have rather less agency. What the picture does is visually represent a metaphor in the following words of Guru Nānak: 'Regard your body as a field, your *man* [mind] the plough, [virtuous] actions the ploughing, and effort the irrigating. [In this field], sow the Name as seed, level it with contentment and fence it with humility' (*Shabad Sorath* 2, *Ādi Granth* 595, translated by Mcleod [1991: 129]).[7]

As a Guru who, unlike Guru Nānak and his first successors, was renowned for his prowess in battle and the chase, Guru Gobind Singh too is depicted with other creatures, in his case most frequently the falcon (*bāz, bāj*) (McLeod 1991: 38, 39, 42, 44, 118-22) and the charger (pp. 38, 42, 119, 122).[8] Similarly, the elephant has its place in Sikh iconography, whether as the decorated ele-

7. The *Ādi Granth*, or *Guru Granth Sāhib*, will be henceforth referred to as AG.
8. For a ruler to carry a falcon was not unusual. See, for example, a late nineteenth-century gouache painting of 'Sangat Singh, Ruler of Jind' in Stronge (1999: 31).

phant donated to Guru Gobind Singh as a thank-offering from Rattan Chand of Assam (McLeod 1991: 111, 131) or the hill *rājās*' killer elephant which Bachitra Singh stabbed through the forehead, as depicted by G. S. Sohan Singh (McLeod 1991: 116, 131). A scene from the life of the sixth Guru, Guru Hargobind, the grandfather of Guru Gobind Singh, depicts him stabbing a roaring tiger, so saving the life of the Mughal emperor, Jahāngīr, who had invited him to hunt tigers with him.

McLeod reproduces a black and white print[9] (Amr̥tsar, 1874–1875) showing Guru Gobind Singh and four mounted male companions pursuing tigers, boars, antelopes and other creatures (Mcleod 1991: 127). Paintings of the Mughal emperor Akbar's hunts near Lahore, showing a profusion of fleeing animals being hunted down by men shooting arrows and inciting panthers to spring on their victims, provide artistic precedent and cultural contextualization (Stronge 1999: 68–69). So too, in paintings with no religious focus, the predilection for hunting and for paintings of royal hunts continued, as illustrated by a Pahārī gouache painting of 'A Sikh Ruler shooting Wild Boar from a Platform', in which blood pours from wounded deer as well as from wounded boar (Stronge 1999: 105).

The contemporary Sikh artists, Amr̥t and Rabindra K. D. Kaur Singh, while generally working on secular themes, consciously develop Indian artistic genres, particularly the Indian miniature, by wittily and perceptively adapting them for topical late twentieth- and early twenty-first-century themes. With regard to animal representation, they continue a visual tradition of white steeds, whether in their rendering of 'The Mahabharata (Krishna and Arjun on the Battle Field)' (Singh and Singh 1999: 76–77) or of a Punjabi bridegroom in the UK riding to his marriage (pp. 40–41), or of a British General of Punjab on horseback visiting Baron Iqbal Singh's family in Punjab prior to Partition (Robson n.d.: 18). Other animals too are exquisitely represented: 'As an animal typically associated with formal portraits of Indian nobility, Lord Iqbal Singh's much loved dog, Lucky, completes this image of the Scottish Sikh Laird' (p. 21). (Interestingly, c. 1815 a painting of Guru Har Rāī had shown him preceded by a small dog, and another c. 1830 depicts two dogs running alongside the mounted Guru Gobind Singh [Stronge 1999: 35, 36].) It was Indian miniature paintings of the royal elephant fight that inspired the Singh twins' 'Battle of the Giants' (Robson: 66–67), depicting 'the clash between opposing teams of American football and rugby', and this composition continues the ploy of creating an animal body as a composite of intertwined human bodies.[10]

9. Item I.M.2 (21)-1917, Lockwood Kipling collection, now held by the Victoria and Albert Museum, London.
10. See, for example, the cover image of Wendy Doniger's study of the history of the Hindus (2009).

THE PLACE OF ANIMALS IN SIKH FOLK TALES AND MYTHICAL NARRATIVES

That animals and birds should figure so prominently not only in secular works by Sikh artists but also in Sikh religious art, including *gurdwārā* reliefs, is unsurprising and—in terms of the Gurus' legacy—unproblematic, at least insofar as (unlike Islam) Sikh teaching nowhere prohibits their figurative representation, and given that many stories of the Gurus and their followers involve, or even centre on, fauna. Thus, the *janam sākhī* tradition includes the story, in the B40 *janam sākhī* (B40 7a-9b; McLeod 1980b: 10–12), of Guru Nānak restoring the ruined crop that had been ravaged by oxen, a 'tale of how divine approval was signified by the suspension of natural laws', as well as the story of the protective cobra, 'a direct borrowing from earlier tradition' (McLeod 1980a: 90).[11]

Rather similarly to the 1699 transformation of the sparrows' character by sipping *amr̥t*, the visual transformation of a bird over a century earlier, during the time of the fourth Guru, also has historical significance for Sikhs. For legend tells how Rajanī, whose husband was crippled, saw a black bird enter the water of the pool in what later became the city of Amr̥tsar, only to re-emerge with white plumage. This transformation emboldened Rajanī to help her husband into the water, from which he duly emerged restored to health. It was the water's credentials that probably led to the founding in its midst of the Sikh shrine which later became the 'Golden Temple', surrounded by the pool of healing water, the '*amr̥t-sar*' (or *amr̥t sarovar*) which gave its name to the burgeoning city.

With Guru Hargobind the focus shifts to horses, as he commanded his Sikhs to give him weapons and horses. Sikhs tell the story of two of these steeds, Dilbāgh and Gulbāgh, which two Sikhs brought from Kabul for the Guru. En route, Mughal soldiers confiscated the horses and put them in the emperor's stable. From here, by two clever and daring stratagems, Bīdhī Chand, a courageous warrior, recovered them for the Guru.

In the story of Bābā Gurdittā, the eldest son of the sixth Guru, Guru Hargobind, it is a cow that figures prominently: despite his father's disapproval of displays of supernatural power, Gurdittā brought back to life a cow which he had accidentally shot while he was hunting. He died shortly thereafter of remorse on incurring his father's displeasure at his indulgence in miracle-working.

Birds and animals repeatedly feature in Guru Gobind Singh's life. For example, foreshadowing the 1699 event, the Gobindpurā *gurdwārā* commemorates an occurrence when the eight-year-old Gobind summoned two nearby sparrows to attack the falcon of a Pīr [Sufi worthy] who coveted his own falcon. In Sikh tradition this was the occasion for Guru Gobind Singh's words: 'It is when

11. Two less familiar *sākhīs* concern 'the city of insects' and 'the monster fish redeemed'. See McLeod (1980: 273).

I make sparrows fight hawks that I am called Gobind Singh' (see, for example, Bedi 2010).

Another *gurdwārā* (Putthi [Bhatthī] Sāhib) was constructed around some clay imprinted by a horse's hoof. The *gurdwārā* commemorates a miraculous feat by Guru Gobind Singh's celebrated blue horse, Nīlā. Needing somewhere to stay, the Guru had asked a local workman, who was firing bricks in a kiln, where he might rest. Mockingly, the man had challenged the Guru (if such he was) to rest on the kiln itself. At the Guru's instigation, Nīlā set one hoof on the clay surround of the furnace which immediately became so cool that the Guru could lie on it (Anonymous n.d. [b]).

A legend with another animal—the hare—is celebrated in another *gurdwārā*, Gurdwārā Shikār Ghāt Sāhib, situated far from Punjab near the river Godavari in the Maharashtrian city of Nanded. Here, it is believed, Guru Gobind Singh killed a hare, thereby liberating the soul of one Bhāī Mūlā who had been cursed since the time of Guru Nānak to continue in the cycle of birth and death until released from this by the tenth Guru. On another occasion, Guru Gobind Singh explained that, in a previous life, a small animal that his falcon had just killed, had been a faithless friend of the falcon's previous incarnation. This cruel death was his due punishment for having reneged on a loan.

Such myths relating to hunting, and their interpretations, suggest a continuing ethical tension among Sikhs over the killing of animals, especially by persons of such high spiritual stature as the Gurus. Popular and traditional paintings leave no doubt that Guru Hargobind and Guru Gobind Singh went hunting. Moreover, a line in canto eight of *Bachitra Nātak*, a composition by Guru Gobind Singh, translates as: 'Many the hunts which we followed in the wastelands, pursuing the bear, the antelope and the boar' (McLeod 1991: 127). However, it is understandable that Sikhs, and especially those who otherwise eschew the killing of animals, apparently feel the need to emphasize the Guru's motive of liberating souls from being reborn or highlight the outworking of the apparently innocent victim's *karma*. Not surprisingly, the matter of goat sacrifice evokes strongly differentiated responses from Sikhs. Nihang and Singh report a continuing practice of sacrificing goats at Nanded as a tradition instituted by Guru Gobind Singh:

> The worship of weapons conducted by Guru Gobind Singh included the reading of the ballads of Chandi and the decapitation [of] a goat as a sacrifice to the divine Mother. The first weapon anointed with the goat's blood was Chandi's standard.
> (Nihang and Singh 2008: 41)

Nihang Sikhs, a warrior order (whose name, Nihang, suggests their ferocity as it is a Persian word for the crocodile), claim continuity with the Sikh tradition that predates the 'reformist' Tat Khālsā movement. It is especially in Nanded, far removed as it is from the Punjab where the majority of Sikhs live, that the older practices still persist. Thus, Rupinder Pamme provides detail of Nihangs' observance of Dassehrā at Nanded:

> During these festivities a goat is decapitated at the shrine with a single blow of the sword known as *jhatka*. The head of the goat is then squeezed for its blood which is collected in a bowl and then a dot of the blood is placed on the weapons. The goat is skinned and the meat or *mas* of the goat is considered to be *maha-prasad* ('great sacramental food') and is distributed to fellow Nihangs.
>
> (Pamme 2010: 124)

If, as they claim, Nihangs Sikhs simply continue the Guru's own practices, it is not surprising that goat sacrifice is also part of some accounts of the 1699 event. For, after each of the five volunteers (*panj pyāre*) had stepped into the Guru's tent, the crowd saw the Guru exit the tent holding aloft a sword dripping with blood. According to one explanation (K. Singh 1977: 83, also McLeod 1997: 52), in order to test his Sikhs' loyalty and courage, he only appeared to have executed the brave volunteers, whereas in reality he had each time decapitated a goat. Others, however, reject this version of events, insisting that this explanation diminishes the Guru's power: he had in fact removed each man's head and then miraculously restored all five heads before the men came out of the tent.

ANIMAL-RELATED ETHICS IN SIKHISM

Controversy over the Gurus' hunting and the slaughtering of goats are of a piece with Sikhism's ambivalence over non-vegetarianism. Sikhs diverge widely both in their attitude to meat-eating (and understanding of Sikh religious teaching on this) and in their actual practice (Brar 2011). In line with Guru Gobind Singh's pronouncement when instituting the Khālsā in 1699, the current widely respected code of discipline, the *Sikh Rahit Maryādā*, prohibits the consumption of animals that have been ritually slaughtered, that is *halāl* meat. While many Sikhs understand this as permission to eat animals that have been killed in other ways, others regard this as a total ban on meat-eating. This is the interpretation of many *amṛtdhārī* Sikhs, and it is especially emphasized by certain spiritual masters (Sants) and in particular Sikh and Sikh-related movements—the Nāmdhārīs, the Akhand Kīrtanī Jathā, Nānaksar and Sikh Dharma of the Western Hemisphere (Nesbitt 2005). In practice, the food served in the *laṅgar* (communal kitchen/canteen) is strictly lacto-vegetarian (with the very small exception of the Nihangs' *mahā prasād*). At the same time, away from the *gurdwārā* and religious occasions, many Sikhs do include meat in their diet, although—in line with Hindu sensitivity—beef is generally avoided. Consistently with the ruling of Guru Gobind Singh, to be religiously acceptable the meat must be *jhatkā*, that is, from animals killed by having their head severed by a single strike from a sword or an axe. Arguably, the prohibition of *halāl* meat was—like Guru Gobind Singh's ban on tobacco and on adultery with Muslim women—motivated by separating his Khālsā socially from Muslims, rather than by animal welfare concerns. Nowadays, quite apart from the pulls of modernity to a non-vegetarian diet, Sikh religious groupings are themselves strongly differentiated by the issue of animal slaughter and consumption, with the Nihangs at one extreme and the Nānaksar *sants*, the Nāmdhārī Gurus, and the teaching of Bhāī Randhīr Singh and his followers in the Akhand Kīrtanī Jathā, as well as Harbhajan Singh Yogī, founder of Sikh Dharma of the Western Hemisphere, at the other.[12]

Leaving aside the enthusiasm of some later Gurus for hunting, the *Guru Granth Sāhib* itself, and stories about Guru Nānak's life, do not advocate vegetarianism. For the Gurus the vegetarian/non-vegetarian debate was a distraction from more fundamental truths. Guru Nānak's verses addressed the contemporary Brahminical Hindu view that anyone who ate meat would be polluted (AG 1289–90). Instead, Guru Nānak pointed out that as humans we are fleshly creatures, inevitably caught up in the chain of life, and he emphasized that plants too are living organisms (AG 472). The Guru emphasized that there are worse forms of blood-sucking—the exploitation of the weak by the more powerful, for instance. There is also a *janam sākhī* story of Guru Nānak roasting venison at a Hindu religious site. Even if not historically verifiable, this episode indicates his followers' assumption that such an action was consistent with both his message and his remembered behaviour. Indeed, none of the ten Gurus preached vegetarianism, and Guru Amar Dās's diet of rice and lentils can be variously understood—for example, as demonstrating his personal abstemiousness rather than as a requirement that his followers become vegetarian.

Any understanding of the evolution of Sikh ethics and conduct towards animals benefits from noting the norms and insights of the Hindu and Muslim context of the Gurus and their followers. So, older Indic (mainly Hindu) respect for the purity of the cow is apparent not only in the widespread avoidance of beef, but also in such practices as, for example, Sikhs' continuing use of milk and water for the daily cleansing of the marble pavement surrounding the pool in which the Golden Temple stands, and for the use of yoghurt in the annual cleansing of the *nishān sāhib* (holy flag hoisted on a pole outside *gurdwārās*).

Although inseparable from considerations of utility and necessity, the love of Nihangs and other Sikhs for their horses was exemplary, as the European observer, Colonel Polier, reported in his writings of 1776–1802:

> The Siques [*sic*]...have mostly two horses a piece, and some three; their horses are middle sized, but exceeding good, strong and high spirited, and mild tempered... and indeed they take the greatest Care to encrease [*sic*] their numbers by all means in their power; and tho' they make merry in the demise of one of their Brethren,

12. As an indication of some Sikhs' strength of feeling, in the nineteenth century some Nāmdhārīs in Malerkotla were executed by the British for having, in their outrage at the slaughter of cows, killed local (Muslim) butchers.

> they condole and lament the Death of a Horse, thus shewing their Value for an animal so necessary to them in their excursions.
>
> (Madra and Singh 2004: 81)

Madra and Singh go on to mention that 'the respect shown to a horse by a Sikh warrior of the eighteenth century is typified by the vernacular term for a horse a *jān bhāī* or life brother' (Madra and Singh 2004: 87). Environmental and ecological issues, as currently debated, did not explicitly figure in the agenda of earlier generations, and in this respect the history of Sikh society is no different from that of other South Asian (and indeed other) faith communities. To take just one example, enthusiasm for hunting tigers, a now endangered species, was shared by Indians and Europeans alike.

While Gopal Puri, a palaeontologist, has asserted unequivocally that 'Sikhs are Lovers of Nature' (1989: 320), Gopinder Kaur has noted a generational drift away from her grandparents' environmentally friendly thrift (2008/9: 48). Moved by late twentieth-century environmental concern, minority Sikh voices are beginning to protest at wholesale environmental destruction and degradation in Punjab. Notably, Pardeep Singh Rai has founded DEEP (Defenders of Ecology and Environment of Panjab, a title abbreviated to an acronym that means 'light' in north Indian languages).[13] However, disregard for environmental issues continues to characterize Sikhs' initiatives, including many in the name of Sikh religion: thus, in recent years, many trees hallowed for their connection with events in the lives of the Gurus have died as a result of marble reconstructions of the historic shrines in which they were honoured (Dogra 2011).

In common with other faith traditions, Sikhism risks being misrepresented by advocates of current agendas. For example, the representation of Guru Nānak as preaching concern for animals (in some curriculum material for young children in UK schools) is anachronistic. Nonetheless, the following verse of the saint-poet, Kabīr, whose compositions form part of the Sikh scripture, affords a glimpse of the way in which animals were treated and of his sympathy with them: 'Without Hari [the Lord] we become the bulls of others; With bruised noses, broken shoulders we eat the chaff of coarse grain' (Kohli 1961: 127).

In conclusion, formulations of ethical positions on animal welfare and natural habitats are few (or non-existent) in Sikhism while practice suggest a profound ambivalence, mostly deriving from differing interpretations of scripture and of the Gurus' deeds.[14] Nevertheless, while there is no equivalent in Sikh religious literature to the creative impulse that issued from the

13. For more information see the NGO website: http://www.defendersofpanjab.org/.
14. To date, Sikhs have—with the exception of Chahal (2005)—not contributed to debates on bio-ethical debates (e.g. genetic modification). One further example is Jagbir Jhutti-Johal's recent work on Sikhism and science where, however, the discourse is limited to procedures involving humans (2011).

poet Vālmīki's empathy with another creature, the *krauñca* bird (the Indian Sarus Crane, *grus antigone antigone*) (cf. Leslie 1998), the recurrence of animal imagery in the *Guru Granth Sāhib* conveys a rare attunement with non-human creation.

ANIMAL IMAGERY IN THE *GURU GRANTH SĀHIB*

Although Sikhs' supreme guide, the *Guru Granth Sāhib*, includes no pronouncements on conservation and sustainability, the writers' imagery is supportive of respect for non-human creation. A reading of the *Guru Granth Sāhib* leaves the reader with a profound sense of the abundant wonders of a minutely observed creation, which for the Gurus expresses divinely instituted order (*hukam*, divine will).

> If God wills, he may cause the tigers, hawks,
> Kestrels and falcons to eat grass.
> He may likewise cause the grass-eating animals to eat meat.
> He thus can create life's pattern as he pleases.
> All creatures live by breathing, but he may sustain
> Them even without it, if he so desires.
> Hence the True one sustains life as it pleases him.
>
> (AG 144, in Kaur-Singh 1994: 141)

The cumulative effect of its poetic compositions[15] is a respectful appreciation of the natural world. One of Guru Nānak's compositions, the *bārahmāhā* ('twelve months') evokes the calendar of rural Punjab: the arrival of cranes (*kūnjān*) in the lunar month of *katik*, the bumble bees (*bhavar*) in the month of *chet*, and in *bhādon* 'the frogs croak and the peacocks squeal / the *Papiha* says 'Preo, Preo', the snakes crawl and bite. / There are mosquitoes on the tank full to the brim...' (AG 1107–10, in Kohli 1961: 118). One of Guru Nānak's verses on the month of *pokh* (December-January) provides the taxonomy of his time: 'His light fills all those born of eggs (*andaj*), born from the womb (*jeraj*), born of sweat (*setaj*) and born of the earth (*utbhuj*)' (AG 1109, in Kohli 1961: 118). Writing about attitudes to nature in Sikhism, Kanwaljit Kaur Singh quotes such unambiguous affirmations of *kudrat* (nature) as:

> God created himself and assumed a Nature,
> Second besides himself, he created Nature,
> Seated in Nature, he watches with delight
> What he creates.
>
> (AG 463, in Kaur-Singh 1994: 132)

15. The *Guru Granth Sāhib* has been composed by six Gurus and by other saint poets (*sants*) whose sentiments and principles resonate with theirs.

> In nature we see God,
> In Nature we hear his speech;
> Nature inspires devotional reveries.
> In Nature is the essence of joy and peace.
> Earth, sky, nether regions comprise nature.
> Air, water, fire, earth, dust are all parts of nature,
> The Omnipotent Creator commands, observes and
> Pervades Nature.
>
> (AG 464, in Kaur-Singh 1994: 133)

> Nature is omnipresent and is beyond value.
> Even if one were to know its value,
> One would become mute while trying to describe it.
>
> (AG 84, in Kaur-Singh 1994: 133)

Kaur-Singh also quotes this statement about creation as a whole:

> All creatures have been given consciousness,
> None has been created without it.
> They follow the path according to their
> understanding, and, judged in the same way,
> They come and go.
>
> (AG 24, in Kaur-Singh 1994: 142)

Verses aplenty introduce animals, birds, fish and insects in relation to the theme that pervades the whole scripture, namely the imperative to centre one's being on remembrance of *nām* (the name and indeed the reality of God):

> As in the sky the white-clothed crane;
> Keeping its mind behind, in its heart continually remembering its young ones;
> So the True Guru keeps the disciple absorbed in the love of Hari, and also keeps him in his heart.
>
> (Gaurī M 4, in Kohli 1961: 128)

> The ocean like a king having mountains of wealth and property,
> Is not equal to an ant, if from its mind He is not forgotten
>
> (Japjī)

> The sparrow...is good and is liked by the Lord if she remembers His Name.
>
> (Vār Malār M1, in Kohli 1961: 128)

> Milching [*sic*] animals eat grass and give nectar (milk) but the egocentric eats best food and doesn't contemplate the name of the Lord.
>
> (AG 1042, in Grewal 1986)

> If I were a doe living in the forest, eating grass
> and leaves, with God's grace, I would find him.
> If I were a cuckoo living in the mango tree,
> contemplating and singing, God would reveal himself through his mercy.
> If I were a female snake, dwelling in the ground, let God's
> word be in my being, my dread would vanish.
> Eternal God is found, light meets light.
>
> (AG 157, in Kaur-Singh 1994: 142)

In Punjabi marriages a moving song that is sung at the time of a bride's departure from her parents to her husband's family continues to evoke the flight of birds. Bird imagery permeates the *Guru Granth Sāhib* too, conveying a wealth of insights:

> The world is like a crow that hath worldly wisdom in its beak.
> (Bilāwal M3, in Kohli 1961: 128)

> On a pond in saltpetre soil, geese have come and descended.
> They dip their beaks in the water but do not drink, they burn to fly away.
> (Farīd, in Kohli 1961: 126)

> Thou art the cage and I am thy parrot:
> What can the He-cat Yama [death] do to me?
> (Gaurī Kabīr, in Kohli 1961: 127)

We find the crane, a popular image for religious hypocrisy, contemplating fish contrasted with the swan in the following lines (that echo local belief that swans can discern precious stones). Imaging the incompatibility of *manmukh* (self-centred) and *gurmukh* (individual focused on God/Guru):

> It becometh not a crane to sit amidst the swans,
> For, even there he hath his eyes on the fish,
> When the swans look around and discriminate, they find
> Nothing in common with the cranes.
> The swans peck at the pearls and diamonds whilst the cranes seek but frogs.
> Seeing this, the cranes fly away lest they be exposed.
> (AG 454, in Grewal 1986: 46)

The profusion of bird-centred images includes the *chatrik* (pied crested cuckoo) craving the first drop of rain, that is, yearning for God/Guru (AG 454, 1007, 538, 538, 96, 858, 1283, 1285). The crow is perhaps least negatively invoked by Farīd, the earliest poet to be incorporated in the *Guru Granth Sāhib*: 'O crow, thou searchest my skeleton, eat thou all my flesh. But touch not the two eyes, for I long to see my Spouse' (AG 1382, in Grewal 1986: 47).

Readers come across the peacock (its supposed love for thunder clouds, and dancing in happiness) in images used by almost all the Guru poets (AG 1272, 173, in Grewal 1986: 480), but also the swallow (Grewal 1986: 48), the parrot, *koel* (a cuckoo, *Eudynamys scolopaeus*), *chakvi* (Ruddy Shelduck), pigeon, sparrow and kite. Larger creatures too are mentioned in connection with devotion to God and the pain of being separated from God:

> Hear thou, o black deer, why art thou attached to the garden?
> (Āsā M1, in Kohli 1961: 127)

> The fish separated from the water weeps in its eyes,
> the fisherman threw a net over it.
> (Āsā M1, in Kohli 1961: 128)

More damningly:

> The creature who is without the devotion of the Lord,
> His body may be considered like that of a swine or a dog.
>
> (M9 in Kohli 1961: 127)

> Slanderers are like animals because they are without the Guru.
>
> (AG 1139, 1163, in Grewal 1986: 37)

Kabīr refers scathingly to the futility of ritual bathing, by reference to frogs. Grewal provides references to the following in the *Guru Granth Sāhib*: the elephant (1986: 37–38), the deer (pp. 38–39), the dog (pp. 39-40), the horse (pp. 41, 43), sheep (p. 42), the ass, buffalo and jackal (signifying disinterestedness and lassitude) as well as the rhinoceros, cat and mouse, and the monkey, which has been ensnared by Māyā (illusion), the juggler (p. 44). Grewal also gathers together references to fish, frogs, snakes, tortoises and crocodiles (pp. 50–53). Mini beasts too appear: the scorpion (p. 52), worms, the black-bee, moth, bee and butterfly (p. 55). Guru Nānak himself evokes the fly:

> The fly dies while it sits on sweet (honey).
> On a wet ball of molasses, the fly comes after wanderings;
>
> (Vār Malar M1, in Kohli 1961: 129)

Similarly, Guru Arjan Dev observed:

> The one which sits on it is stuck in it, the one which is fortunate escapes.
>
> (Vār Mārū M5, in Kohli 1961: 129)

The ant appears in a positive light in Kabīr's comparison of the ant's skill in picking out sugar from grains of sand with the elephant's inability to do so (AG 972, in Grewal 1986: 56). Here Kabīr exhorts his hearers to become like a little ant, 'abandon[ing] the ego of caste' (p. 56).

While some images suggest that non-human animals, like humans, can/must carry out *nām simaran*, others suggest that it is *nām simaran* that distinguishes a human from other creatures. Certainly, contemporary Sikh preachers repeatedly tell their congregations that it is only in one's birth as a human that it is possible to use God's name (*Waheguru*) and to carry out *nām simaran* appropriately.[16] This is consistent with the Gurus' understanding of successive births that 'humans occupy a privileged position in the tree of life and represent the final stage of creation before God realization' (Jhutti-Johal 2011: 17) as expressed in the lines:

> After wandering and wandering for so long, you have come
> In this Dark Age of Kali Yuga, you have obtained this human body, so very difficult to obtain.
> This opportunity shall not come into your hands again.
> So chant the Nam, the Name of the Lord, and the noose of Death shall be cut away.
>
> (AG 258)

16. Jasjit Singh, email communication 27 July 2011.

Despite the encyclopaedic range of fauna in the *Guru Granth Sāhib*, in the Sikh imaginary it is the lion/tiger (*singh*) that predominates. The Gurus' allusions to big cats evoke a range of images and include: 'How can one take refuge in the Lion (the Lord) if jackals (karman) seize him on the way?' (AG 858 in Grewal 1986: 37), and 'If a lion falls on a flock of sheep the master must be answerable'. (AG 360, in Grewal 1986: 37). Guru Arjan Dev said: 'Five lions (desires) and ten senses (tigresses) are overwhelmed and one is set free'. (AG 899, in Grewal 1986: 37).

Subsequent Sikh literature refers to *singh* (lion or tiger), *babbar sher* (lion) and *bāgh* (tiger) as symbolizing the heroic spirit to which Sikhs are to aspire. Thus, Bhāī Kāhan Singh Nābhā's historic pamphlet, *Ham Hindū Nahīn* ('We are not Hindus') told the parable of a potter's donkey which Guru Gobind Singh covered in a lion (or tiger) skin and let loose (see McLeod 1984: 134–35). The donkey roamed about happily, free from his burdens, and terrorizing anyone who came near. This state of affairs ceased the day he was attracted by the braying of a mare from his old stable. There his owner recognized him, tore off the skin and again began whipping him.[17] Interestingly, Bhāī Kāhan Singh Nābhā's interpretation, namely that Sikhs must not 'abandon the sacred faith of the Khalsa' and return to their former caste allegiance' is modified in subsequent retellings, which make no mention of caste. Thus Yogī Bhajan (Harbhajan Singh Yogī) (1979) urged his hearers not to 'follow the few corrupt who have worn the skin of Khālsā with the mind of a donkey', and in religious education teaching material for primary school-age pupils in the London (UK) borough of Redbridge, the moral is that Sikhs 'should live up to the outer symbols of dress and be proud to be Sikhs'.[18] This is consistent with the positive regard for the lion, as evident in the titles of individuals (Mahārāja Ranjīt Singh as Sher-e-Punjāb), of organizations and groups set up in the twentieth century (Babbar Khālsā, Shere Punjāb) and of books, for example *Style of the Lion: The Sikhs* (Singh and Singh 1998).

The lion and tiger also make their appearance in locations related to specific minority Sikh groupings. Thus Nihang and Singh reproduce a painting of Maharājā Narinder Singh of Patiala paying homage to a Nirmalā *sādhū* (c. 1860) seated on a tiger skin (2008: 202), and lion skins are prominent in contemporary *gurdwārās* of the Nirmalā-related Nānaksar tradition whose *sants* are depicted sitting cross-legged, behind the lion's open-mouthed head. As if illustrating the balance (or tension) at the heart of the Sikh ideal of the *sant sipāhī* (warrior saint) both Nānaksar and Nirmalā tradition also honour the celibate state, personified by male devotees referred to as *bahingam* (Nesbitt 1985). The word *bahingam* ('bird') encapsulates the non-attachment of

17. The tale is apparently borrowed and adapted from 'The Ass in a Leopard Skin', one of the many stories incorporated in the *Pancatantra* (see Olivelle 2009: 112–13).
18. See the Early Years Foundation Stage webpage of Redbridge Agreed Syllabus on http://www.redbridgerenet.co.uk (accessed 2 May 2012).

the spiritual life, marking a departure from mainstream Sikh emphasis on *gr̥hasthī*, the married state.

CONCLUSION

Transformation is a recurrent theme in *sikhī* and one that is often conveyed through imagery evoking non-human creatures (e.g. birds, lions, tigers, horses). Animals figure prominently in art and narrative around many of the oldest Sikh *gurdwārās*. In many cases these highlight divergences within Sikh society between the modern and the *sanātan* (traditional, not separated out from wider Indic tradition). As such they mark connecting points with older and circumambient Indic (mostly Hindu) traditions. While an enthusiastic minority of diaspora Sikhs identify strongly with the lore of the lion and of the Nihang, it is as pilgrims and tourists in India that diaspora Sikhs more generally encounter connections with their Gurus, often through *gurdwārās* that enshrine a local association with non-human animals, whether hares or horses.

Indeed, it is the Sikhs' historic devotion to horses that emerges as the strongest brotherly bond between human and non-human animals, even though Sikhs' strongest symbolic identification is with the lion/tiger.

Nānaksar Sikhs' focus on both *singh* and *bahingam*, lion and bird, epitomizes the creative tension in the call to be both saint and warrior, as well as typifying a point of tension between normative and minority tradition. Immersion in the sacred words of the *Guru Granth Sāhib* can encourage successive generations to reconnect with the natural order and perhaps sense that wonder and respect which can strengthen an as yet only incipient commitment to conservation and sustainability. However, it is likely that—as is the case with the vegetarian/non-vegetarian debate—Sikhs will continue to embody divergent responses to ethical issues. The context for ethical judgements, including those relating to animals, will be (for religiously observant Sikhs) the intersection of *sikhī* with Punjabi culture and modernity. They will, along with their contemporaries of whatever religious and cultural background, be influenced by environmental and humanitarian concerns and by popular interpretations of scientists' disclosures about animals' needs and predicaments as humans exploit them or destroy their habitats. In this regard some Sikhs may look for a general direction, if not specific instruction, from their scriptures and in the light of their *rahit* (disciplinary code). Others, who also identify themselves as Sikh, will have only minimal awareness of the Gurus' teaching.

While the name 'Singh' continues to connect all male Sikhs with the Khālsā instituted by the tenth Guru, a smaller minority of Sikhs—increasingly informed by travel and by communications technology—will discover more of their tradition and of the place of sparrows and lions, ants and elephants in the Sikh universe, and they will be moved to marvel afresh at its riches.

ACKNOWLEDGMENT

My thanks to Jasjit Singh and Parmjit Singh for helpful suggestions.

REFERENCES

Anonymous. n.d.(a) 'Keeper of the White Falcon.' *Sikh Information*, http://www.info-sikh.com/PageBaaj.html (accessed 2 May 2012).

Anonymous. n.d.(b) 'The Guru's Blue Horse.' *Sikh Information*, http://www.info-sikh.com/Page-Horse1.html (accessed 2 May 2012).

Bedi, H. S. 2010. 'The Evolution of the Sikh Soldiers.' 3 December available at: www.sikhnet.com/news/evolution-sikh-soldiers-harchand-singh-bedi<http://www.sikhnet.com/news/evolution-sikh-soldiers-harchand-singh-bedi> (accessed 21 August 2013).

Brar, S. S. 2011. 'Misconceptions about Eating Meat.' *Sikh.org*, http://www.sikhs.org/meat.htm (accessed 2 May 2012).

Chahal, S. K. 2005. *Ecology, Redesigning Genes: Ethical and Sikh Perspective*. Amṛtsar: Singh Brothers.

Dave, K. N. 1985. *Birds in Sanskrit Literature*. Delhi: Motilal Banarsidass.

Dogra, C. S. 2011. 'Grand Truncated History.' *Outlook India*, http://www.outlookindia.com/article.aspx?272186

Doniger, W. 2009. *The Hindus: An Alternative History*. Oxford: Oxford University Press.

Dusenbery, V. 2008. '"Through Wisdom, Dispense Charity": Religious and Cultural Underpinnings of Diasporan Sikh Philanthropy in Punjab.' In V. Dusenbery (ed.), *Sikhs at Large: Religion, Culture, and Politics in Global Perspective*: 136–62. New Delhi: Oxford University Press.

Grewal, G. S. 1986. *Imagery in the Adi Granth*. Chandigarh: Punjab Prakashan.

Jhutti-Johal, J. 2011. *Sikhism Today*. London: Continuum.

Kaur, G. 2008/2009. 'Our Environment and Us: A Sikh Perspective.' *Shap World Religions in Education: The Environment*. London: Shap Working Party on World Religions in Education.

Kaur-Singh, K. 1994. 'Sikhism.' In J. Holm and J. Bowker (eds), *Attitudes to Nature*: 132–47. London: Pinter.

Kohli, S. S. 1961. *A Critical Study of Adi Granth*. Delhi: Motilal Banarsidass.

Leslie, J. 1998. 'A Bird Bereaved: The Identity and Significance of Valmiki's Kranca.' *Journal of Indian Philosophy* 26(5): 455–87. http://dx.doi.org/10.1023/A:1004335910775

McLeod, W. H. 1980a. *Early Sikh Tradition: A Study of the Janam-Sākhīs*. Oxford: Clarendon Press.

— (ed.). 1980b. *The B40 Janam-Sakhi*. Amritsar: Guru Nanak Dev University.

— 1984. *Textual Sources for the Study of Sikhism*. Manchester: Manchester University Press.

— 1991. *Popular Sikh Art*. Delhi: Oxford University Press.

— 1997. *Sikhism*. Harmondsworth: Penguin.

Madra, A. S., and P. Singh. 2004. *Sicques, Tigers and Thieves: Eyewitness Accounts of the Sikhs (1686–1809)*. New York: Palgrave Macmillan.

Nayar, K. E. 2011. 'Sikh Women in Vancouver: An Analysis of their Psychosocial Issues.' In D. Jakobsh (ed.), *Sikhism and Women: History, Texts, and Experience*: 252–75. New Delhi: Oxford University Press.

Nesbitt, E. 1985. 'The Nanaksar Movement.' *Religion* 15: 67–79. http://dx.doi.org/10.1016/0048-721X(85)90060-0

— 2005. *Sikhism. A Very Short Introduction*. Oxford: Oxford University Press.

— 2007. 'Sikhism.' In P. Morgan and C. Lawton (eds), *Ethical Issues in Six Religious Traditions*: 118–67. Edinburgh: Edinburgh University Press, 2nd rev. edn.

Nesbitt, E., and G. Kaur. 1999. *Guru Nanak*. Norwich: Religious and Moral Education Press.

Nihang, N. S., and P. Singh. 2008. *In the Master's Presence: The Sikhs of Hazoor Sahib*. London: Kashi House.

Oberoi, H. 1994. *The Construction of Religious Boundaries: Culture, Identity and Diversity in the Sikh Tradition.* New Delhi: Oxford University Press.

Olivelle, P. (ed.). 2009. *The Pañcatantra. The Book of India's Folk Wisdom.* Oxford: Oxford University Press.

Pamme, R. 2010. 'The Pilgrimage to Takht Hazur Sahib and its Place in the Sikh Tradition.' Unpublished PhD thesis, School of Oriental and African Studies, University of London.

Puri, G. S. 1989. 'Nature Consciousness in the Sikh Faith.' *World Religions in Education*: 32–24. London: Shap Working Party.

Robson, J. (ed.). 2005. *Worlds A-part Paintings by the Singh Twins.* London: Twin Studio.

Singh, A. K. D. Kaur, and R. K. D. Kaur Singh. 1999. *Twin Perspectives Paintings by Amrit and Rabindra K D Kaur Singh.* London: Twin Studio.

Singh, J., and T. Singh. 1998. *Style of the Lion: The Sikhs.* Ann Arbor: Akal Publications.

Singh, K. 1977. *A History of the Sikhs, Volume 1: 1469–1839.* Delhi: Oxford University Press.

Singh, N. G. K. 2011. *Sikhism: An Introduction.* New York: I. B. Tauris.

Singh, P. 1989. *The Golden Temple.* New Delhi: Time Books International.

Stronge, S. 1999. *The Arts of the Sikh Kingdoms.* London: V&A Publications.

Tigers, Tiger Spirits and Were-tigers in Tribal Orissa

STEFANO BEGGIORA*

This chapter is based on data collected during fieldwork conducted in and around the town of Phulbani, headquarters of the Kandhamal district (Orissa), between 2001 and 2006. My research was principally focused on investigating the myths and rituals—but also the social structure and cultural heritage—of a local *ādivāsī* (indigenous) group, the Kondhs. While I have discussed elsewhere (Beggiora 2010) the Kondhs' shamanistic rituals and the great cycle of the Meriā, the buffalo sacrifice performed to propitiate the earth goddess on occasion of the annual fertility ceremony in spring, it is my intention to explore here other—perhaps less known—aspects of this Indian minority ethnic community.

Moving from an analysis of the history of the Kondhs, I intend to discuss how local myths, beliefs and ritual practices relate to environment and the local fauna. In particular, I will explore an increasingly obsolete set of beliefs and magical-religious practices that are at the base of therianthropy (human to animal transformation). The belief in the metamorphosis of a human into a non-human animal is difficult to frame in a proper context because of its controversial and often poorly documented features. However, it seems that even today there survives among the Kondhs a strongly rooted belief in the nocturnal transformations of some members of the tribe who take the form of the tiger, thus becoming were-tigers (*pālṭa bāgha*).[1]

* Stefano Beggiora is lecturer in Contemporary History of India in the Department of Asian and North African Studies at Ca' Foscari University of Venice (Italy), where he received his PhD in 2006. Dr Beggiora specializes in South-Asian shamanism and has published several articles and book chapters on Indian ādivāsī (Saoras, Kondhs and Apa Tanis) with particular emphasis on colonial history, laws for the safeguarding of Scheduled Tribes and Castes and the contemporary history of political movements of India. After completing a postdoctoral research project funded by the European Social Fund, he published a book on Indian Economics: *India e Nordest: il mercato del terzo Millennio* (Venezia: Cafoscarina, 2009). Dr Beggiora is author of *Sonum: Spiriti della Giungla. Lo Sciamanismo delle Tribù Saora dell'Orissa* (FrancoAngeli, 2003), *Sacrifici umani e guerriglia nell'India Britannica* (Itinera Progetti, 2010) and many ethnographic documentaries. He is currently working on a book on the transformation of tribal religious life as a result of globalization and the growth of India's economic power.

1. The term *pālṭā*, *pālṭa* or *pālāṭā bāgha* is a colloquial expression widely used in Orissa and is

Those who have previously studied the metamorphosis of a man into a tiger (*Panthera Tigris Tigris*) generally agree on interpreting it as a phenomenon related to magical practices like witchcraft or folk beliefs as vampirism and/or lycanthropy.[2] In colonial times, tales of were-tigers were almost invariably deemed to be superstition, and as such condemned. Yet some of the early explorers in Orissa as well as a few British officers had been more cautious in their conclusions (Macpherson 1865: 376). Therianthropy is not just a functionalist way to explain tiger attacks and the terror that these animals inspire. The belief in *pālṭa bāgha* actually combines the enculturation of indigenous myths on tigers (strong and ubiquitous local symbols) with ancestral ritual practices and elements of Eastern Śāktism and Tantrism. In that, the tiger represents what Marcel Mauss called 'a total social fact' (1966: 76–77).

My analysis of the *pālṭa bāgha* will be twofold. First, I will compare colonial ethnographies with contemporary beliefs. In order to do so, I will examine how the enduring relation between human and non-human animals among the Kondhs finds a justification in ancestral myths of foundations and ceremonies such as human sacrifice, a practice which had been fought by the British during the so-called Meriā Wars (c. 1836–1862) (Boal 1997; Padel 2000). Second, I will discuss how the Kondhs cope with and respond to modernity and the threats that hang over their culture. Caught in a reality amidst the twenty-first century Indian economic boom and virtually uncontaminated eco-systems that survive only thanks to special laws, forest reserves, national parks and projects aimed at the preservation of wildlife species, the Kondhs are struggling to preserve a culture whose very existence is as endangered as the lives of the wild animals that populate the jungles of Orissa.

This chapter will discuss the Kondhs' complex relation with the untamed non-human animal (symbolized by the tiger) as opposed to the human order of the village. While considering the emic point of view of local indigenous societies who look at the non-ordinary behaviour of big cats such as tigers and leopards as a supernatural phenomenon independent from feline resettlement programmes in Eastern India, I will also discuss the way Kondhs understand and interpret issues of animal territoriality and extra-territoriality, the permeability of animal souls and bodies (human and non-human) and notions of interspecies agency, embodiment and power.

---

derived from an Oriya verb meaning 'to transform' (*pālaṭiba*). *Bāgh* is a generic term indicating big cats such as tigers and leopards. In the two main languages spoken by Kondhs, Kui and Kuvi, the expressions *kṛāḍi mlīpa* (or *mlīva*) and *kai kṛani* carry similar meanings. However, as *pālṭa bāgha* is the expression more commonly used by the shamans and hunters of these tribes, I will retain it throughout this chapter.

2. See Campbell (1864: 44–45); Boal (1997: 178); Jena *et al.* (2002: 264); Patnaik (1992: 171); Cammiade (1931: 217–20) and Elwin (1944: 51–53). Other references can be found in the monumental work of Verrier Elwin (1954) on the tribes of Orissa.

POSSESSING THE TIGER: HUMAN PREDATORS AND ANIMAL VEHICLES

Magical and religious beliefs related to the figure of the man-eating tiger are widespread. Although wild tigers (and other big cats) living in areas surrounding human settlements do not normally attack human beings, aggressive behaviour often resulting in the killing—or sever harming—of villagers is not unheard of. Yet in spite of that, the Kondhs consider big cats, and predators in general, sacred agents and invest them with extraordinary powers. Either they are the vehicle of a deity/spirit or, more often, they are explicitly considered the symbol of ancestral and natural entities and as such they represent *de facto* the environment that surrounds and hosts the whole community. For these reasons tigers are traditionally not considered prey for hunters and in the unfortunate event that one of these animals is killed, this is unambiguously interpreted as a sign of misfortune for the entire village. Conversely, if men respect tigers and other wild animals, they should have no reason to fear attacks. This constitutes the basis of a form of harmony between human and non-human animals in the microcosm of the tribe's territory.

The case of the anthropophagous tiger is therefore considered a kind of fracture in the local and universal equilibrium. It is considered an inauspicious event bearing unfavourable, or at least supernatural, connotations. According to the Kondhs, the carnivorous beast would not turn its savagery against human settlements spontaneously, let alone feeding on human flesh. If such an event occurs, this is most likely imputable to some external intervention that has negatively influenced the normal behaviour of the animal. For its ability to manipulate the instinct of the tiger, this actor is considered a subtle entity lacking bodily constrains.

Man-eating tigers are believed not to be moved by the gods. For the Kondhs, aggressive tigers targeting human beings and their settlements are most likely cases of *pālṭa bāgha*. This is explained as a spirit possession where the controller is human and the controlled body is non-human (feline). The Kondhs believe that during the night the soul of a sleeping person has the power to detach itself from the body and to wander through the jungle until it possesses and controls the body of a big cat. In his new embodied form, the 'sleeper' will assault villages, raid the cattle and even attack human beings. The appropriate time for this kind of metamorphosis is midnight, commonly interpreted as the moment of transition from a lighter to a deeper state of sleep.[3]

Local informants report that those who want to become were-tigers should visualize the forest paths that lead into the hunting territory of ferocious felines before going to sleep. Such behaviour would indicate that the

3. This is also symbolic of the habit of tigers and other feline predators who usually hunt at nighttime while during daytime, especially in the hot season, they prefer to remain hidden in the shade and shelter of the forest, away from the noise of villages.

metamorphosis of a man into a tiger is voluntary. However, other informants indicate otherwise and hold that this transformation is involuntary and imputable to illness. As a proof of their point they say that the *pālṭa bāgha* tends not to remember what happened during the night. Once awake, he may retain a vague memory of his transformation into a tiger, or of the possible violent actions he committed in that guise. This, however, is interpreted as an inauspicious nightmare.

The distinction between voluntary (ritual-based) and involuntary (illness-related) metamorphosis deserves a closer analysis. In the case of a human subject who voluntarily embodies a tiger and, even more, attacks a village or specific individuals, it seems safe to say that this event is imputable to social tensions and struggle for power between one or more tribes. Hostilities between different clans or tribes are commonly encountered among Orissan *ādivāsīs*. This is validated by colonial reports, recent history and the oral tradition of the tribe. In this scenario, the voluntary metamorphosis into a tiger is considered either a dramatic yet efficacious offensive weapon or a mean of revenge against an otherwise stronger enemy. In the early twentieth century, the British recorded several cases of feud killings that were preceded by explicit threats from the Kondhs to attack the enemy in the shape of a wild animal. Therianthropy is therefore a deterrent aimed at resolving any potential conflict between tribes or clans (Maltby 1918: 73) but also a validating tool confirming the social power of local myths and rituals.

In the second case, reportedly more common, non-voluntary metamorphosis (including the lack of consciousness of crimes carried out overnight) is related to pathological disorders such as sleepwalking, restless legs syndrome or bruxism (gnashing of the teeth). Further to that, a careful observation of the phase of light sleep referred to as Rapid Eye Movement Sleep is also decisive in identifying who is affected by this particular form of therianthropy, or able to perform it. For the Kondhs, rapid movements, not only of the eyes but those involving involuntary tremors affecting the whole body, reveal the presence of a *pālṭa bāgha* in that they are evocative of the cat's movements while asleep. I was told by local informants that a smoking gun is the unintentional contraction of the facial muscles around the mouth of the sleeper, an expression resembling that of a long-whiskered tiger, or the contraction of the fingers of the hands, a gesture recalling the typical movement of the pads that felines often do while sleeping. In both cases, therianthropy, either voluntary or unconscious, is considered by the tribe a highly dangerous and inauspicious occurrence that needs to be contrasted by means of exorcism.

A tiger attacking a village is an event that requires the prompt intervention of the local shaman (*kuttaka*, or *kuttakaru* if female) in order to normalize the temporary alteration of the microcosm. Such performance, however, is not a straightforward process. The ritual specialist is required to discover the culprit and treat him as a patient. But possession is not always intended as illness. For instance, the possession of the shaman is a 'sacred' condition, as well as that of hybrid figures such as mediums who become the receptacles of the god/goddess. Similarly, the embodiment of a non-human animal is not strictly considered a disease, although it generally entails adverse implications. As a matter of fact, diseases are generally discussed by the Kondhs as forms of supernatural affliction or possession by evil spirits.[4] Here we return to the fracture of the harmony between human and non-human animals. In this case, as we shall see, a no longer human agent tries to take control of a non-human body in order to attack the community.

Cases of *pālṭa bāghas* who spontaneously decide to contact the shaman in order to be healed are very rare. In fact, those who voluntarily transform themselves into were-tigers to harm enemies will try and keep their actions secret so as to avoid being accused of witchcraft and murder. Conversely, those who suffer from a range of psycho-pathological disorders locally interpreted as *pālṭa bāgha* are simply not aware of their actions and the harm they inflict. It is, however, the duty of the shaman to intervene and find an acceptable solution which will counterbalance the village's disrupted order. In order to do so, the healer (either male or female) enters into a state of guided trance and communicates with the spirits. This will allow him/her to investigate the origin of the *pālṭa bāgha* and to establish the nature of his intentions. Once this has been ascertained, the were-tiger must be exorcized through offerings, a ritual performance similar to Hindu *puja*. At the end of the rite, amulets will be prepared. These will preserve the individual from transforming into a tiger in the future.[5] Amulets for preventive and apotropaic use are very popular in the areas inhabited by Kondhs. Although material, forms and style differ, they usually consist of a trapezoidal bronze capsule containing herbs and medicinal plants prepared by the *kuttaka* or *kuttakaru* according to the condition of the subject for which it is intended.[6]

There is a complex pharmacopoeia for the treatment of diseases, or rather to alleviate their symptoms (the causes are always considered of a super-

4. A recent and interesting study establishes a connection between pathological diseases such as rabies and cultural illnesses like lycanthropy (Gomez-Alonso 1998: 856–59). Old European legends would have been originated by the observation of the most common effects of the ailment: restlessness, hydrophobia, strong aggressiveness, photophobia and excessive salivation. It is of particular interest that this kind of disease is transmissible from animal to man. In one circumstance, Sakadadu—one of my Kondh informants—allegedly had a close encounter with a were-tiger, early in the morning when she was in the jungle searching for medical herbs and natural remedies. The tiger was moving her head vertically up and down, something she interpreted as evidence of possession. Alternatively, this could have been a gesture of submission of the *pālṭa bāgha* in front of the shaman's power.
5. The shamans I interviewed state that the treatment in case of 'were-tiger disease' is rather complex. Even after receiving a clear revelation from the spirits about *pālṭa bāgha*, it is not always easy, or possible, to intervene.
6. These are similar to the *jantars* fastened to the arms of Hindus. Such amulets contain the mantra that the astrologer delivers to a customer on the basis of the astrological chart (influence of the planets).

natural kind and therefore one cannot be completely 'healed'). The cure is achieved through exorcism and the aetiological narration (myth) told by the shaman. Medicines to reduce fever, relieve pain, cleanse the wound and so on may also be needed. But the preparation of amulets is the essential part of the healing procedure. For instance, if a person is considered at risk to suffer attacks from a certain kind of spirit bound to the solar element (which cause diseases such as burns, fevers, scalding and leprosy), then the amulet is made with plants, powders and extracts considered refreshing, soothing, watery or 'cold'.[7]

The amulet contains a symbolic counterbalance to the harm inflicted. Some of its elements are extracted from medicinal plants although in many cases it is difficult to identify the exact composition of the mixtures. Among the Kondhs, there exist specific amulets against witchcraft and therianthropy which are distributed to the children of those families where cases of *pālṭa bāgha* have been recorded. Among the Kuttia Kondh, a sub-tribe of the Kondh, these amulets are similar to common necklaces made from coins. Consecrated with a special *pūjā*, the amulet is said to protect the children from what is locally known as 'dream disease'.

In 2002, Sidha Majhi, the *kuttaka* of the village of Deogada (Khandmal district), told me an interesting episode in this regard. A few years earlier his son had gone for hunting in the mountains. There he came across a tiger which he tried to shoot, but the gun misfired. As a result, the cat jumped upon the young man leaving him severely wounded. The boy, in agony, was taken back to the village by a friend. His father, the village shaman, tried to negotiate the young man's health recovery by contacting the spirits.[8] He entered into a state of trance in which Kamaṇi Pēnu, the Black Lady with the white *dhoti*, appeared to him. Kamaṇi Pēnu is the goddess of diseases and remedies, the guide-deity of the Kondh shamans and the tribal form of Ṭhākurāni, the Orissan Hindu disease goddess. The spirit revealed that the boy had been attacked by a *pālṭa bāgha* and that he would surely die. She suggested, however, there might be a cure to save him based on the medication of specific herbal remedies and a healing-technique known as *putkīna* which involves words-blowing during a *pūjā* service. But the Black Lady also said there was a further problem: the were-tiger was still running free. Through dreams, the *kuttaka* had

7. Charms for children are also very common as they are believed to be the unwitting victims of vampirism or of the attacks of wild beasts. In 2006, I witnessed the preparation of such amulets with scapulae of porcupine tied together.

8. Violent death, an always dramatic and inauspicious event, has further consequences. Especially if a corpse is lost, disfigured or eaten by feral beasts (and it is thus impossible to perform a funeral), the soul of the victim will return to the village as a ghost. In such form it will torment (i.e. attack) relatives and friends thus exposing them to the same kind of violent death he or she suffered. For instance, the restless soul of those killed by a tiger will probably push another tiger to kill a second person and so on. Only a shaman is able to contain and restore the disrupted order.

numerous subsequent confirmations of the provenance of the *pālṭa bāgha*. He was a member of a neighbouring village that was known to have hosted several were-tigers. (At the time other tigers had attacked surrounding villages at night and taken away animals from yards and stables.) Sidha Majhi finally decided to put together a brigade of several men who would accompany him to the site of the accident. On the ridge of the mountain, along the course of a stream, he made the necessary arrangements for the sacrifice of a pig whose carcass was then abandoned as an apotropaic offering (cf. Boal 1997: 413–15). After this, the attacks ended abruptly and the boy recovered. During his father's narration, he was present and proudly showed me his arm still bearing the scars of deep and poorly healed wounds.

Ritual healing is not the only option to contain the nefarious presence of the *pālṭa bāgha*. Sometimes the patient refuses to be healed, thus acting against the intervention of the shaman and the will of the community. In this case he is forced to undergo ritual exorcism because, consciously or not, he is putting in danger the very existence of the village. These compelling rituals require the intervention of more shamans as the *pālṭa bāgha* may be immune to exorcism and can fight against the shamans and the community. In this case, I was told, the villagers leave him to his fate: he is ostracized and forced to wander through the jungle. Condemned to a life of poverty and trapped in a spiral of alienation, torn between horrible dreams and ferocious crimes, he would eventually be killed by some animal, or by the enraged members of a nearby village.

This extreme scenario gave me the opportunity to further reflect on the symbolic aspect of the tiger among the Kondhs and the nature of the metamorphosis that transforms men into tigers. As previously reported, during sleep the soul is believed to be detached from the sleeper's body undertaking a long journey leading to possessing the body of a tiger. While the body lies abandoned in a state of deep sleep, insensible to external stimuli, the vital breath keeps the sleeper alive. In the absence of the individual's soul, the human body is in a condition of catalepsy, or apparent death, similar to the shaman's state of deep trance. Sudden awakening from this condition is considered extremely dangerous. If this happens, the body will be shaken by violent tremors and convulsions, a sign that the soul is trying to rush back to the point of departure. If this is not accomplished, the body of the *pālṭa bāgha* can actually die or remain in a perpetual catatonic state. There seems thus to be a condition of reciprocity between the bodies of human and non-human animals. Kondh shamans believe that if the anthropophagous tiger happens to be killed during an attack to a village or by hunters, the same destiny is shared by the body of the *pālṭa bāgha*, who will immediately die. In the case of a successful exorcism performed by shamans or oracles, the soul of the beast remains latent or otherwise subdued by the divine power of the ritual operator. Conversely, those who are victims of an animal driven by an evil spirit turn into 'souls in pain' who gradually lose their individual characteristics and become part of a collective psychic carcass. As for those who are killed by were-tigers, they are transformed into a black *piśāca* (ghost) the size of a thumb and become the spectral tutor of an ordinary tiger. In this case, the animal is powered solely by the desire to kill other human beings, thus multiplying the number of deaths.

MAN-EATERS, MAGIC DEATHS AND TIGER WARRIORS

The attack of an anthropophagous tiger can be identified with the manifestation of the wrath of the earth goddess, Dharani Pēnu. The divine feminine principle which embodies the dynamic and wild chaos of Nature is personified by the feline predator *par excellence*. The depths of the jungle, its dark and unknown territory are symbolically opposed to the centre of the village, the orderly settlement which is home to human beings and domesticated animals. This opposition is embodied by the shaman whose role is to mediate between the empirical and the subtle worlds thereby guaranteeing harmony in the universe. Conversely, the *pālṭa bāgha* and the rituals behind voluntary theriomorphism appear to be a reversal of shamanistic practices as well as indigenous ethics.

In his autobiography, William Macpherson, a British officer in charge during the Meriā Wars, reported an ancient legend current at that time among Kondh villagers (1865: 92, 121, 376). According to the narrative, the goddess Dharani once appeared to men in the guise of a tiger. She said that by assuming the form of the tiger *Mleepa* (English for *mlīpa*, a term derived from the Kui expression *kṛāḍi mlīpa*) one could kill any enemy. So men implored her to teach them the technique of the metamorphosis in order to use it in times of war. The goddess accepted but, in return, asked for a human sacrifice. According to the Macpherson's version, there is a second part of the story which tells about the involvement of the male counterpart of the deity, Bura Pēnu, usually portrayed as more benevolent. The god suggested that the tribes could replace the sacrifice of human beings with that of buffalo. The goddess would be equally satisfied and teach them the technique of the *mlīpa* for use in warfare. This version sheds no special light on the ritual technique behind the belief in therianthropy. However, it emphasizes that the transformation from man into tiger is a secret technique, a gift from the gods that can be used as a magical weapon to fight enemies in battle.

The following is the testimony of Sidha Majhi, the shaman of Deogada village:

> When a man wants to get the power to become a *pālṭa bāgha*, he goes at night near the *jakhri* [the sacred post where offering to the deities are placed] and pours oblations of rice and spirits at the foot of the mast and on the stone [representing] the goddess [Dharani Pēnu]. He prays several times to the goddess to receive that power. Finally, if the goddess agrees, he will become a *pālṭa bāgha* and his soul will

> come out at night from the body. If he is a man, his soul will come out from the front side, if she is a woman it comes out from the back side. However, the rite is secret and the individual that makes such a request to the goddess must take care not to be discovered by anyone. If this does happen, he would need to leave the village immediately and could even be killed. For this reason, the ritual takes place in the evening or at night: the prayer to the goddess is whispered so that nobody walking past could grasp the meaning of the words and the whole event would appear as a common offering.[9]

The report of Sidha Majhi is accurate: it clearly indicates that the origin of the phenomenon is of a ritual nature, a voluntary effort to gain supernatural powers with the obvious purpose of harming others. It also is a clear allusion to the practice of black magic, or witchcraft. Further, it seems that in order to become a *pālṭa bāgha* one does not need secret knowledge. It is a rite accessible to everybody. A person will just need to know how to approach Dharani Pēnu and then wait for the goddess' final decision.

Another informant of mine, the *kuttakaru* of the Kadapana village, Sakadadu Majhi—who is believed to be the most powerful in the area to fight tiger-men—suggests that the non-voluntary nature of the transformation is also very common.

> If the soul of the *pālṭa bāgha* leaves the body frontally, it will follow a straight path over the community. But if it comes out from behind, the soul will be disoriented and will not recognise the village and, as a result the tiger will attack it. This implies that *pālṭa bāghas* are dangerous also for their own people. This is because many are unaware victims and fall ill. For this reason I prepare amulets against nightmares.[10]

According to the *kuttakaru*, being an unaware victim of theriomorphism represents a real pathology that needs to be healed before turning into intentional metamorphosis. In both cases the action of the shaman must be directed towards the departure of the soul from the human body. Sakadadu observed that the majority of phenomena of were-tigers are imputable to evil-eye. She told me that:

> The *pālṭa bāgha* is so dangerous that it is necessary for me to intervene even if a tiger has attacked cattle at night-time only once. The next night, I will try to establish the identity of the culprit through dreaming. Once I know, I can heal him. But if he refuses to be cured, then I'll know that he himself performed the rite [to become a were-tiger]. This is the evidence and through praying I will destroy such power. The spirits always reveal to me who performed the ritual... In such a way I have defeated fifteen tiger-men.[11]

The expression 'defeat the enemies' and 'destroy the power' once again bring us back to some sort of magical battle that the shaman fights against

9. Interview carried out in Deogada village, Khandmal district, November 2002.
10. Interview carried out in Kadapana village, Khandmal district, November 2002.
11. Interview carried out in Kadapana village, Khandmal district, November 2002.

opponent sorcerers. The concept of death-by-magic is well known among the Kondhs and neighbouring tribes. It refers to all those practices of witchcraft that take place before the armed confrontation that should ensure the death of the enemies.

THE BENGAL TIGER IN ORISSA. REFLECTIONS ON REPOPULATION AND THERIOMORPHISM

The forest officers operating around the city of Phulbani (Khandamal district) claim that the hunting territory of an adult tiger covers an area of roughly 50 square kilometres. Due to their shyness and because of the size of the territory they cover, it is normally very difficult to spot these animals. Moreover, because of hunting and the indiscriminate exploitation of the environment, primarily deforestation and pollution, many species are currently threatened by extinction, both in India and in other Asian countries. For environmental and geographical reasons a reliable census is difficult in many of the jungles of interior Orissa. However, years of conservation policy have led to many areas in India becoming repopulated. The growing feline population resulted in the display of anomalous behaviour among tigers and leopards. Not only do these animals come close to villages and the inhabited areas in the plains, but in some cases they even settle down stopping across paths and roads. According to the Palamkhia Chief Ranger, in the area inhabited by the Kuttia Kondh such attitudes are symptoms of discomfort caused by the drastic reduction of the tiger's habitat. This is caused, on one hand, by the demographic expansion of the villages and, on the other, by the increasing population of these animals.

In the area surrounding Phulbani, in 2006—the date of my last survey of the area—some sensational facts occurred that caused apprehension among the locals and were reported with some clamour by the media. A specimen of Bengal Tiger approached a bus stand just outside the town creating panic among the passengers waiting to board on the vehicle. It was reported that a short distance away another tiger was resting undisturbed on the roof of a house. Again in Phulbani, police officers were alerted by a local resident who claimed that a tiger had entered a house through an open door. A government agent active in the area reported that the same year he saw during his night shift a leopard crossing the road while he was patrolling the area on his motorcycle. In all these cases—none of which led to tragic consequences—it seems that the tigers were hardly ferocious. Almost acting like domesticated big cats accustomed to human presence, they have been reported to wander here and there, showing no interest whatsoever in the people around them and displaying no sign of being bothered by the roaring noise of engines. The fact was looked at with amazement only because it occurred, quite unusually, in the lowland area before the foothills of the wildest forest areas, close to the bustle of towns of a certain size.

Unfortunately serious accidents occur more frequently in the tribal areas, where daily tragedies are not rare. But in the area inhabited by the Kuttia Kondhs, other interpretations are given. There, attacks of tigers are often related to the phenomenon of *pālṭa bāgha*. One of these happened on 1 March 2006 in the village of Tidipadar, a small community of 12 families on the road between Tumudibandha and Belghar (Khandmal district). There, a girl living in a women's dormitory went out at night to urinate in the jungle, not far from the houses. This detail seemed important to my witnesses. Women, during their menstrual cycle, are considered carriers of impurities and thus must observe certain restrictions. Young women would usually sleep in separate dormitories at such times. It is believed that the menstrual cycle makes the animals restless and attracts wild beasts.[12] For this and other reasons, menstruating women should abstain from any work, either domestic or outside the house. In this case, I was told, the girl was naturally attracting danger. After moving a short distance into the jungle, the young woman spotted a tiger lurking in the shadow. Terrified, she tried to escape running back towards the dormitory. Because of the darkness and the panic she tripped on some woodpile that had been stored for sale and, stumbling, seriously wounded her head. The noise attracted the attention of other members of the village while probably it scared away the tiger. The shamans of the tribe, while noticing that the beast had not deliberately attacked the young woman, determined that her wounds were to be encoded as the attack of a *pālṭa bāgha*. In other words, the true nature of the beast had been revealed by its unusual behaviour and extra-territoriality. This has yielded a detrimental effect on a member of the community and hence was judged as an attack, even though in this case it has been unsuccessful.

This conclusion, however, required a period of investigation during which three *kuttaka*s from neighbouring villages were summoned. The shamans engaged themselves in rituals involving voluntary possession and entered into a state of trance in order to consult the spirits. After a period of negotiation, they assessed and discussed the responses of the spirits for several hours. Finally, they decided that a purification ritual for the whole village was necessary in order to ensure the girl's wellbeing. The community, alerted to the looming danger, showed serious concern for the situation and came out in support of the decision of the shamans. At the end of the purification ritual, the sacrifice of a pig was celebrated while the *kuttaka*s observed some food restrictions for a short period of time.

A similar case occurred two months earlier in a small village near Belghar. In a pasture area the villagers found a cow that had apparently been killed and torn by a big cat. The dismembered body of the animal had already been half-eaten and no one dared to remove the carcass without first consulting the *kuttaka*s. After some discussion, it was decided that this

12. See Mary Douglas (1978: 12) on bodily and organic processes and social order.

was the result of an attack of a were-tiger. Among the Kondhs the unusual attack on the properties of the village is generally understood as an attack to the community itself. The investigation of the shamans combined traditional knowledge with behavioural information. Villages are accustomed to hunting techniques aimed at tigers. It seems that tigers have quite repetitive habits in chasing their prey, hence it is possible to predict some of their moves. Usually, the tiger is said to cross its hunting territory following a circular path, or a spiral, in either ascending or descending order. Once the traces of the cat are detected it is possible to calculate its movements. I was told that these cats move several times on the same hunting path tracing large circles but would never return to where they started. It thus seemed plausible to the villagers that the tiger would return to finish devouring the carcass of the cow. In this frantic stage of discussion it became clear that determining the direction of arrival of the beast would be vital for protecting the whole village.

After a few moments of disorder, apparently dictated by concerns over the event, the officer in charge of Belghar's Rangers intervened in the discussion. At any rate, the people did not seem to agree on the interpretation of the traces left by the beast. The shamans themselves had difficulty in reconstructing the earlier movements of the tiger. In fact they were more inclined to interpret the incident as a case of therianthropy. To justify their theory, they said that, according to the projection of the circles formed by the possible hunting paths after the attack, it was clear that the tiger would have come across at least one village in the area. In other words, the tiger was actually *from* the village. Eventually the whole community agreed that the attack was imputable to a *pālṭa bāgha*. The shamans therefore celebrated a complex ritual of exorcism in order to ward off the evil entity before purifying the area. At the same time the chief ranger decreed that the situation was too dangerous and that it would be necessary to kill the beast. He therefore formed a group that took position near the carcass of the torn cow. After seven nights of stalking, the beast came back and was shot down with a single rifle's bullet in the neck.

CONCLUSION

During my fieldwork I came across cases similar to the *pālṭa bāgha* of the Kondhs among other *ādivāsī* populations, especially in the North-eastern border areas of Assam and Arunachal Pradesh (Beggiora 2010). Not only did I find a close similarity in the mythical and cosmogonical symbolism related to the origin of the world and the relation between human and non-human spaces, I also found evidence that animal metamorphoses are indeed a shared cultural pattern in several South Asian regions. In many cases I observed how the tiger is looked upon as the personification of the forest and the power of the goddess that help shamans in their fight against demons and evil spirits. I also encountered in the large sub-Himalayan belt—especially in the north-eastern frontier—the widespread belief in diseases carried by tigers and leopards. Despite regional and cultural differences, this closely resembled the dynamics of the *palta bagho* of the Kondhs.

Among eastern tribes, human, non-human and other-than-human entities (spirits and deities) are deeply connected and often they present interesting patterns of inter-penetrability (Osella 1999: 183–210). Any change, any breakdown in the balance between these agents—including their bodies—has a serious impact on society and the territory. Communicating with wild beasts becomes thus essential to preserving a greater order. The tiger, the most important, elusive and powerful of all wild animals, is the symbol of such order while the harmony between the realm of the tamed (the village) and the realm of the untamed (the jungle) is regulated by the way humans and beasts interact.

The recent dispute in the territory of Dongaria between the Kondhs and multinational corporations about mining concessions on the sacred Niyamgiri Mountain is a well-known example of this dramatic situation. Besides the fact that ancestral land is considered an inalienable possession—and besides the infringements on human rights and laws on reserve forests—great discomfort is felt among local indigenous communities for the devastating impact of the mine on the surrounding environment, including its wild fauna.

The *Kui Gāni*, one of the tribal epics of creation, tells the story of how water and light pierced darkness giving rise to the immanent world. Manhood, in an intermediate position in the order of appearance, was born in the shadow of a forest in full ferment. According to the myth, the universe is imagined as a series of overlapping circles, on the one hand, progressing gradually towards a brighter dimension (i.e. the top of the hills and the abode of the gods), and, on the other, moving towards darker realms (i.e. the chthonic space of the ancestors). In such warp, the flow of the many fast-flowing rivers is complex as well as the architecture of the jungle that, like the watery element, is considered alive and constantly changing. Precisely because of this reason all animal species are considered essential for the development and maintenance of the forest. In this sense all animals, from the smaller to the largest specimen, are somehow seen as integral to the existence and economy of the forest. In other words, they are simultaneously architects and builders, constantly working on the changing profile of this immense cathedral. This particular perspective should not be idealized: to survive in the jungle is a daily struggle for human and non-human animals alike. Indigenous communities continue to guard the secret of a critical equilibrium between man and nature and to transmit the ancestral knowledge of an environment in which man is just one among the many agents.

REFERENCES

AA. VV. 1993. *Indigenous Knowledge on Forests. An Enquiry into the Worlds of Kuttia Kondhs & Saoras of Orissa (India).* Cuttack: Printoverse-Maitree Sarani.

Beggiora, S. 2010. *Sacrifici umani e guerriglia nell'India Britannica.* Bassano-Vicenza: Itinera Progetti.

Boal, B. 1997. *The Kondhs, Human Sacrifice and Religious Change.* New Delhi: Inter-India Publications.

Cammiade, L. A. 1931. 'Man-Eaters and Were-Tigers.' *Man* 31: 217–20. http://dx.doi.org/10.2307/2789556

Campbell, J. 1864. *Personal Narrative of Thirteen Years Service among the Wild Tribes of Khondistan for the Suppression of Human Sacrifices.* London: Hurst & Blackett.

Douglas, M. 1978. *Natural Symbols: Exploration in Cosmology.* London: Penguin Books.

Elwin, V. 1944. Notes on a Kondh Tour, *Man in India* 24: 51–53.

— 1954. *Tribal Myths of Orissa.* Delhi: Oxford University Press.

Gomez-Alonso, J. 1998. 'Rabies: A Possible Explanation for the Vampire Legend.' *Historical Neurology* 51(3): 856–59. http://dx.doi.org/10.1212/WNL.51.3.856

Jena, M. K., *et al.* 2002. *Forest Tribes of Orissa: Lifestyle and Social Conditions of Selected Orissan Tribes, Vol. 1: The Dongaria Kondh.* New Delhi: D. K. Printworld.

Macpherson, W. 1865. *Memorials of Service in India.* London: J. Murray.

Maltby, T. J. 1918. *The Ganjam District Manual.* Madras: Government Press (reprint Leman).

Mauss, M. 1966. *The Gift. Forms and Functions of Exchange in Archaic Societies.* London: Cohen and West.

Osella, C. 1999. 'Seepage of Divinised Power, through Social, Spiritual and Bodily Boundaries: Some Aspects of Possession in Kerala.' In J. Assayag and G. Tarabout (eds), *La possession en Asie du Sud, parole, corps, territoire*: 183–210. Paris: Purusharta.

Padel, F. 2000. *The Sacrifice of Human Being. British Rule and the Konds of Orissa.* Delhi: Oxford University Press.

Patnaik, N. R. 1992. *History and Culture of Khond Tribes.* New Delhi: Commonwealth Publishers.

Third Tantra: Environment, Myth, Devotion

Falling Rain, Reigning Power in Reptilian Affairs: The Balancing of Religion and the Environment

IVETTE VARGAS-O'BRYAN*

Nāgas (Tibetan *klu*), theriomorphic or full snake transformative entities, have often been at the margins of scholarly discussions about Tibetan religious, medical and environmental traditions. However, close textual studies and ethnographic research reveal that these figures appear as central subjects in worlds of convergences and collisions. While bridging unlikely partners of religion and medical traditions, serpents and their related figures have wielded a power of resistance and accentuated cultural identity in rituals, myths and social practices. They have played a significant role in shaping the religious history of Tibet and continue to have a strong presence in the daily practice and worship of Tibetans. Drawing from textual sources and ethnographic data collected in Bhutan, Dharamsala (India) and Shangri-la (Zhōngdiàn

* Ivette Vargas-O'Bryan received her PhD in Buddhist Studies from Harvard University in 2003. She is currently Associate Professor of Asian Religious Traditions at Austin College, Sherman, Texas. Her major field is South Asian and Tibetan Buddhist Studies. Her particular interests are in the interaction of doctrine and ritual practice, the rhetoric of illness in Asian literature, and the study of religion and science in Ayurvedic and Tibetan medicine. In 2009, she was a Fulbright scholar in Hong Kong and co-headed the 'Health in Asia' cluster with Dr Zhou Xun at the Centre for the Humanities and Medicine in the Faculty of Arts and Li Ka Shing Faculty of Medicine and the University of Hong Kong. She was Affiliate Researcher at the Institut Français de Pondichéry, India, and scholar-in-residence at the Dharmacakra Center in Nepal. In 2008 she was awarded a Mellon Grant Faculty-Student Collaborative Research Project for the project 'Healing Pluralism and Bodhisattvas in the Tibetan Region' (Dharamsala, India); while in 2007 she received the same grant for the project 'Exotic Exorcists and the Spectacle of Identity: Naxi Nagas in the midst of Modernization' (Lijiang, China and US). One of her edited books on the convergences of religion and medicine is being reviewed by Hong Kong University Press. Professor Vargas-O'Bryan is undertaking two book projects, one on the research/translation work of the Tibetan medical text, the *Bdud rtsi snying po yan lag brgyad pa gsang ba man ngag gi rgyud*, on leprosy and klu diseases, and the other on the history of Gelongma Pelmo and the fasting ritual lineage. She is author of several articles and has contributed to edited books such as *Health and Religious Rituals in South Asia. Disease, Possession and Healing* (Routledge, 2010), *Tibetan Medicine in the Contemporary World* (Routledge, 2008), and *Teaching Religion and Healing* (Oxford University Press, 2006).

county in China) in 2009–2011, this chapter explores the continued awareness of the presence of *nāgas/klus* in contemporary Tibetan communities in South Asia and China, and the persistent need to interact with them in an attempt to balance modern ritual and medical practices with environmental concerns.

MEETING THE ENVIRONMENT OF *NĀGAS* AND *KLUS*

> Tibet is high and its land is pure.
> Its snowy mountains are at the head of everything,
> The sources of innumerable rivers and streams,
> It is the center of the sphere of the gods.
>
> (Karmay 1994: 112)

> The ancient name of this lake was Madhara (Kun-'dzin);
> in Chos kyi nyi ma's time the Newar called it Dhanadaha (Gift-Lake)
> and the Tibetans Ral-gri (Knife-Lake);
> today it is called Taudah (Great Lake).
> It is one mile south of the Chobar gorge
> on a broad terrace above the river level.
> It is strange that earthquakes have not emptied it.
> The local belief is that the wealth of Karkotaka
> and his Nagas lies concealed within the lake,
> which is of profound depth.
> It is said that the Rana overlords of the last century
> attempted to drain this lake to gain its treasure and were foiled.
>
> (Dowman 1983: 248).

In order to understand the role of *nāgas/klus* in Tibetan religious and medical traditions there has to be an understanding of the significance of sacred geography or power places (Tibetan *gnas chen*) in the Tibetan worldview. Sacred geography is the notion that topography is imbued with divinity, or in other words, the belief that any environment or locale is invested with supernatural or holy qualities (Jinpa *et al.* 2005; Huber 1999). Earth, stones, water, plant parts and even the very air itself from such places are imbued with power. As in the case of several religious traditions in South and East Asia, sacred geography embraces a full spectrum of deified landforms and sites associated with divinities, religious practitioners, sacred traditions and miraculous events. This central concern informs not only formal religious as well as medical practices, but local and secular conceptions of dealing with nature and society. In addition, despite modernization, the bifurcation of secular and sacred is often resisted, especially when the empirical or rational does not provide an answer for the unexplained illness, the floods, the earthquake, or the sudden accident, and *karma* alone does not provide a sufficient explanation. Whether one is a lama or a lay physician, the awareness and respect toward the environment is far more than simply ecological and economic concerns, but an awareness of its living nature, an 'eco-divinity' as such, and not one that merely exists for the benefit of humans (Watling 2009; Kinsley 1995). As Buffetrille and Diemberger (2002) have noted in their work on Tibetan sacred sites, places and landscape are a powerful source of imagery and identity in Tibetan cultural areas.

Besides the lore about mountains and pilgrimage sites that have been the focus of recent scholarly research, the beliefs surrounding bodies of water and the stones, caves and trees associated with them have preoccupied Tibetans in religious, medical and political contexts for centuries. These natural formations were clearly believed to be supernatural embodiments or power places for centres of pilgrimage (Tibetan *gnas skor*). However, it is important to note that what is animal and what is nature are not always clearly differentiated, and the more common reptilian embodiment, multifarious and broadly conceived as tadpoles, snakes, slithering worms, fish and half-human/half-snake figures, is what Tibetans call on and wrestle with in their encounters with the environment. A brief overview of *nāgas/klus* in historical texts, myths and the beliefs associated with them provide a picture of the complexity of their roles in Tibetan society and how they are used in specific contexts.

ORIGINS, IDENTITY AND COSMOLOGY

Attempting to define the terms and religious origin of *nāga/klu* reflects the complexity of defining Tibetan religious traditions in general. Although there are three literal meanings of the word *nāga* in Sanskrit and Pali (i.e. supernatural serpent, elephant and ironwood tree), for the purposes of this study I will restrict interpretations of it to two traditions, Buddhism and Bön. When it comes to *klus* and other indigenous beliefs prior to both, these traditions often overlap and their parameters may change according to the context. For the sake of this study, I will rely on particular Bön texts and will refer to it as a syncretic tradition with animistic and, in some cases, Buddhist elements. Buddhist texts, on the other hand, have inherited views from Hindu, Bön and other indigenous traditions to create an image of *klus* reflecting different ideologies and overlapping worldviews.

In Indic mythology, *nāga* appears in diverse literature as a chthonic serpent spirit or half-human/half-serpent that inhabits what could be labelled as the 'underworld', or water sources like lakes, rivers, ponds, or trees. In many respects, the early Buddhist *nāga* inherited much of the early Hindu symbolism. There were many *nāga* cults during the time of the Buddha and they continue to this day. Generally, Buddhist cosmology assigns it to the lowest level of Mount Meru, an ancient mythical mountain important in both Hindu and Buddhist traditions, with the *garuḍa* (mythical bird) enemy on the level above.

In the Tibetan Buddhist context, *klu* became assimilated into the Indian *nāga* concept, perhaps around the time of the eighth century CE, as indicated in the *Abhidharmakośa* during the first transmission of Buddhism into Tibet from India.[1] These *klus* were an ancient class of demi-gods who make up a principal part of the indigenous pantheon of the western Himalaya. Indigenous may refer to an aboriginal Bön but as Tibetan history notes, there are diverse Bön traditions (Baumer 2002). Tucci had noted that when Buddhism eventually became the state religion early on, Tibet was unable to eradicate the ancient *klu* cults and had to make them the object of complex liturgies (1949: 723).

In the Tibetan Buddhist and Bön contexts, *klu* is believed to dwell in the underworld and embody water sources, stones and trees, and is active during the winter season. The *klu* guards the celestial palaces of deities and causes winds and rains. A Bön text, the *Klu 'bum*, a collection of *klu* rituals and myths, records that the orders of *klu* originated from six eggs laid by the cosmic golden tortoise and were connected with Tibetan ancestral cults. They were considered totems of some kind (De Nebesky-Wojkowitz 1956: 290; Kloppenborg *et al.* 1995). The same text also records that there are three categories of *klu*: white, black and multi-coloured (Tucci 1980: 22). These categories of *klu* correspond to the three worlds (*srid gsum*) and are supplementary to their characteristic blue colour, the colour of water. Mimaki and Karmay, in their attempts to organize several Bön works, provided some sort of coherent categorization. They found that *klu* are classified as animals (*dud 'gro*) because of their serpent-like form and their apparitional birth (like the *garuḍa* and the *kinnara*), or as *pretas* (hungry ghosts) (Mimaki and Karmay 1997; Mimaki 2000: 99–101). Tartar (1976: 11–14), in his work on Mongolian myths that also have a strong Tibetan Buddhist flavour, notes that the main spirits of the water (*luus*) are closely linked with the cult of mountains, while in the Chinese context, *klu* is often equated with the dragon (*klung*).

Littered throughout Buddhist scriptures in Asia, the *nāgas* appear making a statement of their eligible status in the Buddhist soteriological realm. For example, the Devadatta chapter of the *Lotus Sutra* tells the story of an eight-year-old female *nāga* who, after listening to Mañjuśrī preach the *Lotus Sutra*, attains Buddhahood in her present form, thus revealing that Buddhahood can be attained in one lifetime, and that women and animals can attain it too (Paul 1985: 185–93). The famous story of the serpent Mucalinda protecting *Śākyamuni* Buddha from the rain as he attained enlightenment under the *bodhi* tree and the tale of the Buddhist philosopher Nāgārjuna retrieving the Mahāyana *sutras* from the *nāgarājās* (kings of the *nāgas*) also attest to the roles of *nāgas* in the form of snakes as protectors of teachings. However, there are several instances in which *nāgas* appear in monasteries and are excluded from Buddhist monastic practice. One famous example is the exclusion of a *nāga* from ordination because the monastic rules (*vinaya*) specifically require (human) initiation. One story in the *Vinaya Khandhaka* (*Vinaya* 1:

1. I thank Geoffrey Samuel for this information.

86–88) that is repeated throughout Buddhist texts led to this particular rule. Once a *nāga*, a powerful serpent who took the form of a human being, was mistakenly ordained as a monk. Shortly after, when asleep in his hut, the *nāga* returned to the shape of a huge snake. The monk who shared the hut was somewhat alarmed when he woke up to see a great snake sleeping next to him. The Buddha summoned the *nāga* and told him he could not remain as a monk, at which the disconsolate snake began to weep. The snake was given the Five Precepts held by the laity or, according to other versions of the story, was urged to observe the *uposatha* day (quarter days of the lunar month as lay Buddhist do) as a means of attaining a human existence in his next life when he could then be a monk. Out of compassion for the sad snake, the Buddha said that from then on all candidates for the monkhood be called '*nāga*' as a consolation, a practice true to this day (Strong 1992: 191; Gombrich 2006: 73).[2]

Early on in Indian Buddhist history and throughout Tibetan history, *nāga*s and *klu*s were treated with ambivalence. How they are perceived therefore contributes to the multiple ways they are treated in society. Most noteworthy is that these figures played critical roles as supporters, protectors as well as adversaries. In his work on the early Buddha's encounters with *nāga*s as reflections of the meeting and compromises of the Buddhist tradition with indigenous beliefs, Cohen underscores the religious rivalry current at the time. If not respected, *nāga*s can turn into adversaries and cause chaos and disease (Cohen 1998: 360–400), an occurrence that medical texts discuss as the disruption of health in terms of individual and societal order. For instance, the *klu*-like *gnyan* figures that appear in Tibetan medical texts (e.g. the twelfth-century medical text *rGyud bzhi*) possess a dual nature and when angered can cause skin and mental diseases. These texts, as well as Buddhist scriptures, see such conditions as easily remediated with strong Buddhist rituals from a Buddha or a *bodhisattva* who can transform the condition and convert the *klu* to protectors of the Buddhist teaching (Vargas-O'Bryan 2011). Furthermore, since *klu*s appear at particular natural areas like springs, lakes, stones and trees, they are looked at as place-specific deities and the diseases caused by him or her are considered diseases of place (Unschuld 1985).

Closely connected with the dual nature of the *klu* is the issue of preservation of Buddhist teachings (*dharma*), Bön and all that is connected with central Tibetan traditions like land, cultural identity and even politics. This issue of preservation is clear in several Buddhist and Bön contexts. Cohen (1998) aptly pointed out the close alliance of *nāga*s with the environment (rain, fertility and kingship) and Buddhist philosophical concepts and indigenous beliefs.

2. In terms of pantheon inclusion, *klu* are found in the retinue of major Tibetan Buddhist deities such as Dpal ldan lha mo, Mgon po, Vaishavana and the guardian of Bsam yas, Tsi'u dmar po (De Nebesky-Wojkowitz 1956: 31, 49, 71, 166; Bellezza 1997: 35–36). They also appear in the entourage of indigenous Tibetan deities like Byang bdud chen po and Bdud nag po sog pa med (De Nebesky-Wojkowitz 1956: 260).

Although issues concerning ritual, cultural identity and political alliances, and the relationship between nature divinities and the *dharma* have been sporadically studied in the past (Karmay 1998: 423–31; Miller 2003: 336–53; Huber 2003: 659–74; Huber 1999), it is only recently that they are being unearthed in the Tibetan context. In these studies, nature divinities are linked with religious rivalry and conversion, righteous kingship, ancestral cults, the promotion of the Buddha *dharma* or particular Buddhist figures or movements, and political alliances. Such examples include foundation and creation myths that link *klu* with ancient ancestral deities (Kloppenborg *et al.* 1995). Besides the obvious example of the awareness by Tibetan monastics and political leaders of the power of *klu*-inhabited springs underneath the Jokhang temple, one of the most sacred places of worship of Tibet, and waterways throughout the old capital and political centre, Lhasa, it is often the case that helpful *nāgas*/*klu*s appear in time of turmoil. During the life of the Sixth Dalai Lama (Tshang dbyangs rgya mtsho, 1683–1706), stories of benevolent *klu*s were told to remind Tibetans how they have lent a hand to Buddhist figures. His predecessor, the Fifth Dalai Lama (Blo bzang rgya mtsho, 1617–1682), built a *Klu Khang* (Klu house) behind the famous Potala Palace in honour and to appease the *klu* residing in the nearby lake.[3]

In addition to stories about nailing down *si mo* (wild demonesses) that embody the land of Tibet with its Buddhist temples (often interpreted as a suppression and conversion of the native tradition to Buddhism) (Gyatso 1987: 33–51; Mills 2002: 123), annual rituals dedicated to *klu*s are closely connected with narratives of renewal, kingship and illness, and their appearance has often been linked with clashes in politics and between religious groups manifested as a disruption in the environment in the form of disease, famine and climate changes (Kapstein 2006).

Besides the obvious designation of Nagaland in India and Bhutan as 'Brug yul ('the land of the dragon'), historically many regions in Asia are directly related to discourses regarding *nāga*s. One example is the Lao language poem *San Lup Bo Sun* (or *San Leupphasun*), which uses enmity with the *garuḍa* as an allegory for Thailand's (Siam) victory in the Laotian Rebellion of 1826–1829 (Ngaosīvat and Ngaosyvathn 1998: 68). In a Cambodian legend, the *nāga*s were a reptilian race of beings which possessed a large kingdom in the Pacific Ocean region. The *nāga* King's daughter married an Indian Brahman named Kaundinya, and from their union sprang the Cambodian people (Gaudes 1993: 333–58). Two main chronicles, *Nīlamatapurāna* and the *Rājataranginī* relate how Kashmir was created out of water and as a land of lakes was under the control of *nāga*s. Traces of *nāga* beliefs are still found in the names of spots in Kashmir like Verinag, Anantanag and Serhnag, places where Buddhism once flourished (Dutt 1985: 12).

3. The second floor of the *khang* is covered with murals depicting *siddha*s (perfected beings) in the form of *klu*s (Winkler 2002: 321–44).

As the above examples and others take note, the presence of *nāga/klu*, especially in serpent form, has been pronounced in Asian affairs, penetrating realms and bridging the gap between the sacred and the profane. In the current context, how *nāga/klu* is connected with nature, particularly in relation with religious and political concerns, cultural renewal and remembrance, and what might be termed as 'moral order' mapped out in the environment is especially prevalent. Although studies of ecology typically focus on the environment as the sum total of local abiotic and biotic factors that share a habitat, on the level of Buddhist and Bön traditions the environment takes on a spiritual significance not always verifiable on an empirical level. Throughout Asia *nāgas*, by converging cultural and religious identity on a natural scale, problematize the category of 'environment' or 'nature', an issue that warrants further investigation.

THE *KLU* AND MEDICAL AND RELIGIOUS HEALERS

Tibetans from diverse communities in South Asia and China often designate *klus* as central figures in their rituals of renewal. One central example is the annual Tibetan New Year's celebrations (*lo gsar*). Note how one Rinpoche clearly delineate the connections:

> During Losar, the Tibetan celebration of the New Year, we did not drink champagne to celebrate. Instead, we went to the local spring to perform a ritual of gratitude. We made offerings to the *nagas*, the water spirits who activated the water element in the area. We made smoke offerings to the local spirits associated with the natural world around us. Beliefs and behaviors like ours evolved long ago and are often seen as primitive in the West. But they are not only projections of human fears onto the natural world, as some anthropologists and historians suggest. Our way of relating to the elements originated in the direct experiences by our sages and common people of the sacred nature of the external and internal elements. We call these elements earth, water, fire, air, and space.
>
> (Rinpoche 2002: xvii)

Such responses to nature as sacred and the connections with fertility, gratitude and renewal are commonplace in Tibetan communities. However, a closer examination in the contemporary context reveals that these views and ritual enactments have a far reaching significance beyond these concerns. The link with the *nāga/klu* and renewal also points to outward expressions regarding underlying political and religious concerns within Tibetan exilic communities in South Asia and Tibetans in China that are in need of attention and remediation. This was evident in the recent message by the Kalon Tripa, Tibet's prime minister-in-exile Lobsang Sangay, who urged Tibetans not to celebrate Losar this year out of respect for Tibetans suffering in China, especially because of the cases of self-immolation, but only to conduct solemn Buddhist rituals (Anonymous 2012).

Aside from requests from a political leader and the annual religious rituals performed by locals, what is more commonly seen in the local contemporary context is the role of the healer to manage chaos and maintain order, especially in terms of healing and renewing balance in a community. In several instances, *klus* figure in medical and ritual settings as characters that appear at times of disorder (often in the form of illness) and are called upon by human healers to restore order and as a reminder of the links between Tibetan culture and Tibetan landscapes and places. Throughout recent research, it was commonly found that it was in the hands of traditional healers, doctors and ritual specialists that order and renewal was sought, and the *klu* connections were explicitly made between Buddhist teachings, the environment and Tibetan cultural identity. So when things go wrong in terms of the individual and cosmic environment, healers know how to manage the problem. Many draw from Buddhist teachings that have a history of using medical metaphors (for example, the common discourse of Buddha as doctor, the *dharma* as medicine, the four noble truths as diagnosis and treatment), others—such as monastics as physicians—operate in the frame of Bön teachings within a highly ritual context.

CAREFUL DOCTORS, MINDFUL LAMAS, MINDLESS BUILDERS

Although the contemporary Tibetan medical system is divided in terms of its practices depending on whether it is in China or South Asia, the medical tradition continues to incorporate environmental concerns in its diagnostic and treatment regiments. Besides Buddhist and Bön scriptures, the foundational textual basis for the medical tradition is the authoritative twelfth-century Tibetan medical four-volume set, the *rGyud bzhi* (*Bdud rsti snying po yan lag brgyad pa gsang ba man ngag gi rgyud*). This text can be generally organized as follows: the 'Root Tantra' (*rtsa rgyud*), the 'Explanatory Tantra' (*bshad rgyud*), the 'Instructional Tantra' (*man rgyud*) and the 'Subsequent Tantra' (*phyi rgyud*). The 'Root Tantra' provides a comprehensive framework for understanding the Tibetan medical system as a whole through an elaborate schema of roots and branches that describe the various aspects of physical health, the causes of disease, their diagnosis and their treatment. The 'Explanatory Tantra' focuses on anatomy and physiology, while the 'Instructional Tantra' is clearly oriented towards clinical practice. Finally, the 'Subsequent Tantra' tackles the intricacies of diagnosis and treatment (Meyer 1992; Meyer 2003). The three latter portions of the text explain how to recognize the causes and symptoms of disease as well as how to treat illness.

The eighty-first chapter of the 'Instructional Tantra' (known as *Man ngag gi rgyud*), which has not been studied thoroughly in current scholarship or translated into any Western language, immediately draws attention to the critical connection between Buddhist and Bön teachings and the environment as a fundamental medical concern. Clearly an almost animistic description of the environment appears in the text. This chapter, entitled *gdug pa klu'i gdon nad gso ba* ('The Cure for the *gdon* disease of the malevolent *klu*'), begins with the well-known Buddhist notion of the degenerate age (Sanskrit *kali-yuga*, Tibetan *snyigs ma'i dus*) when *dharma* is threatened (Nattier 1992) and imbalance is mapped onto the environment:

> Then again Brahmin Rig pa'i Ye shes spoke: 'Kye! Great Brahmin, listen! In the time of the last five hundred degenerate years, when the degenerate *kalpa* arises, human beings are in poverty as their provisions decline. Having ploughed arid grassland for farming, *sa gnyan* [earth demon-god] are turned up. *Chu gnyan* [water demon-god] are disturbed by transforming natural bodies of water into artificial lakes and ponds. *Shing gnyan* [tree demon-god] are deforested and *rdo gnyan* [stone demon-god] are uprooted or overturned. Contaminating hearth, burning impure substances, reckless slaughtering of animals in (spirit homes), and disturbing *gnyan sa* with the hope to subdue enemies by Buddhist and Bön priests who have no time to practice in the proper manner all result in agitating *nāgas*, *gnyan* and earth spirits, gods and *rākṣasah*. Poisons merely spread through touch, sight, breath and thought. The time comes for the rise of *tsi ti dzva la* [i.e. leprosy]. It is disconcerting to see and fearful to think about. Merely hearing about these [events] causes sadness, vision of one's own corpse, and separation from loved ones.'
>
> (G.yu thog Yon tan mgon po (1993 [1982]): 392–93)[4]

The disruption of the ecological balance affects several embodied landscapes: nature (spirit world), human, and society. As the text[5] continues, the focus is on the *nāga*, how to diagnose *nāga* disease (*klu nad*) and how to combat it ritually. The unnatural transformation of water and land, as well as improper ritual behaviour, creates an opportunity for such nature spirits to arise or reveal themselves. Their appearance is thus directly connected with disease. In other words, anything that is not in proper order, including ritual action, provide an opportunity for these place-deities to arise.

The text then continues with the diagnosis of *klu* disease and its treatment, and the description of the outer signs in animal characteristics. It is not just the natural 'bodies', it is also the demonic or malevolent animal transformation of the disease that becomes evident and seems to either surround or possesses the body:

> The outer signs involve examining the visions of dreams,
> and analysing the characteristics of body, speech and mind.
> These characteristics include dreams of water bodies, trees, meadows,
> frogs, tadpoles, fish, snakes, insects, flies, scorpions and spiders;
> or dreaming these creatures either touching or surrounding your body
>
> (G.yu thog Yon tan mgon po (1993 [1982]): 393–37).[6]

4. Author's translation.
5. *Bdud rtsi snying po yan lag brgyud pa gsang ba man ngag gi rgyud* (1993).
6. In the following few pages, the text harkens back to traditional views of *klu* disease with a

The correlations between health (individual and society) and environment become increasingly evident in contemporary medical and ritual contexts. Fieldwork studies in Bhutan, Dharamsala (India) and Shangri-la (China) revealed that not only are such correlations made, but they continue to be critical in today's medical practices and ordinary people's concern with health. In the case of Bhutan in 2009, the importance of keeping balance in the environment was clearly a priority, and this specifically has to do with an acknowledgment of the spirit world in relation to human's and nature's wellbeing.

Bhutan as a country has placed environmental conservation at the centre of its development strategy. Conservation of the environment forms one of the four pillars of Gross National Happiness, which underscores that development cannot be pursued on the premise of economic growth alone, but has to take place in combination with the emotional and spiritual wellbeing of the people. In addition, the Constitution of Bhutan mandates that at least 60 per cent of the country remain forested all the time (Karan 1990). With Tibetan Buddhism as its central state religion and a thriving Tibetan medical tradition, the issue of protecting the environment takes on a more nuanced meaning than what we presume in the West, one that incorporates the spirit world of the *klu*, the land being called 'Brug yul ('the land of the dragon') is a case in point.

During the 2009 IASTAM (International Association for the Study of Traditional Asian Medicine) conference on Asian medicine in Bhutan, Dr Dorji Wangchuk of the National Institute of Traditional Medicine (NITM) acknowledged the importance of respecting the spiritual environment embodied in natural phenomena for the proper functioning of society and health. During a brief interview, he took me to a small hillock behind a series of buildings that were part of the medical complex and showed me a stone surrounded by flowers. There was also a small structure, a *klu khang*, which is typically constructed in rituals for the *klu*. He recounted a story that a small flu-like epidemic attacked the area some years ago. An oracle informed the hospital officials including the physician himself that apparently permission was not acquired from the spirits to build in the area and, as a result, disruption of the land made the *klu* retaliate. The issue of building and breaking ground without permission arises again and again in several Tibetan medical and religious contexts throughout South Asia and China. One example typical of Tibetan ritual contexts regards construction ('breaking ground') for temples, bridges and *maṇḍalas*. In Tibetan Buddhism, the earth ritual (*sa'i cho ga*) is essential for preliminary rites during the consecration of a site for practice like the building of a temple. The ritual is important for the creation of the boundaries of a sacred site and to request the permission of the local deities to build. This may lead to an

---

prescription of '*garuda* pills', with reference to the natural enemy of the *nāga* in Indic Hindu folklore.

annual renewal ritual (Cantwell 2005: 4-21; Huber 1999; Ignacio-Cabezon 1999). Permission of land spirits (*sa bdag*) and *klu*s has to be secured before anything can be established or built.

As in Bhutan and in several Buddhist texts, in the case of the Mentseekhang (Tibetan hospital and medical school) in Dharamsala, there was an immediate recognition that the *klu* must be acknowledged and respected. From stories about accidents during the construction of the hospital (related by the director of the hospital, Dr Tsewang Tamdin) to sickness due to the cutting of trees, spitting or driving over snakes, several physicians admitted being quite concerned that *klus* had to be respected or retaliation was inevitable. Dr Pema Dorjee, a senior physician at the Mentseekhang, was an excellent example of the Tibetan medical tradition's concern with balancing Buddhist beliefs with the environment. On entering his office, one noticed several mandalas and amulets (*btags grol, srung ba'i 'khor lo*) displayed on his desk and walls to protect him, as he would say, from the *klu*. Dr Dorjee was full of stories about construction workers contracting eczema and other skin ailments due to the breaking of land without proper ritual, the land where 'serpent' creatures live.

This view is reminiscent of what was examined in earlier anthropological work done in Nepal. One case in point was a study conducted by Mumford regarding rituals conducted by Tibetan lamas and Gurung local healers on what he interpreted as reciprocal exchange among underworld serpent deities and ritualized apology to them. A lama noted:

> But we in our ignorance,
> by stirring up and muddying the waters
> have destroyed their wealth...
> We ask for forgiveness for cutting trees,
> for digging the earth,
> for turning over rocks,
> for breaking boulders,
> for killing sheep and goats that are owned by klu
> for cutting up snakes' bodies,
> for hooking the mouths of fish,
> for cutting the limbs of frogs,
> for destroying the palaces of the klu and emptying their wells,
> for blocking their springs,
> and for harming the klu themselves...
> For whatever acts have harmed the sa bdag and klu race.
>
> (Mumford 1989: 101)

As Mumford explains:

> [t]he list of offences portrays harm against the *klu* underworld social system... offences against sentient beings of nature 'owned' by the *klu*...particularly water beings, such as fish, frogs, and snakes, and further, offences that have directly hurt *klu* bodies' like the cutting or burning of trees, breaking rocks and other places where they reside.
>
> (1989: 101)

A contemporary example further accentuates the implications of mindless actions in Tibetan medical traditions. A physician at the Mentseekhang in India was convinced that he became seriously ill in Europe after he spit on a tree outside his window. He explicitly stated that *klus* appear in serpent form, they reside in trees and so he offended them. Ritual compensation had to be done. Contemporary Tibetan physicians are sensitive to the view that the disruption of the environment without an awareness of or respect for its spirit inhabitants and the proper performance of ritual treatment are outward violations of the environment and thus in turn, the environment will retaliate.

RITUAL HEALING AND ENVIRONMENTAL AWARENESS

Klu disease and ritual healing have a long history in Tibetan culture and are currently remembered in several ritual performances. One example is the annual performance of the *nyungne* (Tibetan *smyung gnas*, 'fasting') ritual associated with the tenth-century leper nun Pelmo (Dge slong ma Dpal mo), whose hagiographies are recounted while fasting rituals are performed in nunneries and other temple complexes. The ritual is performed during *sagadawa* (Sanskrit *Vaiśakha*), the commemoration of the historical Buddha's birth, death and *parinirvana*. Note a passage from a fourteenth-century hagiography of this nun, who, by performing a fasting ritual associated with the *bodhisattva* Avalokiteśvara, was healed from her illness:

> When she [Gelongma Pelmo] stayed there five days,
> in an experiential vision in which sleep and light were mixed,
> she saw many tadpoles, fish, frogs, snakes, and so forth
> come out of her vagina and anus
> and glide into the earth
> while she recited the six-syllable mantra without distraction.
>
> (Anonymous 1953: folio 13.14-14.6)[7]

In contemporary Tibetan communities there is a keen awareness of the ritual approaches regarding serpent entities and their relation with the environment as ways to restore and maintain a sense of wellbeing. As in earlier studies of physicians' integrative practices at the Mentsikhang in Lhasa (Vargas 2010; Vargas-O'Bryan 2011), in the case of Dharamsala, physicians like Dr Pema Dorjee often sought the advice and ritual sustenance of the local Klu Rinpoche, an expert in *klu pjs* (rituals). Every month, according to the Tibetan calendar, there are designated *klu* days that require specific ritual performance. I have attended several small scale rituals in Nepal, some done for special requests made by Tibetans in the community. However, one such ritual I attended in July 2011 in Dharamsala is typically performed by

7. Author's translation.

the Klu Rinpoche every month for the sake of those in the community who were diagnosed with *klu* diseases by Tibetan physicians or oracles (or both). At this particular session, in a small room in an apartment complex, several people crowded together and sat on the floor below the Rinpoche while two monks chanted from the *klu 'bum*, a large collection of Bön ritual texts dedicated to the invocation and appeasement of the *klu*. In the middle of the room was a clay effigy of a *klu* placed in the middle of a basin. In one corner of the room to the left of the Rinpoche was a tree-like house meant to represent a *klu khang*. At one point in the ceremony, the participants imprinted their fingers on pieces of clay and then pressed the clay against different parts of their bodies that were affected by disease. Thereafter participants dropped the clay into the basin surrounding the effigy in the middle. Later, each participant had to drink from a vase filled with tea water, an elixir of some kind which had been blessed by the Klu Rinpoche and the chanting monks. Subsequently, everyone had to spit into the basin, an act symbolically suggesting the elimination of the illness. At the end of the ceremony, Tibetan monks threw the effigy and the clay pieces into a nearby lake to feed the *klu*. Everyone underwent ritual healing through recognizing the source of the ailment and transforming the ailment through ritual action and purification. This monthly ritual renews the relationship of the *klu* with places in nature, and of course, reminds Tibetans of their presence and the respect due to them through ritual enactment.

In Shangri-la (formerly Gyalthang), China, despite the major efforts in economic development in construction and tourism, the prevalence of tradition was clear in the convergences of religion and the environment. Although Tibetan medicine and Buddhism are heavily advertised as commodities for the tourist market (both Chinese and Western), there is still a major concern by local Tibetan communities to maintain a relationship of respect with their spirit environment. One example was encountered in a small village outside of the new town of Shangri-la in June 2010. The experiences of a successful Tibetan businessman by the name of Tashi,[8] highly respected by both local Tibetans and Chinese cadres, was a case in point. As a typical Tibetan returnee to an economically thriving China determined to invest in business, Tashi was also concerned in revitalizing Tibetan culture in the area in the form of investing in the construction of Tibetan restaurants, art schools, local temples and stupas and the financing of rituals. During the time of the ritual of *nyungne* associated with Gelongma Pelmo, Tashi revealed his concern over the spirits of the land even though he called it local 'superstition'. In a visit to his home nearby the temple, I noticed that the land was surrounded by large oddly shaped trees and a creek meandered around the back of the house. Tashi expressed that at one time the village experienced an unexplained illness that could not be contained by any ordinary means. Everyone in the community

8. Pseudonyms are used in this case.

believed that *klu* inhabited the area around his home, especially the trees and the creek based on dreams recounted by local people. Finally, Tashi requested that local lamas do a prayer and relocate the *klu* to a more appropriate place where they would not be bothered by human intervention. This led to their move to a nearby mountain top, where he would do *pujas* for them on a regular basis. After this relocation, the illness stopped and everything returned to normal.

CONCLUSION: FALLING RAIN AND REIGNING POWER IN REPTILIAN AFFAIRS

As Yeh (2008: 103–37) has made clear in her studies of Tibetan communities in Lhasa, the performance of *klu* rituals at lakes and mountains by Tibetans is both an opportunity to preserve their culture and protest local conditions. Besides transmitting to the future generations an awareness of the importance of environmental issues, often such activities counteract government efforts at conservation that directly impinge on cultural practices and restrict access to Tibetan sacred sites. While heavy monsoon rains took over the natural landscape in Dharamsala ending with amazing streaks of sunshine, it became evidently clear that the environment makes its presence known in so many ways to Tibetan communities. Whether in South Asia or China, from the myths of the land and waters to the rituals of gratitude, permission, respect and healing, *nāgas/klu*s appear to be critical players in Tibetan society creating convergences and asserting its identity in connection with the Tibetan people and their environment. This study expands further and tries to bring together the issues of protection, adversarial relationships, preservation and reciprocity as features that these figures maintained in their continued presence in religious and medical literature and the living folklore of local Tibetan communities. Tibetan physicians and religious ritual specialists (lamas, healers and oracles) as well as Buddhist philosophers each in their own way planted their seeds of recognition by being aware that without these figures, they would have a rather chaotic and 'unnatural' world.

REFERENCES

Anonymous. 2012. 'Kalon Tripa's Losar Statement.' In *Central Tibetan Administration. Restoring Freedom for Tibetans*, http://tibet.net/2012/02/20/kalon-tripa%E2%80%99s-2012-losar-statement/ (accessed 05/04/2012).

Author Unknown. 1953. *Dge slong ma dpal mo'i rnam thar nges 'byung rgyud la skye ba'i chos gtam* (*The Biography of Kamala Bhikshuni, Princess of King Dharma Pal, an Ancient King of Kashmir, India*). Kalimpong: Tibet Mirror Press.

Baumer, C. 2002. *Bön: Tibet's Ancient Religion*. Trumbull, CN: Weatherhill.

Bdud rtsi snying po yan lag brgyud pa gsang ba man ngag gi rgyud [The Quintessential Nectar of the Eight Branches: The Secret Upadesha Section of the Tantra]. 1993. Delhi: Bod kyi lcags po ri'i dran rten slob gner khang.

Bellezza, J. 1997. *Divine Dyads: Ancient Civilization in Tibet.* Dharamsala: Library of Tibetan Works and Archives.

Buffetrille, K., and H. Diemberger (eds). 2002. *Tibet and the Himalayas.* Leiden: Brill.

Cantwell, C. 2005. 'The Tibetan Earth Ritual: Subjugation and Transformation of the Environment.' *Revue D'Etudes Tibétaines 7 Langues et Cultures de l'Aire Tibétaines.* CNRS, Paris, April 2005: 4–21.

Cohen, R. 1998. 'Naga, Yaksa, Buddha: Local Deities and Local Buddhism at Ajanta.' *History of Religions* 37(4): 360–400. http://dx.doi.org/10.1086/463514

De Nebesky-Wojkowitz, R. 1956. *Oracles and Demons of Tibet.* The Hague: Mouton Press.

Dowman, K. 1983. 'A Buddhist Guide to the Power Places of the Kathmandu Valley.' *Kailash: A Journal of Inter-disciplinary Studies*: 183–291.

Dutt, N. 1985. *Buddhism in Kashmir.* Delhi: Eastern Book Linkers.

Gaudes, R. 1993. 'Kaundinya, Preah Thaong, and the "Nagi Soma": Some Aspects of a Cambodian Legend.' *Asian Folklore Studies* 52: 333–58. http://dx.doi.org/10.2307/1178160

Gombrich, R. 2006. *How Buddhism Began: The Conditioned Genesis of the Early Teachings.* London: Routledge.

Gyatso, J. 1987. 'Down with the Demoness: Reflections on the Feminine Ground in Tibet.' In J. Willis (ed.), *Feminine Ground: Essays on Women and Tibet*: 33–51. Ithaca, NY: Snow Lion Publications.

Huber, T. 1999. *The Cult of Pure Crystal Mountain: Popular Pilgrimage and Visionary Landscape in Southeast Tibet.* Oxford: Oxford University Press.

Ignacio-Cabezon, J. 2009. *Tibetan Rituals.* Oxford: Oxford University Press.

Jinpa, G. et al. 2005. Sacred Landscape and Pilgrimage in Tibet: In Search of the Lost Kingdom of Bön. New York: Abbeville Press.

Kapstein, M. 2006. *The Tibetans.* Malden, MA: Blackwell Publications.

Karan, P. P. 1990. *Bhutan: Environment, Culture and Development Strategy.* Columbia, MO: South Asia Books.

Karmay, S. G. 1994. 'Mountain Cults and National Identity in Tibet.' In R. Barnett and S. Akiner (eds), *Resistance and Reform in Tibet*: 112–21. London: Hurst & Co.

— 1998. *The Arrow and the Spindle: Studies in History, Myths, Rituals and Beliefs in Tibet.* Kathmandu: Mandala Books.

Kinsley, D. 1995. *Ecology and Religion: Ecological Spirituality in Cross-Cultural Perspective.* Upper Saddle River, NJ: Prentice Hall.

Kloppenborg, R. *et al.* 1995. *Female Stereotypes in Religious Traditions.* Leiden: E. J. Brill.

Meyer, F. 2003. 'The Golden Century in Tibetan Medicine.' In F. Pommaret (ed.), and H. Solverson (trans.), *Lhasa in the Seventeenth Century: The Capital of the Dalai Lamas*: 99–119. Leiden and Boston: Brill.

Meyer, F., with Y. Parfionovich and G. Dorje. 1992. *Tibetan Medical Paintings: Illustrations to the Blue Beryl Treatise of Sangye Gyamtso*, Vol. 1. London: Serindia Publications.

Miller, R. 2003. '"The Supine Demoness" (Srin mo) and the Consolidation of Empire.' In A. McKay (ed.), *History of Tibet, vol.* 1: 336–53. London: Routledge.

Mills, M. 2002. *Identity, Ritual and State in Tibetan Buddhism: The Foundations of Authority in Gelukpa Monasticism.* London: Routledge.

Mimaki, K. 2000. 'A Preliminary Comparison of Bonpo and Buddhist Cosmology.' In S. G. Karmay and Y. Nagano (eds), *New Horizons in Bön Studies*: 99–101. Osaka: National Museum of Ethnology.

Mimaki, K., and S. Karmay. 1997. '*Bön sgo gsal byed*: Two Tibetan Manuscripts in Facsimile Edition of a Fourteenth Century Encyclopedia of Bonpo Doxography.' *Bibliotheca Codicum Asiaticorum* 13. Tokyo: The Centre for East Asian Cultural Studies for UNESCO.

Mumford, S. 1989. *Himalayan Dialogue: Tibetan Lamas and Gurung Shamans in Nepal.* Madison: University of Wisconsin Press.

Ngaosīvat, M., and P. Ngaosyvathn. 1998. *Paths to Conflagration: Fifty Years of Diplomacy and Warfare in Laos, Thailand, and Vietnam, 1778-1828.* Ithaca, NY: Cornell University Southeast Asia Program Publications.

Nattier, J. 1992. *Once upon a Future Time: Studies in a Buddhist Prophecy of Decline.* Fremont, CA: Asian Humanities Press Nattier.

Paul, D. 1985. *Women in Buddhism: Images of the Feminine in the Mahayana Tradition.* Berkeley: University of California Press.

Rinpoche, T. W. 2002. *Healing with Form, Energy, and Light*. Ithaca, NY: Snow Lion Publications.

Strong, J. 1992. *The Legend and Cult of Upagupta: Sanskrit Buddhism in North India and Southeast Asia.* Delhi: Motilal Banarsidass.

Tartar, M. 1976. 'Two Mongol Texts Concerning the Cult of Mountains.' *Acta Orientalia* 30(1): 1–59.

Tucci, G. 1949. *Tibetan Painted Scrolls*, 3 vols. Rome: Istituto Poligrafico e Zecca dello Stato.

— 1980. *The Religions of Tibet*. London: Routledge & Kegan Paul.

Unschuld, P. 1985. *Medicine in China. A History of Ideas.* Berkeley: University of California Press.

Vargas, I. 2010. 'Legitimizing Demon Diseases in Tibetan Medicine: The Conjoining of Religion, Medicine and Ecology.' In S. Craig *et al.* (eds), *Studies of Medical Pluralism in Tibetan History and Society*: 397–404. Leiden: E. J. Brill.

Vargas-O'Bryan, I. 2011. 'Disease, the Demons and the Buddhas: A study of Tibetan Conceptions of Disease and Religious Practice.' In F. M. Ferrari (ed.), *Health and Religious Rituals in South Asia: Disease, Possession and Healing*: 81–99. London and New York: Routledge.

Watling, T. 2009. *Ecological Imaginations in the World Religions.* New York: Continuum.

Winkler, J. 2002. 'The Rdzogs Chen Murals of the Klu Khang in Lhasa.' In H. Blezer (ed.), *Religion and Secular Culture in Tibet*: 321–44. Leiden: E. J. Brill.

Yeh, E. 2008. 'From Wasteland to Wetland?: Nature and Nation in China's Tibet.' *Environmental History* 14(1): 103–37. http://dx.doi.org/10.1093/envhis/14.1.103

Guardian Spirits, Omens and Meat for the Clans: The Place of Animals among the Apatanis of Arunachal Pradesh

SARIT K. CHAUDHURI*

Non-human animals play a significant role in the construction of the economic, social and religious identity of Tani indigenous tribes (*adivasi*).[1] Located in Arunachal Pradesh, a north-eastern Indian federal state bordering with Bhutan, Burma and China, the Tani nomenclature includes various tribal groups such as the Apatanis, Adis, Nyishis, Galos and Tagins. In these communities animals are important for subsistence but they are also core to the definition and affirmation of internal and external social relationship as well as individual status. Last but not least, animals play an extremely important role in the definition of the religious life of all Tani tribes.

Broadly speaking, animals can be divided in three groups: domesticated (pigs, cows, chickens, dogs, etc.), non-domesticated (monkeys, tigers, leopards) and semi-domesticated. The latter denomination refers essentially to one animal only, namely the mithun (*Bos frontalis*), also known as gayal.[2] Despite their morphological differences, all these animals play key roles in several rituals and mythical narratives. Without the sacrifice of mithuns, for instance, hardly any agricultural festivals of the Tani tribes take place. Similarly, an exchange of mithuns (or other cattle) during marriage or other

* Sarit K. Chaudhuri is currently holding the post of Professor and Head of the Department of Anthropology in Rajiv Gandhi University, Arunachal Pradesh, India. He has been a Postdoctoral Fellow at SOAS where he worked on a collaborative project. For more than 23 years he has been working among the tribes of North East India and published 9 books and 52 papers in journals and books.

1. The term *adivasi* is contended in Arunachal Pradesh. Educated people use *adivasi* to refer to migrant menial workers from minority ethnic communities (Oraons, Mundas, etc.) who work in the tea-plantations of Assam or as domestic helpers. Indigenous communities of Arunachal, who look at themselves as hierarchically superior to outsider ethnic groups, tend to use the English words 'tribe' or 'tribal'.
2. An indigenous bovine inhabiting the forests of north-eastern India, the mithun has such an importance for local culture that it has become the symbol of Arunachal Pradesh. On the state flag, a mithun is flanked by two great hornbills and surmounted by the Ashoka pillar—symbol of India—at whose top are four sitting lions facing the four prime directions.

rites of passage is mandatory. Ritual sacrifices of pigs and birds are also very common while haruspicy (or hepatoscopy) is widely practised by shamans who specialize in reading chickens' livers to foretell the future. These and other ritual performances serve the general purpose of negotiating and communicating with the gods, the ancestors or the world of the spirits.

In this chapter I will discuss how one Tani group, the Apatanis, understand, use and live with animals, and what non-human animals mean in their religious beliefs. The chapter will bring a number of examples drawn from my own fieldwork in the villages of Hari and Mudang-Tage in 2002, 2009 and 2010[3] as well as from previous academic literature. It includes a description of animal sacrifices during large festivals, rites of protection, health-seeking rituals, haruspicy and judiciary rituals.

Myth is also an essential part to justify, and perpetuate, the ritual killing of animals and therefore some foundational sacred narratives will be examined. To each Apatani sacrifice is associated an oral narrative which is transmitted and re-enacted by local shamans or ritual specialists. Such sacred tales provide the aetiology of and the rationale for animal sacrifice and often they offer an arena for discussing the mutual relationship that binds the tribe (human beings) to animals (non-human beings). Finally, this chapter intends to reflect on the oral tradition of the Apatanis and their dependency on other tribal groups and the environment of Arunachal Pradesh. This will allow further reflections on the contradictory nature of animal sacrifice and the way it enhances cultural identity while at the same time it suggests a deep respect for all forms of life.

THE SACRED AND PROFANE DIMENSION OF ANIMALS IN APATANI CULTURE

The Apatanis are one of the well-known tribes of Arunachal Pradesh. Formerly known in colonial literature as Anka Miri, Apa Tanang, Tanae and so forth, they got visibility thanks to the works of Austrian ethnographer Christoph von Fürer-Haimendorf (1962 and 1980). The land of the Apatanis is located in the Ziro valley of Arunachal Pradesh at an altitude of 5,754 feet and surrounded by hill ranges in all directions. Watered by a river known as Kamala that runs in the middle of the valley from north to south,[4] the tribe—according to local myths—is indigenous of another area, a place called Mudo Supung—perhaps the present Tsangpo valley in Tibet. From there they settled in a mythical place called Biri (the current Hong village situated north-east of the

3. Brief fieldwork has also been conducted in different phases in relation to two projects: (1) 'Beads tradition of Arunachal tribes', funded by MAKAIAS, Kolkata; and (2) a research on the Apatani agrarian systems funded by The Asiatic Society, Kolkata, which is still continuing. While engaged in these research projects, I have visited all of the old Apatani villages in the Ziro valley.
4. The river is called Brahmaputra in Assam.

state capital Itanagar) and then dispersed by establishing seven different villages: Hong, Hija, Duta, Mudang Tage, Hari, Bula and Bamin-Michi. (Successively, with the growth of population, three further settlements were created, that is, Siiro, Lempya and Nenchalya.)

The economy of the Apatanis is essentially an agricultural one. Although they possess both domestic (cows) and semi-domestic (mithuns) cattle—but also chickens (*paro*) and pigs (*alyi*)—the Apatanis do not use animal work for tilling the soil or other agricultural-related chores. In fact, the Apatanis, who mainly practice wet rice cultivation, depend on hoe farming. This is a form of working the soil largely based on human labour. Animal husbandry, on the other hand, is practised on a limited scale. The Apatanis tend to animals such as mithuns and cows.

A distinctive trait of Apatani culture is that animals are not only food or an indicator of wealth, like it is the case for other Tani tribes. Traditional beliefs, ancestral myths and ritual practices confirm the role of animals as privileged actors in the world of the Apatanis.[5] Indeed animals are the object of ritual killing, yet this has not to be looked at as a mere act of violence performed for ritualistic or subsistence purposes. Animals are the medium through which human beings can communicate with the gods and the spirits, and put forth their demands. Therefore animals are symbols of justice. Simoons and Simoons (1968: 76) report that:

> One Pair of Hilo deities, who live in the hills, protect man, his crops and 'cattle', presumably including mithun. To these deities, individual offers sacrifices of chickens, pigs, and cattle once a year. Another Hilo pair, who live near Apatani villages, can make people wise and restrained—qualities of high value in Apatani society; to them each household offer animals monthly, which may be chickens, dogs, pigs or 'cattles'... Before going out on a raid, a ceremony is conducted in which a dog, a pig, or a mithun is offered to the paired deities associated with war. They are promised additional sacrifices if the raid is successful. Still another pair of deities is able to help captives escape. They are also appealed to when a mithun is stolen; the owner sacrifices a chicken and urges them to help the mithun break loose and return to its grazing grounds.[6]

The Apatanis believe that animals are meant to be eaten (von Fürer-Haimendorf 1962: 117). But slaughter is always supposed to be regulated by strict ritual norms. Mills, who was touring Arunachal Pradesh in 1945, describes a feast that he gave for the Apatanis. Two mithuns were killed and their meat distributed to seven villages. However, as he noted: 'To the Apa Tani a mithan [*sic*] is far too important an animal to be casually slaughtered,

5. Similar views have been retained in Danyi-Piiloism, a popular nomenclature that recently emerged to indicate indigenous religions using local terms so as to contrast the spread of Christianity in Arunachal Pradesh.
6. With the administrative reform that culminated with the achievement of statehood in 1987, the question of intra-community or inter-community raids or blood feuds in Arunachal Pradesh are no more traceable.

and...the priest had to recite the correct incantations' (Mills 1947: 28. See also Simoons and Simoons 1968: 77). Another very significant incident is reported by von Fürer-Haimendorf (1955: 87–88). As a Government employee, he was assigned the responsibility of establishing friendly relations with both Nyishi and Apatani tribes. During one of his several journeys across Arunachal Pradesh, two Apatani villages contributed with a communally owned mithun to a sacrifice which was meant to confirm their loyalty to and friendship with the outsider. Before the sacrifice, the local ritual specialist informed the mithun of its impeding death and said it was to die for a worthy cause, that is to say the strengthening of friendship relation between Apatanis and a representative of the central government. The animal was not meant to object to its own killing because the gods themselves gave mithuns to the Apatanis for ritual slaughter. When the animal was eventually killed, the meat was divided and distributed to all the households of the two villages, and a share was given to von Fürer-Haimendorf himself (cf. Simoons and Simoons 1968: 78).

Apatanis do not sacrifice only mithuns. Other animals regularly used are fowls, dogs, pigs and common cattle. For many ceremonies, particularly those to resolve individual or small-scale crises, small animals such as chickens are sufficient. For others, the shaman is supposed to take a decision in consultation with his client(s) about what animal is the most suitable choice. Several rituals, however, leave no choice and there is just one animal that must be sacrificed.

The pig rivals the mithun as the most important animal among the Apatanis. Pork is no doubt more prized than the meat of mithuns. Each year hundreds of pigs are acquired from neighbouring tribes such as the Daflas (Nyishis) and Hill Miris in trade. Von Fürer-Haimendorf comments that the demand for pigs at the time of large festivals like *myoko* is as great as the demand for turkeys in England at Christmas (1962: 48). The pig, however, has minimal value in the acquisition of land, the supreme goal for Apatanis. It is also of little, if any, importance in other forms of payment as well as on occasion of ceremonies performed by individuals to enhance their prestige. These are all prerogatives of the mithun.

In the next sections I will discuss animal sacrifice in rites ranging from fertility ceremonies, health-seeking performances, haruspicy, judicial rites and rituals of passage. Oral narratives will also be examined in order to understand the relation between human animals, non-human animals and other-than-animal entities (e.g. deities, spirits, ancestors, etc.).

THE *MURUNG* FESTIVAL

Murung is usually celebrated in the month of January to secure the blessing of benevolent deities (*tigo uiis*) and protection from evil spirits (*gyunyang*). A family-based festivity, the *murung* is naturally restricted to the boundaries of the village where clans and friends collaborate at all stages of the celebration. Every Apatani nuclear family tries to celebrate the *murung* at least once, whereas only the richest clans can afford the expenditure necessary for sponsoring more than one festival. Von Fürer-Haimendorf (1962) defined this particular celebration a 'feast of merit'. On such occasion the wealthy Apatanis confirm their social status. Other reasons, however, converge. For instance, Yabyang (2006) has individuated votive patterns in the celebration of *murung*. This may be performed in response to the prolonged illness of a family member, unusual diseases afflicting domestic animals, etc. According to Kani (1996), a *murung* festival may also be celebrated to counter bad omens and inauspicious dreams.

The celebration of the *murung* involves multiple stages. The first is the observation of chicken livers (haruspicy), a performance conducted by the village ritual specialist in order to ensure that evil spirits will not be any obstacle. If livers are extracted intact, this is believed to be a good sign. Firewood is then collected and mithuns (or, alternatively, cows) are bought or brought from the forest. After this preliminary ritual, the host family will prepare a fermented alcoholic beverage similar to beer while the ritual specialist will get ready to perform the *subu myohing*, a ritual consisting of erecting a sacrificial altar in order to a appease animal (e.g. mithun, cows, etc.) and nature (forest, rivers, etc.) spirits. Rituals are also performed to pacify the sun (*danyi*) and the moon (*piilo*). Two different ritual specialists consult chicken livers in order to establish who will chant the selected incantations on the *lapang* (public platform). The chosen 'priest' (*nyibu*) initiates chanting on the *lapang* and will continue this performance for the whole day in order to ensure that people are protected against any natural calamity for the entire duration of the *murung*.[7]

The first myth to be sung is that of the origins of the Apatanis. During the following ceremonies, called *subu* and *tumu*, the shaman guides the souls of the animals during and after the sacrifice toward *neli* (the netherworld). This is followed by a third narrative: the story of how mithuns and cows were domesticated so as to make sacrifice possible.

Sacrificial animals such as mithun and cows are brought separately in the perimeter of the *lapang* where a male members of the host family smears the horn of the bovines with rice powder (*yatang*) mixed with local beer. Soon after, women belonging to same lineage (*uru*) pour beer over the head of cows and mithuns and distribute rice powder and beer to participants and to those who have gathered to observe the performance.

The ritual beheading of the selected animal is not necessarily performed by a ritual specialist. More often than not this is made by someone having a specific social position within the clan or family. Before the actual killing, there is a mock ritual (*dollo hunii*) through which the sacrificer symbolically offers

7. A translation of such long narratives can be found in Kani (1996).

limbs and other body parts of the ritual victim to the spirit of the animal soon to be sacrificed. Then he will address the ancestors, deities and other spirits. This is followed by the loud beating of brass plates which, on the one hand, is supposed to drive out the souls of sacrificed animals; on the other, serves to the purpose of summoning relatives and friends from nearby villages.

In the next days, the house of the hosting family is visited by neighbours, well-wishers, and so on, who bring gifts (e.g. rice grains, meat, millet and other auspicious items) thus following the local social norms that look at the host family as a provider of meat.

On the day of the sacrifice, the ritual specialist and clan members prepare rice, meat, beer and other counter-offerings for the guests coming from different villages. This is followed by the first animal sacrifice, the ritual slaying of a pig, whose meat is given to family members and close relatives. This is followed by the sacrifice of a chicken. Communal singing and dances are then performed until midnight. (The last part of the ceremony is not restricted to the clan, but is open to the whole village and guests.)

The animal, its death and the sacrificial meat are essential elements in defining community and family kinship during the *murung*. A long procession moves from the village of the host family towards all Apatani villages in the area while the village ritual specialists try to interpret omens. At their return, all those who participated in the festival are offered a complete meal and two pieces of raw meat. Celebration in the form of singing and dancing by young members of the clan may continue for the whole night. The following day, the village shamans are confirmed their prestige and position by the gift of more animals, such as bundles of meat, bacon, dried squirrels, and so on. After observing a period of restriction, the wife of the shaman will sow paddy, and from that moment the cultivation process in the family fields begins.

THE *MYOKO* FESTIVAL

Myoko is generally celebrated in the month of March. It takes place every three years and rotates within three villages. According to the tradition, *myoko* was originally celebrated in a collective form by each Apatani village in the mythical Biri area. Most Apatani intellectuals believe that the Hong village (i.e. Biri) was the first to institutionalize *myoko* rites such as monkey hunting and the construction of a *lapang* (public platform), *babo* (long wooden pole) and *nago* (shrine). These are believed to be the core sacred elements for the celebration of the *myoko* festival.

The hunting of a monkey is necessary for the appeasement of the god Siiki, the father-in-law of Abotani, the primordial female being. Every Apatani village has to hunt a monkey before the actual celebration of festival. Hunters prepare their weapons in advance and observe ritual restrictions that are believed to be conducive to successful hunting. If the hunt is fruitful, the outcome is publicly advertised. The hunters will gather in the house of the altar owner and will be entertained with the meat of the monkey, but also with that of cows. They will be offered rice and abundant rice beer. After this communal meal, the hunters will place the skull and a hand of the monkey on the altar while the ritual specialist will recite a prayer informing the gods that the village will be celebrating the *myoko*.

In earlier days, before the colonial period, the hand of a slain enemy was kept before the *nago* shrine while his tongue was buried under the ritual structure. This performance, called *ropi*, was enacted so as to appease malignant spirits represented by the clan's foes. Quite interestingly, the same ritual was also performed if a ferocious animal like a tiger, a bear, a leopard, and so on, was killed thus showing the belief that ferocious humans (enemies) are alike to animal predators.

When the time of the festival arrives, the *lapang*, *babo* and *nago* are built anew thus replacing pre-existing structures. The community follows strict rules for the erection of the platform, the pole and the sacred altar. This involves a certain artistic effort. The *babo* pole is nicely decorated just as the *nago* is adorned with the finest intricacies. Finally, just as the ritual killing of a monkey opened the *myoko*, the ritual slaying of a pig concludes it. After the complete recitation of a specific hymn (*ropi nii*), the shaman spits rice beer from his mouth on to the *nago bugyang*, a post made of a tree called *kiira*. The spirits must be pleased so once again the shamans of the village—sometimes along with the elders—perform rituals involving haruspicy. This ritual is performed within each household that aspires to offer a pig. Once hepatomancy has been completed successfully (i.e. no bad omen resulting from the reading of livers), pigs are sacrificed at various sacred *lapang*s in the name of *kiiri* and *kiillo* spirits.[8]

ANIMAL SACRIFICE AND ANIMAL HUSBANDRY: THE DEFINITION OF TRIBAL IDENTITY

Von Fürer-Haimendorf (1962: 37–45) was one of the first to give an account of the traditional nature of animal husbandry among the Apatanis in Arunachal Pradesh. He observed that in Apatani economy the breeding of domestic animals plays a secondary role. A very considerable number of mithuns and pigs that the tribe slaughters every year are in fact bought from neighbouring tribes such as the Nyishis and Miris.[9] This custom is of great importance in understanding the relations that the Apatanis held with nearby tribes. In par-

8. The sacrifice of pigs is not mandatory during *myoko*. In fact, it depends upon the decision of the shaman(s). Nevertheless, it is a very popular form of worship in that it is believed to bring long life, prosperity, social recognition of the possibility of obtaining a good matrimony.
9. By Miri von Fürer-Haimendorf was referring to Hill Miris, who now call themselves members of the Nyishi tribe.

ticular it provides elements to reflect on the actual dependency of the Apatanis on the forest as provider of non-domesticated and semi-domesticated animals, and neighbouring tribes as provider of domesticated animals.

A good example is the role played by the mithun. The bovine—irrespective of the way it is obtained—is an important indicator of wealth and economic status in Apatani villages. Moreover, it is usually the medium of exchange for purchasing land. If an Apatani man wants to buy land, he is supposed to sell his surplus grain and get a mithun. This will then be used to buy the land he needs. The price of a bride, but also rents and fines, are also paid with mithuns whereas pigs are the sacrificial animals used on occasion of communal agricultural rites. (If a mithun is used in a similar ritual context, then the festival is used by a family or clan to gain social prestige.)

In 1945 von Fürer-Haimendorf roughly estimated that around two to three thousand mithuns were living in the valley. However, hardly any mithuns were visible. Apatanis told him that if they kept their mithuns near the village or cultivable fields 'there would not be a blade of rice or millet left' (von Fürer-Haimendorf 1962: 37). In fact, the Apatanis still have their own ways of managing mithuns and usually they bring them in the village for festival, fairs or for ritual purposes only.

> Many mithan-owners do not keep their animals in the Apa tani[10] country at all; they give them into the care of Dafla (Nyishi) and Miri friends. Not only are Daflas (Nyishis) and Miris experienced in the keeping of cattle, but their country is also far better suited for mithan than the Apatani valley and they can keep the animal fairly close to their villages without risking a great damage to the crops, their jhum fields being as a rule well fenced in. The reward for keeping another man's mithan is one calf out of three or four according to an agreement...besides the mithan owned by the individuals, there are a number of mithans which are the common property of village or clan, and these are used for sacrifices in the interest of the whole community. Less valuable than mithans, but used in the same manner for sacrifice, as a source of meat and currency, but never milked, are oxen of the small breed common in the plains of Assam.
>
> (Von Fürer-Haimendorf 1962: 38)

When money was not common in the valleys of Arunachal Pradesh, cattle were used as a form of payment between individuals and neighbouring tribes. In a more recent book, von Fürer-Haimendorf noted that:

> The two tribes [the Apatanis and the Nyishis] were economically complementary in so far as the Apa Tanis produced surplus of rice but very little meat, and the Nishis of these villages reared large number of mithans, pigs and goats, but had often to supplement their supply of rice by purchases from Apa Tanis.[11] Alone the village of Tallo sold annually an average of 20 mithans to Apa Tanis, who paid invariably in rice, giving 15-30 carrying baskets of unhusked rice for one mithan

10. Von Fürer-Haimendorf always used 'Apa Tani' instead of 'Apatani' and 'mithan' rather than 'mithun'.
11. These are the Mai, Jorum and Talo villages of the Nyishis.

> or pigs, the price varying according to the size and sex of the animal. Other villages occasionally also bought Apa Tani rice, paying in mithan or pigs, but were less dependant on such purchases than Talo and Jorum, large villages whose jhumland was largely exhausted by long periods of cultivation, while the wet rice they had learnt to cultivate did not cover their requirements.
>
> (Von Fürer-Haimendorf 1982: 53)

Unlike other tribes in Arunachal Pradesh, the Apatanis do not feed their cattle. They never did. Rather they allow bovines to wander over the rice or millet fields once harvesting has been completed. Although they do not pay much attention to their cattle, this is not so as long as breeds are concerned. Even if hybrids have ritual value, the Apatanis hardly promote such idea and prefer to keep mithuns separated by cows.

A further example of animal husbandry as a way to define tribal identity is the use of goats. These are considered by the Apatanis terribly destructive for the crops and therefore they are not valued as an animal per se. Nyishis and Apatanis have contrasting views about having goats roaming in the village, a factor that is mirrored in their rituals, myths and customs. On the one hand, the Nyishis milk goats and let them roam free in the village. On the other, the Apatanis prefer pigs for domestication and keep them in enclosures below their houses. Both animals however can be used for ritual sacrifices. In Von Fürer-Haimendorf's words (1962: 40–42):

> No pigs roam the village streets, for if let loose they would indeed be a serious danger to the rice nurseries, gardens and fields. This necessity of keeping pigs shut up sets a limit on their numbers, for keeping pigs shut up sets a limit on their numbers, for unlike Daflas (Nyishis) or Miri pigs, which find a good deal of food rummaging about the village, the pigs in the Apa Tanis must be fed, and no household can afford more than three or four full-grown pigs at a time... Yet, comparatively few pigs are bred. Apa Tanis find it on the whole more profitable to buy young pigs from Daflas (Nyishis) and Miris, and hundreds of pigs are imported annually into the Apa Tani country... Boars are castrated when two or three months old, and as none are set aside for breeding purpose such sows as are allowed to breed are inseminated by very young boars... The pig is a sacrificial animal indispensable for all communal rites connected with agriculture and there is a good case for the assumption that it is older in Apa Tani culture than the mithan. Pork and bacon are more highly prized than any other meat, and sides of bacon are not only the most acceptable gifts between friends and kinsmen, but are as recognized currency for ceremonial payments.
>
> Fowls are kept by all Apa Tanis for their eggs as well as for their flesh. For the taking of omens and for innumerable minor sacrifices and offerings chicken are needed and on a bamboo structure it is erected on the occasion of a single sacrificial rite one may sometimes count as many as hundred shells of eggs, broken in course of the ritual.

Another important, though rather ambiguous, animal in Apatani culture is the dog. Dogs were originally brought from the plains of Assam but never used for their meat or other practical purposes such as hunting or personal defence. However, dog sacrifices are not unusual at all. Dogs are generally sacrificed in view of hunting expeditions or warfare raids, and they are accepted by the gods during health-seeking rituals, for the recovery of sick people or even as a response to natural disasters or catastrophes. All this indicates that, for the Apatanis, the dog is an important animal from a ritual point of view whereas neighbouring tribes usually despise it and regard it as dirty and impure.

A final example of the use of animals in ritual contexts is that of judicial rituals. Nath (1996: 63) reports that Apatanis used to practise a unique social custom called *lisudu*, a ritual form of judgement in which two families or clans are opposed. During such performance a huge number of mithuns are slaughtered. Each family presents their animals to prove their reasons and validate publically their position. If no more mithuns are available, family members are supposed to buy more. During a *lisudu* trial, the mithuns are gathered and ritually slaughtered while their meat is offered to the entire village. In this way the power and the prestige of the family is confirmed and socially validated by their capacity to take care of the village. While some discuss this as a way to confirm one's own victory in a public arena, others see in it a way to vindicate honour. If, however, the competition crosses a reasonable limit, the *buliang* (council of elders) steps in and stop the fray. Then they try to ensure a compromise to stop the economic ruin of the two competing families.

Von Fürer-Haimendorf too reported of a *lisudu*:

> In 1940 Talyang Bida and Taliyang Pila of Kalung village, who were the sons of two brothers, quarreled over an accusation of theft. Pila's wife had lost some valuable beads and Bida was accused of stealing them. Bida denied any guilt and began the lisudu by slaughtering one mithan at the lapang. The next day Pila killed a mithan at the same lapang, and this went on for twenty days, each slaughtering one mithan on alternating days. The mithan were not their own but were provided by their near kinsmen. Later they paid back some of the mithan but not those contributed by their own brothers and their sister's husbands. Finally, Talyang Bokar, an influential buliang of Kalung, stopped the slaughter, but no compensation was paid by either of the hostile cousins.
>
> (1982: 139–40)

The Austrian ethnographer also provided an alternative analysis of the *lisudu* (Von Fürer-Haimendorf 1962: 41–42). He noted that the mithuns slaughtered on occasion of a ritual trial were distributed between the villagers as well as residents of other settlements in the area. Rich families, apparently, are extremely sensitive about their social prestige and position. As such they often intend *lisudu* as a way to prevent the accumulation of too many resources in the hands of few persons.

ANIMAL SACRIFICE: COPING WITH DOMESTIC AND VILLAGE TRAGEDIES

Among the various events that can possibly strike the life of Apatani villages, fire is one of the most common. The magnitude of such incidents is so devastating, especially if one considers the kind of environment populated by the Apatanis, that it may ruin the economy of a whole area and the lives of several families and clans. Between 2003 to 2007 altogether 37 fire incidents took place as per the District Office record. They caused a loss of about 75 lakh rupees (c. £86,500). Not only do similar events affect food resources and cultivable land. There are also ritual implications. The affected households have to undergo purification rituals (*muchu-darpa kula*) and observe a period of confinement. Such a purification ceremony involves complex and expensive rituals for which they generally call shamans from the neighbouring Nyishi tribe.

The Apatanis understand fire in three different ways: accident, enmity and the evil spirit of fire (Uii-Yamu) which cause major destruction to the households in the villages and may lead to the loss of properties, domesticated animals, grain storage and human life. Despite the degree of damage, there is a specific system of compensation for each kind of fire incident.

Soon after the accident, the owner of the house from where the fire started is required to wait for two or three days so that the houses that were damaged during the fire are reconstructed (or repaired). Soon after reconstruction, the house owner summons a priest or a shaman for an auspicious ceremony, that is, 'testing the egg yolk'. These specialized shamans are usually from the same village. At the presence of the village elders, they start examining an egg yolk in order to see the activity of every possible spirit, both benevolent and malevolent. Once these have been individuated, their requests are listened. They often include the sacrifice of animals such as chickens, dogs, pigs, and sometime cows and mithuns.

The whole day is spent to offer more than 600 eggs. The final decision, however, is taken only in consultation with a Nyishi shaman, as Apatanis believe that rituals involving the invocation of Girii-Yachu Uii (a particular malevolent spirit) should be avoided in that the spirit is too strong and dangerous.

ANIMAL SACRIFICE: RITES OF PASSAGE AND HEALTH-SEEKING PRACTICES

The life of an Apatani is pitted with rituals from the very beginning. The local shaman (*nyibu*) is summoned to protect newborns, pregnant women, women in labour, and so on. Rituals specialists build protective altars that symbolize the mithun and pigs are sacrificed for the same purpose. This is reflected in several myths: 'The sacred lore of the Apatanis reveals that Hiirii was one of the main conspirators against the birth of earth (Chantii), sky (Dotii) and man or Abotani. Then the Nyibu Kolyung Bumya Nyikang [name of a mythical shaman] appeased Hiirii by sacrificing a domestic boar for the proper delivery of both earth and sky' (Yampi 2009: 145–46).

Other significant rites of passage are funerals. These are more complicated if somebody suffered a violent death or in the case of the death of an aged person. The shaman is called to perform *dokho pilya* or *dokho gyamu*, that is, the sacrifice of a hen or dog which is supposed to ensure the traumatized departed soul a safe journey towards *neli* (the abode of the dead). But other sacrifices are required. In the case of an ordinary death, immediately after the completion of the grave or before the corpse is taken out of the house, either a mithun or a cow is to be sacrificed after singing mythical narratives. The animal's role is central in such myths. Not only does it provide sustainment during life. It also acts as a guide in the afterlife thus proving human dependency on cattle.

Apatanis believes in the existence of two forms of netherworlds. These are called *neli* and *tali myoko*. The former is for the souls (*yalo*) of those who died a normal death while the latter is for those who suffered an unnatural or violent death. According to the Apatanis, *neli* is a space very similar to the world previously inhabited by the departed soul. While making his/her journey towards *neli*, a soul is believed to meet Nelkiri, the custodian of the underworld and the guardian of the forefathers. The newly departed soul has to explain how many enemies/ferocious animals have been slain and how many mithuns have been sacrificed. These achievements measure the nature of reception a *yalo* will receive in *neli*. A similar interrogation also happens in *tali myoko* though the quality of life expectancy is always inferior to that of *neli*.

Next in importance are health-seeking rituals. The *su-myoro* is a ritual generally performed in the months of May or June. This requires the ritual slaying of fowls, cows and mithuns. Such offerings are directed towards nature gods and goddesses so as to obtain protection from dramatic events such as diseases, famines and epidemics. Equally important is *yapung*, a rite performed in the last phase of the agricultural cycle when crops are ripe. This ritual is done by sacrificing pigs or fowls to avoid heavy rains, hailstorms or other natural calamities that may then cause diseases. It also demands observation of certain restrictions which are sanctioned with the imposition of fines in cash or equivalent.

CATTLE AND CUSTOMARY LAWS

Traditionally the Apatanis used to settle their disputes through the village council and by utilizing their own customary laws (e.g. *lisudu*). In most of the cases, when it came to deciding an appropriate form of punishment, this was established in the form of giving animals. Today, with the penetration of state machinery and a new judicial system, many people are opting for other forms of repayment. This, however, does not mean that traditional customs have been abandoned. Rather there is an attempt to merge the modern Indian judicial system with the oral laws of the Apatanis. Here follows an example from the Law Research Institute of Gauhati High Court (2007):

> In case of adultery, the village authority imposes punishment and fine on the offender. According to the customary law of the Apatani if a woman is found to have committed adultery, then no fine is imposed on her rather wife's lover will be fined. A wife can be divorced immediately and if her husband keeps her then the man who committed adultery, has to pay the fine of one mithun costing 14,000 rupees which is termed as *hinyang*. However, if husband divorces her on the ground on the ground of adultery then such fine is not required to be paid. In case husband himself is involved in adultery, the case stands on a different footing and he will be required to pay one mithun costing 14,000 rupees along with a *lama dao* (Tibetan sword). In case any unmarried woman gives birth to a child and if the man, responsible for her pregnancy, does not want to accept the child as well as the mother as his wife, then the man would be required to pay the fine in the form of giving one mithun, one cow, one *endi* chadar (wrapper made of *endi* thread having highly valued traditionally) and one *dao* (big knife).
>
> (Barooah 2007: 85–86)

Such multiple cases show how bovines are valued within Apatani society. Precisely because of the socio-cultural and economic value of cattle, any theft case related to mithun and cows (but also other animals such as pigs, dogs, etc.) is presented as a heavily punishable offence (Barooah 2007: 86–88) and examined according to the traditional tribal customs before being passed onto the institutional mechanism of federal law.[12]

CONCLUSION

The intention of this chapter was to illustrate the role of animals in one specific tribe of Arunachal Pradesh, the Apatanis, and particularly to discuss animal sacrifice. I have explored the role of animals in mythical narratives as well as in ritual settings. In particular I have emphasized how animals—through the practice of sacrifice—are essential to the life of the tribe and its clans. Animals are sacrificed to maintain order and cosmic balance between human animals, non-human animals and other-than-human entities. Animals, one can even say, are sacrificed because they are the best offering ever possible. The ritual sacrifice of non-human animals such as mithuns, cows, monkeys, dogs, poultry, and so on, is not a violent act per se. Rather it seems to have a function and meaning that goes beyond mere action, as suggested by Mitchell (2002: 490). The sacrificial killing of non-human animals has implications for the relationships between religion, politics, econ-

12. A descriptive account of various fines in relation to animal theft is given in Barooah (2007: 86-88). The General Body of the Apatanis, made of chiefs and leaders, officers, the council of the elders (*buliang*), law experts etc., had meetings between 1992 and 2003. They decided to compile the laws of the Tribe on the basis of indigenous traditional customs and practices. The detailed text of such laws is given in Barooah (2007: 119–50). One can also appreciate the nature of the transition from oral to textual culture.

omy and society in general. This discourse also brings to the surface important ecological perspectives, mostly based on the way the environment is determined by the way neighbouring tribes such as the Apatanis and the Nyishis negotiate with each other in the available limited physical space. With the impact of Hindu traditions, Christianity and the implementation of national and regional administrative systems, the traditional religious beliefs and practices of the Apatanis are passing through a critical phase. Apatanis, known as one of the most progressive tribes of the state, have widened their cognitive horizon according to a globalized world. In so doing they have reshaped their social boundaries and inter-ethnic relations. Contemporary contexts, within which Apatanis are trying to negotiate, have inevitably reduced their traditional dependence on local ritual specialists or shamans and attenuated sacred and secular space densely linked with non-human animals. The Apatanis, however, have retained many of their traditional festivities, myths and rituals and so they have once again asserted their dependency on non-human animals whose sacrifice becomes a way to perpetuate and assert the cultural identity of their clans.

REFERENCES

Barooah, J. 2007. *Customary Laws of the Apatanis of Arunachal Pradesh with Special Reference to their Land Holding System*. Guahati: Law Research Institute.

Fürer-Haimendorf, C. von. 1955. *The Himalayan Barbary*. London: Press of Glencoe.

— 1962. *The Apatanis and their Neighbours*. London: Routledge & Kegan Paul.

— 1980. *A Himalayan Tribe: From Cattle to Cash*. Ghaziabad: Vikash Publications.

— 1982. *Hailanders of Arunachal Pradesh: Anthropological Research In North-East India*. New Delhi: Vikas Publications.

Kani, T. 1996. *Socio-religious Ceremonies of Arunachal Pradesh*. Guwahati: Purbadesh Mudran.

Mills, J. P. 1947. 'Tours in the Balipara Frontier Tract, Assam.' *Man in India* 27: 4–35.

Mitchell, J. P. 2002. 'Ritual.' In A. Barnard, and J. Spencer (eds), *Encyclopedia of Social and Cultural Anthropology*: 736–42. London: Routledge.

Nath, D. 1996. 'Apatani Agriculture.' Unpublished MPhil dissertation. Itanagar: Department of Tribal Studies, Arunachal University.

Simoons, F. J., and E. S. Simoons. 1968. *A Ceremonial Ox of India: Mithan in Nature, Culture and History*. Madison: The University of Wisconsin Press.

Yabyang, K. 2006. 'A Study of the Murung Festival of Apatanis.' Unpublished MPhil dissertation. Itanagar: Arunachal Institute of Tribal Studies, Rajiv Gandhi University.

Yampi, R. 2009. 'Religious Specialists of the Apatanis: Aspects of their Nature, Structure and Change.' Unpublished PhD dissertation. Itanagar: Arunachal Institute of Tribal Studies, Rajiv Gandhi University.

Karman and Compassion: Animals in the Jain Universal History

EVA DE CLERCQ*

A key outward characteristic of the Jain ideology is its efforts to ensure the welfare of animals. This is one of the first features which European colonizers described when they came into contact with the Jains (Glasenapp 1999: 4; Bender 1976: 116). Accounts of Jains entering the political arena to advocate animal protection are plenty. The most notable was the Śvetāmbara monk Hīravijaya who convinced the Mughal emperor Akbar to order a prohibition on the killing of animals around the sacred places and on festive days of the Jains (Dundas 2002: 145–47; Jaini 1998: 283–84; Glasenapp 1999: 74–77). World renowned are the numerous charitable animal hospitals (*pāñjarāpol*) run by Jains in accordance with Jain ideology (Lodrick 1981). Since 1990, individuals and organizations representing Jain communities in India and in the diaspora are striving to bring the Jain philosophy to the forefront of the global environmentalist movement, as a supreme ecology and defence of animal life, which has existed in India for over two millennia.[1]

This preoccupation with animal welfare is a practical manifestation of the vow of *ahiṃsā*, 'non-injury', central to Jain ethics and ideology. The importance of the *ahiṃsā* principle is related to the belief, which Jains share with other Indic traditions, that a soul migrates between subsequent bodies, either human, animal, plant, infernal or divine, through the workings of *karman*. Causing injury, in the broadest sense, to a being results in the accumulation of demerit (*pāpa*) and a subsequent birth in a less favourable existence. Thus, according to this belief system, we may ourselves be reborn as an animal in a future life, or we may have been an animal in a previous life. The grey dove on

* Eva De Clercq completed her doctorate at Ghent University in Oriental Languages and Cultures (2003) with a critical study of Svayambhūdeva's Paumacariu, a Jain version in Apabhraṃśa of the Rāmāyaṇa, part of which is published as *The Apabhraṃśa of Svayambhūdeva's Paumacariu* (2009, Mumbai: Hindi Granth Karyalay). Since then, she has worked as a postdoctoral fellow on the Jain versions of the Sanskrit epics and Apabhraṃśa language and literature, and spent some years as a research fellow at the University of Würzburg. In 2010 she became Assistant Professor at Ghent University at the Department of Languages and Cultures of South and East Asia, where she teaches Sanskrit and Indian Literature.

1. An overview of international activities of such organizations is provided in Caillat (2009: 123–28). For discussions on Jainism and modern global environmentalism, see the papers in Chapple (2002).

our windowsill or our pet dog may be the incarnation of the soul of a loved one who has passed away. The essence of any creature, its soul, is not valued less than that of a human. It is only because of its specific collected karmic baggage at the time of its last death, that this soul has been reborn in an animal existence. Nevertheless, a life as an animal, a *tiryañc* (literally 'going horizontally', and referring to animals and plants), is considered the lowest form of existence. The *tiryañc* category of beings is divided into widely varying subgroups, depending on the number of sense faculties and on whether or not they have the capacity to reason, ranging from the *nigoda*, one-sensed, submicroscopic organisms at the bottom end, to five-sensed animals such as fish, birds, reptiles, amphibians and mammals at the top end (Jaini 1998: 108–11).

Like the famous Buddhist *jātaka* tales, Jain stories of transmigrating souls in animal existences are popular didactic tools for bringing across the theory of karm, and abound in Jain narrative literature, including the so-called 'universal history' of the Jains, a corpus of texts which narrate the traditional history of all creatures, naturally emphasizing humankind. Their focus is the biographies of a specific number, mostly 63, of heroes, the *śalākāpuruṣas* or *mahāpuruṣas*, 'great men' who are believed to have lived in the current era. These texts, which are called *purāṇas* or *caritas*, are considered a counter-tradition for the rise of Purāṇic Hinduism and as such include Jain variants of popular Hindu gods, protagonists and stories, such as Rāma and Kr̥ṣṇa (Jaini 2000: 375–428; Cort 1993). The 63 *śalākāpuruṣas* comprise 24 *tīrthaṃkaras*, 'ford makers' or *jinas*, 'conquerors', prophet-like persons, born after long intervals in time, who realize omniscience (*kevala*) and subsequently spread the Jain faith in the world, 12 *cakravartins*, 'universal emperors' who each bring the six parts of Bhārata under a single dominion, and nine triads of *baladevas, vāsudevas* and *prativāsudevas*, who live simultaneously. The *baladeva* is the half-brother of the *vāsudeva*, who is destined to kill their common enemy, the *prativāsudeva*. Rāma and Kr̥ṣṇa belong to these triads as respectively the eighth *baladeva* and ninth *vāsudeva*. A full list of the 63 *śalākāpuruṣas* is provided in Table 1.[2] Longer lists include additional categories, such as the mothers and fathers of the *tīrthaṃkaras*, 24 *kāmadevas*, 11 *rudras*, 9 *nāradas* and 14 *kulakaras* under the *śalākāpuruṣas*.[3]

Table 1. The 63 *śalākāpuruṣas*

Tīrthaṃkara	Cakravartin	Baladeva	Vāsudeva	Prativāsudeva
R̥ṣabha	Bharata			
Ajita	Sagara			
Sambhava				

2. When different, the Śvetāmbara accounts, based on Hemacandra's *Triṣaṣṭiśalākāpuruṣacarita* are marked with an asterisk (*), the Digambara accounts, based on Jinasena's and Guṇabhadra's *Mahāpurāṇa*, are marked with a plus sign (+).
3. As in the Digambara treatise on cosmology *Tiloyapaṇṇatti* 4.1473.

Abhinandana				
Sumati				
Padmaprabha				
Supārśva				
Candraprabha				
Suvidhi (Puṣpadanta)				
Śītala				
Śreyāṃsa		+Acala/*Vijaya	Tripṛṣṭha	Aśvagrīva
Vāsupūjya		+Vijaya/*Acala	Dvipṛṣṭha	Tāraka
Vimala		+Bhadra/*Dharma	Svayambhū	+Meraka/ *Madhu
Ananta		Suprabha	Puruṣottama	+Madhu/ *Madhusūdana
Dharma	Maghavan	Sudarśana	Puruṣasiṃha	+Niśumbha/ *Madhukrīḍa
	Sanatkumāra			
Śānti	(Śānti)			
Kunthu	(Kunthu)			
Ara	(Ara)	+Ānanda/ *Nandiṣeṇa	+Puruṣapuṇḍarīka/ *Puṇḍarīka	+Bali/ *Niśumbha
	+Subhūma/ *Subhauma	+Nandana	+Datta	+Prahlāda
Malli	*Padma	*Nandimitra	*Datta	*Balīndra
Munisuvrata	+Mahāpadma *Hariṣeṇa	Padma (Rāma)	Lakṣmaṇa	Rāvaṇa
Nami	+Hariṣeṇa			
	Jayasena			
Nemi	Brahmadatta	Balarāma	Kṛṣṇa	Jarāsandha
Pārśva				
Mahāvīra				

Literary compositions on the Jain universal history contain different definitions of what a Jain *purāṇa* should entail (De Clercq 2005). Some authors explicitly mention that it should treat the *gatis*, the four modes of existence: (1) human, (2) hell being, (3) divine being or (4) *tiryañc*. This chapter will present an overview of the various kinds of animal presences in these Jain universal histories, literally, in the encounters between *śalākāpuruṣas* and animals, and figuratively, in the symbolic value of certain animal occurrences, and will conclude with an excursus on animal sacrifice.[4]

4. We leave out the abundant poetic metaphors and similes in the compositions under scru-

ANIMALS AS SYMBOLS

In the biographies of its heroes, particularly in the stories of the most revered *tīrthaṃkaras*, Jain authors make ample use of pan-Indian animal symbolism. They hereby deliver implicit additional emphasis on certain aspects of *tīrthaṃkara* identity, and position the Jain heroes, and ultimately the entire Jain doctrine, in wider South Asian society and culture.

DREAMS OF THE MOTHERS

A typically Jain feature regarding the biographies of the *śalākāpuruṣas* is that, when their soul descends into the womb of their mother, the mother has a number of dreams, or rather a succession of images which appear to her in a dream. These images seem to relate to the place in the hierarchy held by the *śalākāpuruṣa* category, though there is no complete consensus among authors from the different branches of Jainism. Śvetāmbaras list the number of images of the mother of a *tīrthaṃkara* and a *cakravartin* as 14, of the mother of a *vāsudeva* as seven, and of a *baladeva*'s mother as four.[5] According to Digambara authors, the mother of a *tīrthaṃkara* sees 16 images in a dream, but there is disagreement with regard to the other *śalākāpuruṣas*.[6] All authors however agree that the first three images seen by the mother of a *tīrthaṃkara* are always of an elephant, a bull and a lion. Some authors explicit that these animals are white, and sometimes the elephant is described as having four tusks, resembling Indra's divine mount Airāvata. The significance of this dream motif is evident from the fact that it recurs in an important temple ritual, in which the *pañca-kalyāṇakas*, five auspicious events in the life of a *tīrthaṃkara*, are re-enacted and celebrated. One of these auspicious events is the dream experienced by the mother (Jaini 1998: 196–99). It is also a favourite subject in Jain pictorial and sculptural art. The elephant, bull and lion as the first elements perceived by the mother are very telling for how the Jains view and honour their spiritual leaders. All three are well-known as symbols of kingship and empire, at least since the time of the Aśokan pillars, where these three were favoured as capitals (Geer 2008: 26). Even though the vast majority of Jains since centuries have belonged to merchant classes, all the *tīrthaṃkaras* were born in royal families. According to Śvetāmbara accounts, Mahāvīra's soul first descended into the womb of a Brahmin woman, only to be

---

tiny. Compositions, narrating (part of) the Jain universal history, included in this study are the *Mahāpurāṇa* of Jinasena and Guṇabhadra, the *Harivaṃśapurāṇa* of Jinasena Punnāṭa, the *Paumacariyam* of Vimalasūri and the *Triṣaṣṭiśalākāpuruṣacarita* of Hemacandra.

5. This is the case in the best known and authoritative Śvetāmbara *purāṇa*: the *Triṣaṣṭiśalākāpuruṣacarita* by Hemacandra.

6. Guṇabhadra's *Mahāpurāṇa* (14.123-29) mentions six dreams for the mother of a *cakravartin*. The *Harivaṃśa Purāṇa* of Jinasena Punnāṭa (34.13-15) describes seven dreams of the mother of the *vāsudeva* Kṛṣṇa. For an overview of different accounts, see Chandra (1970: 384–87).

later transposed by divine intervention into the womb of a *kṣatriya* lady, underlining the importance of the *kṣatriya* identity of *tīrthaṃkaras*.[7] Every *tīrthaṃkara* is by birth destined for a political career, but instead chooses to renounce earthly kingship to become a spiritual leader. The symbolism of the elephant, bull and lion seen by the mother in a dream can be seen as reflections of the royal affiliations of the *tīrthaṃkaras*.[8]

MARKS OF THE TĪRTHAṂKARAS

Aside from the animals in the dream of the mothers, there is another way in which animals occur as symbols in some biographies of the *tīrthaṃkaras*. Hemacandra describes how every *tīrthaṃkara* is born with a particular *lāñchana*, 'mark', a list of which is provided in Table 2.[9]

Table 2. *Tīrthaṃkaras* and their marks

Tīrthaṃkara	Mark
Ṛṣabha	bull
Ajita	elephant
Sambhava	horse
Abhinandana	monkey
Sumati	*curlew (krauñca)/+cuckoo (koka)
Padmaprabha	red lotus (padma)
Supārśva	*svastika/+nandyāvarta
Candraprabha	(half) moon
Suvidhi/Puṣpadanta	makara (crocodile)[11]
Śītala	*śrīvatsa / +svastika
Śreyāṃsa	rhinoceros

7. Note that this episode is absent in the Digambara biographies of Mahāvīra. There he directly descends into the womb of the kṣatriya woman Triśalā.
8. In Śvetāmbara accounts, the dreams of the mother of a *tīrthaṃkara* and of a *cakravartin* are identical. Three *tīrthaṃkaras* of the present era experienced a fruitful career as a full *cakravartin* before renouncing the world and becoming a *tīrthaṃkara*. The Digambara accounts, which only list six dreams announcing the birth of a *cakravartin*, do not refer to any of these three animals, instead mentioning other generally considered auspicious symbols. With regard to the *tīrthaṃkaras* Śānti, Kunthu and Ara, who were *cakravartins* prior to becoming *tīrthaṃkaras*, Guṇabhadra's *Uttarapurāṇa* lists the 16 dreams for a *tīrthaṃkara*. For more on the notions of kingship in Jainism, see Babb (1993, 1994 and 1996).
9. *Tiloyapaṇṇatti* 4.604-605 uses the term *cihna*, 'mark' instead of *lāñchana*. Shah (1987: 83) translates the term as 'cognizance'. When accounts differ, Śvetāmbara variants based on Hemacandra's *Triṣaṣṭiśalākāpuruṣacarita* are marked with an asterisk (*), Digambara accounts based on the *Tiloyapaṇṇatti* are marked with a plus sign (+).

Vāsupūjya	buffalo
Vimala	boar
Ananta	*hawk/+porcupine[12]
Dharma	thunderbolt
Śānti	deer
Kunthu	(he-)goat
Ara	*nandyāvarta/+fish[13]
Malli	jar (kalaśa)
Munisuvrata	tortoise
Nami	blue lotus
Nemi	conch
Pārśva	serpent
Mahāvīra	lion

In 16 out of 24 cases, these marks are animals. The origin and meaning of this motif remains vague, though they appear to be a later phenomenon, since such marks are not mentioned as regular attributes of *tīrthaṃkaras* in the earlier biographies predating Hemacandra, except the *Āvaśyakaniryukti* (early sixth century), which states that Ṛṣabha was born with the mark of a bull on his thigh.[13] The addition of this motif in the *tīrthaṃkara* biographies appears to stem from the prominence of these *lāñchanas* in iconographic representations of the *tīrthaṃkaras*, where they are engraved on the pedestal of the icon and are generally the only identifier differentiating between the 24 *tīrthaṃkaras.*[14] According to Shah (1987: 85) they begin to occur regularly in artistic representations of the *tīrthaṃkaras* from the fifth century onwards. Prior to that, from the second or first century BCE, a mark associated with a particular *tīrthaṃkara* seems to have been positioned on a pedestal or a pillar in front of a *tīrthaṃkara*

10. According to Shah (1987: 84), the *Pratiṣṭhāsāroddhāra* (1228), a Digambara manual by Āśādhāra on the installation of *tīrthaṃkara* images has a crab as the emblem of Puṣpadanta.
11. *Tiloyapaṇṇatti* 4.605 reads *sāhī*, interpreted by the Hindi commentator as 'porcupine' (see also Turner 1966-1985: §12766 śvāvidh-). Hemacandra's text is quite clear (śyena, in *Triṣaṣṭiśalākāpuruṣacarita* 4.4.29). According to Shah (1987: 84), *Pratiṣṭhāsāroddhāra* mentions a bear as the emblem of Ananta.
12. *Tiloyapaṇṇatti* 4.605 reads *taragakusumā*, 'floating flower'. The Hindi commentator interprets this as fish.
13. Note that Hemacandra also specifies that Ṛṣabha was born with the mark of a bull on his thigh. For the other *tīrthaṃkaras* he is not specific with regard to where or how this 'mark' should be visualized.
14. The exception is the image of Pārśva who is typically represented together with the serpent Dharaṇendra.

shrine or image, as is evidenced from *āyāgapaṭas* from Kaṅkālī Ṭīlā dating from the first century CE (Shah 1987: 87; Quintanilla 2000: 86). In a subsequent phase, the mark was portrayed twice at the end of the pedestal flanking a *dharmacakra*, 'wheel of the faith', and only after that the emblem became central and the wheel was dropped. Cort (2010: 213–14) considers the fact that, excepting Pārśva, images of the different 24 *tīrthaṃkaras* would be unintelligible, were it not for the presence of the mark in the seat of the icon, as a deliberate strategy connected to the theological concept of the *tīrthaṃkara* as a transcendent divinity, at the same time singular and plural. This idea is supported by the fact that the Śvetāmbara term *lāñchana* holds the connotation of 'stain, blemish', whereby the abstract transcendent divinity is somehow stained by the addition of the embodying marker. Striving towards coherence between the textual and iconographic representation of the *tīrthaṃkaras*, Hemacandra seems to have been the first to include references to the different marks in his biographies. With regard to the choice of a specific mark for a specific *tīrthaṃkara*, Shah refers to a verse in Āśādhāra's *Pratiṣṭhāsāroddhāra*, which says that the mark on a *jina* icon is that 'which is recognized individually on account of [his] family, greatly honorable in the world'.[15] Shah interprets this as denoting the charges of heraldry (*dhvajas*) which, according to him, every *kṣatriya* family possessed.[16] It thus seems that, with the gradual extension of the list of *tīrthaṃkaras* to 24 and a growing need to differentiate among them in iconographic representation, the idea rose to assign an insignia to each *tīrthaṃkara*. Not only did this pragmatically enable artists to embody the individual *tīrthaṃkara*, but in so doing it again underscored the warrior descent and nature of the *tīrthaṃkara*.

ANIMAL ENCOUNTERS IN THE UNIVERSAL HISTORY

ANIMALS AS PREVIOUS EXISTENCES

A significant part of the biographies of the great heroes in the Jain *purāṇas* concerns their previous existences. Accounts of previous births as animals are relatively rare among the śalākāpuruṣas. This seems to relate to the relatively low status of an animal existence, as opposed to the comparatively high spiritual maturity of most of these heroes. The last *cakravartin* Brahmadatta, for instance, long before his birth as a *śalākāpuruṣa*, experienced an existence as a deer, in which he was killed by a hunter, followed by a life as a swan, in which he died at the hands of a fisherman.[17] Even though he reached a superior state of martial valour as a *cakravartin*, he was not very evolved

15. *vaṃśe jagatpūjyatame pratītaṃ pṛthagvidhaṃ tīrthakṛttāṃ yad atra.* Author's translation. *tal lāñchanaṃ saṃvyavahārasiddhayai bimbe jinasyeha niveśayāmi* (from Shah 1987: 108).

16. Warriors having individual emblems are described in *Mahābhārata* 4.50.4-22, 7.80.2-29, 6.17.18-39 and 6.45.7-33 (cf. Brockington 1998: 185).

17. *Triṣaṣṭiśalākāpuruṣacarita* 9.1.16-20 (Johnson 1931-1962: vol. 5, 318).

spiritually, committing grave sins which lead to a rebirth in hell.[18] A parallel situation occurs in the previous lives of the *Rāmāyaṇa* characters. After an existence in which the souls of four protagonists Rāma, Lakṣmaṇa, Sītā and Rāvaṇa coexisted and interacted, and in which the enmity between the souls of Lakṣmaṇa and Rāvaṇa for the sake of Sītā is introduced, Rāma's soul goes through a number of existences as a human or in heaven, completely separated from the souls of Lakṣmaṇa, Sītā and Rāvaṇa, who are reborn in subsequent animal existences in a forest, fighting each other incessantly: deer, boars, elephants, buffaloes, oxen, monkeys, and many unnamed others.[19] In concordance with Brahmadatta's case, the *baladeva* Rāma attains omniscience and escapes *saṃsāra*, 'the cycle of transmigration', forever, whereas Lakṣmaṇa and Rāvaṇa are born in hell, Sītā in heaven. Thus, there appears to be a tendency in the Jain *purāṇas* that animal existences in the not too distant past indicate a lower level of spiritual development. There are, however, important exceptions to this tendency in the accounts of *tīrthaṃkaras* who were animals in a relatively recent previous life.

The narrations of the previous existences of the most popular of the *tīrthaṃkaras*, Mahāvīra, Pārśva, Nemi and Śānti, tend to be the most drawn out and complex. In a previous life, Mahāvīra was Tripṛṣṭha, the first *vāsudeva* of this era. It is predicted that the first *prativāsudeva*, Aśvagrīva, will be killed by whoever kills the lion living near his rice fields. Aśvagrīva asks Tripṛṣṭha to protect the rice fields from the lion. Tripṛṣṭha goes to the lion's cave and challenges the animal. The lion attacks and Tripṛṣṭha tears him into two pieces in a very heroic way and accompanied by auspicious occurrences, such as a rain of flowers, fragrant wind, and so on.[20] When Tripṛṣṭha has later fulfilled his destiny by killing the *prativāsudeva* Aśvagrīva, he dies and is reborn in one of the hells. After that, he is himself reborn as a lion on a mountain near the Gaṅgā (Ganges river). Because of the sins committed as a predatory animal, the lion after death is born in hell, after which he is again reborn as a lion in the Himālaya. One day, as he is eating a deer which he had just caught, two *munis* (ascetic sages) pass by. They halt and instruct the lion about its previous existence as Tripṛṣṭha and his subsequent lives as a hell-being and as a lion near the Gaṅgā. The lion remembers and begins to weep. After hearing the narration of his other previous existences, the lion bows to the *munis*, encircles them in reverence and takes up the vows of a layman. He commences a fast, dies and is reborn in heaven.[21] Later, he will be born as Mahāvīra, marked with a lion.

18. *Triṣaṣṭiśalākāpuruṣacarita* 9.1.600 (Johnson 1931–1962: vol. 5, 355).
19. Vimalasūri's *Paumacariyam* 103.1-123. Note that Hemacandra 7.10.24 only mentions the existence as deer. This account is absent in Guṇabhadra's *Uttarapurāṇa*. For variations in the different Jain Rāma stories, cf. Chandra (1970: 187–91).
20. *Triṣaṣṭiśalākāpuruṣacarita* 4.1.394-406 (Johnson 1931–1962: vol. 3, 28–29); the account of Tripṛṣṭha killing the lion is absent in the *Uttarapurāṇa*.
21. *Mahāpurāṇa* 74.120-219; *Triṣaṣṭiśalākāpuruṣacarita* 10.1.182 (Johnson 1931–1962: vol. 6, 14). Note that Hemacandra does not give a description of the life of Mahāvīra as a lion.

Another popular account of a *tīrthaṃkara* as an animal in his previous existence is found in the biography of Mahāvīra's predecessor, the twenty-third *tīrthaṃkara* Pārśva. After concluding a life as a pious man in 'painful meditation' (*ārta-dhyāna*), while being stoned to death by his own brother, the soul of Pārśva is born as an elephant in the forest. In this elephant existence, he is reminded of his previous life by a *muni*. The elephant accepts the layman's vows and is killed by a *kukkuṭa* serpent, who was his murderous brother from his previous life. He is subsequently born in heaven.[22] This story demonstrates the frequently recurrent motif of *ārta-dhyāna* as leading to an animal existence. Jains classify meditation (*dhyāna*) into four types, two of which can occur spontaneously, but may be detrimental to one's spiritual advancement, and which are therefore to be avoided. The first of these two is *ārta-dhyāna*, the preoccupation with something unpleasant or painful, such as thinking of a lost thing or person, thinking of something disagreeable, physical or mental pain, or longing for unattainable objects (Jaini 1998: 252; Glasenapp 1999: 236–37). The motif of a person dying while performing *ārta-dhyāna*, and being reborn as an animal on account of it, is common in Jain narratives.[23]

More importantly both stories of Pārśva's and Mahāvīra's previous existence as an animal exemplify that all five-sensed animals, possessed of a mind, are capable to advance on the path towards spiritual liberation. A being in heaven and in hell is never able to make spiritual progress, which is reserved exclusively to humans and the higher category *tiryañc*. After hearing a *muni* give instruction, or otherwise remembering its previous existence, an animal can take up a form of the layman's vows, such as fasting, refraining from injuring other beings, and so on. Its reward is a better existence in its next life, either as a human, so that it may continue its spiritual advancement, or as a being in one of the heavens.[24]

When comparing the animal existences of the two *tīrthaṃkaras* with those of the *cakravartin* Brahmadatta and the *vāsudeva* Lakṣmaṇa and *prativāsudeva* Rāvaṇa, one can distinguish a hierarchy paralleling their positions as *śalākāpuruṣas*. It is probably no coincidence that Pārśva and Mahāvīra were an elephant and a lion, the most regal of the animals, in a former life, again underlining the royal aspect of the *tīrthaṃkara*. The existences of the lower *śalākāpuruṣas* as deer, swans, and so on, appear, in comparison, much more trivial. Moreover, there seems to be a greater multiplicity and random-

22. *Triṣaṣṭiśalākāpuruṣacarita* 9.2.56-108 (Johnson 1931–1962: vol. 5, 359–63); Bloomfield (1985: 39); *Mahāpurāṇa* 73.12-24. The popular stories of Pārśva's previous existences are performed during the annual *Pauṣ Daśmī* festival. For a description, see Babb (1996: 26–32).

23. See, for instance, the story of Daṇḍaka in *Triṣaṣṭiśalākāpuruṣacarita* 1.1.435 (Johnson 1931-1962: vol. 1, 45). On *ārta-dhyāna* leading to a rebirth as a *tiryañc*, see Varni (1997–2000: vol. 1, 275).

24. From Jaini's study (2000: 253–66) it appears that the concept of animals pursuing spiritual progress by taking over the behaviour of pious laymen was also common in Buddhism.

ness of animal births among the lower *śalākāpuruṣas*, absent in that of the *tīrthaṃkaras*.

EFFECT OF THE TĪRTHAṂKARAS *ON ANIMALS*

There are many instances in the universal history of animals being in the presence of a *tīrthaṃkara* and benefitting after hearing a sermon. Such accounts emphasize that Jainism is a universal ideology, the benefits of which can be experienced by all creatures.

This universality is evident from the *samavasaraṇa*, the 'universal preaching hall' which is constructed by the gods every time a *tīrthaṃkara* holds a sermon. When a *tīrthaṃkara* has reached omniscience, the gods hurry to the place where he or she is located. They cleanse the surface of the earth, sprinkle it with fragrant water, cover the area with gold, gems and flowers, and build jewelled arches in the four directions. Then they construct an inner rampart of gems, a second rampart of gold and a third outer rampart of silver. In the middle of the *samavasaraṇa*, a tree is placed over a jewelled platform with a throne for the *tīrthaṃkara* to sit. Gods and humans take place in the enclosure closest to the *jina*, within the first rampart. Animals take place within the second rampart, and the space within the third rampart is reserved for the animal vehicles of the gods.[25] Every creature becomes blissful listening to the words of the *jina*, abandoning their instinctive enmities and fears, as described by Ṛṣabha's son on the occasion of the first *samavasaraṇa*:

> This elephant has come to your assembly and, drawing with his trunk the lion's paw, frequently scratches his temple. Now the buffalo rubs the neighing horse with his tongue frequently from affection, as if he were another buffalo. The deer here, with pricked-up ears and his tail waving from pleasure, his face bent, smells the tiger's face with his nose. This young cat embraces the mouse running at his side, in front, and behind, as if it were his own offspring. This serpent, fearless, coiled in a circle, sits like a friend in the vicinity of a large ichneumon. O Lord, whatever creatures have been eternal enemies, they remain here free from hostility. For this is your unequaled power.[26]

A remarkable story of an animal receiving instruction takes place at the *samavasaraṇa* of the twentieth Tīrthaṃkara Munisuvrata in Bhṛgukaccha, modern day Bharuch. The first disciple (*gaṇadhara*) of Munisuvrata asks who has adopted the Jain *dharma* at the *samavasaraṇa*. Munisuvrata replies that no one has adopted it, except the high-bred horse of the king. The king requests to hear the story of the horse and Munisuvrata explains that in its previous

25. These vehicles are regarded as a low category of gods, the Abhiyogas. See Varni (1997–2000: vol. 1, 130). Some descriptions, such as that of Jinasena in his Ādipurāṇa (chapter 22 and 23) go into great detail on the construction of the *samavasaraṇa*.
26. *Triṣaṣṭiśalākāpuruṣacarita* 1.3.543-49 (as translated by Johnson 1931–1962: vol. 1, 198–99).

life, the horse was a pious merchant who had a golden statue of a *jina* made. One day he went to a Śaiva temple where priests were moving jars of ghee, crushing the many ants that had clustered beneath the jars. When the merchant noticed this, he began gently to remove the ants with his garment out of compassion. Feeling insulted, one priest crushed the ants with his feet. The merchant nevertheless gave ear to the instruction of a Śaiva *ācārya* there, performed the Śaiva rites and was therefore reborn as a horse, nevertheless by nature possessing good character. Munisuvrata adds that he has come to that place to enlighten the horse. The king then sets the horse free and from then on, this place, Bhṛgukaccha, is the sacred place Aśvāvabodha, a famous Śvetāmbara pilgrimage site.[27] A rebirth as a high-bred horse is here considered to be among the best of animal births. The merchant is said to owe this to his liberality and the fact that he had installed a golden icon of the *tīrthaṃkara*. His birth as the horse of a king enabled him to come into the presence of Munisuvrata and ultimately progress spiritually on the Jain path to salvation.[28]

Independent of a *samavasaraṇa* is the following important encounter with an animal from Pārśva's biography. As a prince, before renouncing the world, Pārśva one day went to view the penances of an ascetic. He noticed a snake trapped in a piece of wood in a fire. He ordered the wood to be taken from the fire. The snake was already burnt and with compassion, Pārśva recited the *namaskāra mantra* to it. As a result of the auspiciousness from hearing the mantra, the snake died in meditation and was reborn as the Nāgakumāra god Dharaṇendra. Later he protected Pārśva when he was attacked by his transmigratory enemy, who created a storm to hinder his ascetic practice. This story is moreover behind the famous iconographic representation of Pārśva with Dharaṇendra.[29]

An account from Mahāvīra's biography illustrates his compassion for all living beings and the overall enlightening power of the presence of a *tīrthaṃkara*. While roaming, Mahāvīra one day passes a place where an angry serpent lived. People advise him not to go near the animal. Mahāvīra knew of the circumstances under which this soul had the misfortune of being born a serpent: he was an ascetic who one day kicked a frog and chose to ignore it. When his disciple remarked that he had 'forgotten' to confess his injury to the frog, the ascetic angrily rushed upon the boy with murder on his mind, but ran into a pillar and died. After an existence as a god, the soul of the ascetic was born as a man, the bad-tempered abbot of a group of ascetics. One day, while angrily trying to kill someone, he fell on his own axe, splitting his own head. He was then born as the angry serpent. Mahāvīra enters the

27. Its story is narrated in the pilgrimage manual *Vividhatīrthakalpa* of Jinaprabhasūri (fourteenth century) as *kalpa* 10. Note that the Digambara texts are completely silent about this episode. The pilgrimage site Aśvāvabodha appears to be exclusively Śvetāmbara.

28. *Triṣaṣṭiśalākāpuruṣacarita* 6.7.198-220 (Johnson 1931–1962: vol. 4, 85–87).

29. *Triṣaṣṭiśalākāpuruṣacarita* 9.3.217-27 (Johnson 1931–1962: vol. 5, 392); *Mahāpurāṇa* 74.101-19 and 74.139-41. For studies of Pārśva's association with Dharaṇendra, see Dhaky (1997).

wood inhabited by the snake to meditate. The snake attacks Mahāvīra again and again, but Mahāvīra remains unmoved. When Mahāvīra addresses him, he remembers his previous life, repents and starts to fast. Passers-by begin to honour the serpent, rubbing it with ghee. This attracts ants that come to eat away the ghee. After a fortnight of staying immovable, the serpent dies from being eaten by the ants and is reborn in one of the heavens.[30]

Some famous encounters with animals are found in the biography of the sixteenth *jina* Śānti, albeit in his previous existence as prince Megharatha. One day a cockfight is held. Two cocks fight for a very long time without one prevailing. On Megharatha's request, his austere father, the king, narrates the story of their previous births to explain their current condition. They once were two befriended merchants who deceived their customers. Because of their deceit, they died in *ārta-dhyāna* and were reborn as elephants. In a first elephant existence, they quarrelled, fought and died, to be reborn again as elephants in separate herds. When they one day saw each other, they rushed towards each other, battled and both died. They continued to fight in subsequent battles as buffaloes, rams and eventually cocks. The cocks renounce the world, fast and die, to be reborn as gods. Remembering their previous existence, they create an aerial car and invite Megharatha, whom they consider their benefactor in their life as cocks, for a journey around the world. This is an illustration of the benefits one may incur when taking care of animals.[31]

The most famous story of Megharatha's greatness is narrated later. One day a dove fell into his lap seeking refuge with him. The bird, in a human voice, asked to be rescued, and the king conceded. Thereupon a hawk approached, asking the king to turn the dove loose, because it was his food. The king refused because it is against the *kṣatriya* code to deny refuge to a creature asking for help. He moreover rebuked the hawk for pursuing momentary satisfaction by eating meat, which inevitably results in a rebirth in hell. He suggested the hawk should find inanimate food. The hawk declined and then himself formally asked refuge with the king, who was now obliged to care for him. The bird reiterated his request for meat. Megharatha offered his own flesh to the hawk, to the same amount as the weight of the dove. The dove prospered and became heavier, so every time Megharatha had to offer more of his own flesh to the hawk, until he ultimately presented his entire body for food. When his retinue observed this, they protested that they also needed his protection, for which he had to keep his body in good condition. Thereupon a god appeared who explained that the whole ordeal was arranged by him, as he wanted to test Megharatha's famous compassion. The dove and the hawk fought each other because of an enmity from a former life. Remembering their previous

30. *Triṣaṣṭiśalākāpuruṣacarita* 10.3.225-80 (Johnson 1931–1962: vol. 6, 54–58).
31. *Triṣaṣṭiśalākāpuruṣacarita* 5.4.66-187 (Johnson 1931–1962: vol. 3, 279–86). A variant story can be found in *Mahāpurāṇa* 63.150-223.

life and instructed by Megharatha, they took to fasting and when they died, they were reborn as gods.[32]

In both cases the animals are freed from an apparent vicious cycle of confrontation by Megharatha's intervention. The second story is an adaptation of the famous story of king Śibi found in the *Mahābhārata* and the Buddhist *Jātakas*.[33]

EFFECT OF ANIMALS ON THE TĪRTHAṂKARAS

Aside from spiritual progress made by animals from encountering a *tīrthaṃkara*, sometimes a *tīrthaṃkara* himself benefits from meeting an animal. The twentieth *tīrthaṃkara* Munisuvrata, for instance, was impelled to renounce the world upon seeing an elephant in the forest abstaining from food. The elephant had remembered its previous existence in which he was a man who had chosen the wrong faith and was therefore reborn as an animal. Disgusted with transmigration, the elephant began to fast to achieve spiritual advancement.[34]

The most famous and dramatic encounter with animals leading to a *tīrthaṃkara*'s renunciation is that of the twenty-second *tīrthaṃkara* Nemi. In due course a marriage was arranged between handsome young prince Nemi and princess Rājīmatī. While Nemi was in his chariot, on the way to his bride to be married, he was distracted by the sound of the animals waiting to be slaughtered for the wedding banquet:

> As Nemi went along, he heard the pitiful cries of animals and asked his charioteer: 'What is this?' though he knew well. The charioteer replied: 'Lord, do you not know? These various animals have been brought here to provide food for your marriage. Earth-dwellers, goats, et cetera and sky-dwellers, partridges, et cetera, belonging to village and forest, these will die, master. These are being watched by guards inside enclosures, crying out. For fear of life is a great fear of all.'
>
> Then Nemi, a hero of compassion, said to his charioteer, 'Drive my chariot to the place where these animals are.' The charioteer did so; and the Blessed One saw many animals, their hearts terrified at losing their lives. Some were fastened by ropes on the neck, some on the feet, some had been thrown into cages and some had fallen into snares. Their faces upturned, their eyes pitiful, their bodies trembling, they looked at Nemi friendly from (his) appearance. 'Protect! Protect!' they said to Nemi, each in his own language. Neminātha, giving orders to the charioteer, had them released. When the animals had gone to their respective places, the Lord had the chariot turned back towards his own house. Śivā, Samudravijaya, Kṛṣṇa, Rāma, and others left their own conveyances and were in front of Nemi. Śivā and Samudravijaya, their eyes filled with tears, said: 'Why have you suddenly

32. *Triṣaṣṭiśalākāpuruṣacarita* 5.4.253-313 (Johnson 1931–1962: vol. 3, 291–95); For Guṇabhadra's variant account: *Mahāpurāṇa* 63.253-79.
33. For a comparison of different versions of this story, see Meisig (1995).
34. *Mahāpurāṇa* 67.31-37. This motif is absent in Hemacandra's biography of Munisuvrata.

> turned away from this festival?' Nemi said: 'Just as these animals were bound by bonds, so we are bound by bonds of karma. Just as there was release from bondage for them, so I shall take initiation to make my own release from the bondage of karma—the sole source of happiness.'[35]

After these words, young Nemi abandoned his marriage plans and immediately renounced the world, to the dismay of his relatives and his waiting bride Rājīmatī. The sheer contrast between the splendour and cheerfulness of the royal wedding organization, on one hand, and the anguish of the innocent animals waiting to be slaughtered, on the other, is what makes this episode so striking and Nemi's decision so touching. Its popularity is evident from the literary adaptations and the ample illustrations found in manuscripts narrating this story.[36]

EXCURSUS: THE ORIGIN OF ANIMAL SACRIFICE ACCORDING TO THE JAINS

In this chapter we discussed how Jain authors used standard South Asian animal symbolism to underscore the *kṣatriya* identity of the *tīrthaṃkara* and how factual animal presences in the lives of the *śalākāpuruṣas*, particularly of the *tīrthaṃkaras*, emphasize the universality of the Jain doctrine, as effective for all living beings trapped in *saṃsāra* through the workings of *karman*, and appeal for awareness and compassion for souls stuck in lowly *tiryañc* existences. Though *ahiṃsā* and a general benevolence towards animals are common to most South Asian religions, the Jains stress its importance to an extreme.

One tenet, in which Jainism views itself as very distinct from Brahmanical ideology, is its rejection of animal sacrifice. The story behind the origin of animal sacrifice is told in the Jain universal history by Nārada to the eighth *prativāsudeva* Rāvaṇa.[37] In his youth Nārada once took instruction with a teacher, together with two other pupils. One day two ascetics prophesied that only one of the teacher's pupils would go to heaven, the other two would go to hell. To test his pupils, the teacher gave each a cock made of dough and ordered them to kill it where nobody could see. Nārada's fellow students went and secretly destroyed the dough cocks. Nārada went away with his dough cock and reflected, ultimately deciding that he could not destroy it, securing his place in heaven. Of the three pupils, one became a king, the other, who was

35. *Triṣaṣṭiśalākāpuruṣacarita* 8.9.171-84 (as translated by Johnson 1931–1962: vol. 5, 258–59). Colette Caillat (2009: 143) provides the translation of the parallel passage in the *Uttarādhyāyanasūtra*. See also *Harivaṃśa Purāṇa* 55.85-100 and *Mahāpurāṇa* 71.158-68. Note that according to Guṇabhadra this was prearranged deliberately by Kṛṣṇa to kindle Nemi's longing for renunciation.

36. For instance, the messenger poem *Nemicarita* by Vikrama (fourteenth century). See Jaini (2000: 372).

37. *Triṣaṣṭiśalākāpuruṣacarita* 7.2.363-502 (Johnson 1931–1962: vol. 4, 141-51); *Paumacariyam* chapter 11.

the son of the teacher, became a teacher himself, expert in the Vedas. Their old teacher became a Jain mendicant. Years later, Nārada returned and overheard his fellow student, the son of his teacher, explain that according to the Ṛgveda, sacrifice must be made with an *aja*, meaning a goat. Nārada interrupts that he is making a mistake and that *aja* signifies three year-old rice, which is called thus, because it no longer reproduces (*a-ja*). They argue and make a wager that whoever is wrong, must have his tongue cut out. They decide to leave it to the third pupil, who was by now king. Secretly, the wife of the old teacher, mother of the Veda expert, goes to the king to request his favour. The king concedes, and she asks him to answer the question regarding the meaning of *aja* in sacrifice wrongly. Reluctantly, the king yields and, out of loyalty to his teacher, testifies that *aja* means goat. From then on, Brahmins have been sacrificing goats, countless innocent animals have been pointlessly put to death and countless ignorant sacrificers have collected inauspicious *karman*, because of a lie to protect the tongue and the honour of a mistaken Veda teacher. This story exemplifies how Jains view themselves as advocates of animals in a world where, as they see it, many do not view animals as equal to other beings.

REFERENCES

Babb, L. A. 1993. 'Monks and Miracles: Religious Symbols and Images of Origin among Osval Jains.' *Journal of Asian Studies* 52(1): 3–21. http://dx.doi.org/10.2307/2059142

— 1994. 'The Great Choice: Worldly Values in a Jain Ritual Culture.' *History of Religion* 34(1): 15–38. http://dx.doi.org/10.1086/463380

— 1996. *Absent Lord: Ascetics and Kings in a Jain Ritual Culture.* Berkeley: University of California Press.

Bender, E. 1976. 'An Early Nineteenth Century Study of the Jains.' *Journal of the American Oriental Society* 96(1): 114–16. http://dx.doi.org/10.2307/599898

Bloomfield, M. 1985. *The Life and Stories of the Jaina Savior Pārçvanātha.* Delhi: Gian Publishing House.

Brockington, J. 1998. *The Sanskrit Epics* (Handbuch der Orientalistik, Indien—12). Leiden: E. J. Brill.

Caillat, C. 2009. 'Les jaina et le règne animal.' In N. Balbir and G. Pinault (eds), *Penser, dire et représenter l'animal dans le monde indien*: 123–55. Paris: Librairie Honoré Champion.

Chandra, K. R. 1970. *A Critical Study of Paumacariyaṃ.* Muzaffarpur: Research Institute of Prakrit, Jainology and Ahimsa Vaishali.

Chapple, C. K. (ed.). 2002. *Jainism and Ecology: Nonviolence in the Web of Life.* Cambridge: Harvard Divinity School.

Cort, J. 1993. 'An Overview of the Jaina Purāṇas.' In W. Doniger (ed.), *Purāṇa Perennis: Reciprocity and Transformation in Hindu and Jaina Texts*: 185–206. New York: State University of New York Press.

— 2010. *Framing the Jina. Narratives of Icons and Idols in Jain History.* Oxford: Oxford University Press.

De Clercq, E. 2005. 'The Jain Rāmāyaṇa-Purāṇa: Paumacariyam – Padmacarita – Paumacariu.' In P. Koskikallio (ed.), *Epics, Khilas and Purāṇas: Continuation and Ruptures (DICSEP III)*: 597–608. Zagreb: Croatian Academy of Science.

Dhaky, M. A. 1997. *Arhat Pārśva and the Dharaṇendra Nexus* (B. L. Series No. 11). Delhi: Bhogilal Leherchand Institute of Indology.

Dundas, P. 2002. *The Jains.* Reprint 1992. London: Routledge.

Geer, A. van der. 2008. *Animals in Stone. Indian Mammals Sculpted through Time.* Leiden: E.J. Brill. http://dx.doi.org/10.1163/ej.9789004168190.i-462

Glasenapp, H. von. 1999. *Jainism—an Indian Religion of Salvation: An English Translation of Der Jainismus—eine Indische Erlösunsreligion by Shridhar B. Shrotri*. Delhi: Motilal Banarsidass.

Jacobi, H., and M. S. Punyavijayaji (eds). 1962–1968. Ācārya Vimalasūri's Paumacariyaṃ with Hindi translation (2 vols.) (Prakrit Text Society Series Nos. 6 and 12). Varanasi and Ahmedabad: Prakrit Text Society.

Jain, P. (ed.). 1954. *Mahāpurāna* (Vol. II): *Uttar Purāna of Acārya Gunbhadra—with Hindi translation* (Jñānapītha Mūrtidevi Jaina Granthamālā—Sanskrita Grantha No. 14). Kāshī: Bhāratīya Jñānapitha.

— (ed.). 1963–1965. Ādipurāṇa of Āchārya Jinasena (2 vols.) (Jñānapītha Mūrtidevī Jaina Granthamālā Sanskrit Granth Nos. 8–9). Kāshī: Bhāratīya Jñānapītha.

— (ed.). 1978. *Harivaṃśa Purāṇa of Jinasena* (Jñānapīṭha Mūrtidevī Jaina Granthamālā Sanskrit Grantha Nos. 27). New Delhi: Bharatiya Jnanpith.

Jaini, P. S. 1998. *The Jaina Path of Purification*. Reprint 1979. Delhi: Motilal Banarsidass.

Jaini, P. S. (ed.). 2000. *Collected Papers on Jaina Studies*. Delhi: Motilal Banarsidass.

Johnson, H. (trans.). 1931–1962. *Triṣaṣṭiśalākāpuruṣacaritra* (6 vols.) (Gaekwad's Oriental Series, Nos. LI, LXXVII, CVIII, CXXV, CXXXIX & CXL). Baroda: Oriental Institute.

Lodrick, D. O. 1981. *Sacred Cows, Sacred Places. Origins and Survivals of Animal Homes in India*. Berkeley: University of California Press.

Meisig, M. 1995. *König Śibi und die Taube. Wandlung und Wanderung eines Erzählstoffes von Indien nach China*. Wiesbaden: Harrassowitz Verlag.

Quintanilla, S. R. 2000. 'Āyāgapaṭas: Characteristics, Symbolism, and Chronology.' *Artibus Asiae* 60(1): 79–137. http://dx.doi.org/10.2307/3249941

Shah, U. P. 1987. *Jaina-Rūpa-Maṇḍana—Volume I*. New Delhi: Abhinav Publications.

Śrīcaraṇavijayajī Mahārāj, Śrīpuṇyavijayajī Mahārāj, Śrīramaṇakavivijayajī Gaṇī and Vijaya śīlacandrasūri (eds). 1990–2006. *Triṣaṣṭiśalākāpuruṣacaritamahākāvyam* (4 vols.). Ahamadābād: Kalikālasarvajña Śrīhemacandrācārya Navama Janmaśatābdī Smṛti Śikṣaṇ Saṃskāranidhi.

Sukthankar, V. S. (ed.). 1933–1966. *The Mahābhārata* (19 vols.). Poona: Bhandarkar Oriental Institute.

Turner, R. L. 1966–1985. *A Comparative Dictionary of the Indo-Aryan Languages* (4 vols.). London: Oxford University Press.

Upadhye, A. N., and H. Jain (eds). 1951–1956. *Jadivasaha's Tiloya-Paṇṇatti* (2 vols.) (Jivaraja Jain Granthamala No. 1). Sholapur: Jaina Samskriti Samraksaka Samgha.

Varni, J. 1997–2000. *Jainendra Siddhānta Kośa* (5 vols.) (Moortidevī Jain Granthamālā: Sanskrit Grantha Nos. 38, 40, 42, 44 and 48). Reprint 1921–1983. New Delhi: Bharatiya Jnanpith.

Vijaya, Jina (ed.). 1934. *Vividha Tīrtha Kalpa of Jinaprabha sūri* (Singhi Jaina Series No. 10). Śāntiniketan: Sañcālaka, Siṅghī Jaina Granthamālā.

Fourth Tantra: Devotion, Wisdom, Awe

Horses that Weep, Birds that Tell Fortunes: Animals in South Asian Muslim Ritual and Myth

DAVID PINAULT*

Muslim views of the spiritual status of non-human animals—at least those views that are derived primarily from Islamic scriptures—differ notably from the significance assigned to animals in Indic religions. God created the earth in such a way as to fill it with *ayat Allah* ('Allah's signs', Qur'an 40.81) for the moral guidance of humans. Consider Q. 16.79: 'Haven't they looked at the birds held aloft in the sky? Nothing keeps them there except Allah. In this are signs for a people who believe.' The study of animals' behaviour is expected to lead to faith in God.

The Qur'an indicates that animals may also provide moral guidance for human acts of worship. In response to those Meccans who opposed the prophet Muhammad, Qur'an 16.48-49 offers the following admonition: 'Haven't they considered what God has created? ...All those beings in the heavens and on the earth, animals and angels alike, prostrate themselves to Allah, and they are not prideful.' The Arabic word for 'prostrate'—*yasjudu*—is derived from the same verbal root as the word *sajdah*, which denotes the Islamic prostration in prayer to be performed by all believers. The implication is clear: animals, like angels, are instinctive Muslims, and they offer a model of pious behaviour for humans to imitate. In fact, the Qur'an indicates that even trees and grass perform the *sajdah* in honour of God (55.6).

But a key difference between humans and other created beings is that humans must choose whether to worship God. Animals, in company with the trees and grass, are involuntary Muslims. Their piety is natural and not the product of conscious choice or moral effort. For this reason they lack

* David Pinault is Professor of Religious Studies at Santa Clara University. He received his PhD in Arabic and Islamic Studies from the University of Pennsylvania. He is the author of numerous articles, book chapters and encyclopaedia entries on topics ranging from medieval Arabic literature to Shia ritual in South Asia. His books include *Horse of Karbala: Muslim Devotional Life in India* (Palgrave/St Martin's Press, 2001), *The Shiites: Ritual and Popular Piety in a Muslim Community* (St Martin's Press, 1992) and *Story-Telling Techniques in the Arabian Nights* (Brill, 1992). His most recent publication is *Notes from the Fortune-Telling Parrot: Islam and the Struggle for Religious Pluralism in Pakistan* (Equinox, 2008). Professor Pinault has also served as a volunteer at a wildlife rescue centre on the island of Java operated by the NGO ProFauna Indonesia. Currently he is a member of ProFauna's Advisory Board.

the ability possessed by humans to earn either paradise or hellfire in the afterlife.[1]

This ability to make moral choices and thus gain salvation is what elevates humans above non-human animals according to Islam. Hence it is unsurprising that the Qur'an describes creatures such as cattle, horses, mules and donkeys in utilitarian terms, as beings created by God to be used by humans (Qur'an 16.5-8).

In turn the existential situation confronting humans—the need to make moral choices and face the eternal consequences of these choices in hell or heaven—is linked with the Islamic doctrine of *tawhid* (the monotheistic assertion of Allah's absolute oneness). If no deity exists save Allah, then humans cannot escape responsibility for their actions by looking to another divine being for intercession. From an ethical perspective, *tawhid* serves to heighten humans' sense of moral accountability—an accountability to which non-human animals are not subjected.

This scripturally derived Islamic view of humans and non-human animals may be compared with what is found in religions that originated in the Indian subcontinent. First may be noted the blurring of distinctions among the realms of humans, gods and animals. Among the *avatara*s of the Hindu deity Vishnu are humans (Rama and Krishna), animals (a fish, a turtle, and a wild boar) and a human-animal hybrid (the lion-man Narasimha). The Buddhist *jataka*s describe earlier lives of the Buddha (before he existed as the historical figure Siddhartha) in which he lived a merit-earning existence as—among other non-human animals—a monkey, a parrot, a golden mallard, and a self-sacrificing hare.

Such stories suggest another important distinction. Hinduism, Buddhism and Jainism all possess stories conveying a common insight. Animals and humans share the existential condition of being struggling wayfarers, subjected to *karma* and *samsara* (the ongoing incarnational sequence of life, death and rebirth), propelled along the helical vortex of time. Therefore, animals—and this is an important difference from Islamic doctrine—share with humans the opportunity to make moral and salvation-related choices that will improve their spiritual status after their current earthly existence.

For example, the Hindu *Bhagavata Purana* (8.2-4; cited in Nelson 2006: 187–88) tells the story of Gajendra, an elephant that is attacked by a crocodile in a lake and dragged underwater. Desperate, Gajendra recites a hymn in honour of Vishnu. The god rewards the elephant for its piety by freeing it from the crocodile and granting it *moksha* (deliverance from *samsara*).

Chapple's study of animals in Jainism tells of myths 'where animals perform deeds that guarantee themselves an elevated status' (2006: 242). Two cobras rescue Parshvanatha (the twenty-third Jain Tirthankara) and are rewarded with rebirth in the heaven of the guardian nature-deities. A lion listens to a

1. For a discussion of faith and moral volition with regard to humans and non-human animals, see Foltz (2006: 15–17).

sermon by Jain monks on nonviolence and becomes a renouncer, curbing its carnivorous instinct to kill other creatures for food. It starves to death and is rewarded with rebirth as Mahavira (the twenty-fourth Tirthankara).

And the Buddhist *Vinaya Pitakam* tells the tale of a *naga* (serpent deity) that wanted so badly to experience enlightenment that it took the form of a human and enrolled as a novice at a monastery. The *naga*-monk did well until one night, thinking itself alone in its cell, it let down its guard briefly and fell asleep: 'And in his sleep he took on his natural form. His snake's body filled the whole room, and his coils came out through the windows' (1.86-87; translation by Strong 1995: 61–62). This—understandably—upset the other monks and led to the *naga*'s expulsion, for only humans are allowed to be monks. To console the snake, the Buddha suggested a course of spiritual discipline that would free it from its current incarnation and help it earn rebirth as a human.

Although such tales imply that animals have a lower spiritual rank than humans, nonetheless they also demonstrate that non-human animals share with humans the desire for spiritual advancement. In fact the moral struggle for animals is even harder. A Jain *pujari* (ritual specialist) whom I interviewed on this subject explained that if a human behaves badly, indulging in a lifetime of violent behaviour, his or her karmic punishment may entail rebirth as an appetite-laden creature such as a tiger. The tiger's flesh-eating instincts will make it hard to resist the desire to kill; indulging such desires then will lead to another rebirth that is even more bestial and appetite-driven. 'The tiger-karma wants to pull you further down', as my informant explained; but to advance spiritually, one must resist these impulses.[2]

Such stories suggest an unbridgeable gulf between Islam and the South Asian traditions of Hinduism, Buddhism and Jainism. But here it must be borne in mind that South Asian Islam in practice (as distinguished from an exclusively scripturalist understanding of Islam) exists—alongside other religions of the subcontinent—as one point on what I would call a 'darshanic' continuum of ritual and myth.

Labels such as 'Islam' or 'Hinduism' notwithstanding, South Asian religion can be characterized as darshanic (from the Sanskrit term *darshan*: the 'auspicious sight' of a deity, as defined by Diana Eck, where worship involves the opportunity 'to stand in the presence of the deity and to behold the image with one's own eyes, to see and be seen by the deity' [Eck 1985: 3, 87]). Darshanic religion involves seeing, but also adorning, clothing and touching some figural representation of the divine. It is imagistic in orientation, permitting one to have direct contact with the sacred. And despite Islam's well-known aniconism and prohibition against any veneration of images, I will argue here that certain South Asian Muslim practices that make use of

2. Interview with Mr Jayesh Khona of the Jain Bhawan, Milpitas, CA, May 2004. I thank Mr Khona for his kindness in providing this information.

animals—specifically, Shia rituals involving the veneration of consecrated horses during the annual Muharram observances—display a strongly darshanic dimension.

SORROW SHARED BY ALL CREATURES IN THE COSMOS: WEEPING HORSES IN SOUTH ASIAN SHIA RITUAL

Shia Muharram rituals commemorate the battlefield death of the prophet Muhammad's grandson, Husain ibn 'Ali (d. 680 CE). Together with other members of *ahl al-bayt* (the prophet's family), Husain was killed at a site in the Iraqi desert known as Karbala. The date of his death, Ashura (the tenth day of the Islamic month of Muharram), is the focal point of the annual liturgical calendar for Shias throughout the *ummah*. According to Shia belief, in exchange for Husain's suffering and martyrdom at Karbala, God granted him *shafa'ah* (the power to intercede on behalf of sinners).

How can believers today access this power of intercession? The question is addressed by the sixteenth-century Qur'an commentator Husain Wa'iz al-Kashifi in his devotional work *Rawdat al-shuhada'* ('The Garden of the Martyrs'), where he explains the importance of physically manifested emotional involvement in the communal remembrance of Husain:

> As it has been stated in various writings: 'Paradise is awarded to anyone who weeps for Husain or who laments in company with those who weep for Husain'... 'Paradise is awarded': for the following reason, that every year, when the month of Muharram comes, a multitude of the lovers of the Family of the Prophet (*jam'i az muhibban-e Ahl-e Bayt*) renew and make fresh the tragedy of the Martyrs, and they bewail the offspring of the Lord of Prophecy.
>
> (al-Kashifi 1979: 12)

Especially important to note from Kashifi's text are the words *muhibban-e Ahl-e Bayt*: 'lovers of the Family of the Prophet'. The means par excellence for expressing this love is what is known as *matam*: ritualized gestures of grief, which may range from loud weeping, to slapping one's chest or head, or cutting oneself with a knife or flail in acts of self-flagellation known as *zanjir-zani*. Sunni critics condemn *matam* as *bid'ah*: a heretical innovation for which no warrant exists in the Qur'an or *hadith* (the accounts of the sayings and doings of Muhammad). They note that Islam forbids believers to harm their bodies, and that the spurting blood associated with flagellation is *najis* (ritually polluting), rendering practitioners unfit for prayer.

But Shia devotees claim that their excessive behaviour testifies to their status as unsurpassed lovers of the prophet's family. Those who engage in *matam* earn *savab* (religious merit) and hence access to Husain's *shafa'ah*; and those who stimulate others to lament Husain—for example, preachers at the *majalis* (lamentation gatherings) that are held throughout Muharram—themselves earn *savab* as well.

But it is not only preachers who show us the way. Animals, too, provide an example. Kashifi suggests the cosmic dimension of the tragedy of Karbala by quoting a Muharram lamentation poem:

> Earth and heaven weep at the death of Husain;
> From the Throne on high to the dirt far below, all beings weep.
> Fish in the ocean depths, birds in the sky's upper heights:
> All weep in mourning for the King of Karbala.
>
> (al-Kashifi 1979: 12)

This sentiment is reflected in a devotional work published in Karachi in the 1970s called *The Importance of Weeping and Wailing*. The author, Syed Mohammed Ameed, cites traditions to the effect that the entire cosmos participated in bewailing Husain's death at Karbala. The sky shed tears of blood for 40 days; wild beasts roamed the jungles in agitation; *jinns* recited poems of lamentation; 70,000 angels descended to Husain's grave to weep; the earth emitted blood in grief. (Readers of the Christian Gospels will recall the cosmic response to Jesus's crucifixion: the sky darkens; the earth quakes; the Temple curtain is torn in two.)[3]

In Ameed's interpretation, God caused these actions to be manifested in the world in order to make clear to us humans the overriding importance of remembering Husain and commemorating his death in mourning. 'The inescapable conclusion', argues Ameed, 'is that weeping and wailing for Husain is a matter of extraordinary importance in the eyes of Allah. Otherwise he would not have made all His creatures to weep according to their own natural forms' (Ameed 1973: 7–10).

Ameed's implied argument—that animals and other non-human creatures provide Shias with a *sunnah* (behaviour that has exemplary or paradigmatic quality) that should be imitated—is analogous to what we have seen earlier in the Qur'an, where animals perform the *sajdah* in their worship of Allah and thereby provide a model of piety to be imitated by believers (cf. Pinault 1992: 102–103).

For South Asian Shia communities today, the *sunnah* of animals participating in *matam* rituals can be seen annually in processions that feature Zuljenah (Fig. 1).[4] This is the name of the stallion that Husain is said to have ridden into battle at Karbala. According to Shia devotional sources, on the day of Ashura, Husain left his family's encampment and rode off alone to confront the enemy. Zaynab (Husain's sister), Sakina (his young daughter), and the other 'women of Karbala' were unable to see what befell him due to the dust of combat and the crowd of enemies on the desert plain. The women learned of his death only when Zuljenah returned alone from the battle, riderless, bleeding and pierced with arrows (Fig. 1). This moment is richly elaborated in devotional texts. Here is Kashifi's version:

3. See, for instance, Mt. 27.45-53; Mk 15.33-38; and Lk. 23.44–45.
4. Zuljenah is the term in Urdu; the Arabic equivalent is *Dhu al-janah*.

> Its mane stained with the blood of that worthy man, tears streaming from its eyes, it headed toward the tent of Imam Husain. As for the women of the Imam's household: when they saw it approaching with a bloodstained face, and that its rider was not to be seen, a cry rose up from their very hearts... They began lamenting. Zuljenah lowered its head, and teardrops fell from its eyes... The horse beat its head against the earth [in grief] so many times that it died.
>
> (al-Kashifi 1979: 353)

'The horse beat its head against the earth': a significant gesture. Zuljenah, in Kashifi's telling, is itself engaged in the act of *matam*. Characters from the Karbala drama perform paradigmatic actions: if even Husain's horse struck itself in grief, so, too, should we who hear the story.

This notion of the horse's paradigmatic sorrow is reinforced by Kashifi's assertion, 'Teardrops fell from its eyes'. Zuljenah understood what had happened to its master and wept for that reason. This part of the myth of Karbala—the belief that the animal that witnessed its master's death was moved with compassionate sorrow—remains important to many South Asian Shias today, a point to which I return below.

Figure 1. Shia poster art: the Horse of Karbala. Zuljenah, the Imam Husain's stallion, is shown arrow-pierced on the battlefield. The text reads, 'Hail, Husain, martyr of Karbala'. In the upper right, in both Arabic and Urdu, is a hadith attributed to the prophet Muhammad: 'Husain proceeds from me, and I proceed from Husain'. Purchased in Delhi, 1989.

Zuljenah continues to figure prominently in modern-day lamentation poetry. The following is an Urdu *nauha* (lamentation poem) from a chapbook I purchased at a Shia shrine in Lahore. In the text the otherwise anonymous poet identifies himself by the name Javeed:

> When the Winged One, Zuljenah, returned riderless
> from the battlefield to the tents,
> Every weeping eye looked about for the master.
>
> At the final hour the horse took this message from the battlefield:
> 'The *ummah*, the members of Husain's own faith,
> have thrown down and trampled on the living image of the Prophet!'
>
> It rubs on its own forehead
> this blood of the Martyr of Sorrow
> and cries out in anguish: 'O Lord of the Two Worlds!'
>
> The whole body of this mute creature
> is wounded by arrows.
> Against him, too, the tyrants have directed their violent impulse.
>
> This is the Buraq of Karbala, on which the Shah mounted.
> The king permitted his own head to be cut off
> and then soared forth in a *mi'raj*, a heavenly flight,
> like that once attained by the Prophet.
>
> The animal's ability to recognise truth
> is greater than man's.
> At Karbala, Zuljenah's conduct is exemplary.
>
> Why shouldn't Faithfulness now kiss the feet of this horse?
> The mute poet Javeed has received blessings from those in sorrow,
> from the Karbala Martyrs.
>
> (in Reza n.d.: 19; translation by D. Pinault)

Two features of this poem are especially noteworthy. The first involves the poet's reference to Zuljenah as the 'Buraq of Karbala'. Buraq was the mythical winged creature which (according to Islamic legend) was ridden by the prophet Muhammad on his *mi'raj* (ascension to heaven) (cf. Qur'an 17.1). Shia devotionalism makes frequent reference to Muhammad's intimacy with his grandson. Here the poet highlights this closeness by suggesting that Husain's actions imitated those of his grandfather. Just as Buraq bore the Prophet in the *mi'raj*, so, too, did Zuljenah bear the Imam in the battle that led him to Paradise.

The second feature I wish to examine involves the *takhallos* or signature-closing at the poem's end, where the poet inserts his own name into the text. (This is a device familiar from classical Persian poetry.) Note that the poet describes himself as 'mute' (*be-zaban*). At first this can be taken as a conventional show of modesty and self-abasement: good poets, after all, should be anything but mute. But then return to stanza four and observe that Zuljenah, too, is referred to as *be-zaban*. So the poet is assimilating himself to the status of Husain's horse. Like Zuljenah, Javeed implies, he, too, is wounded and in sorrow. And like the horse he, too, despite his creaturely limitations, will do what he can to convey the tragic truth of Husain's martyrdom.

During the Muharram season, numerous cities and villages in Pakistan and India serve as the venue for public processions that feature what is known as the *shabih-e Zuljenah* ('the likeness of Zuljenah'). A stallion symbolizing Husain's horse is caparisoned and led through the streets. Here I will focus on Zuljenah rituals I witnessed in two locations: the town of Leh (Jammu and Kashmir, India) and the city of Lahore (Pakistan).

Leh is located in the Ladakh district, which shares a border with Chinese-controlled Tibet. Ladakh is known as 'Little Tibet', because of its substantial Tibetan cultural presence and Buddhist-majority population. But Leh also has Sunni and Shia Muslim communities. The Buddhist majority in Leh occasioned a kind of ritual cooperation I never witnessed in Pakistan: the Muslim-minority population of Sunnis and Shias collaborated in staging the town's Zuljenah *jalus* (procession). The purpose of this collaboration? As one Shia informant told me, 'To send the message to other communities: *ham Musulman log sab eik hein*: we Muslim folks are all one'. The Sunnis, however, made sure that their ritual performance differed noticeably from that of the Shias, as will be discussed below.

In the Muharram preparations that I witnessed, on the ninth of Muharram (the day before Ashura), Shias from Leh drove a livestock truck to the nearby village of Chushot to bring a stallion that was used every year for this ritual. Once in Leh, the horse was stabled overnight in the courtyard of a hotel belonging to a Shia community leader. The next morning, the day of Ashura, the *mujavir* (the 'attendant' who was to accompany the stallion throughout the procession) lit incense sticks and stuck them in the ground before the horse. Then he groomed the horse, fitted an embroidered halter over its head, and tied a votive cloth around its neck.

Just as the *mujavir* was about to lead away the horse to begin the procession, the elderly mother of the hotel proprietor pushed through the crowd of onlookers, cried out in an anguished wail, and buried her face against the horse's neck. Later the woman's son explained to me, 'It's the tradition for the women of the house to cry when Zuljenah goes out'. A change had been effected: until then, bystanders had been patting the animal playfully, joking with each other, asking me to take photos of themselves with the horse. With the mother's cry, everyone grew quiet: a kind of consecration had occurred. The horse had become *shabih-e Zuljenah*: the likeness of Imam Husain's riderless mount.

It was then led through the streets to the town's principal Shia mosque. In a walled yard beside the mosque, men of the Anjuman-e Imamia streaked the stallion's body and mane with red paint, to suggest the wounds inflicted on both Zuljenah and its rider. Then they caparisoned it with a silk saddlecloth, a saddle, and a sandalwood Qur'an stand, atop which was positioned a copy of the Qur'an.

After this, they tethered two live pigeons to the saddle and perched them atop the horse. They, too, had been daubed with red paint and are part of the folklore of Karbala. According to Shia legend, a pair of doves passed over Karbala and alighted to dip their wings in Husain's blood (Fig. 2). Thereafter they flew to Mecca and Medina; the blood dripping from their wings announced the Imam's martyrdom to the inhabitants (Pinault 2001: xix, 131–32, 143).

Fully caparisoned, the horse then became the focal point of the Ashura procession. Leading the *jalus* was a cluster of Sunnis (who had positioned themselves as far as possible from the horse). They didn't wail or chant dirges or slap themselves. Instead they shouted slogans such as *Allahu akbar* (God is great) and *La ilah illa Allah* (There is no god save Allah), a kind of non-denominational assertion of Islam, for the benefit of the many Buddhist onlookers in the crowd. Farther back in the procession and closest to the horse were young Shia men who faced the *shabih-e Zuljenah* and scourged themselves, leaving a trail of blood along the route of the march.

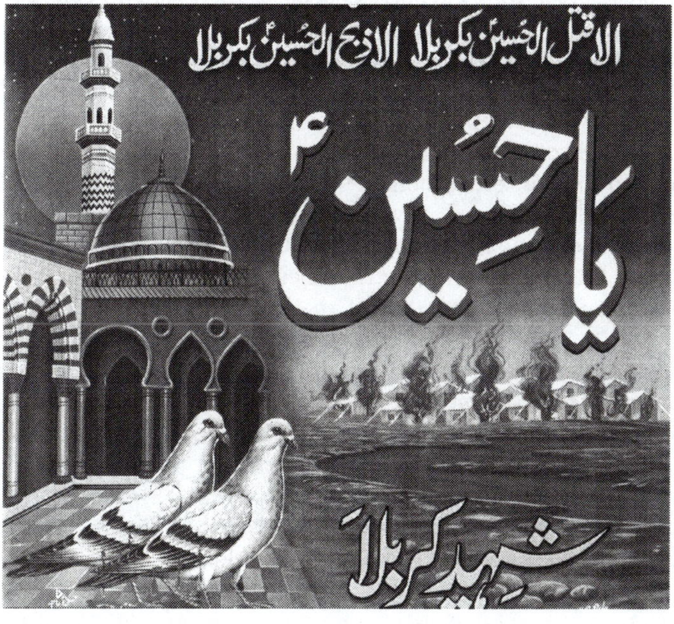

Figure 2. Shia poster art: a legend of Karbala. On the right, the martyrs' tents in flames. On the left, two doves, which are said to have dipped their wings in Husain's blood. Thereafter they flew over the city of Medinah. The blood dripping from their wings announced the Imam's death. Purchased in Delhi, 1989.

The horse clearly constituted the focal point of sacredness. As it was led from one street to another, a cry sometimes went up: *Zuljenah a raha hae* ('Zuljenah is coming!'), as the horse came into view, and a wave of lamentation swept over the crowd—thus replicating the moment when Zaynab and Sakina first saw the horse return from battle without its master. As noted earlier, such displays of lamentation help mourners gain access to Husain's intercession; thus the horse can be understood as a means towards personal salvation. And in the processions I witnessed, the riderless horse powerfully evoked the presence of the martyred Imam, but without the use of potentially idolatrous icons or other human likenesses of Husain.

Not that the *shabih-e Zuljenah* escaped charges of idolatry. In the processions I witnessed, women came forward to press their babies against the horse or pass them under its belly (for the purpose of praying for the infants' health); men bowed before the horse and fondled and kissed its saddlecloth. A Sunni religious leader complained to me about the Shia participants: 'They're praying to the horse... This is the kind of thing that Hindus or Buddhists might be expected to do, but not good Muslims.'

But Shia participants were quick to reply. One of the horse's custodians reminded me that a copy of the Qur'an is placed atop the saddle in every procession. 'So when people bow, they're really bowing to the word of God, not just to some horse.' Thus the horse is made to carry its own defence against charges of heresy.

What of the horse's own reaction to what it experiences yearly at Ashura? Again and again in my Ladakhi fieldwork, Shia informants insisted that the horse chosen to represent Husain's mount understood the meaning of the event it helped commemorate. For that reason, I was told, the horse sometimes wept during the procession, not because of distress at being led through agitated crowds and ranks of bloodstained flagellants—as a cynic might claim—but out of sympathetic solidarity with the Karbala martyrs.

Many of the rituals—and controversies—involved in Ladakh's Zuljenah procession can also be found across the border in Pakistani cities such as Lahore (Fig. 3). Particularly impressive is the scale of Lahore's celebrations. The Ladakhi town of Leh, with a population of 10,000, makes do with a single *jalus*. Lahore, with a population in excess of 11,000,000, has dozens of Zuljenah processions from the fifth to the tenth of Muharram, each taking place within individual neighbourhoods throughout the city. To give an idea of the popularity of these neighbourhood-based parades: in the course of a single afternoon during the 2002 Muharram season, I witnessed in quick succession four different Zuljenah processions in four different localities of Lahore.

In one procession I saw in 2002, atop the horse's saddle was fixed a gold chhatri (an ornamental parasol used to honour royalty—a custom borrowed from Hindu India). Among the boys who chanted dirges and the men who pounded their chests in time to the chant, vendors kept pace with the horse, selling garlands of red carnations (reminiscent of how flower garlands are sold at Hindu shrines in India for honouring statues of the gods).

Buyers draped the garlands over the saddle and chhatri and then pressed their hands to the horse's muzzle, its neck, flank, whatever part of its body they could reach in the throng. 'Savab ke lie', came the explanation when I asked about this: to earn religious merit. Parents with children in their arms stepped forward—just as I saw in Ladakh—to pass the youngsters under the horse's belly. 'For the sake of the children's health and wellbeing', I was told.

Figure 3. Zuljenah procession, Lahore, during the 2002 Muharram season. Photo by David Pinault.

'Lahore is a city of shrines and pilgrimage places', as one resident told me. 'That's why the Deobandis and other *tablighi* types don't have so much success here.' (He was referring to Muslim missionary-reformers who want to 'purify' Islam of any practices that smack of paganism.) And Lahore in fact is crammed with shrines honouring assorted miracle-workers, holy women, Sufi saints, and martyred Imams. People go to such places to pray for intercession, healing, and blessing. The Zuljenah *jalus* is so popular because during Muharram a 'likeness' (*shabih*) of the sacred goes out among the people. The shrine becomes mobile, transportable, accessible for every neighbourhood and street corner. Wellbeing and the opportunity to earn religious merit come within the reach of all.

As in Ladakh, I noticed the darshanic quality of Lahore's processions, how the 'likeness of Zuljenah' affords worshippers the 'auspicious sight' of something divine. *Darshan*, as noted above, is a term from the lexicography of Hinduism; and the Shia-Hindu comparison is necessarily inexact. Hindu statues (*murtis*), when ritually 'activated' with *prana* ('breathlife'), allow worshippers reciprocal eye-contact with sculptures that have been infused with the life-force of the divinity whose features are reflected in a visible and palpable image.[5]

No such claim, of course, is made by Shias on behalf of Zuljenah. Rather, the presence of the sacred is suggested by the pathos of its absence: the aniconic reference to Husain in Zuljenah's empty saddle, the reminder of violent death in the red paint staining the horse's mane. Here the emotion is intensified because viewers must visualize Husain's martyrdom for themselves (as Athenian audiences had to do in the offstage deaths reported by messengers in ancient Greek drama).

As in Ladakh, Lahore's Zuljenah processions face charges of heresy. Some of the sharpest rebukes have come from fellow Muslims within Pakistan's Shia community. Such Shias are often clerics who are Khomeinist and Teheran-oriented. The ayatollah Ruhollah Khomeini emphasized *taqrib* ('rapprochement' between Shias and Sunnis) so as to downplay theological and ritual differences among Muslims and achieve tactical alliances with Sunni radical movements in the Arab Near East and elsewhere in the Islamic world.

In December 2002 I visited the Shahid 'Arif al-Husaini Madrasa, a Khomeinist Shia academy in Peshawar, in Pakistan's North-West Frontier Province. Accompanying me was a young Shia named Rizvi—a zealous practitioner of the bloodiest forms of *zanjir-zani* and an enthusiastic participant in Zuljenah processions. The madrasa's director, Allama Javad Hadi, lectured us at length about the unislamic quality of various Muharram practices that are dear to South Asian Shias, most notably the making of *tazias* (gilt-wood cenotaphs of the Karbala martyrs that are carried in parades); self-scourging; and Zuljenah processions. These, he proclaimed, were all Hindu-tainted heretical innovations. Best to focus on the five Pillars of practice incumbent on all Muslims. But Rizvi wasn't overawed by the cleric. '*Rozah* [Ramadan fasting], *namaz* [prayer], *hajj* (pilgrimage): all Muslims do these things', he replied, and I could tell he was angry. 'Even the Wahhabis do these things. But without *matam*, *zanjir-zani*, Zuljenah, the *tazias*, there'd be nothing left of Shiism. There'd be nothing to mark us as different from the Sunnis.'

This reflects a sentiment I encountered frequently in both India and Pakistan. Precisely because of the contested and controversial quality of the Zuljenah parades, Husain's horse and its present-day 'likenesses' have become useful elements of a ritual system that helps maintain the distinctive communal identity of South Asian Shias.

5. '*Prana*, the "breathlife", is infused into the image in the central rite called *pranapratistha*, establishing the breathlife' (Eck 1985: 52).

HOW TO ISLAMICIZE AN ORACLE: PIETY AND ORTHODOXY IN THE WORLD OF FORTUNE-TELLING PARROTS

Like the Zuljenah processions, the use of parrots for divination has come under attack from Islamist reformers who condemn the practice as hopelessly tainted by Hinduism. And in fact parrot fortune-tellers (Fig. 4) are found among both Muslim and Hindu populations, in an arc ranging from the Pakistani Punjab to India and Southeast Asia.

My first encounter with a fortune-telling parrot occurred in Hyderabad, India in 1991. I saw an elderly Hindu (his forehead marked with the paste-stripes of a Vishnu devotee) seated on the sidewalk in a busy commercial district. Beside him was a large shrouded cage. When I approached, he removed the shroud, revealing a handsome brilliant-green parrot. On a mat before the cage was arranged a row of overlapping envelopes.

Figure 4. Fortune-telling parrots, Lahore, March 2002. The Urdu text on the placard says: 'Islamic oracle-book. Parrot oracle: 5 rupees. Qur'anic oracle: 10 rupees. Don't hesitate over spending 5 rupees! Go ahead, have your fortune read. Don't complain about your fate; try your luck! Amulets made here for every purpose.' Photo by David Pinault.

The parrot-master explained that for five rupees his bird would select an envelope the contents of which might offer me counsel or a glimpse of my future. By way of sample the man opened several envelopes and showed me what was inside. Each envelope contained a devotional card picturing Shiva, Lakshmi, Krishna or one of the other Hindu gods. The master opened the cage door and the parrot hopped out. It paced back and forth over the line of envelopes, then paused and made its choice. With its beak it tugged free an envelope and fluttered to the shoulder of its master. The man opened the envelope.

It held two cards. One showed a copy of the Qur'an, surmounted by Arabic lettering that proclaimed 'the glorious Book'. The second card depicted a familiar scene from Christian iconography: Christ on the cross, flanked by the sorrowing figures of Saint Joseph and the Blessed Virgin Mary. As a Catholic who happens to be a researcher in the field of Islamic studies, I found the parrot's choice of cards to be a good summary of my religious identity and my professional life. I was impressed.

The diaspora of fortune-telling parrots extends to Singapore, in a locality known as Little India. All the parrot-masters I encountered there were Tamil Hindus, whose families originated in India's Tamil Nadu State. As in Hyderabad, the bird's technique was to select a fortune from a row of envelopes. But in Singapore each envelope contained not only a Hindu-deity devotional card but also a slip of paper bearing a fortune printed in Tamil on one side and in English on the other. This bilingualism seemed necessary, given the clientele, which included local Malays, Chinese and Indians, as well as tourists from around the world.

My first parrot-fortune in Singapore announced: 'The wheel of fortune turns to the phase of a yogi, abiding only in his prayer. Whatever will be your wish, it will be granted. Your enemies will vanish and you will be as powerful as an enchanted steed, because of the merit of the prayer.' The next card selected for me announced, 'You are currently worrying about a specific problem. In fact your life in the recent past has been full of hardships.' It went on, however, to offer the reassurance that these problems were 'mainly due to the unfavourable position of your star' and that 'all your worries will soon become things of the past'.

The fortune-telling parrots of Pakistan's Punjab function similarly—up to a point. Like their counterparts in India and Singapore, the parrot-masters I met in Lahore and Rawalpindi have trained their birds to select a fortune from a row of envelopes arrayed before prospective clients on the footpath. In Lahore most such vendors advertise their presence via Urdu-language placards, each of which typically is illustrated with a brightly painted parrot that holds in its beak an envelope. One such placard I saw reads '*Islami fal-nama* ('Islamic book of oracles/omens'). *Tota-fal panch rupae* ('parrot oracle, five rupees'). *Qur'ani fal das rupae* ('Qur'anic oracle, ten rupees').

The term *fal-nama* links the parrot-masters of Lahore with the centuries-long history of divination in popular Islamic culture. In the medieval era, *fal-*

nama ('book of omens') referred to a genre of texts that guided diviners in interpreting dreams, taking auguries from the behaviour of animals, finding the mystical significance of numbers and letters, and so on.

One placard-advertisement I saw in Lahore made the claim that this practice of 'Islamic divination' was created by the 'holy prophets and noble companions of the Prophet Muhammad'. Another assured customers that the oracles on offer were 'free of any taint of frivolous matters (*jo fazool baton se pak hayn*)'. Such advertising hints at a certain anxiety and defensiveness concerning the orthodoxy of divination and parrot fortune-telling in contemporary Pakistan, a point to which I return below.

As the placard described above indicates, the more expensive service available in Lahore involves a *Qur'ani fal*. This entails an oral consultation, wherein the fortune-teller refers to a 'Qur'anic oracle book' in guiding the client.

If the client opts for the *tota-fal*, then the oracle is chosen by the parrot rather than by human agency. As mentioned above, the bird selects a fortune from a row of envelopes. Each envelope contains a slip of paper comprising a photocopy of a divinatory pronouncement from an Urdu oracle-book. Following is an oracle selected for me by a parrot outside Lahore's Data Darbar Sufi shrine: 'Your situation is certainly complicated, but God will make it easy. No harm will come to you from any enemy. But you, for your part, should not stir up any conflict or quarrel. If you comply with this and are patient, your heart's desire will be fulfilled.' The pronouncement concludes with an invocation found on many Lahori printed oracles: *Aur kaho in sha' Allah ta'ala* ('And say: If God most exalted wills it'). A second Lahori oracle described my current status as 'not good' but then advised me, 'Endure these days with patience and gratitude and do not neglect your acts of worship'.

Like the parrot-fortunes I encountered in Singapore, the oracles I was offered in Lahore and Rawalpindi follow a certain pattern. They refer in general terms to the client's current difficulties but are melioristic in tone. They offer an optimistic view of the future, coupled with common-sense advice as to behaviour (be patient, don't pick fights, etc.). The Pakistani *fal*-texts also remind clients to fulfil their religious obligations ('do not neglect your acts of worship') while reassuring them of Allah's ultimate protection. Overall, the language is formulaic, the tone one of orthodox Islamic piety.

Pakistanis with whom I spoke varied in their reactions when they learned of my parrot-interests. Islamist-revivalist types generally disapproved, saying that parrot fortune-telling was justified by neither scripture nor prophetic *sunnah*. Self-styled Deobandis told me that Lahori Muslims borrowed this custom of parrot fortune-mongering from the Hindus. The linkage with Hinduism was certainly not intended as an endorsement. Parrot-masters I interviewed in Lahore complained that their business has dropped off in recent years, due to what they described as criticisms by preachers and Muslim reformers. One parrot-man I spoke to pointed to the painted sign he used as advertising. He read the text aloud: *Tota-fal. Islami fal-nama*' ('Parrot oracle.

Islamic oracle-book'). 'See?' he said. There was defiance in his voice; fear, too, I thought. 'Islamic', it says.' He emphasized that he cited the Qur'an in the advice he gave people. 'I'm a good Muslim.'

When I repeated this argument later to a Lahori mullah, the cleric let me know he wasn't impressed. 'That kind of talk', he frowned, 'doesn't change the fact that all this parrot-business is Hindu.'

GECKOS, ANTS, ELEPHANTS: ANIMALS AND THE QUESTION OF DENOMINATIONAL LOYALTY IN SOUTH ASIAN ISLAM

As can be seen from the above, the intersection of the realms of animals and religion in South Asian Muslim culture is fraught with concerns about communal identity. Questions of denominational identity extend also to the realm of *jinns*.

The Qur'an asserts that *jinns*, like humans, must choose whether to submit to Allah. Unlike humans (who are made from clay), *jinns* were created from the element of fire. Islamic folklore elaborates on this distinction to claim that *jinns*, normally invisible, are capable of shape-shifting and taking on the form of various creatures (cf. Qur'an 72.1-15; 55.14-15).[6]

In Lahore I met several men who proudly bore the job title *'amil ruhani* ('spiritual practitioner'): they earned a living as healers, exorcists and sorcerers. Many of the afflictions they dealt with were attributed to *jinns*. God created ten times as many *jinns* as humans, I was told. The overwhelming majority of these *jinns* are malevolent *kafirs* ('infidels' or 'unbelievers'), and almost all these *kafir jinns* are Hindu. Such *jinns*, my informants claimed, are responsible for idolatrous practices in India. Some *jinns* take on the form of the deity Ganesha, assuming the likeness of elephants. Others assume the shapes of various other animal deities venerated in Hinduism. These disguised *jinns* are what Hindus mistakenly worship as gods (cf. Pinault 2008: 154–55).

Many homes in Lahore are believed to be infested with *jinns*. A young *'amil* ('practitioner') I met in March 2004 told me of how he rushed to a Muslim home one night in response to an 'emergency call'. The lady of the house told him her daughter-in-law was 'feeling afflicted' every night. He walked about and studied the house and determined that 'Hindu *jinns*' were living in a tree in the family's yard. (Popular Urdu fiction tells of *jinns* that perch in trees and drop down onto humans who unwisely linger nearby) (cf. Pinault 2008: 122–94). When he confronted them, the *jinns* indicated they had no intention of leaving. 'We've lived here a long time', they insisted—an interesting claim, which (when taken together with present-day Pakistani urban myths about Hindu *jinns* haunting old bridges and abandoned temples), may reflect

6. For an example from *The Thousand and One Nights* of *jinns* taking on the form of animals, see al-'Adwi (n.d.: 63–64).

Muslim awareness of the fact that, prior to partition in 1947 and the emergence of Pakistan, cities such as Lahore once had sizable Hindu populations.

Hostile *jinns* can take various animal forms when infesting a home. I heard of one case in which *jinns* assumed the shape of ants and swarmed all over the rooms of a house. On the other hand, the young healer who'd discovered Hindu *jinns* in a tree told me that he himself had domesticated a number of Muslim *jinns* that took the shape of gecko lizards when he dispatched them to roadsides and the homes of individuals about whom he wished to acquire information. When I asked why they chose the shape of geckos, he replied that geckos are small, they're common, and they're everywhere. They slip in and out of houses easily and unnoticed: the perfect spies, for collecting information useful to an *'amil.*

No *'amil* I interviewed speculated on the spiritual interiority of animals or what it might be like for a gecko or elephant to undergo the experience of sharing its awareness with a *jinn*. Instead, the perspective I encountered was utilitarian: *jinns* are believed to assume the forms of animals simply as vehicles in which to move about human society and communicate with humans. This is analogous to a motif found in medieval Islamic folklore, where a malicious *jinn* may enter a pagan idol, speak through its mouth, and lead unbelievers astray (cf. al-'Adwi, II, 42–43). Like the idol, animals are construed as convenient forms through which to navigate the material world.

This apparent uninterest in what animals may think or feel in spiritual encounters is likewise demonstrated in a Lahori Muslim ritual known as *chil-gosht ka sadqah* ('almsgiving/charity involving pariah-kite meat'). Impoverished immigrants from throughout the Punjab earn a living by offering scraps of meat as votive-food to the pariah kites that wheel over Lahore's Ravi River Bridge. Motorists commuting over the bridge stop their cars and pay to have the meat offered in their names to the birds. Participants I interviewed explained the religious rationale. Persons who are worried by some care or problem may rid themselves of their trouble by touching the meat and thereby transferring the trouble to the kite that descends to snatch the morsel. As the bird flies off with the meat in its talons, so, too, does the problem disappear (cf. Pinault 2008: 108–21). This popular ritual, a variant on the ancient practice of scapegoating, is comparable to another urban ritual in contemporary Lahore, whereby a goat is sacrificed as a way of 'ritually transferring harmful influence to an animal' (cf. Ewing 1997: 97–103). Again, such rituals suggest a largely utilitarian view of animals in terms of their usefulness as disposal units for human cares.

CONCLUSION: THE QUESTION OF ANIMAL CONSCIOUSNESS AND SPIRITUAL AUTONOMY IN THE CONTEXT OF SOUTH ASIAN ISLAM

In the introduction to their book on the status of animals in religion, Waldau and Patton emphasize the importance of acknowledging the spiritual autonomy of animals and perceiving that 'animals are, in their own right, the *subjects* of experience, beings with consciousness...rather than the *objects* of human perception or usage' (2006: 11).

South Asian Islamic sources evince little interest in animals as 'beings with consciousness' except insofar as these beings prove themselves instinctive Muslims whose behaviour confirms the beliefs of pious humans. An example can be seen in the life of the Moghul prince Dara Shikoh (d. 1659), who wrote of his encounter with a Sufi mentor: 'Once I sought his advice on some matter... At the time we were quite alone, as none ever accompanied me while I went to visit him. My horse, tethered to the branch of a tree, all of a sudden began to speak and confirmed his statement. He [the Sufi sheikh] smiled and remarked that my own horse affirmed what he had said' (cf. Hasrat 1982: 111).

An analogous incident appears in Farid al-Din Attar's life of Ebrahim ibn Adham (d. c. 782 CE), ruler of the Afghan city of Balkh. As a young man, Ebrahim enjoyed a life of princely self-indulgence, until Allah conveyed to him a warning that caused him to become a Sufi ascetic. The warning came while Ebrahim was out hunting in the desert: 'At that instant a deer started up, and Ebrahim prepared to give chase. The deer spoke to him. "I have been sent to hunt you. You cannot catch me. Was it for this that you were created, or is this what you were commanded?"' (cf. Attar 1966: 65). In such stories, animals serve as transmitters of divine injunctions while disclosing nothing to suggest they possess independent consciousness or spiritual autonomy. Like the idol used by the *jinn* in medieval folklore, they are the mouthpiece for unseen forces.[7]

Animals figure prominently in South Asian Muslim ritual and myth, to such an extent that they are imagined as agents that play a role in Islamic religious life (in ways that exceed the circumscribed roles assigned them in the Qur'an). The most poignant example of this agency is the Zuljenah parade stallion, which is thought capable of empathetic suffering and participation in Shia lamentation practices. But this doesn't constitute spiritual autonomy. The rituals and texts surveyed in this chapter present the realm of animals—whether horses, parrots, ants or geckos—through the lens of the very human concerns of orthodox piety, sectarian identity and communal-denominational loyalties.

REFERENCES

al-'Adwi, M. Q. (ed.). n.d. *Alf laylah wa-laylah*. 2 vols. Baghdad: Maktabat al-muthanna.
Ameed, S. M. 1973. *The Importance of Weeping and Wailing*. Karachi: Peermahomed Ebrahim Trust.
Attar, F. 1966. *Muslim Saints and Mystics: Episodes from the Tadhkirat al-Auliya'*. Translated by A. J. Arberry. London: Routledge & Kegan Paul.

7. Analogues can be found in world literature. In Homer's *Iliad* (19.405-17), Achilles's horse Xanthos is briefly endowed with speech by the goddess Hera so that it may warn its owner of his impending death. In Gustave Flaubert's story *La légende de Saint-Julien l'hospitalier*, a stag being pursued by a ruthless hunter is divinely enabled to speak so that it may warn him of the consequences of his violence.

Chapple, C. 2006. 'Inherent Value without Nostalgia: Animals and the Jaina Tradition.' In Waldau and Patton: 241–49.

Eck, D. 1985. *Darshan: Seeing the Divine Image in India.* Chambersburg, PA: Anima Books.

Ewing, K. P. 1997. *Arguing Sainthood: Modernity, Psychoanalysis, and Islam.* Durham, NC: Duke University Press.

Foltz, R. C. 2006. *Animals in Islamic Tradition and Muslim Cultures.* Oxford: Oneworld.

Hasrat, B. J. 1982. *Dara Shikuh: Life and Works.* Delhi: Munshiram Manoharlal.

al-Kashifi, H. W. 1979. *Rawdat al-shuhada'.* Teheran: Kitab-forushi islamiyah.

Nelson, L. 2006. 'Cows, Elephants, Dogs, and Other Lesser Embodiments of Atman: Reflections on Hindu Attitudes toward Nonhuman Animals.' In Waldau and Patton: 187–88.

Pinault, D. 1992. *The Shiites: Ritual and Popular Piety in a Muslim Community.* New York: St Martin's Press.

— 2001. *Horse of Karbala: Muslim Devotional Life in India.* New York: Palgrave.

— 2008. *Notes from the Fortune-Telling Parrot: Islam and the Struggle for Religious Pluralism in Pakistan.* London: Equinox.

Reza, S. H. (ed.). n.d. *Bayaz-e matam (hissah savvom): muntakhab wa-tazah nauhon ka majmu'ah.* Lahore: Ja'fariyah kutubkhanah.

Strong, J. S. 1995. *The Experience of Buddhism: Sources and Interpretations.* Belmont, CA: Wadsworth Publishing.

Waldau, P., and K. Patton (eds). 2006. *A Communion of Subjects: Animals in Religion, Science, and Ethics.* New York: Columbia University Press.

Winged Messengers, Feathered Beauties and Beaks of Divine Wisdom: The Role of Birds in Hindi-Urdu Allegorical Love Stories

THOMAS DÄHNHARDT*

> There is not an animal
> (that lives) on the earth,
> nor a being that flies
> on its wings, but forms
> part of Communities like you...
>
> (Qur'an 6.38)

In the ancient Mediterranean world, among the Romans, the ritual of *avis spicere* was a way to observe and interpret different kinds of birds flying high in the sky to gain knowledge about the will of the gods. It was an essential ritual entrusted to the *augurs*, a small but highly influential class of priests whose function was that of 'taking the auspices', thereby determining whether the recognized signs were to be deemed as either auspicious or inauspicious for the peace, fortune and wellbeing of the Empire (*pax, fortuna et salus Imperii*), or for the individual destiny of a human.[1]

Moving eastwards, several centuries later in the Arabian desert, Muḥammad ibn 'Abd Allāh, the messenger of Allah, revealed to mankind the inherent truths of Islam as preserved in the Holy Qur'an. In the understanding of Muslims, the Book puts a definite seal on the divine wisdom conveyed to

* Thomas Dähnhardt was educated in modern Indian languages (Hindi and Urdu) at Ca' Foscari University of Venice (Italy) and received his PhD from the Department for Religious Studies at SOAS (University of London) in 1999 for a comparative study on the doctrines and methods taught by a Hindu offspring of the Naqshbandi Sufi order in nineteenth and early twentieth century Northern India. After working as a Research Fellow at the Oxford Centre for Islamic Studies (OXCIS) he is currently teaching Hindi and Urdu literature in the Department of Asian and North African Studies at the University of Venice (Italy). His chief areas of interest include the Indo-Islamic culture and the different phenomena of cross-cultural identity resulting from the numerous points of contact between Islam and Hinduism, especially in the field of Sufism, *bhakti* and devotional literature. He is the author of *Change and Continuity in Indian Sufism: A Naqshbandi-Mujaddidi Branch in the Hindu Environment* (New Delhi: DK Publishing, 2002) and of several articles and book chapters on South Asian Sufism and Islamic literature (in Hindi and Urdu).

1. On augury and divination see Mortensen (2006: 425).

humanity through a long series of prophets going back to the origin of mankind itself. Among these prophets we find mention of Solomon (Ar. Ḥaḍrat Sulaymān), the king-prophet already praised in the Talmud for his outstanding degree of wisdom, who had been granted by the Lord the gift of the language of the birds (*mantiq al-ṭair*).

> And Solomon was David's heir. He said: 'O ye people! We have been taught the speech of Birds, and on us has been bestowed (a little) of all things: this is indeed Grace manifest (from Allah)'.
>
> (Qur'an 27.16)

The allegorical story told in this *sūra* sees among its protagonists the hoopoe, the messenger between Solomon and Bilqīs, the legendary ruler of Saba. The bird's role consists of guiding the infidel queen onto the path of *tawḥīd*. This story inspired the Persian Sufi poet Farīd al-Dīn al-ʿAṭṭār (1142–1220) many centuries later to compose his most famous work, *The Conference of the Birds*. In this Sufi allegory, the hoopoe (*hudhud*) acts as messenger and guide of a multitude of different bird species (among which figure the nightingale, the parrot, the peacock, the goose, the partridge, the heron, the mythological *humā* bird and the falcon), each of them full of pride for themselves (*khudī*) and their role in this world. Eventually, the hoopoe convinces them to abandon their rank and set out on a journey in search of their king, the awesome *simurgh*, a giant eagle-like creature portrayed since ancient times as a royal symbol by successive Persian dynasties. Nourished and pulled forward by the love the birds have discovered in the bottom of their heart, their quest leads them through seven valleys (the seven stages, or *maqāmāt*, of the Sufi path) and many succumb during the tiresome journey until eventually only 30 of them reach the presence of the mythical ruler who resides on the top of the mountain Qāf, a symbol of the cosmic axis (*quṭb*). Revealing his real nature, the simurgh shows the exhausted creatures the illusory reality of their separate existence (*fanā*) and leads them to realize their true identity through everlasting permanence with the Supreme Being (*baqā al-baqā*) here personified by Simurgh himself. This tale was to occupy a place of utmost prominence in Persianate Sufi literature for centuries and arguably continued to be a model for the Sufi authors of many allegorical love stories written in the Indian subcontinent.[2]

About a century later, during the heyday of the Delhi Sultanate, the Indo-Persian Sufi poet Amīr Khusrau (1253–1325), who used to refer to himself as *Ṭoṭa-i Hind*, the parrot of India, in self-conscious appreciation of both his outstanding eloquence and the deep affection for his homeland India, composed a number of works in which he actively operated in favour of an Indo-Islamic cultural symbiosis. In order to proof that India is indeed a country resembling

2. This story has been rewritten many centuries later (1712) in an Indianized version in Dakhini Urdu by the poet Wajdī with the title *Banjhī bacha*.

paradise (*firdaws, khuld-i barīn*), Amīr Khusrau indicates in the third chapter of his *mathnawī*, the *Nuh Sipihr* ('The Nine Celestial Spheres', 1318) the common ancestor of mankind, who according to some traditions chose to live in India after being brought down from heaven, and the peacock, the celestial bird who adopted India as his preferred habitat. Thus, in the imagination of one of the most acclaimed Indo-Persian poets, India appears to be a climate well suited for the cohabitation of humans and birds, sharing the common destiny of being forced out of the Garden of Eden after falling prey to the charm of a snake.

The works of Amīr Khusrau reflect the composite cultural environment of the Sultanate period that was to flourish during later Mughal rule. It provided a fertile ground for the production of literary works that brought together elements pertaining to both the Indian and the Islamic cultural milieu. The scope of these works ranged from offering mere entertainment to didactics, ethics and the spiritual refinement of the individual. In some cases, the latter aspects were combined to form an inextricable tissue of symbols, metaphors and other suggestive images creating narratives of universal appeal to Indians of all social and religious extractions.

Such characteristics are especially recognizable in allegorical love romances, a literary genre ideally suited for transcending the borders of religious and social divisions. In these poems, humans and animals alike play a specific role aimed at relating the world of our everyday experience with the realm of the transcendent. By adopting the parameters outlined in the treatises that codify Sanskrit and Persian artistic performance, Indo-Muslim poets combined the aesthetic principles of Indian literary tradition with the spiritual didactics of Sufism to instil a poetical taste and sense of inner participation (Skr. *rasānubhāva*) among their audience. This was to culminate in the experience of a link between the heart of the performer and that of the auditor (*sahṛdayatā*). For Sufis, this fundamental concept of Indian representative arts as outlined in the *Nāṭyaśāstra* and further codified by Abhinavagupta's *Abhinavabhāratī* met well with their purpose of conveying subtle meanings pertaining to the main objective of human life which, in India and elsewhere, was traditionally envisaged as the chance to recognize, approach and ultimately achieve intimacy (*qurbat*), identity or union (*waṣl*) with the object of love and of worship.

In Urdu literature, especially in the Deccan but later also in Northern India, the kind of composition best suited for this purpose was the Persian-style *mathnawī*. Typically, works of this genre would tell stories that alter descriptions of erotic, passionate love (*'ishq-o maḥabbat, śṛṅgāra rasa*) with episodes praising the spirit that entices the brave and enduring warrior-lover to move into battle for the sake of conquering country and heart of his beloved (*vīram-rasa*). Combining elements of the *mathnawī* with aspects found in the *rāso-rāsika* literature that flourished in the Rājput courts, this kind of narrative was further 'Indianized' in the mediaeval Hindi literature of Northern

India and became known as *premākhyān* or *premgāthā* (lit. love story). In the course of time, the *premākhyān* became a specific genre of allegorical love romance in which notions and imagery pertaining to Hindu mythology and the Indian environment in general were employed as a background against which its authors developed concepts pertaining to the Sufi doctrine of Divine wisdom (*'ilm al-ilāhī*).

The central theme of these poems is love in separation (*viraha-prema* or *firāq*) which acts as the dynamic force setting into motion the distant lovers and, with them, the entire Universe. Everything that exists in nature is interpreted as a sign hinting at the attainment of the ultimate goal whereby every creature ultimately becomes the actor of Divine Will and contributes in its own right to the eventual success of the human protagonists. The poets of these stories do not depict the multitude of creatures as independent actors but as agents of the all-pervading Divine Consciousness that directs the sincere and wholly committed lover-devotee to the source of all beatitude.

Unsurprisingly, in the fascinating realm of imagination created by these works in imitation of the cosmic play of creation, conservation and reintegration, a specific role is assigned to all living species populating the Universe:

> Seest thou not that it is God whose praises all beings in the heavens and on earth do celebrate, and the birds (of the air) with wings outspread? Each one knows its own (mode of) prayer and praise. And God knows well all that they do. Yea, to God belongs the dominion of the heavens and the earth; and to God is the final goal (of all).
>
> (Qur'an 24.41-42)

These include animals, plants and even minerals.[3] In the universalistic view held by traditional cosmology and reflected in the works of Sufi poets, all creatures occupy a distinct place and play a specific role in the Universal order (*dharma* or *dīn*). They thereby contribute, each in their own peculiar way, to the potential success of the key-players on the stage.

In the *premākhyān*, unlike 'Aṭṭār's poem, the protagonists are humans and the hero (*nāyaka*) reaches his ultimate perfection in the transcendent state of perpetual closeness (*qurbat*) with his Beloved (*ma'shūq* or *priya*). In the hierarchical order that governs the various degrees of existence, the multitude of animals as well as trees, shrubs, flowers and herbs and, to a minor extent, rocks, gems and metals, ultimately converge in their common scope of assisting humans in attaining perfection (*rasāyana*, the science of alchemy).

Among the innumerable animal species sharing the human plane of existence birds undoubtedly hold a prominent rank. Whereas Hindu mythology envisages birds mainly as semi-celestial creatures acting as vehicles (*vāhana*) of the gods thereby complementing the specific nature of the latter, the 'sec-

3. In Hindu cosmology, the world in which we live is referred to as *mānava-lokā* (the 'place of the human being') whereas the Qur'an states: 'And He has subjected to you, as from Him, all that is in the heavens and on earth...' (45.13).

ular' literatures of the Subcontinent contemplate innumerable bird species in order to confer a distinct flavour to the different landscapes, continents (spatial symbolism) and seasons (temporal symbolism) of creation. This is especially true for the love stories in which the colour of the birds' plumage and the beauty of their voice can be used to underline, contextualize and emphasize key moments of or stages in the lovers' quest for each other. The *premākhyān* thus provide the ground for combining the aesthetic aspect elaborated in classical Indian *kāvya* literature with the Sufi symbolism of love as it developed in the Persianate cultural environment.

By the time it reached India, the Persian poetic tradition had already developed a highly sophisticated register transposing the plane of transcendent, divine love (*'ishq-i ḥaqīqī*) into the allegorical description of human love (*'ishq-i majāzī*) with the purpose of translating supernatural realities into an intelligible language. Birds such as the ever-recurring nightingale (*bulbul*) were employed as an allegory of the human soul (*nafs*) trapped in the cage of the physical body yearning to regain its primordial freedom in the unlimited realm of the spirit. All those passionate of Urdu poetry know only too well the *ghazals* of, for instance, Mīr Dard, Ghālib, Ātish and Inshā, where descriptions of the nightingale consuming itself in its longing for the lover in the rose-garden of its unfulfilled desires abound.

Indeed, birds comprise a great variety of species, each of which bearing its own characteristic features. The roles assigned according to the specifics delineated so far insert birds into a context of interaction with the (human) world that unfolds along complementary lines, either horizontal or vertical. The horizontal perspective allows birds to act as messengers between two separate entities sharing the same plane of existence thereby stimulating and assisting them in the gradual process of their reconciliation. The vertical axis allows for the opening of a channel of communication between the immanent and the transcendent planes. In a descending perspective, like in the case of the Roman augurs, the role of birds closely resembles that assigned to the angels who share many functions with the Hindu *devatā*.

In Hindu mythology two important deities of the *trimūrti*, Brahmā, the god of creation, and Viṣṇu, the Preserver, are often depicted as riding birds when intervening in the affairs of the world. In this projection of celestial forces on the earthly plane, *haṃsa*, the wild goose that acts as mount of Brahmā,[4] symbolizes the pure and unconditioned Spirit (*Brahman*) which, directed by its Master, descends and permeates the realm of existence when alighting on the primordial waters of the yet undifferentiated world.

4. In the *Rāmāyaṇa* and the *Mahābhārata* as well as in some pieces of *kāvya* literature this bird is mentioned as *rāj-haṃsa* and seems to refer to the whooper (*Cygnus cygnus*) and the mute swan (*Cygnus olor*), or indeed the royal goose (*Anser indicus*). *Haṃsa* appears to be a generic term applicable to a large variety of bird species belonging of the Anatidae family, including an unspecified variety of swans, geese and ducks (Dave 2005: 422–29).

But birds are also perceived as earthly creatures endowed with the quality of rising (and hence potentially raising others) to the higher dimensions (*loka*) of the Universe. In this sense, birds indicate the possibility of a return and re-absorption of the spirit into the primordial Unity of its celestial principle.[5]

In mediaeval love romances too the *haṃsa*, the noblest of all birds, sometimes represents the archetype of that very human desire that envisages the return of the spirit to its pristine origin, beyond the mental projection of the perishable world, where it is relinquished from all bonds tying ordinary creatures to the apparently endless cycle of birth and rebirth (*saṃsāra*). The Indian wild-goose (sometimes also described as a swan) plays a role resembling that of the Persian *bulbul* and *hudhud*. In the *Madhumālatī*, for instance, one of the celebrated Sufi allegorical stories composed during the first half of the sixteenth century in Northern India by a disciple of the renowned sheikh of the Shaṭṭārī order, Muḥammad al-Ghawth (d. 970/1562), when the queen-mother of the story's heroine discovers Madhumālatī's illicit love affair with Manohar, the prince-hero, she uses a magic spell to transform her daughter into a wondrous non-specified bird (*pakṣī*).[6] Released from all ties with her former life in the royal palace, the restless bird sets out in search of her beloved '...abandoning her parental palace, her wealth and worldly goods and all her friends, companions and relatives...her kingdom, the comfort of her bed, sleep at night, and food in the day... Day and night she wanders restlessly, maddened by love' (*Madhumālatī* 354–55).

In this context, it is worth quoting Manohar's declaration of love to Madhumālatī: 'I have heard that on the day the world was born, the bird of love was released to fly. It flew through all the three worlds, but unable to find a fit resting place it turned and entered the innermost heart...' (*Madhumālatī* 116). Here, the beautiful Sufi image comparing the bird-spirit to Allah, Who, according to a famous *ḥadīth* created the world out of the desire to see His own image reflected in it, is woven into the concept of the threefold universe (*triloka*) common to both Islamic and Hindu cosmology.

Just as the birds encouraged and guided by the hoopoe in Aṭṭār's poem, the transformation of Madhumālatī from a human being into a bird compels/allows her to leave behind the limitations of her precedent life and embark on the search for her beloved. During her quest she is spotted and caught by another prince named Tārācand, whose mind is enchanted and attracted by the birds' outstanding beauty. Eventually, Tārācand becomes Madhumālatī's guide on the path that will eventually lead her to the fulfilment of her Love: 'The pearls [of the Prince's broken crown] fell and rolled through the net; the bird...turned to look properly. Although it wished to fly away...it was mysteri-

5. See how Hindu sacred literature describes *haṃsa*'s flight northwards, escaping the unbearable heat of the Indian summer season, directed at Lake Mānasarovar—hidden between the peaks of the Himālaya—in order to meet his beloved mate (*Aitareya Arānyaka*, 8.23).
6. A *haṃsa* but, judging by its behaviour, also a nightingale or a parrot.

ously attracted to the pearls. In utter surprise, the Prince cries out: This bird indeed lives on pearls!' (*Madhumālatī* 361).

Notwithstanding the occasional parallels to the symbolic role assigned to *haṃsa* in Hindu sacred literature, in the secular *kāvya* literature the bird appears to be appreciated primarily for aesthetic reasons. The image of *haṃsa*'s immaculate plumage and the grace of the movement of its wings have been commonly used as a poetic device both in classical Sanskrit poetry and in the literature of the Indian vernaculars to symbolize outstanding, even super-human, beauty. In the thirteenth century lyrical poem *Haṃsa-sandeśa*, ascribed to Vedānta Desikā, the *haṃsa* plays the role of messenger between Rāma and Sītā, the archetypical Indian love couple protagonists of Vālmikī's *Rāmāyaṇa*. The author dwells extensively on the description of the *haṃsa*'s grace and beauty which is best displayed while in flight to convey his message between the lovers.

The *haṃsa* also appears in a description of Lake Mānasarovar, situated at the feet of Mount Meru, as found in the fourth chapter of the famous romance *Padmāvat* (Jayasi 1995; de Bruijn 2012). This latter is probably the best known among the *premākhyān* written in the Awadhī variant of Eastern Hindī by Malik Muḥammad Jāyasī (c. 1477–1542), a Sufi poet reputedly affiliated to the Indian Chishtī Sufi order. The central figure of the story is Padmāvatī, the lotus-born heroine whose luminous beauty (*ḥusn-i nūrānī*) depicts her as a reflection of divine beauty (*jamālī*) in human shape. In one of the opening scenes describing Padmāvatī taking her bath and playing games with her mates along the shores of the Mānasarovar, the young ladies are observed in their gay activity by the *haṃsa* who, after crouching down on the shores of the sacred lake, feels ashamed of itself when comparing its beauty to that of the maids (*Padmāvat* 4.6).

The beauty (*ḥusn*, *ramaṇīyatā*) that distinguishes many bird species is proverbial in several narratives. The peacock's (*mora* or *puchārī*) magnificence, for instance, is recognized in both heaven and earth (*Madhumālatī* 202)[7]: the peacock displays beauty in multitude, as the colours of its feathers combine the splendour of the celestial vault with the multiple colours of the manifested world.

The intervention of celestial forces in the affairs on earth is represented in Hindu mythology by Garuḍa, identified alternatively with the white-necked or Brahminy kite (*Haliastur indus*) or with a unspecified kind of eagle.[8] Asso-

7. The bird's heavenly origin is contemplated in Persia and in India, as exemplified by Amīr Khusrau. On the one hand, the peacock is evocative of the contemplative observer of God's divine beauty (*jamāl*). On the other, it is a source of pride for the selfish-minded one, whose senses are entangled in the snares of the world thus trapping him/her in the chains of negligence and ignorance (*ghaflat*).

8. This seems to be different from the extremely shy white kite or black-winged kite (*Elanus caerulus*) the sighting of which is frequently described in Indian literature as auspicious sign. See, for instance, the description of Manohar and Madhumālatī's wedding procession where the appearance of this bird is interpreted an assurance of success (*Madhumālatī* 184).

ciated with the sun just like his Persian counterpart, the *simurgh*, and hailed since Vedic times for carrying nectar (*amṛta*) from heaven to earth, in later Purāṇic literature and in the *Mahābhārata*, Garuḍa acts as vehicle of both Viṣṇu and his descent (*avatāra*) Kṛṣṇa.

Clearly, Garuda's role is derived from his representing the celestial influences issuing from the seven heavenly spheres (*svarga*) while confronting the forces of chaos that emanate from the seven inferior worlds (*pātāla*). No wonder that this role confers on Garuḍa the title of 'king of the birds'. He is the ancestor of the bird race and feathered tribes (*suparna*) and the unrelenting antagonist of all snakes (*nāga*). Garuḍa appears as a fearless warrior and insatiable devourer of snakes who intervenes in the cosmic order with the aim of defying the forces of darkness represented by snakes and other reptiles thereby re-establishing the subtle balance between the celestial and the chthonian forces at play in the unfolding of the cosmic drama.[9] Although we find no specific reference to Garuḍa in the *premākhyān*, the perpetuation of this primordial conflict in mediaeval literature lives on in the figure of Nāgmatī, the first wife of Ratansen in the *Padmāvat*. As her name suggests, she embodies the serpent-natured and dark-complexioned counterpart of the radiant, bird-like female protagonist Padmāvatī, her antagonist and rival in love.

These examples provide evidence that birds, just as angels in Semitic cosmology, are ideally suited to act as mediators between the realms of the divine and the human as well as messengers. Such motif is a recurrent one. Among others, it is found in the famous Arabic love tale of *Lailā wa Majnūn*, which reached India through the Persian version of the poet Niẓām al-Dīn Ganjavī (1141–1203).[10] In the story, the hero, Qais, after going mad (*majnūn*) for being refused to marry Laylā, retires to live naked in the wilderness among wild beasts. There, he keeps composing verses dripping of unfulfilled love dedicated to his sweetheart which he entrusts to the birds of the forest with the request to forward them to his beloved.

The already mentioned potential of birds as messengers is further corroborated by the capacity of some species to communicate their knowledge through the use of an articulate voice, singing sweet songs, chirping melodious tunes or even utter words pertaining to the human language. There derives the idea that birds are indeed both sources of wisdom and transmitters of secret messages. The secrets they reveal and the advice they are able to give are in most cases deemed genuine whereas the multitude of languages they speak testifies to the degree of their wisdom.

In the cultural climate of India, this latter role is most typically personified by the parrot (Skr. *śuka* or Per. *ṭoṭa*). His ability to speak, or at least to repeat

9. It is worth mentioning also the myth told in the *Bhagavata-Purāna* 8.2-4 concerning the liberation of the elephant king Gajendra (*Gajendra-mokṣa*) from the jaws of a crocodile by Viṣṇu mounting Garuḍa.
10. One of the most famous modern versions of *Lailā wa Majnūn* (in Urdu) was composed by the great Lakhnawī poet, Mīrzā Muḥammad Hādī Ruswā (1857–1931).

simple words, makes the parrot an ideal messenger, faithful friend and advisor to whom all kinds of secrets can be safely entrusted. Its colourful feathers, effable manners and ability to imitate human words and gestures have made the parakeet one of the favourite domesticated animals of the Subcontinent, where the bird's proverbial intelligence and alleged wisdom is often put to use for the purpose of fortune-telling and other stratagems pertaining to divination (Pinault 2008).

In Hindu mythology the parrot is the vehicle of Kāmadeva, the god of passionate love and erotic pleasure, who aids the lovers in achieving the realization of their longing (Benton 2006: 139–42). These connotations makes it a suitable actor in love stories where it can interpret different roles ranging from that of a narrator of erotic tales to that of savant advisor and trusted messenger of the lovers.

The cross-cultural importance of the parrot is also evident in vernacular literature where its role is praised, for instance, by al-Ghawwāṣī, the poet laureate of the Deccani ruler Sultān 'Abd Allāh Qutb Shāh of Golkonda (r. 1626–1672). Al-Ghawwāṣī composed in the seventeenth century a *mathnawī* titled *Ṭūṭī-nāma* (Tales of a parrot) in Dakhinī Urdū (cf. Kadiri 2010). He presumably based his version on the famous work bearing the same title ascribed to Ḍiyā al-Dīn Nakhshabī (d. 1350), the renowned fourteenth-century physician and disciple of the Chishtī teacher Shaykh Farīd al-Dīn Mas'ūd 'Ganj-i Shakar' of Ajodhan (569/1179–663/1265). This latter work is a translation of an older Persian version and adaptation of the Sanskrit *Śukasaptati* (Haksar 2010, Orsini 1992). Interestingly, the Sufi inspired works of these authors associate the parrot, just as 'Attār did in his famous *mathnawī*, with al-Khiḍr, the mysterious guide of Moses mentioned in the Qur'an (*sūrat al-kahf*) who, endowed with the most intimate science of Allah (*'ilm al-ladunnī*), became the prototype of the super-human instructor of all Sufis (cf. Dahnhardt 2004).

In the narrative of the original Sanskrit, perpetuated in innumerable popular versions all over the Subcontinent, the parrot acts principally as a storyteller. Its narration aims at preventing Prabhāvatī, the lonely wife of a rich merchant, from giving in to the temptation of meeting her lover during the prolonged absence of her husband. The parrot appears here in his role of narrator and entertainer who, while indirectly helping to maintain the link of fidelity between husband and wife, ultimately allows for the happy reunion of the couple.

The importance of the parrot or parakeet (Hindi: *śuka* or *totā*) in Indian and Persianate Sufi literature is further extended in the *Padmāvat*. Here, the parrot is one of the protagonists interpreting multiple roles as messenger, erudite preceptor of the heroine and spiritual guide of the hero. The savant, golden-coloured parakeet or parrot is named Hīrāman (lit. diamond-like mind), a name that is indicative of its role and nature since, we are told, the diamond is in itself colourless (like *buddhi* or *'aql*, the intellect) but in its spotless beauty are reflected the colours of the entire spectrum just as the mind reflects all the impressions it receives from the surrounding world. The very name of the animal indicates the intimate affinity between him and his Master or the lotus-like princess Padminī, herself the embodiment of divine beauty (*jamāl*) and divine perfection (*kamāl*). As such, the description of both, the human and the non-human animal hero, bears witness to a direct relation with the symbolism of light (*nūr*) elaborated in Sufi cosmology where, termed as the 'light of Muhammad' (*nūr al-muḥammadī*), it represents the connecting link between the transcendent and the immanent dimensions of Universe.

In the story, the parrot originally belongs to Padmāvatī, the daughter of Gandharvasen, the ruler of Siṃhala. The celestial beauty of this legendary island becomes evident at the beginning of the story. While describing the island in terms reminiscent of the Garden of Eden, Jayasī informs us that Siṃhala is covered by thick forests inhabited by various species of birds which, although speaking many different languages, all share one common topic in their conversations:

> While sitting on branches dripping with nectar (*amṛta*), the fire-tailed myzornis chirps and the pigeons bill and coo: Only one, only You! (*ekehī, eke tuhī*); the starling and the (wild) parrot sing melodious songs, the ringdove clamours, the large hawk cuckoo (*papīha*) calls on his beloved: *Pīv, pīv!* The warbler (*phudkī*), mad with joy, begins to invoke his beloved: *Tuu, tuu*; the cuckoo (*koyala*) repeats his lonely verse, the racket-tailed drongo (*bhṛṅga rāja, Dicrurus paradisaeus*) speaks many different languages; the nightjar calls out: *dahī, dahī* (I burn, I burn with love), while the wild pigeon (*kapota*) laments its defeat against its rival in love. The peacock calls on the mate to diplay his beauty, the crow (*kāga*) keeps chatting and makes a great many noises. This forest is plenty of birds and each of them in its own language invokes the name of God. At the centre of the island is said to be situated the lake Mānasarovar. Everything in this lofty abode appears to live in constant memory (*dhikr*) of the supreme Lord.
>
> (*Padmāvat* 1.5)

The symbolism of love is used to describe the primordial harmony (*dharma*) that reigns in the realm where Padmāvatī and her parrot Hīrāman reside. By contrast with the above description of the wilderness, the narrative then turns to the parrot kept as tamed animal by Padmāvatī in a cage inside the royal palace.

> God had endowed this animal with such a radiance that its eyes were shining like gems and its face was gleaming like pearls and rubies: it was a splendid parrot of gold-like colour, the two were [i.e. the parrot and Padmāvatī] as if gold had molten with the flux. Inseparable, they always enjoyed the company of each other, engaged in the study of the Veda and the treatises concerning Divine knowledge; while listening to their subtle talks, Brahmā himself assented with a nod of his head.
>
> (*Padmāvat* 3.5)

While in the relation between a non-human animal and its human *protegé* the parrot embodies a luminous beauty reflecting that of his lady-master, his function at court consists of instructing her to exoteric sciences. From his beak flow words of erudition and the bird is described as omniscient. Yet notwithstanding the intimate tie linking the two beauties, the real, most intimate nature of the savant bird emerges more clearly when it relates itself to the realm of the created world, the natural attraction for which is indicated by the parrot's innate desire (*ḥubb*) to acquire freedom in the forest. The desire of the parrot to evade from the cage and fly out into the world seems here to convey the meaning expressed in a well-known *ḥadīth qudsī*: 'I was a Treasure but was not known, so I loved to be known. Then I created the creatures and made Myself known to them, so they came to know Me' (in Chittick 1998: 70).

Threatened with death by jealous (human) enemies at court, the loyal animal is moved by the desire to regain his original freedom and so escapes into the forest where it is welcomed and revered by wild birds. But alas, the wisdom of the extraordinary bird pertains to a higher order which sets him apart from the limited horizon of the other birds living in the forest.

Eventually the parrot, failing to recognize the danger of an approaching hunter in disguise, is caught and taken to the market of Siṃhala for sale. Entangled in the snares of the material world represented by the bazaar, the parrot is bought by a poor Brahmin who recognizes the value of the learned bird and takes it with him to the capital of Ratansen. Impressed by the beauty and wisdom of the parrot, Ratansen acquires it from the Brahmin and introduces it to the royal chambers of the palace at Chittaur.

At this stage, after being transposed into the depth of the material world, the parrot starts to act as (divine) instructor (*gurudeva*, *shaykh al-kāmil*) and targets Nāgmatī, the antagonist of Padmāvatī. Hurt in her pride by the savant parrot who reminds the selfish queen: 'On a lake never visited by *hamsa*, they call the heron a swan' (*Padmāvat* 8.2), Nāgmatī becomes aware of the danger represented by the bird's presence at court and once again orders are issued to kill the animal. But Ratansen acknowledges the bird's true nature and welcomes him as preceptor and master: 'Hīrāman is a savant parrot, his words are like dripping nectar...a savant's tongue is always sincere...and since it abhors any perversion, it leads onto the straight path and offers an upright opinion' (*Padmāvat* 8.6).

From this moment onwards, the parrot assumes the role of spiritual guide of the Rājput ruler. Through the description of the beauty of his former patron Padmāvatī (*Padmāvat* 9), the bird acts as a messenger of divine love instilling a passionate attraction in the heart of his new adept. Revealing his own identity, the bird informs his eager disciple: 'I, Hīrāman, was her parrot: I grew up in her service and have learnt the human speech, otherwise what destiny would have befallen this humble fist of feathers' (*Padmāvat* 9.2). Ratansen is then instructed of the need to renounce the world and die to oneself in order to aspire to success on the path of love (*prema-mārga*). The initiation proper consists of an exaltation of the heroine's beauty, achieved through the traditional literary device of a 'head to toe' description (*nakha-śikha varṇana*) of Padmāvatī's physical beauty delivered by the parrot. The king thus decides to abandon his reign and set out on the long journey to Siṃhala during which the parrot guides his disciple and indicates to him the way to the promised destination. Here the bird embodies the wisdom of the human *sheikh* or *guru* who leads his disciple (*murīd, śiṣya*) through the treacherous tracts of the initiatory path. As the parrot points out: 'Only he can be a guide who has himself witnessed the path; only he can fly who has himself grown wings on his body, otherwise he resembles a twig that causes its leaves to fall or a blind leading another blind...' (*Padmāvat* 12.13).

Significantly, once Ratansen has fulfilled his mission (the marriage with Padmāvatī), the parrot disappears from the narrative (*Padmāvat* 26). In fact, another, unspecified, bird-messenger (*dūta, saṁdeśavāhaka*) appears on the scene. Its role consists of recalling the now realized hero back from his celestial abode in Siṃhala to his earthly mission in Chittaur (*Padmāvat* 31). After suffering the pain of separation throughout the twelve months of the six Indian seasons (*bārahmāsa*), Nāgmatī, the abandoned queen and antithesis of Padmāvatī, leaves her royal chambers and ventures out to consult herself with the birds of the forest:

> Like a peacock (as we have seen, a bird closely associated with snakes, as both are typically associated with the Indian raining season) I have come to live in the forest to question you about my beloved husband...my beloved has turned me into a *kharabān*...however, I continue to survey his path, like a green pigeon [*hārīt*]: but alas, to which bird could I possibly entrust my message? Oh white dove, fly out to my beloved and tell him: Even though in your heart you may be angry with me, that woman knows nothing but your name! And you too, little weaver bird [suhar], and you, dear skylark [*chātak*], if you will lead me to re-embrace my beloved husband you will be equal to a hawk. I am your cuckoo who invokes the name of his beloved repetitiously: call it out, you too, O *maharī*, and throw out your inflamed cry. Come, my dear starling [*mainā*],[11] come close, ye dear goose: oh jay, the torment of love has pierced my heart! But oh: as soon as I talk about this pain of mine, the birds too burst into fire...
>
> (*Padmāvat* 30.18)

Finally, when Nāgmatī is about to faint, a tiny bird approaches her in the heart of the night, enquiring about her state. To this creature, representing the torment of the queen's heart exemplified by the many different birds invoked before, Nāgmatī entrusts the message of burning love that bursts out her afflicted soul. The bird, after setting out on its mission transforms itself into a ball of blazing fire burning everything it encounters along its path until it eventually reaches Siṃhala and delivers the message of love to its addressee

11. The *mainā* (also myna in English) belongs to the family of the starlings and is renowned for its skills of imitation.

thereby instilling in the Prince's heart a strong feeling of nostalgia for his beloved homeland (*waṭan*).[12]

With the delivery of Nāgmatī's message to Ratansen ends the fascinating and mysterious task assigned to birds in this love story. From that moment onwards begins the journey of return of Ratansen, which leads him back to his reign and fortress where he is to reconcile the love of his two wives and eventually achieve his ultimate perfection after meeting death in battle. Although this final act of self-sacrifice finds its corroboration in the Rājput code of chivalry, it is also in line with the Sufi doctrine that contemplates the intimate friend of God's (*walī*) return to the realm of creation (*rujū'*). In imitation of the example set by the Prophet, he thus accomplishes perfection (*kamāl*) through extinction of his individual existence (*fanā al-fanā*). As such, a death like Ratansen's represents the ultimate mission of the perfected human being.

Back to the *Madhumālatī*, we have already mentioned that here it is the heroine who is transformed into a bird. This condition releases her from the bonds of the royal palace and thus facilitates her search for her beloved Manohar. Moved by the unbearable pain (*dard*) of being separated from her beloved (*viraha*), this bird is so described by Manjhan:

> She flew faster even than the wind, many set out to pursue her but no one could catch her...her feathers were green, her legs were red, her beak was beautiful and her eyes were large and gleaming like...pearls; ...such a rare bird had never been seen before in the Kali age.
>
> (*Madhumālatī* 357)

Thus, in visualizing the exceptional creature that apparently combines the qualities of the *haṃsa* and the parrot as described in the *Padmāvat* (or for that matter the *bulbul* and the *hudhud*), beauty (*ḥusn*) and virtue (*ikhlāq*) go side by side and convey the idea of a super-human, nay super-natural creature roaming through the realm of creation in search of the perfect human and receptacle of unconditional love. Eventually, the bird decides 'to sacrifice its life on the path of love' and lets itself be caught in the fowler's net, 'that it might fulfil its ultimate desire, Manohar' (*Madhumālatī* 361). After undergoing a series of trials as a bird, the heroine eventually regains her original human shape, ready for the final and definite encounter with her beloved. In this subtle play of transformation, the role of man and bird has found its resolution and the separate, distinct identity of both is ultimately transcended in the mystery of the night during which the two lovers meet achieving everlasting union.

From an observation of the role played by birds in the Sufi love-poems, it appears evident that birds too have been subject to the same process of indigenization that the *mathnawī* underwent in the Subcontinent. Like other

12. See Mirabāī's *Padāvalī*: 'Putting crows to flight my days have passed in vain... (*Padāvalī* 115). Crows too act as messengers sent by the woman in love to her distant lover. In India, the direction taken by the bird (in this case, the crow) once put to fly is an indication for the *virāhinī* of the way from which the beloved may eventually return.

features of Indo-Persian culture, the literature produced by the Sufis who authored love stories gradually substituted both Persian and Hindu narratives, as they were better suited to reach and stimulate the imagination of both the indigenous and the indigenized mind. In its scope but also in style, technique and, of course, imagery, the *premgāthā* perpetuates the didactical pattern of the Persian-style Sufi *mathnawī* but, further to that, it adds images and symbolic connotations pertaining to the cultural code of the Indian subcontinent. In this process, the transcendent power of human and super-human love exemplified by the actors involved in the story invites the audience to move beyond the cultural borders defined, for instance, by conventions of language.

Although the role played by birds emerging from the descriptions found in the allegorical Sufi narratives is largely based on and derived from well-established precedents encountered in the cultural environment of both India and the Persianate Middle-East, their adaptations testify the canny use made by its authors in bringing together notions pertaining to the repertoire of the respective poetic traditions with the aim of creating an allegorical poem which describes fundamental aspects of the path of spiritual realization. Reminding us of the example set somewhat nearer to my own cultural environment by St Francis of Assisi roughly during the same period, these stories demonstrate that here and there and everywhere those capable of understanding the language of the birds were thus given the privilege of communicating with the most intimate friend and beloved of all, the Lord himself.

REFERENCES

Benton, C. 2006. *God of Desire: Tales of Kamadeva in Sanskrit Story Literature*. Albany, NY: State University of New York Press.

Chittick, W. C. 1998. *The Self-disclosure of God: Principles of Ibn Al-*ʻArabī's *Cosmology*. Albany, NY: State University of New York Press.

Dahnhardt, T. 2004. 'Encounters with Khidr: Saint-Immortal, Protector from the Waters and Guide of the Elected Ones beyond the Confluence of the Two Oceans.' In A. Rigopoulos (ed.), *Guru: The Spiritual Master in Eastern and Western Traditions: Authority and Charisma*: 105–20. Venezia: Cafoscarina.

Dave, K. N. 2005 (1985). *Birds in Sanskrit Literature*. Revised edn. Delhi: Motilal Banarssidas Publishers.

de Bruijn, T. 2012. *The Ruby in the Dust: Poetry and History of the Indian Padmāvat by Sufi Poet Muhammad Jayasi*. Leiden: Leiden University Press.

Haksar, A. N. D. (trans.). 2010. *Shuka Saptati: Seventy Tales of the Parrot*. Calcutta: Rupa & Co.

Holy Qur'ān, The. Text, translation and commentary by 'Abdullāh Yūsuf 'Alī. 1413/1992. Beirut: Al-ʻInāyat Baṭabʻa wa nashr ʻUlūmiya.

Jayasi, M. M. 1995. *Il poema della donna di loto (Padmavat)* (edited and translated from the original Awadhi into Italian by Giorgio Milanetti). Venice: Marsilio.

Kadiri, M. 2010. *Tota-Kahani: Or Tales of a Parrot, in the Hindustani Language (1852)*. Translated by S. H. B. Haydari. Whitefish: Kessinger Publishing.

Manjhan, S. 2000. *Madhumālatī, an Indian Sufi Romance*. Edited and translated by A. Behl and S. Weightman. Oxford: Oxford University Press.

Mortensen, E. 2006. 'Raven Augury from Tibet to Alaska.' In P. Waldau and K. Patton (eds), *A Communion of Subjects: Animals in Religion, Science and Ethics*: 423–36. New York: Columbia University Press.

Orsini, F. (trans.). 1992. *Le storie del pappagallo—Śukasaptati*. Venice: Marsilio.

Pinault, D. 2008. *Notes from the Fortune-Telling Parrot: Islam and the Struggle for Religious Pluralism in Pakistan*. London: Equinox.

Radhakrishnan, S. (ed.). 1994. *The Principal Upaniṣads*. New Delhi: HarperCollins.

The Biggest Star of All: The Elephant in Hindi Cinema

RACHEL DWYER*

The Indian elephant, *Elephas maximus indicus*, or the *ibha, gaja, hastin, karin, matanga, naga, varana, kanjara, padmin, dvipa, dantin, sindhura*, to give him but a few of his Sanskrit names, has been part of Indian civilization and culture for more than three thousand years. However, little has been written about elephants in cinema where they have featured for nearly a hundred years. This chapter looks at how the elephant's cinematic image developed from their earlier representations to create a new way of looking at the elephant and considers why this is increasingly important at a time when the animal's future is in the balance.

ELEPHANTS IN INDIAN CULTURE

The elephant permeates all aspects of Indian culture (Ram 2007; Sukumar 2011). Elephant images are found as far back as the Indus Valley Civilization (c. 3300–1300 BCE), then on Mauryan imperial insignia (third century BCE) and on Ashokan pillars, whether topping the pillar at Sankissa or as carvings, notably on the Sarnath pillar whose lions form the National Emblem of the modern Republic of India. Elephants support the great temples of Ellora; and appear on 'Arjuna's Penance' in 'The Descent of the Ganges', the famous sculpture at Mahabalipuram (c. seventh/eighth century), where there is also the statue of an elephant outside the Nakula-Sahadeva *ratha*.[1] Statues of ele-

* Rachel Dwyer is Professor of Indian Cultures and Cinema at the School of Oriental and African Studies (SOAS), University of London. She took her BA in Sanskrit at SOAS, followed by an MPhil in General Linguistics and Comparative Philology at the University of Oxford. Her PhD research was on the Gujarati lyrics of Dayaram (1777–1852). She has published ten books several of which are on Indian cinema. Professor Dwyer has recently completed *Beyond the Boundaries of Bollywood: The Many Forms of Hindi Cinema*, co-edited with Jerry Pinto (Oxford University Press, 2011) and *Bollywood's India: Indian Cinema as a Guide to Modern India* for Reaktion Books, London, is forthcoming 2014. Her next project is on the Indian elephant.

1. A monolithic chariot named after two of the five Pandava brothers, the heroes of the *Mahabharata*. The place is a UNESCO World Heritage site and is located c. 60 km south of Chennai, Tamil Nadu.

phants have been erected in the Ambedkar Park in Noida by the former Chief Minister of Uttar Pradesh, Mayavati, whose party has the elephant as a symbol. Folk images of elephants decorate buildings and are used as block prints on fabric; miniature paintings feature hunts and processional elephants, while in *shatranj*, a form of chess, the bishop is *alfil* (from Arabic: *al-fi'l*), the elephant.

Elephants also feature in Indian mythology from the story of the emergence of Indra's mount, the seven-trunked white elephant Airavata, from the churning of the Milky Ocean, alongside the other *dikpalas* or supporters of the world. The association of elephants with rain and fertility is also prominent, as it appears in the image of Gajalaksmi, an aspect of the goddess Lakshmi who bathes with elephants, while other myths, such as that of the flying elephants grounded by the irate sage Dirghapatas associate them with the sky. Ganesh, the elephant-headed god with the body of a child, is one of India's most popular gods as the Remover of Obstacles (Vighnesha), invoked at the beginning of any work or task (Courtright 1985).

Elephants are popular motifs not just in art, but are themselves art objects as wearers of ornaments and caparisoning for ceremonies, ranging from jewellery such as necklaces, anklets, and trunk ornaments, to functional objects such as howdahs and ankushes (goads), and regalia. Ivory and other trinkets made from killing elephants, which were once abundant, are now banned internationally but the trade has not unfortunately ceased (Walker 2009).

Elephants formed one of the four divisions of the ancient army, famed in the west after King Poros and his elephants fought against Alexander the Great, but they were also draught animals and used as executioners (Digby 1971). These war elephants shaped Indian architecture, as forts had elephant gates (*gajadvara*), gates large enough to let an elephant through, as well as having spikes to stop elephants being used as battering rams. Inside the forts were the *pil-khanas*, the elephant stables, which had to house the thousands of elephants of the Mughal emperors. War elephants were also highly prized. Digby mentions that Akbar the Great was a connoisseur of elephants and had many favourites in his stable (1971: 65).

Elephants feature abundantly throughout Indian literature. They are characters in the animal fables, the *Hitopadesha* and the *Panchatantra*, although they do not have the features for which they are prized today, seeming instead to be a rather foolish animal, outwitted by the cunning jackal. In Sanskrit *kavya*, or court literature, the elephant was often compared to humans. One of the most celebrated comparisons is that of a woman as *gajagamani* (she who has the gait of an elephant) to mean a particularly graceful, swaying walk. Heroes are compared to elephants as figures of strength. King Dushyanta in Kalidasa's *Shankuntala* is compared to an elephant. As Edgerton (1985: 4 n.4) points out, he is compared to a particular kind of elephant, the *girichara* (mountain-ranging) elephant which is known to be a particular kind of 'sturdy, brave and warlike' elephant. Elephants are likened to clouds in Kalidasa's epic *Meghaduta* and in the poetry of Amir Khusrau (Digby 1971), and they complement the aesthetic beauty of the landscape in Kalidasa's *Raghuvamsha.*

Folk tales of elephants are found (e.g. Narayan 2009), and women are compared to elephants in erotic literature such as the Sanskrit *Anangaranga.* Kipling's *Just So* stories of the elephant include 'How the elephant got his trunk', and 'Toomai of the elephants' is the story of a boy's maturing through his work with his tusker, Kala Nag. This enthusiasm was shared by his father, John Lockwood Kipling, who has a chapter on elephants (1904), where he notes the names given to elephants—*Moti Gaj* (Pearl Elephant), *Kala Naag* (Black Snake), and *Dulary* (Beloved).

Indian scientific literature also includes writings on the elephant. The *Gajashastra*, composed in Sanskrit over several centuries, beginning with the *Arthashastra* which has information about the king's elephants. Medical treatises, the *Hastyayurveda*, also deal with elephants. Later works which specialize in elephant knowledge include the *Hastividyarnava*, produced in Assam in 1734 (Barkath 1976) and the *Matangalila* (Edgerton 1931), which has been translated into Malayalam. It seems that these were compiled from the knowledge of mahouts and were used by the British in their forestry work for capturing, training and maintaining elephants. These texts—which are still in use today—contain information about 'castes' of elephants, different types of elephants, how they need to be looked after and their diet throughout the changing seasons, as well as the distinguishing features of elephants which make them particularly auspicious. These texts develop a huge vocabulary for elephants, ranging from words for elephants at different stages of life, the parts of the body, the stages of musth,[2] as well as stable stories. This material is still used today on contemporary websites (Elephant Spotlight) where detailed analysis of the form of the elephant and his characteristics are mentioned. They have pictures of famous elephants, who are awarded honorific titles, as well as awards for best posture, trunk length, tails, many of which build on the older science exposed in the *Gajashastra.*

THE ELEPHANT IN INDIAN CINEMATIC CULTURE

This brief survey of the elephant in Indian culture shows that there are well-established aesthetics of the elephant which date back to the earliest history, demonstrating that there is a significant background that can be drawn on to examine the representation of the elephant in Indian movies. Cinema, which is located in the ever-moving dynamic between tradition and modernity,

2. A periodic condition in bull elephants. The rise in testosterone levels causes highly aggressive behaviour and makes elephants particularly dangerous. Elephants in musth can be recognized by the discharge a thick secretion called temporin from the temporal ducts on the sides of the head.

drawing on Indian cultural forms framed by western technology and in a constant dialogue with other media, has been constantly changing throughout the century since the first all-Indian film was made in 1913, D. G. Phalke's *Raja Harischandra.* This chapter does not explore all of India's many movies, nor indeed does it survey all Hindi films, but rather presents some films which feature elephants, where the elephant steals the scene to be the biggest star of all.

One of the earliest films to star an elephant made in the west was Alexander Korda's *Elephant Boy*, directed by Robert Flaherty and Zoltan Korda, 1937. Robert Flaherty, the famed documentary maker of *Nanook of the North* (1922) and *Man of Aran* (1934), shot extensive wildlife footage in India. Korda, worried about how to market the movie, decided to graft on the story of Kipling's 'Toomai of the elephants'. Though the magnificent tusker, Irawat, who plays Kala Nag, was much admired, he did not play a character as such but was the companion of the orphaned boy whose care of the elephant brought him status and respect in British and Indian society. The film established the first international Indian superstar, Sabu, a mahout's son from Mysore, and was successful commercially and acclaimed critically. The movie won awards at the Venice Film Festival the same year as the Marathi devotional film, *Sant Tukaram*, directed by V. S. Damle and S. Fattelal, creating an image of a religious, pre-British India, depicting the gentle masculinity of a saint, very different from that of Korda's hyper-masculine film which has no female characters.

Walt Disney's *Dumbo* (1941) is one of the most popular and successful cartoons of all time. This is a modern animal fable story, showing how difference can be an advantage, as the huge ears which bring about the separation of baby and mother elephant and the cruel treatment of the baby while his mother is in captivity eventually lead to his success and his mother's raised status. The baby elephant is portrayed as 'cute' and is demonstrably emotional as a human baby. But he never speaks, and his mother speaks only once to give him his name, Jumbo Jr, which the malicious, talking, elephants change to Dumbo. These two mute animals, Mrs Jumbo and Dumbo, remain more animal than other animal characters in the film. They speak through their expressions and bodies, and communicate in a direct manner, perhaps linked to the love children have for non-speaking objects, such as stuffed animals. Although Mrs Jumbo does not speak, she seems to be the unidentified source for the Oscar-winning, tear-jerking lullaby, 'Baby mine', which is not synced to her mouth.

Yet, in spite of the huge success of these two films, it is not clear that they had any direct impact on the depiction of elephants in Indian films. Indian cinema is aware of and has been directly influenced by other cinemas, in particular Hollywood, while animals have featured in Hollywood since the earliest days to the present (*Puss in Boots*, 2011), as they have in Indian films. The latter has featured other 'famous' animals such as the tonga-pulling horse Dhanno in *Sholay* (directed by Ramesh Sippy, 1975), the hawk Allah Rakha in Coolie (directed by Manmohan Desai, 1983), pigeons which carry messages and have flashbacks (*Maine pyar kiya*, directed by Sooraj Barjatya, 1989), or Tuffy the dog who takes messages at God's instruction (*Hum aapke hain kaun...!*, directed by Sooraj Barjatya, 1994). Although these animals seem to follow language, act consciously or take directions from the divine, the elephant has a particular role in bringing these previous symbolic meanings to the film as well as starring in it to the extent of eclipsing the major human star.

Europeans associated the elephant with the wonder of India. Having been curious about the animal at least since Hannibal, and throughout history (Sukumar 2011), the elephant provided spectacle in many of the early films. The Colonial Forestry Department made a documentary film of a *kheddah*, the capturing of elephants in a stockade (Sanderson 1907); a cruel practice which continued in Mysore until 1971, and beyond in some areas. Elephants feature in films to show the high, usually royal, status of the characters as they are associated with power and authority as well as wealth. The King of Jaipur lent his elephants for the shooting of the Indo-German co-production, *Light of Asia* (directed by Franz Osten, 1925), to help to convey the status of Gautama Buddha's family, while films on the Mughals—from *Mughal-e Azam*, directed by K. Asif (1960) to *Jodhaa Akbar*, directed by Ashutosh Gowariker (2008)—have featured elephants as war animals as well as symbols of strength. Superstar Rajnikant has a pet elephant in *Muthu*, by K. S. Ravikumar, 1995 (Tamil), to show his wealth, although given the film's pastiche of Rajni's superstar status, the elephant may well be a royal association.

Religious genres have shown ceremonial elephants representing religious power and feeling, notably the Malayalam biopic of the divine elephant, Guruvayoor Kesavan, directed by Bharathan, 1977, and in *Navrang*, of V. Shantaram. 1959, where during the poet's Holi song, an elephant emerges from a statue of Ganesh to dance.

White elephants also feature as mystical creatures. The eponymous white elephant of the National Award winning film, *Safed haathi*, directed by Tapan Sinha (1978), appears in the forest to help a boy who has had a difficult life. *The White Elephant*, of Aijaz Khan (2009), is the story of a sacred elephant who transforms people's lives. Elephants make brief appearances in many films as forestry animals, such as in *Munimji*, directed by Subodh Mukherji (1955), where the elephant hates lies; *Pakeezah*, of Kamal Amrohi (1971), where a herd of elephants disrupts the boat ride; or trained elephants in films such as *Rajendrudru Gajendrudru*, directed by S. V. Krishan Reddy and Ranga Rao Kurra, 1993 (Telugu) and *Kumki*, of Prabhu Solomon, 2012 (Tamil).

There is one film in which elephants have starred, eclipsing even the major human star of the day, Rajesh Khanna. This is *Haathi mere saathi* ('The Elephants are my Companions', hereafter abbreviated to *HMS*), directed by M. A Thirumugham and produced by 'Sandow' M. M. A. Chinappa Devar, 1971.

It was the first film of the screenwriting duo, Salim (Khan)-Javed (Akhtar), who wrote many classics of Hindi cinema including *Sholay* (1975) and *Deewaar* (1975), although the dialogues were written by Inder Raj Anand. *HMS* was the biggest box office hit of its year and made the most money of any film by that date.

The film's fame lives on today as the name of a 2011 campaign to raise awareness of elephants by the Ministry of Environment and Forests in partnership with Wildlife Trust of India. While the film's title song is best remembered, the music by Laxmikant-Pyarelal broke records for HMV as the first Indian record to win a silver disk and lyricist Anand Bakshi and the team were given a special award from the Society for Prevention of Cruelty to Animals (SPCA) for the song '*Nafrat ki duniya ko chhod kar pyar ki duniya mein khush rehna mere yaar*' ('Having left this world of hatred, may you live happily in the world of love, my friend') about cruelty to animals.

The film's story is as follows. A young boy, Raju, is thrown from his father's car in an accident. The father prays to the god Ganesh who sends four elephants, Ramu, Damu, Mahesh and Ganesh, to look after him and take him home. When his father succumbs to his injuries, the elephants become Raju's family, helped by a loyal retainer. Raju's real family and family servants swindle him out of his considerable inheritance and he is forced to take to the street, abandoning hope of marrying Tanu, whose wealthy father would approve of only a rich man. The elephants and he look after one another, becoming street performers, until their success enables him to start a zoo, 'Pyar ki duniya', the world of love. Tanu and Raju eventually marry and have a son.[3] However, after finding she can't have another child, Tanu, in worse case post-natal depression, becomes obsessed that Ramu will kill their son and makes Raju choose between family and the elephants. Raju chooses Ramu though beats him for allegedly attacking his son. Then Ramu breaks into Tanu's house to protect the boy from a snake; however, Raju's competitors try to shoot him and Ramu takes the bullet. Tanu realizes her mistake and Raju builds a memorial to Ramu at which the whole family—four-legged and two-legged—prays.

Raju was played by Rajesh Khanna who was the biggest star of Hindi cinema at the time, while Tanu was played by Tanuja, from the Samarth dynasty to which Nutan and Kajol belong. However, they were eclipsed by the four pachyderms, in particular by Ramu, who has the major role with others in support, presumably to be family rather than just a friend, even though the title of the film is *saathi*, 'companion', rather than family. Although the elephants are meant to be male, I think Ramu is a cow as they all look like small female, well-trained circus elephants. Bull elephants, tuskers in particu-

3. While Raju grows up to have his own family, the elephants in the film are childlike and asexual, and do not mate or reproduce. Elephants follow a similar life cycle to humans, with reproduction beginning in their teens but these elephants are devoted to Raju and are more like ideal servants, loyal and faithful.

lar, are more prestigious. As captive elephants they do not live in groups and the owners have to deal with musth, whereas cows form groups with a matriarch, which seems to be Ramu's role. The elephants are all named after gods: Ganesh, Mahesh is Maheshvara (Shiva) while Ramu and Damu are diminutives of Rama and Damodara (Krishna).

The story of the jungle boy is familiar, most notably because of Kipling's *The Jungle Book* about Mowgli who lives with the animals until he has to return to human settlement as he grows up, or similar stories such as Tarzan. However, in *HMS* the narration is reversed as the elephants come to live in the city rather than the boy being raised in the jungle. *HMS* is about domesticating the wild and bringing humans and animals closer together in the opposite direction. The boy does not become like an animal and learn to live by the Law of the Jungle, rather the elephants become human and domesticated.

Tanu does not trust the elephants to be truly human, even though Raju believes they are his family, and fears Ramu's closeness, demanding he be treated like a wild animal and chained. It is striking that her distrust begins to emerge after the romantic honeymoon and could be read as her fear of her husband's animal nature or simply as a mistrust of her husband's family.

Tanu is associated with cars throughout the film, a symbol of wealth and modernity. The famous title song where Raju meets Tanu has the elephants towing her car then pushing it to a garage. Tanu has a huge imported car of her own which she drives but she also has a car with a driver once she is married and her father drives his own car. Raju is nearly killed at the beginning of the film in a car crash and he prefers to travel with his elephants, who also represent feudal wealth: the servant remarks that even kings cannot afford to keep elephants these days.

In *HMS* the animals remain better than the humans and the film mentions that the worst animal is the two-legged one. Tanu's father, Ratanlal, lies to her; people are obsessed with money (apart from the doctor whom the elephants bring to Raju); the family and servants are cheats. Raju watches his wife leave home after he slaps her, but when he beats Ramu with a chain, and breaks down, the elephant caresses him with his trunk. The elephants love without expectation of return and they do not stop loving whatever happens. The three surviving elephants forgive Tanu, as does Raju, perhaps because he has learnt about love from the elephants. The world of animals is the *pyar ki duniya*, the world of love, and the film has many sequences in which even lions and tigers are portrayed as gentle, loving creatures.

The elephants are shown to be very human in the film, where they are moral and ethical. They put Raju's welfare above their own and pray to Ganesh for his welfare and seek out a doctor when he is sick. Ramu sacrifices his life knowingly, in order to bring the family back together, even though he has not done any wrong himself. He shows the inhumanity of humans and how they must learn from the example of animals to be selfless and forgiving. Raju already knows how to be like this as he has been brought up by the elephants as much as humans but the others do not have this knowledge even after spending time with animals and have to be shocked into accepting this. The elephants understand emotion and seem to follow language though they do not speak. There are many close-ups of the elephants, in particular of their eyes as if seeing what they think and they communicate with each other and with Raju. At the end of the film, when Tanu asks Raju to forgive her, there are close-ups of the elephants' eyes which seem to return his gaze to grant their permission. Ramu is particularly emotionally expressive as he weeps, gets distressed, sympathizes, smiles. However, he is misunderstood by Tanu, abused by Raju and Raju's competitors attempt to murder him with a needle in a banana, before they kill him when they try to shoot Raju.

Despite Tanu's fears, the elephants bring little of the wild with them. However, they are closely connected to the divine. They are directed to rescue Raju by Ganesh at the beginning of the film when Raju's father prays to the god to bring his child home. The elephants also worship Ganesh when Raju falls ill. Although clearly associated with Ganesh, when Ramu dies, Raju takes his corpse to a temple, a mosque and a church. He is then buried with a *chador* (usually associated with Muslim tombs) and the grave is heaped up with flowers. In the closing scene, Ramu's statue is garlanded and prayed to by the whole family, including the other elephants and zoo animals in the manner of a revered or deified Hindu figure.

HMS is always discussed as a children's film. However, unlike most children's films, the key actors are adults and there is no major role for a child. The film has plenty of adult romance and takes an adult perspective. Given the huge success of *HMS*, it was inevitable that a remake would be made. The same team made a film called *Maa* in 1976, persuading the stars of 1975's blockbuster *Sholay*, Dharmendra and Hema Malini, to take the star roles. The film is about the capturing of elephants and other animals for a circus. Warned by his mother not to separate children from their mothers, Dharmendra insists it is his business and captures a baby elephant. The animal's mother is so distraught that she attacks Dharmendra, whose mother intervenes and is eventually killed by the elephant. The woman dies making his son promise that he will reunite the baby elephant with its mother. The baby hates Dharmendra and seeks revenge. While eluding capture making Dharmendra sing and dance for him before trying to escape, he gets his leg stuck in a railway track. Our hero stops the train when it is only feet away and touches the elephant's feet to beg forgiveness. The elephant and he fight villains, escape a plane crash, then the baby is reunited with his mother. Dharmendra sees the elephant as his own mother and realizes how much all creatures love their children and will keep his mother's word never to separate mothers and babies again. The film did not enjoy much commercial success although it has potential as a cult classic.

FROM ANIMAL TO GOD: GANESH IN INDIAN CINEMA

Ganesh, who is not an elephant but a god in the form of a human child with a elephant's head, has featured in movies at different levels (Dwyer 2006).[4] Many films feature the worship and celebration of Ganesh, not just in the opening credits where he is invoked as the Lord of Beginnings, but often for a dramatic sequence in many films. The Bombay Ganapati festival is particularly popular in cinema as it allows for big song and dance spectacles showing crowd scenes as well as the deity himself. Among many examples would be *Agneepath*, directed by Mukul Anand (1990); *Satya*, directed by Ram Gopal Varma (1998) and *Don*, of Farhan Akhtar (2006).

A new genre is the emergence of an animated Ganesh in recent years where the elements of his childlike nature are emphasized, forming a definite children's genre which is only loosely established in India. The success of animation in India has helped as Ganesh himself is usually animated, while the development of children's genres has been encouraged by the importation then domestic affirmation of children's media whether television channels or children's gaming. Cartoons had long been popular for the Anglophone elites in the *Amar Chitra Katha* series (McLain 2009), but Hindi-speaking animation appeal to a wider audience. Ganesh, who lives with his brother and his parents, has great appeal to children and his elephantness can also add to this.

These films include *Bal Ganesha*, directed by Pankaj Sharma (2007), where, naughty, childlike Ganesha snowboards around Mount Kailash where his parents Shiv and Parvati live. This was followed up by *Bal Ganesha 2* (2009), which presents key episodes from his story.

My Friend Ganesha, directed by Rajiv S. Ruia (2007), is similar to other devotional films except it is aimed at children and Ganesh himself is animated. A young boy, Ashu, whose parents are too busy to have time for him, spends time with his *bai* or maid, Gangubai. One day he saves a mouse from drowning and Gangubai tells him about Ganesha and his rat, Mushkaraj. The boy wants a friend so the *bai* suggests Ganesha who appears to him. Ashu then persuades his family to bring Ganapati home for the festival and the 'remover of obstacles' helps solve the family's problem and bring them close together again. This film is clearly a superhero type production, where the bullied boy becomes a superhero like Superman, Batman, or Krrish, when helped by Ganesha. However, it is also interesting as the Maharashtrian maid reminds the upwardly mobile family of their traditions and shows them how to incorporate religion into their new, westernized, lifestyle. These themes were seen in the next two outings of this version of Ganesh: *My Friend Ganesha 2* (2008) and *My Friend Ganesha 3* (2010), where a rich boy mistreated by relatives after

4. Mythological and devotional films were among the foundational films of Indian cinema but are now mostly B-grade at best although special effects suggest they may emerge as major genres. They have also been popular as television serials.

his parents die runs away with a truck-driver and his wife and engages Ganesha's help to fight for justice.

WHAT IS SPECIAL ABOUT FILM FOR PRESENTING THE ELEPHANT?

These feature films present the elephant as a star, or at least as a character, and so the human and divine qualities of the animal may be emphasized more than in earlier representations. Furthermore, in the older representations as well as in mythology or in the arts, the elephant was not anthropomorphized and it is unclear exactly when this starts.

The form of the film may or may not require anthropomorphizing of the elephant. Kala Naag is not anthropomorphized in *Elephant Boy*, where he is seen through the eyes of his mahout as a pet who behaves like him, notably in the wonderful opening scenes of the morning toilet and breakfast. The pachyderm, however, is not sentimentalized, and is employed as a work animal by the Forestry Department. At the end of the film, he is shown to have a private life as an elephant away from the camp, such as during the forest dance. Perhaps this is in part because Flaherty shot many sequences for a wildlife documentary and it was only made into a narrative feature film when Alexander Korda grafted it onto Kipling's story. Rossellini's elephants in his *Matri bhumi* (1959) were shown as Forestry Department workers rather than as anthropomorphized animals.

When the elephant stars in a film it needs to be anthropomorphized, usually in the way that circus elephants are, where they perform tricks in which they imitate human behaviour by walking on two legs or—as in *Haathi mere saathi*—where they play football, answer the phone, find a doctor, and worship Ganesh as well as working as elephants by dragging and pushing the broken-down car, rather than eating, walking and being an elephant.

Yet even documentaries may anthropomorphize animals. Sir David Attenborough anthropomorphizes elephants in part of the moving tribute to the great Echo, the Amboseli elephant, who featured in documentaries over several decades (and whom I was once privileged to observe close up). While tamed or zoo animals usually have names, it is often thought that wild animals should not be named and fieldworkers, mostly women, have been attacked by (mostly male) scientists, such as Duane Quiatt, for naming the animals they were researching.[5] The close observation over decades by the US conservationist Cynthia Moss and her research team has given us greater insights into elephant families (Moss *et al.* 2011), and the team has been clear that they are emotionally attached to the elephants and they do give them seemingly human traits in their descriptions. It is investigations such as these into the social life of the animals which have changed our understanding of elephants.

5. See Jane Goodall and the chimpanzees of Bombe and Cynthia Moss and Amboseli elephants (Diski 2010).

The interest in the emotional lives of animals (Bekoff 2007; Masson and McCarthy 1995) has occurred alongside the growth in the study of emotions in the 'psy' disciplines (psychology etc.) and in the arts. Together with the study of emotion in literary texts and reading (e.g. Brown 2010; Robinson 2005), the study of emotion in film has been vast, ranging from research on melodrama to the cognitive study of the emotions in film and in film viewing, where emotional involvement is seen as a primary motivating factor in attention and aesthetic response (Smith 1995 and Dwyer 2013).

While fieldwork is about the emotional lives of animals themselves, the emotional relationship between humans and animals has to be considered in particular with watching animals, especially on film. It is very difficult to spend any time with an animal and not to anthropomorphize it, as we do not have any other clear way of emotionally bonding with animals. While objections are couched in scientific terms for the experiments, it is seen as sentimental to anthropomorphize animals. Animals are seen to embody emotions and sentiments to such an extent that they become icons of that emotion on greeting cards, in advertisements and in other media. Yet even if it is sentimental, or even kitsch to do so, as Salomon (2004) argues, a display of tender sentiments is not unpleasant. If the sentiment brings a greater acknowledgement of the animals' presence and creates sympathy for its plight, it seems to be something good and positive. In other words, if showing an image of a cute baby elephant can be used to prevent poaching, it is for the good.

It seems that one of the problems for the serious study of animals is this association of anthropomorphism with children. Animals are often thought to belong in children's genres of literature and film. Yet Lever's 2008 'autobiography' of Cheeta was far from cute and is highly unsuitable for children, while in art Damien Hirst's (unnamed) animals and those of M. F. Husain are not intended primarily for the young. Novels which grant elephants subjectivity (Gowdy 2000), or character (Nicholson 2009; Saramago 2010) are not childish or kitsch.

The Indian aesthetic theory of the nine *rasas* (lit. 'juice', also 'feeling') has underlined the importance of emotion. In *Haathi mere saathi*, Ramu evokes all of these: *shringara* (love) as he is a loveable animal (elephants are rarely portrayed as romantic or sexualized in Indian culture in general); *vira* (heroism) as he is heroic and makes the ultimate sacrifice for his master; *hasya* (comedy)—he is naughty sometimes and does funny things like playing football; *raudra* (furious) when he is wrongly accused of being dangerous to the family; *karuna* (pity) when he is beaten by Raju and when he dies; *bhayanak* (terror) when he frightens Raju's wife, Tanu; *bibhatsa* (disgust) for the way that humans treat him; *adbhut* (wonder) for this amazing and loyal creature; and *shanta* (peace) when he is deified at the end of the film.

The problem of anthropomorphizing can be re-examined by thinking about the boundaries between humans and elephants. Initially this seems a silly question as the differences are vast. However, there is a clear affinity between humans and elephants and it is worth exploring whether the role of the animal in Indian culture can deepen our understanding of what is it to be human and what it is to be an elephant.

Questions of what divides animals from humans have been addressed by many western philosophers, notably Cavell *et al.* (2008), Derrida (2008) and Haraway (1992). While some historians examine what is to be human (Bourke 2011), others have explored this in fiction, for example, Nobel laureate novelist J. M. Coetzee (1999 and 2004). While most concur that there is a difference between humans and animals—this varies from Derrida's 'abyssal rupture' to a biological continuum—biological studies continue to blur the boundaries as new findings show that the psychology of animals is more complex than hitherto realized: for example, some animals can understand past and future and others recognize themselves.

The human and animal divide in India is relatively understudied, except as a thread running through the work of Wendy Doniger, most recently (2009) in her studies of animals in Hinduism, where she looks at monkeys, snakes, tigers, cats, herons but particularly dogs, horses and cows. According to the concept of *samsara*, souls (*atman*) transmigrate from human to animal bodies (and vice versa), thus blurring divisions between them. (This lack of a clear division forms part of the ethics of non-violence, *ahimsa*.)

There is no doubt that humans are fascinated by elephants, finding them 'picturesque' and sources of 'aesthetic enthusiasm' (Digby 1971: 52; see also Scigliano 2002). They are one of children's favourite animals, while adults remain in awe of them. Images of the elephant are ubiquitous not just in countries which have native elephants but throughout the world. It is often thought that this is to do with their absolute difference from humans in terms of their vast size and their distinctive features such as the trunk, the tusks and the large ears. However, recent studies (Payne 1999; Wemmer and Christen 2008; Bradshaw 2009; Moss *et al.* 2011) have shown that the divisions Derrida suggests between animals and humans—speech, reason, experience, mourning, culture, understanding technology, clothing, and so on—are also found among elephants, perhaps clothing being the only undisputed difference.

Not only are the boundaries between animals and humans unclear but also those between animals, humans and gods. Gods can take on animal and human forms, (notably Vishnu's ten incarnations which include animals, as a fish or a boar, both animal and human as the Lion-Man, Narasinha, and human as Rama and Krishna). Ganesha embodies the human, animal and divine in one form, as a god with a human body but an elephant head. Elephants as animals have a divine or semi-divine status and Ramu's deification at the end of *Haathi mere saathi* is very similar to what happened to the famous elephant, Guruvayoor Kesavan (1904–1976), whose statue outside the famous Guruvayoor temple is honoured on his death anniversary with a procession of elephants.[6]

6. Anonymous (2008). See also Seth (2009).

A film, *Guruvayoor Kesavan*, was released in Malayalam in 1977 and later there was a television series about this one elephant. The film shows the elephant dedicated to the temple, presents key episodes from his life and, at the end of the film, Kesavan foresees his death and, with a lotus in his trunk, approaches Krishna as Guruvayoorappan.

CONCLUSION

The Indian elephant is a wild forest animal that increasingly finds itself in conflict with humans as the ever growing population clears elephant forest habitat to grow food crops which attract the animals to an easy food supply.

While organizations including the World Wildlife Fund, the Wildlife Trust of India and Friends of the Asian Elephant have made some progress on issues of captive elephants in zoos and circuses, few people seem to know that the Indian elephant has been recognized as an endangered species since 1986 by the International Union for the Conservation of Nature. Poaching is not the huge problem that it is in Africa, but the Indian elephant's biggest threat is habitat loss and degradation along with its inability to migrate along traditional routes. There is now half the number of elephants today than that at independence, with estimates agreeing at around 20,000–25,000 wild elephants and a captive population of around 3,500 (temples, zoos, circuses, wildlife departments).

India has some of the strongest legislation to protect elephants but it is not well enforced. The elephant was made the heritage animal in 2010, and there are plans for a National Elephant Conservation Authority—Gajah—with a Consortium of Elephant Research and Estimation; and a new land conservation category of Elephant Landscapes. These, ten in number, will include the existing 32 Elephant Reserves, which should be granted Ecologically Sensitive Area status under the Environment Protection Act (Rangarajan *et al.* 2010). The lack of awareness of the elephant is shown by the failure of many in India, including the Tourist Board, to differentiate the Indian from the African elephant (Jebaraj 2010). The tamed animal and its divine and human representations from toys to Ganesha to films, which present the cute and cuddly kitschy aesthetic, are the ways that the Indian elephant is best known today. If these representations encourage people to respond to the elephant, learn its plight and encourage us to protect elephants this must be a good thing. The elephant, once seen as an Orientalizing symbol of India is now regarded as a way of understanding what it meant to be human, animal and divine. However, it is deeply worrying that today the elephant itself is physically disappearing and may soon remain visible only in art and other representations such as cinema.

REFERENCES

Anonymous. 2007. 'Homage to Guruvayur Kesavan.' *The Hindu*, Wednesday, 21 November 2007. http://www.hindu.com/2007/11/21/stories/2007112155801100.htm (accessed 8 May 2012).

Barkath, S. 1976. *Hastividyarnava sarasamgraha*. Edited by P. C. Choudhury. Gauhati: Publication Board, Assam.

Bekoff, M. 2007. *The Emotional Lives of Animals: A Leading Scientist Explores Animal Joy, Sorrow, and Empathy—and Why They Matter.* Foreword by Jane Goodall. Novato, CA: New World Library.

Bourke, J. 2011. *What It Means to Be Human: Reflections from 1791 to the Present*. London: Virago Press.

Bradshaw, G. A. 2009. *Elephants on the Edge: What Animals Teach Us about Humanity.* New Haven: Yale University Press.

Brown, L. 2010. *Homeless Dogs and Melancholy Apes: Humans and Other Animals in the Modern Literary Imagination.* Ithaca, NY: Cornell University Press.

Cavell, S. *et al.* 2008. *Philosophy and Animal Life.* New York: Columbia University Press.

Coetzee, J. M. 1999. *The Lives of Animals*. Princeton, NJ: Princeton University Press.

— 2004. *Elizabeth Costello*. London: Vintage.

Courtright, P. B. 1985. *Ganesha: Lord of Obstacles, Lord of Beginnings.* New York: Oxford University Press.

Derrida, J. 2008. *The Animal that therefore I Am.* New York: Fordham University Press.

Digby, S. 1971. *War-Horse and Elephant in the Delhi Sultanate: A Study of Military Supplies.* Oxford: Orient Monographs.

Diski, J. 2010. *What I Don't Know about Animals.* London: Virago Press.

Doniger, W. 2009. *The Hindus: An Alternative History.* New York: Penguin.

Dwyer, R. 2006. *Filming the Gods: Religion in Indian Cinema*. London: Routledge.

— 2013. 'Happy Ever After: Hindi Films and the Happy Ending.' In N. Sorin-Chaikov (ed.), Топография счастья от Американской мечты к пост-социализму (*The Topography of Happiness from the American Dream to Postsocialism*). Moscow: New Literary Observer (Novoe Literaturnoe Obozrenie).

Edgerton, F. 1985. *The Elephant-Lore of the Hindus: The Elephant-Sport (Matangalila) of Nilakantha.* Delhi: Motilal Banarsidas. First printed in 1931.

Elephant Spotlight. 2007, http://elephantspotlight.com/test/eid17-ElephantAlbum.htm (accessed 8 May 2012).

Gowdy, B. 2000. *The White Bone: A Novel of Elephants*. London: Flamingo.

Haraway, D. 1992. *Primate Visions: Gender, Race and Nature in the World of Modern Science*. London: Verso.

Jebaraj, P. 2010. 'African Jumbo in Incredible India Ad.' *The Hindu*, 28 September 2010. http://www.thehindu.com/news/national/article799389.ece (accessed 8 May 2012).

Kipling, J. L. 1904. *Beast and Man in India*. London: Macmillan and Co.

Lever, J. 2009. *Me Cheeta: The Autobiography.* London: Fourth Estate.

McLain, K. 2009. *India's Immortal Comic Books: Gods, Kings, and Other Heroes.* Bloomington: Indiana University Press.

Masson, J. M., and S. McCarthy. 1995. *When Elephants Weep: The Emotional Lives of Animals.* New York: Delta Books.

Moss, C., H. Croze and P. C. Lee (eds). 2011. *The Amboseli Elephants: A Long-Term Perspective on a Long-Lived Mammal.* Chicago: University of Chicago Press. http://dx.doi.org/10.7208/chicago/9780226542263.001.0001

Narayan, T. C. (trans.). 2009. *Lore and Legends of Kerala: Selections from Kottarathil Sakunni's* Aithihyamala. New Delhi: Oxford University Press.

Nicholson, C. 2009. *The Elephant Keeper*. London: Fourth Estate.

Payne, K. 1999. *Silent Thunder: The Hidden Voice of Elephants*. London: Phoenix.

Rangarajan, M. *et al.* 2010. *Gajah. Securing the Future for Elephants in India. The Report of the Elephant Task Force*. Delhi: Ministry of Environment and Forests, http://moef.nic.in/downloads/public-information/ETF_REPORT_FINAL.pdf (accessed 8 May 2012).

Ram, V. 2007. *Elephant Kingdom: Sculptures from Indian Architecture.* Ahmedabad: Mapin.

Robinson, J. 2005. *Deeper than Reason: Emotion and its Role in Literature, Music and Art.* New York: Oxford University Press. http://dx.doi.org/10.1093/0199263655.001.0001

Salomon, R. 2004. *In Defense of Sentimentality.* New York: Oxford University Press. http://dx.doi.org/10.1093/019514550X.001.0001

Sanderson, G. P. 1907. *Thirteen Years among the Wild Beasts of India: Their Haunts and Habits from Personal Observation, with an Account of the Modes of Capturing and Taming Elephants.* Edinburgh: John Grant.

Saramago, J. 2010. *The Elephant's Journey.* London: Harvill Secker.

Scigliano, E. 2002. *Seeing the Elephant: The Ties that Bind Elephants and Humans.* London: Bloomsbury.

Seth, P. 2009. *Heaven on Earth: The Universe of Kerala's Guruvayur Temple.* New Delhi: Niyogi Books.

Smith, M. 1995. *Engaging Characters: Fiction, Emotion and the Cinema.* Oxford: Clarendon Press.

Sukumar, R. 2011. *The Story of Asia's Elephants.* Mumbai: Marg Foundation.

Walker, J. F. 2009. *Ivory's Ghosts: The White Gold of History and the Fate of Elephants.* New York: Grove Press.

Wemmer, C., and C. A. Christen. 2008. *Elephants and Ethics: Towards a Morality of Coexistence.* Baltimore: The Johns Hopkins University Press.

FILMOGRAPHY

Agneepath/The Path of Fire, dir. Mukul Anand, 1990.
Bal Ganesha/Young Ganesha, dir. Pankaj Sharma, 2007.
Bal Ganesha 2/Young Ganesha 2, dir. Shamir Tandon, 2009.
Deewaar/The Wall, dir. Yash Chopra, 1975.
Don, dir. Farhan Akhtar, 2006.
Dumbo, dir. Samuel Armstrong *et al.*, 1941.
Elephant Boy, dir. Robert Flaherty and Zoltan Korda, 1937.
Guruvayoor Kesavan, dir. Bharathan, 1977 (Malayalam).
Haathi mere saathi/The Elephants are my Companions, dir. M. A Thirumugham.
Hum aapke hain koun...!/What am I to You?, dir Sooraj Barjatya, 1994.
Jodhaa Akbar, dir. Ashutosh Gowariker, 2008.
Kumki/Trained Elephant, dir. Prabhu Solomon, 2012 (Tamil).
Maa/Mummy, dir. M. A Thirumugham, 1976.
Maine pyar kiya/I've Fallen in Love, dir. Sooraj Barjatya, 1989.
Man of Aran, dir. Robert Flaherty, 1934.
Matri bhumi/Mother Earth, Roberto Rossellini , 1959.
Mughal-e Azam/The Great Mughal, dir. K. Asif, 1960.
Munimji/The Accountant, dir. Subodh Mukherji, 1955.
Muthu, dir. K.S. Ravikumar, 1995 (Tamil).
My Friend Ganesha, dir Rajiv S. Ruia, 2007.
My Friend Ganesha 2, dir Rajiv S. Ruia, 2008.
My Friend Ganesha 3, dir Rajiv S. Ruia, 2010.
Nanook of the North, dir. Robert Flaherty, 1922.
Navrang, dir. V. Shantaram, 1959.
Pakeezah/The Pure One, dir. Kamal Amrohi, 1971.
Prem sanyas/Light of Asia, dir. Franz Osten, 1925.
Puss in Boots, dir. Chris Miller, 2011.
Raja Harischandra/King Harischandra, dir.D. G. Phalke, 1913.
Rajendrudru Gajendrudru, dir. S. V. Krishan Reddy and Ranga Rao Kurra, 1993 (Telugu).
Safed haathi/The white elephant, dir. Tapan Sinha, 1978.

Sant Tukaram, dir. V. S. Damle and S. Fattelal, 1936.
Satya, dir. Ram Gopal Varma, 1998.
Sholay/Embers, dir. Ramesh Sippy, 1975.
The White Elephant, dir. Aijaz Khan, 2009.

Fifth Tantra: Awe, Fear, Death

Dark Shades of Power: The Crow in Hindu and Tantric Religious Traditions

XENIA ZEILER*

The crow, *kāka*, is a highly symbolic animal in South Asian religious traditions. Its representations in mythology, iconography and ritual range from one as revered divine companion and ritual assistant to one as feared and inauspicious omen and bearer of evil.[1] The ambivalence of the crow's perception first became clear to me while studying Tantric goddesses and their transformation following processes of inclusion into popular and mainstream Hindu traditions. In my recent works on the goddess Dhūmāvatī (Zeiler 2011, 2012), I was able to observe how the crow is a constant presence, whether in medieval textual or contemporary traditions. Yet what seemed particularly striking to me is that crows in present-day religious traditions are still perceived in an ambiguous way very similar to the representations constructed in ancient and medieval texts. As accompanying animals of deities, that is to say in strict mythological settings, crows were and still are well-regarded and revered. But as subjects on their own, and therefore beyond mythological frames, that is to say as living birds, crows are often looked upon with anxiety and fear.

This chapter discusses the crow in the religious traditions which dominate its perception in South Asia, namely Hinduism in general and Tantrism in particular (Gupta, Hoens and Goudriaan 1979: 5–12). As details of the crows' representations and perceptions in both systems tend to overlap, the chapter first aims at singling out characteristic mythological, iconographical and ritual representations of the crow in each tradition. This differentiation is then taken as a foundation to analyse the reciprocal influences of both religious tradi-

* Xenia Zeiler studied South Asian Classical and Ancient Studies at Humboldt-University Berlin and Jawaharlal Nehru University, New Delhi. She concluded her PhD in Cultural and Religious History of South Asia (Classical Indology) at the South Asia Institute, University of Heidelberg, in 2009. Her dissertation analysed the Tantric background of the goddess Dhūmāvatī and her recent transformation processes, including her rise to an urban deity in Benares. She has published several articles and book chapters, mainly on the goddess Dhūmāvatī and the Mahāvidyās. Her research interests include Ethno-Indology, transformations in contemporary urban Hinduism and Hinduism and Modern Mass Media. Since 2008, Xenia Zeiler has been a Lecturer for South Asian Religions at the University of Bremen, Germany.

1. For an analysis of the crow's symbolism and its ambivalence in different religious traditions, see Armstrong (1958: 77–88), Schmidt (2002: 2–10) and Mortensen (2006).

tions upon each other in shaping perceptions of the crow in contemporary South Asia. Although Brahmanic Hinduism and Tantrism share some deities and ritual practices (cf. Brown 2001), I will herein focus on Tantric rituals as alternative to Brahmanism and its praxis. In particular, I will reflect on ways in which the crow is represented in Tantric traditions with respect to issues of ritual purity,[2] ritual power and 'dark' ritual-empowering potency in destructive ritual procedures (Bühnemann 2001). For this, my analysis will be directed towards the crow as ritually related to the goddess Dhūmāvatī.

The chapter is divided in two main sections. First, I will begin with a discussion of the crow in Brahmanic Hinduism with special reference to the issue of the bird's ambivalence and its alleged inauspicious potential. In this section, I will also explore and analyse how the crow is discussed in contemporary Internet forums and online discussions. This will be conducive to stress the importance of modern mass media, and especially the World Wide Web, in the (re)shaping of religious beliefs and practices in contemporary South Asia, with special reference to non-human animals. The second section of the chapter analyses Sanskrit and Hindi textual material on perceptions of the crow in Tantric traditions and consists of three parts. Initially, I point out the influences of Hindu beliefs on the Tantric thought-world by discussing the crow as the animal companion (or vehicle, *vāhana*) of divine beings. Then, I document and examine a specific Tantric trend, that is the role of the crow as a ritual-empowering dark assistant. This is essential for developing my argument of a 'crow potency' specifically employed in Tantric ritual. Finally, I discuss the application of 'crow potency' in destructive Tantric *uccāṭana* rituals, that is, ritual performances aiming at the dispelling and/or eradication of enemies.

'IS THE CROW A GOOD SHAKUN?'[3] THE CROW IN HINDU TRADITIONS

Representations of the crow in Hindu traditions range from those of a cooperating assistant and messenger to those of an inauspicious omen and bearer of bad luck or evil.[4] Textual, iconographical and ritual traditions point at three

2. For a detailed discussion of Tantric rituals and for the frequent ritualistic use of products and utensils considered impure in Brahmanism and in the Tantric Kaula tradition, see Gupta, Hoens and Goudriaan (1979: 121–62).
3. The title of this section is taken from an online forum thread that appeared on the popular Q&A website Sawal on 2 January 2009. Śakuna in Sanskrit primarily denotes a bird (either a good or bad omen), or any auspicious object.
4. Mortensen (2006: 425) notes that '[r]avens have been known as birds of augury from Rome to the Celtic world, from Arabia to Scandinavia. The term augury refers to divination through the interpretation of the flight and speech of birds. In Europe the raven [*Corvus corax*] has a decidedly mixed reputation, and although conflation with the symbolic meaning of the ominous crow (*Corvus brachyrhynchos*) is prevalent in both Asia and Europe, the further northeast we move in Asia, the more the raven becomes a more neutral or positive messenger.'

major aspects. First, the crow is related to ancestor worship. This is the only case in Hinduism in which a markedly positive character is ascribed to crows. The bird is considered to be the embodiment of the recently departed souls (*preta*) (Knipe 2005: 67–68) or a messenger of Yama, the god of death. Feedings of crows (Witzel 1992), a particular way of honouring the bird, is essential in rituals for ancestors, and in *śrāddha* (funerary) rituals the act of feeding crows is prescribed on the tenth day of *piṇḍadāna*.[5] A typical example of this practice is the Nepali festival of Tihar, which stresses the role of crows as messengers of Yama and of the ancestors, and includes a ritual act of mass crow feeding on its first day (Majupuria 2000: 170).[6]

Second, crows are represented as vehicles (*vāhana*) of both gods and goddesses. Yet significantly all the deities that are connected to crows share a certain characteristic background—one of inauspiciousness. Gods and goddesses with whom crows are closely affiliated in Hindu mythology and iconography are the goddess Jyeṣṭhā, the god Śani and, at times, the goddess Nirṛti and the god Yama. Jyeṣṭhā, a goddess prevailing in South India—especially during the seventh and eighth centuries CE and disappearing from textual and iconographical sources after the eleventh century—is described as having an unconventional character with a strongly inauspicious or even dangerous side (Leslie 1992: 113–27). She is repeatedly put in relation with a crow *vāhana* even though the bird serves more often than not as the ensign on the goddess' banner rather than as an actual mount or seat.[7] Jyeṣṭhā is *kākadhvajasamāyuktā* ('having a crow in her banner') and *kākkaikkoḍiyāḷ* ('crow-bannered') (p. 117). In fact, in the iconography of the goddess, the crow is often depicted at her side and therefore it is not a vehicle in a stricter sense.

Śani, the personification of the planet Saturn, is also believed to have a very harmful and inauspicious character. More specifically, he is believed to be the source of several diseases, bad luck and ghost possession on humans. Popular Hindu traditions often include an appeasing worship of Śani in rituals for the dispelling of ghosts, especially in *ojhāī*, healing rituals or exorcisms that borrow from both local/regional folk traditions and Tantric practices (Zeiler 2011: 293–95). Just like Śani, the extremely inauspicious and dangerous Vedic goddess Nirṛti[8] and the god of death Yama are often closely associ-

5. The *piṇḍadāna* (offering of balls of rice to deceased ancestors) is one amongst the several essential rituals of ancestor worship. The procedure aims at supporting the deceased in their passage from the realm of the living to the abode of the ancestors.

6. Crow feeding as a prominent feature of Tihar is increasingly commented on in modern mass media. For an example from Nepali Press, see Anonymous(a) 2010.

7. This is a feature shared with the Tantric goddess Dhūmāvatī. For a discussion on similarities of the goddesses Jyeṣṭhā, Nirṛti and Dhūmāvatī see Zeiler (2011: 166–69).

8. Nirṛti is constantly referred to as an inauspicious goddess in Vedic and early Sanskrit textual traditions and, at times, she is ritually identified with a crow. For instance, the *Kauśikasūtra* describes a ritual to dispose of the goddess' evil influence. Among other things the sacrificer

ated with the crow, who is highly esteemed in some Hindu textual sources.[9] For instance, Yama praises it so in the *Rāmāyaṇa*:

> Then, o Rāma, the Lord of justice [Yama] spoke to the crow, which was sitting in the first row of the sacrifice: 'O bird, I wish you well. You shall certainly enjoy that you are spared from the different afflictions exposed on birds. My wish grants you, o bird, that the fear of death has no access to you. You shall live as long as the humans do not kill you. All humans, who live in my realm and who are starving, shall be refreshed when you have eaten and when you are refreshed.'
>
> (Rāmāyaṇa, Uttarakāṇḍa 18)

In conclusion, it seems that crows are paired predominantly with dangerous and inauspicious deities. Hindu mythology forms a pronounced framework for the crow's representation as *vāhana*, while Hindu rituals and iconography preferably place the birds in dark, fearsome and inauspicious contexts.

Third, the crow is often looked upon as an inauspicious omen and the bearer of bad luck or evil, especially in popular practices and beliefs. Though this particular feature is widely accounted for (Majupuria 2000: 170; Sivaramamurti 1974: 31), it becomes especially apparent in recent discussions on the Internet. Media in general and the Internet in particular play an increasing role in the negotiation and (re)construction of religious topics in Hindu traditions, including the role of animals as religious subjects. It is therefore not surprising that several Internet discussions on South Asian religions also reflect on the crow and its position, function and mythological background in Hinduism. The most recurring questions (or concerns) on the Internet are about how to deal with crows in general (Moksha 2009 or Anonymous(b) 2011), how to counter their alleged inauspicious potential (Anonymous(c) 2005; Kapoor 2009) and where to find information about their connection with death (Tulasi 2010) or the ancestors (Anonymous(d) 2011 or V. Kamat 2012). In 'How I sent my Father to Heaven', Vikas Kamat (2012) so describes Hindu funerary rituals and the role of crows:

> There is a belief that unfulfilled desires of the dead prevent the soul from liberating. This is indicated by the refusal of the crow to eat the *pinda* [rice balls]. I invited the crow to eat the *pindas*, saying that crows were my father's favorite birds. The crows came near the food, but did not bite. The gathered relatives asked me if I

---

has to pierce with an iron nail the thigh of a black crow, which is identified with Nirṛti. The crow is then allowed to fly away and is expected to stick to one's enemies (Dhal 1995: 131–32).

9. In the *bhakti* (devotional) tradition, the crow is considered a wise and learned animal. In the *Uttarakāṇḍa* of Tulsīdāsa's *Rāmcaritmānas* it is told the story of the sage Kākabhuśuṇḍī who was transformed into a crow by Śiva. Kākabhuśuṇḍī teaches the *yoga* of devotion to Garuḍa, the King of birds: 'In the north there is a beautiful purple mountain called Nīlagiri, where lives the amiable Kākabhuśuṇḍī, [1] supremely conversant with the path of devotion to Rāma, enlightened, full of all good qualities and very aged. He unceasingly recites the story of Rāma and all sorts of noble birds reverently listen. [2]' (*Rāmcaritmānas* 7.61.1-2).

> knew of any of unfulfilled wishes of father. I promised publicly that I'd continue to run his website, and that I'd preserve his cameras and letters. As if they understood, lot more crows approached, but none would bite yet. The crowd exclaimed that there must be something else, and I promised to my father that I'd take good care of mother. Again, as if they heard my thoughts, the crows ate away the rice balls... The obliging crows reported that father indeed reached the heavens! In gratitude, I honored the brahmins by giving them gifts, and fed the relatives. This is known as Samaradhana or celebration and marked the end of mourning.

While such discussions take place on a variety of Internet forums, the majority of information on the crow's background depicted in blogs (Anonymous (e) 2011), homepages (Kamat 1994), social networks and shared video platforms is drawn from Hindu folk narratives, iconography and mythology, and occasionally, Bollywood. Such discussions give us a sense of contemporary concerns, perceptions, beliefs and practices. Additionally, they contribute to reshaping the existing religious field thereby often generating new tendencies, ideas and perspectives.

The overall picture of the information presented here points to the ambiguous perception of crows in Hinduism. The specific backgrounds of crows in ancient and medieval Hindu traditions as messengers of Yama or their connection with the world of the ancestors and as *vāhanas* of dangerous and inauspicious deities lead to a bipartite perception of the bird in contemporary popular culture. But such a divergent presentation of the crow is not restricted to Hindu praxis and mythology alone. Tantric traditions too depict crows in an ambivalent fashion. And in one domain they do so by leaning on a well-known Hindu notion, that is, the concept of *vāhana*.

REVERENCE AND AWE: THE CROW AND THE TANTRIC GODDESS DHŪMĀVATĪ

In Tantric contexts non-human animals figure as companions, advisors, mounts or supporters of different deities, in a way very similar to Brahmanic Hinduism. Yet animals in Tantrism are also believed to have special skills and powers. This is particularly true of the crow, a bird already associated with exceptional dark or magical forces in several Hindu mythological contexts. It is precisely such power, or potency, that becomes an essential tool for ritual efficacy in most Tantric traditions.

While crows only play a restricted role in Hindu mythology, they are of particular interest in Tantric ritual praxis. Hindu texts refer to the crow in a rather stereotyped fashion. The bird is more often than not an inauspicious being (with the exception of the birds' role in ancestor rituals). Conversely, in Tantrism the sphere of influence of the crow is not inauspicious *per se*. Indeed, Tantric mythology and ritual praxis too refer to ominous dark aspects in crows. But they do so in a strikingly different way as compared to Hindu classic mythology.[10] Tantric texts emphasize an ambivalent potential in crows as beneficial to certain rituals and occasionally incorporate the power of the crow—or 'crow potency', as I will call it—in ritual instructions.

This becomes clear by analysing the most prominent occurrence of the crow in Tantric settings, that is, the bird's association with the strikingly fierce goddess Dhūmāvatī. Throughout Tantric traditions, the crow is the only animal associated with the deity, whereas in Brahmanic Hinduism, the bird is affiliated with different gods and goddesses. As such, the crow figures prominently in the goddess' recorded iconography and ritual, and each and every detailed Tantric reference to Dhūmāvatī mentions the crow as her companion.

Like for any other Tantric deity, Dhūmāvatīs' ascribed character, attributes, likes and dislikes are best surveyed in her *dhyānamantras*. These short hymns, which are ritually used for mental consolidation and meditation, also list the respective animal companion. The most influential *dhyānamantra* for Dhūmāvatī is first recorded in the *Phetkāriṇī Tantra*, a ritual text in Sanskrit presumably composed between the fourteenth and the sixteenth century CE.[11] Here follows the original text and its translation:

> *Vivarṇā cañcalā duṣṭā dīrgghā ca malināmbarā |*
> *vimuktakuntalā rukṣā vidhavā viraladvijā ||*
> *kākadhvajarathārūḍhā vilambitapayodharā |*
> śūrpahastātirukṣākṣā dhūtahastāvarānvitā ||
> *pravṛddhaghoṇā tu bhṛśankuṭilā kuṭilekṣaṇa |*
> *kṣutpipāsārddhitā nityambhayadā kalahāspadā ||*
> (*Dhūmāvatī-dhyānamantra, paṭala 7 of the Phetkāriṇī Tantra*)

> She is pale and fickle, angry, of high stature and wears dirty clothes. Her hair is discoloured. The widow is rough and has intermittent teeth. She sits on a cart which has a crow in the banner. Her breasts hang down. In the hand she holds a winnowing fan and her eyes look very cruel. She has unsteady hands and her hand shows the gesture of wish-fulfilling. She has a big nose, is exceedingly deceitful and has crooked eyes. Permanently afflicted by hunger and thirst she arouses horror and has her abode in conflict.[12]

10. The same applies to other Indo-European cultures and religious traditions. See, for instance, the role of crows and ravens in beliefs and practices on magic in ancient Greek and Roman traditions (Schmidt 2002: 149–55).
11. For a discussion of the *Phetkāriṇī Tantra*, including hypotheses about its date of composition and the chapter on Dhūmāvatī (*paṭala* 7), see Zeiler (2011: 41–47 and 2012: 172–74). The text so far has not been translated or critically edited. For a short summary of its contents, see Goudriaan and Gupta (1981: 115–16), who refer to it as 'among the most important sources of Tantric magic' (p. 113).
12. Author's translation.

This *dhyānamantra* dominates all textual sources on Dhūmāvatī and bears witness to the understanding and reception of the goddess and that of her animal companion. The *dhyānamantra* is repeatedly reproduced in nearly all classical Sanskrit texts on Dhūmāvatī as well as in the modern popular Hindi and academic secondary literature.[13] Its statements are the only foundation for nearly all modern iconographical depictions of the goddess (see Figures 1 and 2).[14] This influential short textual sequence leaves no doubt about the close connection of the crow with the goddess Dhūmāvatī. Not only is the crow the only animal connected to the goddess, it is also a primary iconographical identification mark of the *devī*. As a matter of fact, the bird seldom serves as a mount for Dhūmāvatī or as a draught animal pulling her chariot. Rather, nearly all existing iconographical depictions of the goddess exactly correspond to the contents of the *dhyānamantra* stated above: the crow accompanies the goddess and functions as her symbol on her flag.

The *dhyānamantra* is of particular interest because it instantly reveals why the crow was chosen as companion of this particular goddess. To connect the crow to a goddess showing an exceptional high potential of roughness, cruelness, deceitfulness, horror and conflict—all symptomatic attributes of Dhūmāvatī according to her *dhyānamantra* as well as hymns and ritual instructions contained in most textual descriptions[15]—surely is no coincidence. Quite to the contrary, it seems reasonable to infer that it is precisely because of a widely accepted concordance between the goddess and her animal companion's character that the two were paired. Even without the *dhyānamantra* (or any other text on Dhūmāvatī) commenting on reasons why the crow is special to the *devī*, it is evident that an alleged dark inauspicious or evil perception of crows underlies this choice. I argued before that such an ominous potential is a predominant characteristic in the bird's image in different Hindu traditions. The crow is clearly associated with a gloomy, threatening and portentous background. Its presence in the Tantric pantheon is one of awe and fear rather than one of admiration or reverence based on sympathy or devotion (e.g. the Nepali Tihar festival or the episodes from the *Rāmāyaṇa* and the *Rāmacharitmanasa*). Other aspects, however, figure predominantly. In the next section I will show how the crow, when isolated by its association with Dhūmāvatī, becomes a powerful element in Tantric ritual praxis.

13. For a detailed listing and discussion of classical Sanskrit, Hindi and secondary academic literature, see Zeiler (2011: 13–15, 41–74, 75–87).

14. Bühnemann (2000: 123) has reported on several paintings of Dhūmāvatī from different periods and regions. Nearly all paintings and every modern Hindi compilation known to me depict the goddess according to this *dhyānamantra*.

15. Dhūmāvatīs' textual tradition before the late nineteenth century is discussed in Zeiler (2012: 169–76). For an analysis of the transformation of the goddess in modern and contemporary India, see pp. 169–91 in the same article.

Figure 1. Dhūmāvatī. Poster above the entrance to the goddess' temple in the mohallā Dhūpcaṇḍī in Benares, October 2011. Photo by Xenia Zeiler.

Figure 2. Dhūmāvatī. Oil Painting at the inner walls of the temple Lakṣmīkuṇḍa in Benares, May 2003. Photo by Xenia Zeiler.

CROW POTENCY IN TANTRIC RITUALS

Crows in Tantric traditions do not only figure in mythological narratives based on the concept of *vāhana*. Nor are rituals involving crows restricted to the ritual tradition of Dhūmāvatī. Beyond these affiliations, crows appear in a number of Tantric rituals, including magical practices. Numerous textual sources bear witness to the usage of (dead) crows or their blood, feathers, or body parts (e.g. wings) in rituals. The blood of a crow or the ashes extracted from the burning of a whole crow or from a crow's wing are understood and propagated as powerful offerings in Tantric contexts. Not surprisingly, the rituals in question originated in the *vāmācāra* ('left-hand') Tantric traditions and are largely built on the idea of ritual self-defence or wish-fulfilling. Very often they are placed in the context of the *ṣaṭkarman* rituals—six rituals for magical purposes, usually performed to secure attraction, subjugation, immobilization, eradication, pacification or killing.[16] In particular, rituals involving crows are undertaken for protection from opponents. Such rites aim at rendering an enemy harmless through *stambhana* (immobilization), or at ruining or killing him through *uccāṭana* (dispelling/eradication) or *māraṇa* (killing). In such contexts, a ritual empowering the assistance of the crow is employed—a form of animal involvement which I will define 'crow potency'.

Such a label may be applied to rituals related to the use of animals in relation to several deities. Though the rituals in question are basically Tantric in nature, they were incorporated in non-Tantric texts too. The *Purāṇas*, for instance, show some evidence of similar magical practices. The *Matsya Purāṇa* offers an interesting case study. The text incorporates a ritual for destructive purposes which uses crow potency in the worship of the Navagrahas, a group of deities personifying the nine planets.[17] The text specifically dictates a procedure aimed at bringing about misfortune to an enemy. The adept, meditating with dishevelled hair on the enemy's misfortune, is instructed to present three pots filled with the blood of recently killed crows.[18] Yet more often than the ritual offering to the Navagrahas, crow potency is an essential part of the Tantric ritual worship of the god Hanumān. The *Mantramahodadhi*, an important text dated 1588 CE,[19] outspokenly refers to the evil potential of crows when prescribing:

> A sacrifice performed in a sacrificial pit in the shape of a half moon, and by means of products associated with evil such as the wings of crows and sticks from the śleṣmātaka tree [*Cordia latifolia*], is also very harmful towards an enemy. One should perform it with dishevelled hair during the night while facing the South, and repeat it 300 times. After that the enemy will die.[20]

This is a rare statement in Tantric ritual texts, which bears witness to the reasons why crow potency is considered important. It also specifies why such a concept is applied for destructive purposes and self-defence. What

16. For a detailed analysis of the individual *ṣaṭkarman* rituals, see Goudriaan (1978: 251–412). For a summary on *ṣaṭkarman* rituals in *the Mantramahodadhi*, see Bühnemann (2001).
17. Sūrya (the sun), Candra (the moon), Maṅgala (Mars), Budha (Mercury), Bṛhaspati (Jupiter), Śukra (Venus), Śani (Saturn), Rāhu (ascending lunar node) and Ketu (descending lunar node).
18. *Matsya Purāṇa* 93.151, quoted from Goudriaan (1978: 87).
19. For dating, authorship and a detailed overview on commentaries, translations and editions of the *Mantramahodadhi*, see Bühnemann (2000: 5–13).
20. *Mantramahodadhi* 13.12, in Goudriaan (1978: 89).

is made clear here is, first, that crows (and surely not only their wings) are associated with evil. The instruction states this in a firm and unequivocal way; it even depicts it as an unquestionable fact. Further to that, and perhaps more importantly, the statement highlights the precise ritual concept underlying the application of crow potency in Tantric rituals. As for many other magical rituals the idea is that evil counters evil. Accordingly, individuals considered harmful or evil have to be defeated by entities or objects associated with evil.

Such ideas prevail in contemporary texts on Tantric ritual. Crow potency, for instance, is incorporated in a strongly Tantric-influenced modern ritual manual dedicated to the god Hanumān. The *Hanumān Upāsanā* by Radha Krishna Shrimali (published c. 1990) gives a background of this ritual slightly differentiating from the ones stated above, mainly because its efficacy depends on the worship of a *yantra* (ritual diagram) specifically designed to dispel ghosts. In order to draw a ghost out of a possessed person it is advised to arrange the *yantra* in the following way:

> It is to be drawn, on the eighth night of a dark lunar fortnight, on a piece of cloth obtained on the preceding Sunday or Tuesday from the shroud of a corpse at the cremation ground and is to be written with black ink made of the drug *dhatūrā* (a poison sacred to Śiva) using a crow's feather or iron needle.[21]

During this ritual, crow potency is applied in a distinctive, although non-violent, fashion. Even though this surely has many reasons, one seems crucial. The probably most important explanation for this unusual procedure lies in the purpose of the ritual itself. As I argued before, Śani is feared for having terrible effects on humans. Like Yama, Śani is regarded a judge and is traditionally believed to be the one who evaluates one's deeds in life, thus contributing to the choice of punishments and rewards. Furthermore Śani's influence is at the core of ideas and beliefs on ghost (*bhūta*) possession and exorcism, that is, the ritual dispelling of evil spirits. To draw a ghost out of an afflicted person often means to appease Śani. The ritual requires utensils believed to pacify the deity. Using a black crow's feather and/or an iron needle as writing tools (Lutgendorf 2001: 292–93 n. 20), the text reinforces the very nature of Śani which is symbolically rendered through a specific colour (black) and material (iron):

> Lord Saturn is tall, black, long-limbed, and emaciated, with reddish-brown eyes, large teeth and nails, prominent veins, a sunken stomach, a long beard, matted locks, and profuse coarse, stiff body hair. He is lame and his limbs are rigid; his constitution is Vata. Intensely harsh, he is cruel in authority, and his gaze, which is directed downward, is utterly terrifying... His metal is iron, and his gem is blue sapphire... If you hope to prevent Saturn from mangling your life, as he has mangled so many lives, make regular offerings of black sesame seeds, sesame oil, and

21. Shrimali (c. 1990: 35–36), in Lutgendorf (2001: 281).

> sugar on Saturdays to an iron image of that planet; also, make Saturday donations of sesame an iron to the needy. I make my sincere obeisance to that Lord Saturn whose color is that of pure collyrium, who is son of the Sun and Shadow, and who is brother of Yama, the god of righteousness and death.
>
> (Śanimāhātmya: *pradhanakarma*, in Svoboda 1997: 87–88)

CROW POTENCY IN *UCCĀṬANA* RITUALS

The power of the crow, or crow potency, is referred to in the specific context of *uccāṭana* rituals (Nihom 1987: 104–105), a set of practices performed to ruin or overthrow enemies. Even though such ritual instructions are fundamentally Tantric in nature, they are not only mentioned in Tantric sources. Like many other Tantric practices, *uccāṭana* rituals infiltrated Hindu non-Tantric texts such as, for instance, some *Purāṇas*. Besides the example I drew from *Matsya Purāṇa*, there are other texts that speak of crows and their blood or body parts. The *Garuḍa Purāṇa*, for instance, includes ashes and blood of crows as important tools in a list of devices for *uccāṭana* rituals.[22] The *Agni Purāṇa* too reports of the use of crow blood:

> By means of a sacrifice mixed with the blood of an ass one will eradicate the enemy (*uccāṭayet*); by means of a sacrifice to which the blood of a crow has been added, there occurs the destruction of the foe (*utsādanam*).[23]

Rituals utilizing crows are at times even connected to Dhūmāvatī. A small number of rituals addressing the goddess also mention crow potency in the way described above. This may appear inconsistent at first sight, as crows have a venerated status as *vāhana* or companion of the *devī*. Nevertheless, rituals in honour of Dhūmāvatī more often than not do use crow potency, as the goddess is explicitly connected to śatrunigraha (restraining an enemy) and *uccāṭana*. Both forms of ritual aim at rendering enemies inoffensive or harmless, which is the exact ritual background for crow potency in Tantric ritual practices.

The *prayoga* (ritual application) of the eight-syllable *Dhūmāvatīmantra* (*dhūṁ dhūṁ Dhūmāvatī svāhā*) in the *Mantramāharṇava*, an important late nineteenth-century source on Dhūmāvatī (Zeiler 2011: 56–59; Bühnemann 2000: 3, 18), mentions crow potency twice. Both references are placed in a strictly ritualistic context. Crow potency is here applied to a ritual instruction aiming at destroying enemies. The *Dhūmāvatītantra* chapter of the *Mantramāharṇava* presents details for a complete ritual procedure in honour of the goddess and is entirely tailored to her special sphere of action, that is

22. *Garuda Purāna* 177.69–73, in Goudriaan (1978: 361).
23. *Agni Purāna* 137.12-13, in Goudriaan (1978: 555). To include 'ass potency' in *uccāṭana* rituals is unusual. This is the only reference known to me of placing donkey potency and crow potency side by side.

to say the obliterating of enemies.[24] It is composed according to the typical design of Tantric ritual instructions and starts with the characteristic opening sequences previous to the actual *prayoga*. Here, the initiating procedure for the following ritual is given, namely *mantra*, *viniyoga* (application [of the mantra in ritual]), *ṛṣyādinyāsa* (mental appropriation/assignment beginning with the *ṛṣi*, i.e. the sage), *karanyāsa* (mental appropriation/assignment of the hand) and *hṛdayādiṣaḍaṅganyāsa* (mental appropriation/assignment of the six limbs beginning with the heart). The *prayoga* itself begins with a ritual opening followed by instructions for the installation of the *pīṭha* (seat) of the goddess, the worship of the presiding Śaktis and *āvaraṇapūjā* (worship of the outer fence). The latter focuses on the attendants of the goddess in the first and second protective barrier of the *yantra*. This includes all parts of the *yantra*, which are individually stated here: the *ṣaṭkoṇa* (six-angled figure), the eight petals of the lotus, the *bhūpūra* (outer part of a *yantra*) and the ten Dikpālas (guards of the cardinal points). Next, the adept is advised to head naked for the cremation ground and to start the repetition of 100,000 *japa* (muttered prayer) of the eight-syllable *Dhūmāvatīmantra* (Zeiler 2011: 60–64). Only after the perfection of the *mantra* (Bühnemann 2000: 22–24) with a *homa* (oblation) consisting of sesame seeds and purified butter, water oblations and the feeding of Brahmans, the actual *prayoga* instruction starts. This gives a number of different ritual instructions to render an enemy ineffective, starting with how to infect an adversary with fever and how to gain power over him (Zeiler 2011: 63–64). Then, crow potency is incorporated:

> If one burns a crow in the fire of a cremation ground, takes her ashes, implies the mantra on this and throws it at the head of the opponent, he will be ruined immediately.[25]

After two further statements on how to annihilate and destroy an enemy (Zeiler 2011: 64), another procedure utilizing a crow is mentioned:

> After merging *nīm* and a wing of a crow, he shall recite one hundred and eight times. Then he may put this in the smoke with the name of the one to be subordinated (and) immediately he conquers the enemies.[26]

It is evident that these two examples from the *Mantramāharṇava* keep in line with the standard procedure of crow potency in Tantric *uccāṭana* rituals. Other texts account for this in slightly variegated rituals to be performed in honour of Dhūmāvatī. The *Tantrasāra Saṃgraha* advises burning a crow in the fire of a cremation ground and scattering the ashes uttering the *mantra*

24. See Zeiler (2011: 60–74) for the first translation from Sanskrit and a detailed analysis of the *Dhūmāvatītantra*.

25. *Mantramāharṇava, Dhūmāvatītantra, prayoga* of the eight-syllable *Dhūmāvatīmantra* 8, author's translation.

26. *Mantramāharṇava, Dhūmāvatītantra, prayoga* of the eight-syllable *Dhūmāvatīmantra* 12, author's translation.

of Dhūmāvatī in the enemy's house in order to kill him.[27] The *Śaktisaṃgama Tantra* speaks of a *kākakramaḥ* (crow procedure) as part of a ritual for Dhūmāvatī that will enable the ritualist to kill any person once he succeeds in transforming 'his own mind into a crow' (*svacittaṁ kākavat kṛtvā*).[28] The crow—it so appears—is used in Tantric ritual procedures related to Dhūmāvatī while, at the same time, is the goddess' companion and emblem.

The Tantric mythological, iconographical and ritual tradition of Dhūmāvatī depicts and propagates the crow in two divergent, even opposing ways. This is not surprising if we sum up the textual findings of crow potency in Tantric *uccāṭana* rituals. In particular, if we observe the respective worship of all individual gods or goddesses as related to *uccāṭana* rituals, we will find no major difference between ritual instructions and the underlying procedure. Rituals aiming at the destruction of enemies are constructed on the same foundations, be they related to Dhūmāvatī, Hanumān, Śani, the Navagrahas or other deities.

But crow potency used for dark ritual purposes and the offering of crows (or their body parts) in rituals is not restricted to Hindu Tantras only. Early Buddhist Tantric texts mention the crow in ritual procedures which highly resemble the Hindu Tantric ritual patterns of *uccāṭana*. The similarities are quite striking and cover several aspects of the rituals in question. For example, the eighth to ninth-century Buddhist *Cakrasamvara Tantra*[29] states:

> Next, there is the accomplishment of all ritual actions through the five *ha* syllables, by means of which there is rapid engagement in power through the cognized only. One should rub one's hands on which are the five syllables, haṃ hau ho hai haḥ. Drawing blood from his mouth with a [word of] command, one's foe dies instantly. Should one anoint the skull that is the receptacle of one's own blood with the blood of one's ring finger, as soon as it dries, the victim perishes. Should one, angered and with reddened eyes, repeat [the syllables] excitedly, the king will quickly be killed, along with his army and his mount. Make an offering of the ḍākiṇī sacrifice (bali), with cat, mongoose, dog, crow, crane, and jackal; there is no doubt that in this Tantra this quickly yields power.[30]

The specific purpose of the ritual as well as its actual application closely corresponds to the Hindu Tantric idea underlying crow potency in ritual performance. What is sought for is the death of the enemy, what is promised is a quick success, what has to be done is to ritually offer a crow. The basic ideas at the core of such proceedings in Buddhist Tantric traditions seem to be based on very old perceptions of the crow and its dark potency in South Asian religious traditions.

27. *Tantrasārasaṁgraha* by Nārāyaṇa (17.56), in Goudriaan (1978: 364).
28. Śaktisaṁgamatantra, Tārākhaṇḍa 28.1-7, in Goudriaan (1978: 363).
29. For an introduction and dating, see *The Cakrasamvara Tantra* (2007).
30. *Cakrasamvaratantra* 46.1-5, in Gray (2006: 30). For an annotated translation of this passage, see *Cakrasamvara Tantra* (2007: 358–59).

CONCLUSION

Hindu traditions show an ambiguous perception of crows. Ancient and medieval Hindu texts depict crows as messengers of Yama, psychopomp birds linked to the realm of the ancestors or as *vāhanas* of dangerous and ominous deities—mostly goddesses. In the context of ancestor worship the birds are revered but as mythological *vāhanas* they are unmistakably related to the very dangerous and inauspicious character of the deities they accompany. This conflicting view prevails in contemporary popular Hindu traditions as well.

In Tantric traditions there is evidence of a twofold, somehow contradictory, perspective on crows. On the one hand, the bird serves as the exclusive *vāhana* of the fierce goddess Dhūmāvatī. Like any other *vāhana*, the bird is venerated because of its close relationship with a deity. As the goddess' mythological and iconographical companion, the crow is regarded as an object of human reverence, even if this is based on awe rather than on devotion. On the other hand, crows play an important role individually, that is without the presence of divine beings, especially as far as certain ritual practices are involved. In these contexts, the power of the crows—widely reputed ominous—is used for ritual purposes. In Hindu and Buddhist Tantric traditions alike, dead crows or their body parts are presented as ritual offerings in similar contexts, that is to say empowering the ritualist to render enemies harmless or even to outspokenly harm and/or kill them. Such potential, which I call 'crow potency', is especially applied in *uccāṭana* rituals.

Brahmanic Hinduism and Tantric traditions have contributed from different angles to constructing a highly ambivalent imagery around the crow. This includes mythology, ritual practice and iconography. Both share basic ideas of an alleged dark or inauspicious power. Yet crows are also independent agents. While in the mainstream Hindu tradition they serve as mediators between the world of the humans (*naraloka*) and the world of the ancestors (*pitṛloka*), in Tantric traditions they are of crucial importance for aggressive rituals aiming at controlling or vanquishing an adversary. In contemporary South Asia, the birds' prominent role in esoteric rituals is well-known and crows are feared also because of their presence in Tantric ritual practices. This, of course, adds to a general negative perception of crows in popular mainstream Hindu society—a perception already prevalent in ancient and medieval Hindu texts which link the bird solely to inauspicious deities.

Of course, the crow is not the only animal related to inauspiciousness and evil in South Asia. For several reasons, dogs, jackals, lizards and other species are regarded as inauspicious and/or impure in textual and living traditions. But perhaps with the exception of dogs (White 1992) crows are frequently and constantly perceived as ominous and dangerous animals. It thus appears that the crow can be seen as a key for a more general understanding of the concepts of inauspiciousness, evil and danger. While most Hindu traditions try to pacify the dangerous potential of the crow and to render its alleged inauspiciousness harmless, most Tantric traditions accept or even welcome the bird's dangerous potential and try to utilize animals regarded as ominous or inauspicious for ritual purposes. By studying the crow and its underlying representations we can add one more facet to the understanding of the divergent interpretations on notions of (in)auspiciousness and (im)purity in South Asian religious traditions. So far there are not as many studies on inauspicious, dangerous or evil animals as those available on animals regarded as auspicious or benign. It seems that alleged 'dark' animals are often overlooked in favour of research on more benevolent animals which are clearly predominant in South Asian mythology, iconography and, especially, worship.

The discussion of the crows' representations in this chapter revealed a number of findings on this subject. While non-Tantric traditions fear the crows' inauspicious potential, some Tantric traditions actively take advantage of it. The crows' explicit involvement in Tantric rituals, especially in *uccāṭana*, also highlights concepts of (in)auspiciousness and (im)purity. Especially in left-hand Tantrism, the concepts of auspiciousness and purity as prevalent in Brahmanic Hinduism are obliterated. Many substances and materials regarded as impure or dangerous in Brahmanic Hinduism—for instance alcohol, meat or blood—are utilized in Tantric ritual *precisely* because of their reputation in Brahmanic Hinduism. The main reason why inauspicious animals, like the crow, were incorporated in Tantric rituals probably follows a similar reasoning. The involvement of inauspicious and/or impure substances and animals obviously was one possibility to distinguish Tantric ritual practice and to highlight the magical potential in it. Additionally, by manipulating animals, as it has to be done for rituals using crow feathers, ashes or blood, Tantric traditions outspokenly turned against the Brahmanic Hindu concept of non-violation (*ahiṃsā*). 'Crow potency' thus became a radical indicator of the dissenting character of Tantra and Tantric rituals.

REFERENCES

Anonymous (a). 2010. '1st Day of Tihar Gives Hindus Plenty to "Crow" about.' *The Himalayan*, 11 April 2010. http://tinyurl.com/9xy7yta (accessed 8 May 2012).

Anonymous (b). 2011. 'Considerations of Omens through Birds: The Crow.' http://www.urday.in/birds.htm (accessed 5 January 2012).

Anonymous (c). 2005. 'Why is Crow Inauspicious? Does That Apply Only to Hindus or Everybody if It is True?' http://tinyurl.com/9djzcrn (accessed 5 January 2012).

Anonymous (d). 2011. 'Why the Crows are Referred as our Ancestors? What about Other Birds?' http://in.answers.yahoo.com/question/index?qid=20110407055841AA8uJtZ (accessed 5 January 2012).

Anonymous (e). 2001. 'Sacred Animals in India,' http://www.indianetzone.com/26/sacred_animals_plants_indian_customs.htm (accessed 5 January 2012).

Armstrong, E. A. 1958. *The Folklore of Birds: An Enquiry into the Origins and Distribution of Some Magico-Religious Traditions*. London: Collins.

Bhattacharyya, B. (ed.). 1941. Śaktisaṁgama Tantra. *Vol. II. Tārākhaṇḍa.* Baroda: Oriental Institute of Baroda.

Brown, C. M. 2001. 'The Tantric and Vedāntic Identity of the Great Goddess in the Devī Gītā of the Devī-Bhāgavata-Purāṇa.' In T. Pintchman (ed.), *Seeking Mahādevī: Constructing Identities of the Hindu Great Goddess*: 19–76. Albany, NY: Albany University Press.

Bühnemann, G. 2000. *The Pantheon of the Mantramahodadhi. Vol. 1. The Iconography of Hindu Tantric Deities.* Groningen: Egbert Forsten.

— 2001. 'The Six Rites of Magic.' In D. G. White (ed.), *Tantra in Practice*: 447–62. Delhi: Motilal Banarsidass.

Dhal, U. N. 1995. *Goddess Laksmi. Origin and Development.* Delhi: Eastern Look Linkers.

Goudriaan, T. 1978. *Māyā Divine and Human: A Study of Magic and its Religious Foundations in Sanskrit Texts, with Particular Attention to a Fragment on Viṣṇu's Māyā preserved in Bali.* Delhi: Motilal Banarsidass.

Goudriaan, T., and S. Gupta. 1981. *Hindu Tantric and* Śākta *Literature.* Wiesbaden: Otto Harrassowitz.

Gray, D. B. 2006. 'Skull Imagery and Skull Magic in the Yoginī Tantras.' *Pacific World: Journal of the Institute of Buddhist Studies* 8: 21–39.

Gupta, S., D. J. Hoens and T. Goudriaan. 1979. *Hindu Tantrism.* Leiden: E. J. Brill.

Kamat, K. 1994. 'Animals of Indian Mythology.' Originally published as: 'Attitude of our Ancestors towards Animals.' *The Quarterly Journal of the Mythic Society* 85(2). http://www.kamat.com/kalranga/prani/animals.htm (accessed 5 January 2012).

— 2012. 'How I Sent My Father to Heaven.' http://www.kamat.com/indica/culture/death/heaven.htm (accessed 5 January 2012).

Kapoor, P. 2009. 'In Hindu Mythology, the Crow is Regarded as an Inauspicious Bird. What is the Reason for This?' http://qna.rediff.com/questions-and-answers/in-hindu-mythology-the-crow-is-regarded-as-an-ina/15240351/answers/15242296 (accessed 5 January 2012).

Knipe, D. M. 2005. 'Die Konstruktion eines provisorischen Körpers für den preta in hinduistischen Bestattungen.' In J. Assmann, F. Maciejewski and A. Michaels (eds), *Trauerrituale im Kulturvergleich*: 62–81. Göttingen: Wallstein.

Leslie, J. 1992. 'Śrī and Jyeṣṭhā: Ambivalent Role Models for Women.' In J. Leslie (ed.), *Roles and Rituals for Hindu Women*: 107–27. Delhi: Motilal Banarsidass.

Lutgendorf, P. 2001. 'Five Heads and No Tale: Hanumān and the Popularization of Tantra.' *International Journal of Hindu Studies* 5(3): 269–96. http://dx.doi.org/10.1007/s11407-001-0003-3

Majupuria, T. C. 2000. *Sacred Animals of Nepal and India.* Bangkok: Craftsmen Press.

Mitra, R. (ed.). 1876. *Agnipurāṇa.* Calcutta: Asiatic Society of Bengal. <cited?>

Moksha G. 2009. 'Answer to "Is the crow a good Shakun?"' http://sawaal.ibibo.com/puja-and-rituals/crow-good-shakun-666831.html (accessed 5 January 2012).

Mortensen, E. 2006. 'Raven Augury from Tibet to Alaska.' In P. Waldau and K. Patton (eds), *A Communion of Subjects: Animals in Religion, Science and Ethics*: 423–36. New York: Columbia University Press.

Nihom, M. 1987. 'On Buffalos, Pigs, Camels, and Crows.' *Wiener Zeitschrift für die Kunde Südasiens* 31: 75–109.

Paṇḍits of the Ānandāśrama (ed.). 1907. *Matsyapurāṇa.* Poona: Ānandāśrama.

Phetkārinītantram. 1992. In G. Kavirāja (ed.), *Nirvānatantram, Toḍalatantram, Kāmadhenutantram, Phetkārinītantram, Jñānasankālinītantram, Savrttiko Devīkalottarāgamasca, Yogatantra Granthamālā* 4. Vārāṇasī: Sampūrṇānanda Saṁskr̥ta Viśvavidyālaya.

Schmidt, G. 2002. *Rabe und Krähe in der Antike. Studien zur archäologischen und literarischen Überlieferung.* Wiesbaden: Reichert Verlag.

Shah, U. P. (ed.). 1975. *The Vālmīki-Rāmāyaṇa: The Uttarakāṇḍa.* Baroda: Oriental Institute.

Shrimali, R. K. n.d. *Hanumān Upāsanā.* New Delhi: Diamond Books.

Sivaramamurti, C. 1974. *Birds and Animals in Indian Sculptures.* New Delhi: National Museum.

Śrīkr̥ṣṇadāsa, K. (ed.). 1906. *Garuḍapurāṇa.* Bambaī: Śrīveṅkaṭeśvara Press.

Śrīkr̥ṣṇadāsa, K. (ed.). 1962. *Mantramahodadhi by Mahīdhara.* Bambaī: Śrīvenkaṭeśvara Press.

Śrīkṛṣṇadāsa, K. (ed.). 2001. *Mantramahārṇavaḥ*. Bambaī: Śrīvenkaṭeśvara Press.

Svoboda, R. E. 1997. *The Greatness of Saturn: A Therapeutic Myth*. Twin Lakes, WI: Lotus Press.

Tantrasārasaṁgraha by Nārāyaṇa. Aiyangar, M. D. (ed.). 1950. Madras: Madras Govermental Oriental Series, 15.

Tulasi. 2010. 'Does Hearing Crow Caw Means Death?' http://en.allexperts.com/q/Hindus-946/2010/8/Crow-1.htm (accessed 5 January 2012).

Tulsīdāsa. 1994. Śrī Rāmacharitmanasa (The Holy Lake of the Acts of Rāma). Delhi: Motilal Banarsidass.

White, D. G. 1992. 'You are What You Eat: The Anomalous Status of Dog-Cookers in Hindu Mythology.' In R. S. Khare (ed.), *The Eternal Food: Gastronomic Ideas and Experiences of Hindus and Buddhists*: 53–94. Albany, NY: State University of New York Press.

Witzel, M. 1992. 'Meaningful Ritual: Structure, Development, and Interpretation of the Tantric Agnihotra Ritual of Nepal.' In A. W. van den Hoek, D. H. A. Kolff and M. S. Oort (eds), *Ritual, State, and History in South Asia: Essays in Honour of J. C. Heesterman*: 774–827. Leiden: E. J. Brill.

Zeiler, X. 2011. *Die Göttin Dhūmāvatī. Vom tantrischen Ursprung zur Gottheit eines Stadtviertels in Benares*. Saarbrücken: Verlag Deutscher Hochschulschriften.

— 2012. 'Transformations in the Textual Tradition of Dhūmāvatī: Changes of the Tantric Mahāvidyā Goddess in Concept, Ritual, Function and Iconography.' In I. Keul (ed.), *Transformations and Transfer of Tantra in Asia and Beyond*: 165–94. Berlin/New York: De Gruyter. http://dx.doi.org/10.1515/9783110258110.165

Fear, Reverence and Ambivalence: Divine Snakes in Contemporary South India

AMY L. ALLOCCO*

Snake worship is both old and widespread in India, with roots stretching back to Vedic materials. The *Atharva Veda*, for example, includes a number of hymns (such as 5.13, 6.12, 6.56, 6.100, 7.56, and 7.88) whose mantras are intended to ward off snakes and their bites and/or to counteract their venom, whether through the use of syllables, sanctified water, particular grasses or anthill sand. It is likely that fear of snakes (*nāgas*) and their poison was an early motivation for their propitiation, or that some of snakes' unique characteristics, such as the periodic shedding of their skin, led to their being ascribed magical powers and eventually being deified. Whatever initially catalysed religious and ritual interest in snakes, it is clear that Indic traditions have long regarded them as divinities linked with water, fertility and anthills.

The plentiful references to *nāga* worship and discussions of snake deities in colonial sources on South India (Dubois 1983 [1899]; Elmore 1995 [1913]; Thurston 1989 [1906] and 1912; Whitehead 1999 [1921]) demonstrate that these associations attracted the notice of British civil servants, missionaries, clergy members and ethnographers. These authors comment on the regional varieties of snake worship, trace out its underlying mythologies, elaborate on the relationships between snakes, anthills, and the class of local goddesses connected to disease (especially pox-viruses), and speculate about its links to cultures beyond India. Their contributions are par-

* Amy L. Allocco is Assistant Professor of Religious Studies at Elon University in North Carolina, USA. Allocco, who earned her PhD from Emory University, focuses her research on contemporary Hinduism, gender, and ritual traditions in the state of Tamil Nadu in South India, where she has been studying and conducting ethnographic fieldwork for more than 15 years. Her current book project analyses contemporary snake goddess traditions in South India and the repertoire of ritual therapies performed to mitigate *nāga dōṣam* (snake blemish), a malignant horoscopic condition understood to cause delayed marriage and infertility. Allocco has been awarded fellowships by the American Institute of Indian Studies (AIIS), the American Association of University Women (AAUW), Fulbright International Institute for Education (IIE), and Fulbright-Hays to support her research and writing. She is co-editing a volume titled *Ritual Innovation in South Asian Religions*, is the author of several book chapters and has published articles in the *Journal of Feminist Studies in Religion* and *Method & Theory in the Study of Religion*.

ticularly notable because many of the South Indian perceptions of and customs related to *nāgas* resonate strongly with those found in this part of the subcontinent today, particularly the enduring link between *nāga* traditions and fertility. Edgar Thurston quotes one Surgeon-Major Cornish who observed in the 1871 Madras Census Report that 'probably so long as the desire of offspring is a leading characteristic of the Indian people, so long will be the worship of the serpent, or of snake-stones, be a popular cult' (1989 [1906]: 283). This and several similar examples recounted by Thurston and others effectively underscore the close connections that existed during this period among snakes, anthill worship, and women's petitions for fertility, phenomena which remain intimately related in contemporary South India.

Other accounts offer a stronger sense of the prophylactic dimension of snake worship, present as early as the *Atharva Veda*, whereby *nāgas* are honoured not for the blessings they may confer but instead to preclude them from harming humans. A number of authors note that killing a snake is regarded as a sin and detail the lengths that individuals may go to in order to avoid injuring a snake, as *nāgas* are believed to deliver formidable curses with far-reaching implications. According to L. K. Bala Ratnam, 'No orthodox person would ever kill or hurt serpents even if bitten by them. For it is a common belief that those who intentionally or unintentionally injure them would be chastised by leprosy, itch, childlessness, or opthalmia' (2000: 633). Remarkably similar ideas persist in South India, where the karmic consequences of one's conduct toward snakes continue to be understood as truly literal. Snakes are believed to retaliate in kind for sufferings endured; for example, farmers who kill snakes in their fields, householders who disturb mating snakes, or those who knock down anthills wherein snakes were living will be similarly deprived of livelihood, progeny, and shelter. Writing about practices in south-western India, C. Karunakara Menon asserts, 'Next to cow-slaughter the killing of snakes is considered the most heinous sin a Malayali may commit', and notes that 'when a snake is seen inside, or in the neighbourhood of a house, great care is taken to catch it without giving it the least pain' (1901: 24). Both Bala Ratnam and Thurston record the example of the individual who cut down the trees in a traditional snake grove becoming afflicted with a skin condition and consulting with an astrologer, who attributed the illness to the wrath of the offended *nāga* (Bala Ratnam 2000: 636–37; Thurston 1912: 126–27). There are significant homologies between the beliefs about *nāgas*' curses chronicled in these early- and mid-twentieth-century sources and those that circulate in contemporary South India. Maligned snakes are most commonly thought to curse their antagonists with childlessness while diseases and conditions affecting the skin and eyes are counted among their secondary set of afflictions.

It is perhaps unsurprising, then, that even potentially dangerous snakes may have been allowed free passage rather than run the risk of offending them and inspiring their curses. The following excerpt illustrates that not only was this true even among seemingly defenceless schoolchildren,[1] but that the venomous visitor was treated to milk offerings and worship.

> The worship of serpents, especially the deadly cobra, is common all over South India. In one village of the Wynaad I came across a Mission school which was visited almost daily by a large cobra, which glided undisturbed and harmless through the school-room. Neither teachers nor pupils would have dared to kill it. Constantly they fed it with milk. In many towns and villages large slabs of stone with figures of cobras, often two cobras intertwined, carved in bas-relief are seen on a platform under a large tree. They are worshipped especially by women who want children.
> (Whitehead 1999 [1921]: 22)

Whitehead's observations bear a striking resemblance to the beliefs, traditions and practices I encountered in my own fieldwork on the wide repertoire of Hindu *nāga* traditions in contemporary South India.[2] These similarities are especially evident in terms of the gendered nature of *nāga* worship, its overt connection to fertility, and the ubiquity and lavish nature of ritual attentions paid to snake sculptures, which are commonly installed under sacred trees. In fact, my interest in *nāga* traditions was initially piqued by the impressive groupings of stone snake images (*nāga cilai* or *nāgakkal*) that stood underneath a sacred *peepal* tree (*araca-maram; Ficus religiosa*) at a popular Hindu goddess temple in Chennai, Tamil Nadu's capital (Fig. 1).

During the Tamil month of Āṭi (July–August), a vibrant festival season dedicated to the Hindu Goddess, I witnessed crowds of women arranging abundant offerings in front of these *nāga* images and began to trace out the web of narratives that they represent: the reasons why snake stones are typically offered and installed; the myths connecting snakes, anthills, and local goddesses; the stories of the individual women worshipping; and beliefs about the Nāga Caturtti (Snake's Fourth) festival, which is celebrated during Āṭi. Building on preliminary research investigating snake worship during the summers of 2004 and 2005, I returned to South India for 14 continuous months of ethnographic research focused on *nāga* traditions in 2006–2007. I supplemented this fieldwork with additional research carried out during the summers of 2008 and 2011, which brought the total number of Āṭi festival cycles that I have observed and participated in to six. While the vast majority of my ethnographic research and textual study was carried out in Chennai, I also spent

1. Bala Ratnam quotes an unnamed correspondent to the *Madras Mail* who recounts a story about being hosted overnight at a *śūdra*'s home in Kerala where similar attitudes toward potentially deadly snakes were in evidence. The correspondent observed several young cobras slithering about near where his host's children were playing and was told that the building in question had for three generations been home to the snakes, who had never harmed members of the *śūdra*'s family (2000: 633–35).

2. Fieldwork was generously supported by an American Institute of Indian Studies Junior Fellowship; research grants from Emory University's Graduate School of Arts and Sciences and Fund for International Graduate Research; and a Hultquist Stipend as well as other faculty development and research funds awarded by Elon University.

extended time working at other Tamil temples and visited several key sites in Kerala and Andhra Pradesh.

Figure 1. A woman adds her offerings to those left by other female devotees at this grouping of stone snake images under a sacred peepal tree at a popular Hindu goddess temple in Tamil Nadu's capital city. Photo by Amy L. Allocco (Muṇṭakakkaṇṇi Ammaṉ Temple, Chennai, 2011)

GENDER AND GENDERED DEVOTIONAL RELATIONSHIPS WITH THE SNAKE GODDESS

In contradistinction to most places in northern and central India where *nāgas* are regarded as male entities,[3] in contemporary South Indian Hinduism they are gendered as female and thus understood as snake goddesses (singular, *nāgattammaṉ*). In addition to their primary association with fertility, snake goddesses are also worshipped for prosperity and protection, and figure among the class of local goddesses linked with pox and related diseases.[4] In part because in/fertility, illness and healing, and familial well-

3. The most important exception to this generalization is the goddess Manasā, whose worship is concentrated in north-eastern India, especially West Bengal and Assam.
4. This class of goddesses is primarily populated with various forms of Mariyamman, some of which overlap with the snake goddess. One such example is the Śrī Nākamāriyammaṉ Puṟṟu Kōyil in Chennai, where the goddess is identified both as a snake goddess and a local form of Mariyamman, and is present in anthropomorphic form in the inner sanctum, as an anthill, and in the form of the divine snake who lives inside the anthill. There are many sources on

being are generally understood to fall within women's sphere of concern, the ritual propitiation of *nāgas* is overwhelmingly the practice of women in Tamil Nadu today. While many of them approach the snake goddess at specific times in order to secure her blessings in one or more of these areas, other women participate in ongoing, reciprocal ritual relationships with her, and it is almost exclusively women who embody the snake goddess in possession and speak her prophecy (*aruḷ vākku*). Female devotees undertake a wide range of vows to honour and propitiate this female divinity; they fast, conduct cycles of *pūjās* (devotional worship) and promise her pleasing gifts of saris, jewellery and other items if their wishes are fulfilled. These vows typically intensify during the Āṭi festival season, when they may include firewalking, ritual piercings, carrying milk pots in procession, ritually feeding the goddess her favourite foods and dancing her presence in possession performances.

One such devotee is Pushpa,[5] an elderly woman who works as a helper and sweeper at Aruḷmiku Nāgāttammaṉ Ālayam (literally, The Holy Snake Goddess Temple) in Chennai. This temple stages several of its own ritual events during the month of Āṭi and serves as the starting point and destination for many milk pot and other processions that animate the celebrations of smaller goddess temples in that area of the city. Pushpa spoke passionately about her devotion (*bhakti*) to this goddess and was unequivocal about her desire to continue to reside near the temple, thus making it possible for her to pass her advanced years in this goddess's service.

> There is lots of power [śakti] in this snake goddess. If you have faith in her she will do everything for you—everything depends on your faith. For me everything is her; everything is this goddess. When you believe in her with your whole heart she will never leave your side. Now I am 71; I was born and brought up near her temple. I have always lived near her—I never lived outside of this neighbourhood. My children have grown up and are living separately in different places, but I wanted to live where I was born and brought up. So, I came and sat in this goddess's place and have served her here ever since.

Pushpa understands herself and the goddess as mutually responsible for and responsive to one another and believes that this snake goddess is pleased by the service she renders at the temple. Despite the fact that Pushpa regards herself as a loyal devotee and describes her chosen goddess in both intimate and expansive terms, she also noted that if displeased, the deity is capable of displaying her anger and punishing those who offend her. Pushpa suggested that while the goddess appears in her beautiful 'ladylike' form to devotees who have earned her pleasure, those who have inspired

Mariyamman and her myths, including Beck (1981); Craddock (2001); Egnor (1983); Harman (2004); Meyer (1986); Nabokov (2000); Ramanujan (1999b); and Younger (1980).

5. All names used in this chapter are pseudonyms and the translations of this and other interviews and print sources are the author's.

her ire see her most commonly in what Pushpa called her 'true form', that of a slithering snake.

FORMS OF THE SNAKE GODDESS IN CONTEMPORARY SOUTH INDIA

The snake goddess takes multiple manifestations and is accessible to devotees in a range of physical forms. She is perhaps most often represented anthropomorphically, typically as a black stone head with a crown of snake hoods arranged around her face. When she is installed in the inner sancta of temples in this form she may be accompanied by a full-body image as well, either carved from the same black stone or cast in a variety of metals. Temple priests daily bathe and anoint these anthropomorphic *nāgāttammaṉ*s, dress them in lustrous silks, and adorn them with jewellery, vermilion (*kuṅkumam)* and turmeric (*mañcaḷ*) powders, and flowers. Devotees bring similar offerings to snake goddess temples to those they present at other shrines; these include coconuts, fruit, flower garlands and blossoms, milk, incense, oil lamps, and camphor.

The snake goddess takes the form of an anthill (*puṟṟu*, sometimes referred to as a termite hill or white-ant hill), which is conceived by some to be a *svayambhū* (self-manifest) eruption of the goddess from the earth (Fig. 2). These conical, earthen mounds may be relatively small or grow to be as many as six or more feet in height and are often decorated with vermilion and turmeric powders, *nīm* fronds, and flower garlands. Anthills feature tunnel-like passages where snakes are believed to enter and exit and it is at these openings that devotees place milk offerings (poured into small dishes or halved coconut shells) and whole eggs so that they may be enjoyed by the divine *nāga*s thought to dwell within. The emergence of these natural signifiers of the goddess is often the initial indication that she has chosen to reveal herself in a particular place. Many oral narratives and written temple histories (*sthala purāṇam*) concerning the origins of individual snake goddess temples note that the anthill appeared first, worship followed, and that a shrine with an anthropomorphic image was constructed much later.

The actual serpents who are believed to dwell in the recesses of such anthills are recognized as a third form that the snake goddess takes. Although Tamils acknowledge that anthills are built by ants or termites and not by the divine snakes themselves, many of my consultants described how anthills are sanctified and rendered worthy of worship by virtue of the presence of the goddess who in her reptilian form takes the anthill as her temple or house. A female healer in Chennai (2007) described these related manifestations: 'The goddess came and sat in an anthill. We see her there as a snake. Both the anthill and the snake are the goddess. Sometimes she is a snake, sometimes she is an anthill. Always she is śakti.'

Figure 2. A small stone *nāga* image is joined by a trident, also markers of the goddess, in front of an anthill (*puṟṟu*) at an urban snake goddess temple in Tamil Nadu. Divine reptiles, who figure among the snake goddess's multiple forms, are believed to dwell inside this anthill and to enter and exit via the hole that can be seen in front. Photo by Amy L. Allocco (Śrī Nākāttammaṉ Ālayam, Chennai, 2007)

The identification of snakes with the goddess directly informs individual attitudes toward these potentially dangerous creatures and undergirds the belief that to harm or kill a snake is to invite serious repercussions. As we shall see below, these attitudes and beliefs are frequently gendered in that female devotees describe themselves as more readily able to recognize a snake as a form of the goddess than their male counterparts.

Finally, the snake goddess also takes the form of the snake stones discussed above, which may be granite slabs on which snake images are carved or three-dimensional sculptures of snakes (Fig. 3). Typically installed under sacred trees in the courtyards of Tamil temples, *nāga* images exhibit a variety of representations: they may show one polycephalous snake, two intertwined snakes, or a single coiled snake with one extended hood. Snake stones are enlivened in *pratiṣṭhā* rites which kindle breath and life (*uyir*) in these stone forms. Devotees and priests identify these images as *nāgāttamma<u>n</u>* only after this ritual has been performed. Like any permanently installed temple image, these stone *nāgas* require daily worship after breath is instilled in them. These images are not only exceptionally common in contemporary Tamil Nadu, they also function as the snake goddess's most accessible form, since her mostly female devotees regularly 'feed' them with milk, bathe, anoint, and decorate them with their own hands in embodied displays of devotion that are relatively less possible with some of the goddess's other forms.

Figure 3. A grouping of stone snake images under a sacred tree in the courtyard of a Hindu goddess temple in Chennai. Photo by Amy L. Allocco (Alaiyammaṉ Kōyil, Chennai, 2005)

The snake goddess's multiple forms are by no means mutually exclusive; they share space at many temples and are joined by other signifiers of the goddess, which include sacred trees and her trident. Pushpa, the devotee who serves at Aruḷmiku Nāgāttammaṉ Ālayam, discussed the goddess's range of physical forms with me as well as her capacities and powers. Her remarks crystallize a view of the goddess's all-encompassing nature and cast herself as the humble devotee in relation to the tremendous power of her chosen deity.

> We worship the goddess's head inside the temple and we worship the snake inside the anthill. The anthill is like a temple for her and it is also the goddess's form, so

> we worship both... Very good people come here and very sick people come, too. Some have disease and some have *dōṣam* [literally 'blemish', a negative horoscopic condition]; the goddess's work is to make them well... Every day she comes in my dreams. We cannot predict when she will visit us in our dreams but if you want her to visit you then you should stand there [in front of her shrine], think of her, and ask her to come and protect you. Then if you have leg pain, hand pain, or any other sort of difficulty you can take a little sacred ash or anthill soil from here and apply it with faith and your pain will go away. She has every sort of power. We are nothing compared to her—she embodies all of the power. I told you this many times already: for me everything is her; everything is this goddess.

FEAR, REVERENCE AND AMBIVALENCE: *DŌṢAM* ON THE RISE

While Pushpa's comments convey the reverence she feels toward the particular snake goddess to whom she is devoted and portray this divinity as awe-inspiring and consummately powerful, they also reference the fact that some of those who appear before the snake goddess come with diseases and astrological afflictions and thus hint at the ways in which *nāga*s are ambivalently imaged in Tamil Nadu. This ambivalence fits with how snakes are depicted in the colonial and other sources discussed in the first section of this chapter, where these creatures are represented as having the capacity to bless as well as curse. More specifically, they are thought to bestow fertility when pleased with offerings and veneration and to block conception in retribution for maltreatment. Thus, while *nāga*s are certainly understood as divine beings and thus invite worship, in many cases these rituals have a prophylactic element aimed at averting potential—or mitigating actual—curses.

This prophylactic dimension principally stems from the popular belief that disturbing, harming, or killing a snake, whether knowingly or inadvertently, in this life or in a previous birth, produces a condition called *nāga dōṣam* (snake blemish).[6] This astrological flaw, which manifests in inauspicious planetary configurations in an individual's horoscope (*jātakam*), is primarily faulted for delayed marriage and infertility but may also be blamed for an array of additional negative effects.[7] *Nāga dōṣam* is indicated when the shadow planets Rāhu and Ketu[8] occupy unfavourable positions in the horoscope that is cast in relation to an individual's birth time and which is under-

6. Outside my study (Allocco 2009), little has been written about *nāga dōṣam* (cf. Goslinga 2011: 113; Kapadia 1995: 68–91). While I use the standard Sanskrit *nāga dōṣam* throughout, in Tamil print sources the term is variously rendered as *nāka tōcam, nāka tōṣam* and *nāka tōśam.*
7. While the link between *nāga*s and fertility is clearly very old, it is likely that because marriage is widely regarded as a necessary prerequisite for conception, the experience of delayed marriage or complicated marriage prospects was subsequently mapped onto *nāga* traditions and associated with *nāga dōṣam.*
8. Rāhu and Ketu are, respectively, the north and south lunar nodes, where the moon's and the sun's paths cross in the sky.

stood to reveal many of the important events—such as when one will marry and how many offspring one will have—that will shape that person's life course. Rāhu and Ketu are widely regarded as hostile planetary entities who may exert either periodic or permanent malignant influences on individuals. As such, they receive worship in their stations among the nine planets (*navagrahas*) both from those who wish to avert their gazes and those who suffer from *nāga dōṣam* or others among their afflictions. Those affected by *dōṣam* also turn to the snake goddess to atone for past sins committed against snakes and to rectify the blemishes (namely late marriage and difficulty conceiving) that these shadow planets induce.

Because the karmic consequences of harming a snake can travel across an individual's rebirths and may even be transferred among members of a lineage, one does not typically know that s/he has *nāga dōṣam* until its ill effects manifest. In contemporary South India this condition reveals itself most often when that individual has reached marriageable age but experiences difficulty in securing a suitable partner; in such cases the sufferer's family consults with an astrologer, who can diagnose *nāga dōṣam* by examining the individual's horoscope and can prescribe remedial rituals (*parikāram*) to relieve this condition. These curative measures range from relatively simple and inexpensive practices like worshipping established snake stones and making offerings to anthills at neighbourhood shrines to more complex rites such as hiring a priest to consecrate, install, and enliven a new *nāga* image or undertaking a pilgrimage to a temple known to be powerful a *dōṣa-nivartti sthala*, or site for relieving or removing *nāga dōṣam*.

My research demonstrates that *nāga dōṣam* is receiving considerable attention in Tamil Nadu today and that the rituals to rectify this horoscopic blemish are being performed by Hindus from across the caste spectrum. This astrological problem is indigenously described as 'increasing' in prevalence and as an affliction associated with 'modern times'. During the period I was conducting fieldwork I translated dozens of articles focusing on *nāga dōṣam* and the temples offering rituals to mitigate it from Tamil-language devotional magazines as well as a number of detailed religious booklets discussing the underlying causes of, negative effects resulting from, temples associated with, and ritual treatments for this condition. *Nāga dōṣam* surfaced repeatedly in casual conversations with old friends and new acquaintances alike, and consistently presented itself in more focused fieldwork interviews with priests, devotees, and astrologers. A recent *dōṣam* diagnosis was offered as the reason underlying their worship by many of the women I encountered as they offered milk and eggs at anthills and decorated snake stones installed under spreading banyan and *nīm* trees in temple courtyards. Further, I spoke with dozens of individuals who had recently travelled to religious sites regarded as important centres for the ritual treatment of this astrological blemish, such as Rameswaram and Thirunageshwaram in Tamil Nadu and Kalahasti in neighbouring Andhra Pradesh. Although the specific ritual procedures available at each of these temples are different, those who undertake pilgrimages to these sites usually avail themselves of the services of male priests in order to do some combination of offering and consecrating a new snake stone; sponsoring a fire sacrifice (*hōmam*); participating in a worship ceremony honouring Rāhu (and sometimes Ketu); offering sterling silver *nāga* images to Brahmins; taking a prescribed number of ritual baths; and/or worshipping established stone *nāga* images.

Significantly, *nāga dōṣam* is understood to be increasingly common in Tamil Nadu today as urbanization and shifting social patterns deprive snakes of their natural habitats and their traditional worship, and this prevalence is to a large extent responsible for the growing prominence of and innovation in snake worship traditions. Many of the narratives I collected emphasize that as humans clear additional land for cultivation and habitation they are increasingly encroaching on territory that naturally belongs to snakes, and that by destroying snakes' dwelling places humans are inhibiting those snakes from mating, reproducing and providing a safe domicile for their offspring. One priest in Chennai (2006) explained, 'In the olden days when farmers worked in the fields, in villages and in fields many snakes would be seen. Those areas were inhabited by many snakes. We were farming in their place. We were farming where they lived. So many farmers happened to kill snakes, fearing that the snakes may kill them. The *dōṣam* caused by killing a snake is seen in their horoscopes.' These disturbances and intrusions form part of a larger complex of human selfishness, non-performance of rituals, the breakdown of the joint family, shifting gender roles (especially the increase in women working outside the home and thus being unable to dedicate themselves to ritual responsibilities, including worshipping snakes), and other changes that my consultants indexed to 'modern times' and which they understand as linked to the recent rise in diagnoses of *nāga dōṣam*.

Because the repertoire of rituals to remediate *nāga dōṣam* necessarily overlap with *nāga* worship, such traditions are increasingly visible and expanding in popularity in South India today. There is mounting interest on the part of the mostly female devotees who worship snake stones and anthills, as is evidenced by the burgeoning crowds who come to adorn them on ritually auspicious occasions. Some of the local goddess temples where I carried out my research had to close their doors periodically throughout these days to wash the pooling milk offerings from the stone *nāga* installations and remove the unsteady heaps of offerings piled before these forms of the snake goddess. These temples faced the problem of more interest in dedicating new snake images than they could accommodate because of space constraints and thus were developing creative solutions to respond to the ritual demand. Further, ritual practices connected with the *Nāga Caturtti* festival are now appealing to a cross-section of women whose families have not traditionally marked this occasion, as well as being met with renewed attention from women whose families have customarily celebrated this festival. One grandmother noted wryly that because *Nāga Caturtti* now has associations with *nāga dōṣam* and its observance is thought to positively affect one's marriage prospects (and subsequent ability to conceive), it is one religious occasion in which she has no difficulty getting her unmarried granddaughters to participate.

NĀGA CATURTTI: SNAKE'S FOURTH FOR THE PROTECTION OF CHILDREN

The *Nāga Caturtti* (literally, Snake's Fourth) festival honours snakes and entreats them for fertility and protection.[9] It is celebrated by many in Tamil Nadu on the fourth day after the new moon (*caturtti*) during the ritually heightened *Āṭi* month, although different systems of calculation and various versions of the ritual almanac mean that some celebrate it on the fifth day (*pañcami*) or at other times in the year.[10] While many observe this festival with traditional aims in mind, such as to assure the protection of their children, to secure generalized blessings and prosperity from snakes, and to avert snake bite, some informants and particular Tamil-language sources posit an explicit connection between worshiping *nāga*s and relief from *nāga dōṣam*. Such a correlation signals that *Nāga Caturtti*'s ritual context is amenable to expanded meanings and additional innovations in light of its association with the increasingly prevalent issues associated with this astrological condition. The range of benefits that accrue from this *pūjā* is explicated both in select Sanskrit ritual digests, such as Lakṣmīdhara's *Kṛtyakalpataru*, and described in particular *Purāṇa*s, like the *Agni Purāṇa*. *Nāga Caturtti* is observed coincident both with the rainy season, a period in which snake bites are more likely due to the fact that snakes are often displaced from their subterranean homes during the monsoon, and when many Tamil farmers are sowing paddy seeds and may encounter snakes in agricultural fields. One Sanskrit scholar described to me how snakes' anthill residences become

9. For descriptions of the practices associated with this festival, see Alter (1992); Aravaanan (1977); Fuller (1944); Kane (1997); Mandlik (1869); Panda (1986); Sinha (1979); Sutherland (1991); Tewari (1991); Wadley (1975).
10. Some non-Brahmin castes such as Mudaliyars and Chettiars in Tamil Nadu celebrate *Nāga Caturtti* in October or November. These and other variations may be attributable to different versions of the *pañcangam* (lit. 'five limbs'), the almanac that prescribes the appropriate dates for festivals and is used in fixing the dates for auspicious occasions, that are followed by different castes. In many parts of India this festival is celebrated on the fifth day after the new moon, or *pañcami*, in commemoration of the day that Hindu mythology says the *nāgas* were born to Kadru, sage Kasyapa's wife. In Tamil Nadu many celebrate this festival as *Nāga Caturtti* on the fourth day after the new moon and follow it with *Garuḍa Pañcami* the next day.

flooded at this time, which forces the reptiles to venture out in search of more weather-proof dwellings, and which accounts for the increased incidence of snake bites.

While many observe *Nāga Caturtti* by performing *pūjās* at local anthills and stone *nāga* installations at neighbourhood temples,[11] others supplement these public practices with domestic rituals designed to honour snakes and cast a net of protection around their residences such that snakes will desist from entering them. The devotional worship of anthills and snake stones follows the usual contours and most commonly includes offerings of milk, eggs, flowers, and fruit. It is customary to take some anthill soil (*puṟṟumaṇ*), which is widely believed to have medicinal properties, as *prasādam* (a substance infused with the deity's grace) at the conclusion of one's *Nāga Caturtti pūjā* and to consume a pinch of it. In keeping with the offspring-centred focus and aims of this ritual occasion, one woman I know dabs some in her bellybutton for the protection and prosperity of her only son. Domestic observances often feature wall drawings of *nāgas*, typically made with moistened turmeric powder (Fig. 4), on the home's exterior, as well as images of snakes rendered in white rice flour at the home's entrance. Such drawings may be decorated with a tufted cotton garland, flower blossoms, and tiny pinches of turmeric and vermilion before spoonfuls of milk and water are offered on the *nāgas*' protruding, forked tongues. Situated outside the house, such images are intended to communicate to reptilian visitors that although they are esteemed guests who deserve propitiation on this festival day, they should refrain from entering the home's inner precincts throughout the year. In the *pūjā* space inside the home a small silver *nāga* image (Fig. 5) may be treated to ritual attentions including being bathed with milk, turmeric-water, honey, and rosewater before being dressed with shimmering fabrics, adorned with flowers and jewellery, and treated to oil lamp, incense, and various food offerings. Prayers and mantras are recited, requesting protection from the snakes being honoured, and some female devotees will abstain from certain foods as part of their festival observances.

11. Many Tamils told me that although their *pūjās* are confined to snake images and anthills, wherein snakes are believed to dwell, elsewhere in India people worship live snakes on this festival occasion. Members of the so-called 'snake charmer' community in Bedepara, West Bengal told me that they coax snakes to coil around their bodies in a performance of devotion to the goddess Manasā during the Jhapan festival. That they are not harmed by these snakes is interpreted as a sign that Manasā is pleased by their worship and has graced their community with her protection. Although Manasā also enjoys vibrant worship at the local level in Assam, one folklore scholar there told me that he knows of no instances of live snakes being worshipped there on *Nāga Pañcami* or other occasions. Vogel describes the ways this festival is observed in different parts of India and mentions the worship of Manasā in connection with *Nāga Pañcami* (1926: 275–80).

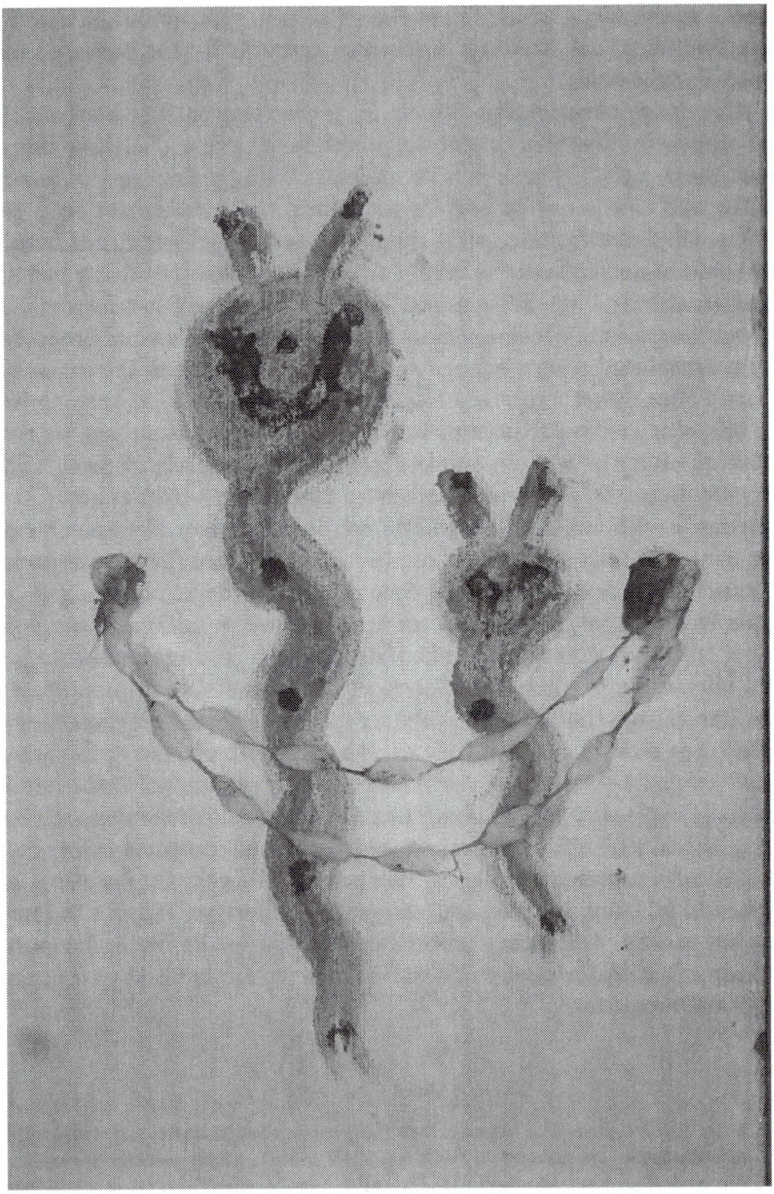

Figure 4. *Nāga* wall drawings on a home's exterior made by a female worshipper in honour of the *Nāga Caturtti* festival. Photo by Amy L. Allocco (home of Susheela, Chennai, 2007)

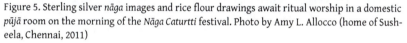

Figure 5. Sterling silver *nāga* images and rice flour drawings await ritual worship in a domestic *pūjā* room on the morning of the *Nāga Caturtti* festival. Photo by Amy L. Allocco (home of Susheela, Chennai, 2011)

I encountered several iterations of the central myth underlying the *Nāga Caturtti* festival in Tamil-language print sources as well as oral narratives. While the details and characters vary significantly, the myth's basic structure and central event are largely consistent. After a farmer kills several baby snakes while ploughing his field, the grieving *nāga* mother sets out to take revenge by killing the famer's family members. After fatally biting most of them she discovers one of the famer's female relatives performing *nāga pūjā* and abandons her vengeful plan. She agrees to restore the farmer's family members to life and promises that families whose women worship snakes on this festival day will be blessed with wealth and happiness. Although this aetiological myth does not mention the possibility of *nāga dōṣam* accruing to the farmer's family members, preferring to dwell instead on the fruits of his female relative's *bhakti*, an article concerning this festival (celebrated here on the fifth rather than the fourth day after the new moon) that appeared in the Tamil-language newspaper *Tiṉa Maṇi*'s weekly pull-out feature on religion in 2007 explores the connection between performing worship for *nāga*s during this festival and experiencing relief from *sarpa dōṣam* (a term that is used interchangeably with *nāga dōṣam*).

> The *Nāga Pañcami* vow is a *pūjā* done to seek the blessings of the serpent. If the snake planet occupies the second place, fourth place, or fifth place in one's horoscope then that person is said to have *sarpa dōṣam*. To attain peace one should worship the *nāga*, pour milk on the anthill, and perform *nāga pratiṣṭhā*. If you disturb

the female and male snake when they are together [mating] or if, even without your knowledge, you kill a cobra, these acts will cause *dōṣam* for you. *Dōṣam* causes women to be barren, causes the separation of the wife and husband, and causes other confusion in the family.

(Moulisvaran 2007)[12]

Though difficult to quantify very precisely, the impact of vernacular print sources (as well as astrology, television and call-in radio shows) on the popular awareness of—and anxiety about—*nāga dōṣam* has been significant and accounts in large part for contemporary South India's considerable appetite for snake goddess temples and shrines, *dōṣam*-removal rituals, and participation in the *Nāga Caturtti pūjā*. As the above translation suggests, the motif of human action interfering with a snake's breeding (and thus denying it the continuation of its lineage) surfaced frequently in narratives and provides important clues toward explaining why the offended *nāga* seeks its retribution by obstructing human fertility. Karma is interpreted quite literally as indexed to sinful acts perpetrated: impeding a snake's reproduction at any point along the continuum—from interfering with its conception to harming newly-hatched *nāga* babies—invites precisely the same kinds of fertility problems to be visited on the responsible individual through the curse of *nāga dōṣam*. In keeping with broader Hindu understandings of karmic consequences, in terms of maltreatment of snakes the repercussions can travel over an individual's multiple rebirths, and/or affect up to seven generations of the person's family.

Interestingly, although women account for a disproportionate number of *nāga dōṣam* cases in contemporary South India, several of my female consultants averred that because they are not active participants in her worship and thus do not know the snake goddess as they do men are less capable of recognizing a snake as the goddess and thus more likely to harm or kill it. Such mistakes would render males, and by extension their families, more vulnerable to the curse of *nāga dōṣam*. Indeed, I recorded a number of narratives about men who misinterpreted a snake passing through their houses or lands as a dangerous and threatening intrusion rather than a divine visitation. The majority of these stories feature a protective father who almost killed a snake that entered his house while his family was eating or sleeping, only to be restrained from doing so at the last moment by his wife, who recognized the snake as a form of the goddess and who subsequently worshipped her with offerings of milk and eggs.[13] A female devotee named Amudha described visitations, both to her home and in her dreams, from the snake goddess in her reptilian form.

On Fridays we buy eggs and milk and go to the temple and give them to her [the goddess]. We usually do this every other Friday. If I fail to do so, the snake will come in my dreams and I will feel uneasy. When my daughter was two years old

12. Author's translation.
13. In his essay on women's narratives, Ramanujan describes strikingly different perceptions of snakes in what he calls 'woman-centred tales' and 'man-centred tales' (1999a: 445).

> I was nursing her and the snake came into our house. It came from the [nearby snake goddess] temple. It was night; ten o'clock. I had just served food for my husband, and while I was 'feeding' my child it came in. At that time we had no 'power connection' in my house. It was very dark. I did not say, 'There is a snake there', because my husband might beat it. I just said, 'Look here, look here', very softly, and told my husband that Amma [the goddess] has come. That Friday we went to the temple and told her, 'You should not appear in our home like this. We will come and feed you in the temple.' I said that I would buy egg and milk and give to her. So, twice in a month I buy egg and milk and keep it at the anthill.

As is characteristic of many of these examples, the snake goddess's appearance inspired mixed feelings. Although this devotee reports that she ultimately instructed the goddess not to visit her at home in reptilian form, it is clear that she feared her husband would not recognize their guest as the divine being that she had ably identified the snake as and worried that he might react with the sort of violence that would put the family at risk of incurring *nāga dōṣam*. Moreover, it is clear that in this case, at least, the divine snake's visitations were prompted by the wife's ritual neglect of the goddess and thus might be motivated by the goddess's desire to remind her devotee of their mutual dependence.

CONCLUSION

The fact that female devotees may participate in abiding ritual relationships with the snake goddess in her multiple forms notwithstanding, a certain degree of ambivalence is suggested by the examples of the women whose *Nāga Caturtti* wall drawings and rice flour images of snakes are intended to communicate that these reptiles should not transgress their domestic thresholds and that of the devotee who requests that in return for committing to being more diligent in coming to the temple with her offerings the goddess should not continue to visit her in snake form at her home. While my consultants would be united in professing that the snake goddess deserves their ritual attentions and, like Pushpa, many of them would extol her capacities and agree that 'everything is her; everything is this goddess', many of them would admit that the spectre of *nāga dōṣam* inspires anxiety and that at least some of the worship the snake goddess receives in contemporary South India is linked to a new consciousness about and fear of this astrological condition and its deleterious effects. The colonial-era sources make it clear that the links between *nāga* worship and fertility aims have been around for some time and that these religious practices have been consistently gendered in nature. It is also evident that snake worship in the Subcontinent has long had a prophylactic dimension whereby reverence may be linked to fear and propitiation stems in part from the belief that *nāga*s can bless when pleased and curse when angered. These divergent reactions to human conduct most commonly manifest in terms of in/fertility, with the boon of children being the most sought-after blessing at snake goddess temples and infertility being the most dreaded among the negative effects of *nāga dōṣam*. Since the recent interest in and popularity of ritual practices associated with *nāga*s has been catalysed by a range of changes, including urbanization and shifting social, religious and economic patterns, that we have not yet seen draw to a close, it is likely that the new significances assigned to snakes and *nāga* traditions have also not reached their conclusion. Surgeon-Major Cornish's 1871 assertion that interest in snake worship will be sustained as long as India remains preoccupied with fertility seems, then, to be quite perceptive, promising us additional developments in beliefs concerning *nāga*s and ritual practices dedicated to divine snakes in South India.

REFERENCES

Allocco, A. 2009. 'Snakes, Goddesses, and Anthills: Modern Challenges and Women's Ritual Responses in Contemporary South India.' Unpublished PhD dissertation, Emory University. http://dx.doi.org/10.1525/california/9780520076976.001.0001

Alter, J. S. 1992. *The Wrestler's Body: Identity and Ideology in North India*. Berkeley: University of California Press.

Aravaanan, K. P. 1977. *The Serpent Cult in Africa and Dravidian India*. Madras: Paari Nilayam.

Atharva Veda Saṁhitā (Śaunaka Śākhā), 4 vols. Edited by Vishva Bandhu *et al.* (1960–1964). Hoshiarpur: Vishveshvaranand Vedic Research Institute.

Bala Ratnam, L. K. 2000 (1946). 'Serpent Worship in Kerala.' In R. M. Sarkar (ed.), *Through the Vistas of Life and Lore: Folkloric Reflections on Traditional India*: 621–42. Calcutta: Punthi Pustak.

Beck, B. E. F. 1981. 'The Goddess and the Demon: A Local South Indian Festival in its Wider Context.' *Purusartha* 5: 83–136.

Craddock, N. E. 2001. 'Reconstructing the Split Goddess as Śakti in a Tamil Village.' In T. Pintchman (ed.), *Seeking Mahādevī: Constructing the Identities of the Hindu Great Goddess*: 145–69. Albany, NY: State University of New York Press.

Dubois, J. A. 1983 (1899). *Hindu Manners, Customs, and Ceremonies*. New Delhi: Asian Educational Services.

Egnor, M. T. 1983. 'The Changed Mother, or What the Smallpox Goddess Did When There Was No More Smallpox.' *Contributions to Asian Studies* 18: 24–45.

Elmore, W. T. 1995 (1913). *Dravidian Gods in Modern Hinduism*. New Delhi: Asian Educational Services.

Fuller, M. 1944. 'Nag-Panchami.' *Man in India* 24: 75–81.

Goslinga, G. 2011. 'Embodiment and the Metaphysics of Virgin Birth in South India: A Case Study.' In A. Dawson (ed.), *Summoning the Spirits: Possession and Invocation in Contemporary Religion*: 109–23. London: I. B. Tauris.

Harman, W. P. 2004. 'Taming the Fever Goddess: Transforming a Tradition in Southern India.' *Manushi* 140: 2–13.

Kane, P. V. 1997 (Reprint 1941–1962). *History of Dharmaśāstra*. Poona: Bhandarkar Oriental Research Institute.

Kapadia, K. 1995. *Siva and Her Sisters: Gender, Caste, and Class in Rural South India*. Boulder, CO: Westview Press.

Mandlik, R. S. V. N. 1869. 'Serpent Worship in Western India: The Nāga-panchamī Holiday as it is Now Observed; Serpent Worship, the Nāgas and Sarpās.' *Journal of the Bombay Branch of the Royal Asiatic Society* 36(9): 169–200.

Menon, C. K. 1901. 'Serpent Worship in Malabar.' *Calcutta Review* 113: 19–25.

Meyer, E. 1986. *Aṅkāḷaparamēcuvari: A Goddess of Tamilnadu, Her Myths and Cult*. Stuttgart: Steiner Verlag Wiesbaden GMBH.

Moulisvaran, J. 2007. 'Nāka Pañcami! Karuṭa Pañcami!' *Tiṉa Maṇi*, 17 August 2007.

Nabokov, I. 2000. *Religion against the Self: An Ethnography of Tamil Rituals*. New York: Oxford University Press.

Panda, S. C. 1986. *Naga Cult in Orissa*. Delhi: B. R. Publishing Corporation.

Ramanujan, A. K. 1999a. 'Towards a Counter-System: Women's Tales.' In V. Dharwadker (ed.), *The Collected Essays of A. K. Ramanujan*: 429–47. Delhi: Oxford University Press.

Ramanujan, A. K. 1999b. 'Two Realms of Kannada Folklore.' In V. Dharwadker (ed.), *The Collected Essays of A. K. Ramanujan*: 485–512. Delhi: Oxford University Press.

Sinha, B. C. 1979. *Serpent Worship in Ancient India*. New Delhi: Books Today.

Sutherland, G. H. 1991. *The Disguises of the Demon: The Development of the Yakṣa in Hinduism and Buddhism*. Albany, NY: State University of New York Press.

Tewari, L. G. 1991. *A Splendor of Worship: Women's Fasts, Rituals, Stories and Art*. Delhi: Manohar.

Thurston, E. 1989 (1906). *Ethnographic Notes in Southern India*. New Delhi: Asian Educational Services.

— 1912. *Omens and Superstitions of Southern India*. London: T. Fisher Unwin.

Vogel, J. Ph. 1995 (1926). *Indian Serpent-Lore or The Nāgas in Hindu Legend and Art*. New Delhi: Asian Educational Services.

Wadley, S. S. 1975. *Shakti: Power in the Conceptual Structure of Karimpur Religion*. Chicago: The University of Chicago Press.

Whitehead, H. 1999 (1921). *The Village Gods of South India*. New Delhi: Asian Educational Services.

Younger, P. 1980. 'A Temple Festival of Mariyamman.' *Journal of the American Academy of Religion* 48(4): 493–517. http://dx.doi.org/10.1093/jaarel/XLVIII.4.493

The Silent Killer: The Ass as Personification of Illness in North Indian Folklore

FABRIZIO M. FERRARI*

Śītalā ('the Cold One') is a mother goddess who heals from poxes and other diseases. When anthropomorphically rendered,[1] she appears as a three-eyed fair-complexioned virgin (*kanyā*). Although in certain iconography she has been depicted as a menacing woman holding daggers (Fig. 1), traditionally she has a more gentle aspect. Śītalā holds an earthen pitcher (*kalsī*) and a broom (*jhāṛu*), and is crowned with a winnowing fan (*śūrpa*). All these objects bear witness to her healing power. The vessel contains cold healing water. With the broom the goddess wipes away the germs of diseases. The winnowing fan, a reminiscence of her agricultural origin, is used to cool ill devotees with fresh air.[2] Besides such trademark attributes, Śītalā is often seated side-saddle on a 'donkey' (Fig. 2). Despite its ubiquity, the equid—whether wild ass or donkey[3]—is a rather marginal character. Laudatory invocations in Sanskrit, vernacular narratives, devotional/auspicious poems and folk myths do

* Fabrizio M. Ferrari was educated in Indology at the Ca' Foscari University of Venice (Italy) and received his PhD from SOAS in 2005 for a study on popular Hinduism in West Bengal. He taught South Asian Religions and Religious Studies at SOAS and is now Professor of Religious Studies at the University of Chester. He has published articles and book chapters on disease goddesses and healing rituals. He is the author of *Oltre il confine, dove la terra è rossa. Canti d'amore e d'estasi dei bāul del Bengala* (Ariele, 2001) and *Guilty Males and Proud Females: Negotiating Genders in a Bengali Festival* (Seagull, 2010). He wrote the first monograph in English on the Italian anthropologist and historian of religion Ernesto de Martino (*Ernesto de Martino on Religion. The Crisis and the Presence*, Equinox, 2012) and has edited the volume on *Health and Religious Rituals in South Asia: Disease, Possession and Healing* (Routledge, 2011). His research is mainly directed towards the study of religious folklore in the frame of Marxist anthropology. He is currently writing an extensive research monograph on the goddess Śītalā.

1. Śītalā is also profusely worshipped in the form of big human heads, earthen pots (*ghaṭ*) and black roundish stones (*śilā*). These are besmeared with red *kumkum* powder and often surmounted with small gold-plated or metal crowns, or large eyes.
2. The movement of the winnow is also a ritual practice used by folk-healers to get possessed by the goddess and negotiate health.
3. The words 'ass' and 'donkey' are nowadays used interchangeably. However, they are not synonyms. The term 'donkey' was originally used to indicate a domesticated 'ass' (cf. Parpola and Janhunen 2011: 62, 101). 'Ass' is henceforth used to indicate both the Indian wild ass (or half-ass, i.e. hemione) and domesticated asses.

not indulge in descriptions, nor do they explain its presence. The animal is non-gender specific, has no proper name and is speechless. In this chapter I will argue that the ass is not just a mere mount but can be considered the embodiment of disease and misfortune, while Śītalā, rather than being a 'disease goddess', is a controller and a healer.

Fig. 1 Silver pendant showing Śītalā on a donkey holding two daggers. Provenience: Jharkhand. Author's collection.

Fig. 2 Śītalā in full regalia on a donkey. Popular poster art. Purchased in Varanasi (November 2010).

ILLNESS AND ASS-MOUNTED GODDESSES IN SOUTH ASIA

Since Vedic times Hindu gods and goddesses have been portrayed on animal or human/animal hybrid vehicles. Yet *vāhanas* in Hindu mythology are not just means of transportation. While some reflect the personality of the deity they carry (e.g. Durgā's tiger/lion), others are independent characters with specific features and powers, and—occasionally—forms of worship (e.g. Garuḍa and Nandī). In the mythology of the so-called 'pox goddess' nothing explains the presence of the donkey/ass. Although in several narratives she wanders solo (Bang 1973: 86) and countless *mūrtis* (icons) have no vehicle, the presence of the ass—a suspiciously quiet animal valued only for its strength—has become customary in commercial reproductions, ritual manuals (*pūjā-paddhati*), stories of vows (*vratkathā*) and laudatory verses (*cālīsa-saṃgraha, śītalā ārtī*).

The earliest iconographic evidence of Śītalā as an ass-riding goddess is with all probability an eleventh-century statue at the Sun temple (*Sūrya-kuṇḍa*) in Modhera (Mahesana district, Gujarat). Naked on her ass, an unusual twelve-armed Śītalā holds weapons like Durgā along with her distinctive basket. Tiwari (1996: 452) reports that:

> a good number of shrines and sculptures of Śītalā are found from Gujarat (Moḍherā, Vaḍnagar, Sejakpur), Rajasthan (Osiāñ, Arthūṇā), Bengal and even Tamilnadu during the 11th and 12th centuries CE. The Saccikamātā Mandir at Osiāñ (Rajasthan) contains an inscription dated in *saṁvat* 1234 (CE 1177) on the northern façade of its sanctum which records the installation of the images of Caṇḍikā and Saccikā goddesses along with Śītalā.[4]

As for literary sources, Śītalā is first mentioned as an ass-riding goddess in Nārada Purāṇa (1.117.94-98), a text that can be dated between the ninth and the tenth century CE. Another important source, though much later, is the *Bhāvaprakāśa* (sixteenth century), a medical compendium authored by Bhāva Miśra, where a complete hymn, the *Śītalāṣṭakastotra*, is dedicated to Śītalā (*Madhyakhaṇḍa* 60: 31–42). This is perhaps the most popular written reference to the goddess as we know her today,[5] and is subsequently found in a number of sources in different languages, including *smārta* texts and the popular *vratkathās* (stories of vows). The Bengali *Śītalā-maṅgal-kābyas*, didactic and eulogistic poems composed between the late seventeenth and the nineteenth century, are with all probability the most extensive genre celebrating Śītalā. Such works are of extreme interest for being the only literary source where the ass-riding (*gardabhāhinī, rāsabhasthā*) Śītalā is actually a killer.[6] The presence of the ass, and its relation to disease (*rog, vyādhi*), remains however unexplained.

A possible rationale for the association of the ass with 'disease goddesses' may be found in Vedic literature. Though asses are strong and fast rides that carry Agni (*Taittirīya Saṃhitā* 5.1.5; *Vājasaneyi Saṃhitā* 11.13) and the Aśvinas,

4. In his article on Śītalā in Indian art, Tiwari mentions other notable images: a twelfth-century statue from Sejakpur (Gujarat), an eleventh/twelfth century statue held in the Archaeological Museum of Amer (Jaipur, Rajasthan), an image from the Nilakanteshwara Mandir in Arthuna (Banswada, Rajasthan), a twelfth-century statue from the Jasmalnath Mahadev Mandir of Asoda (Gujarat) and a twelfth/thirteenth century bronze statue held in the Musée Guimet Paris (France) (Tiwari 1996: 457–59).

5. The origin of this hymn is obscure. Bhāva Miśra indicates it has been extrapolated from the *Kāśī Khaṇḍa* (c. fourteenth century CE), a section of the *Skanda Purāṇa*. Yet as Nicholas (2003: 179) observes, all published editions of the text do not include it. Śītalā is however mentioned in the *Avantya-khaṇḍa* (7.134.2; 7.135.1-7; 12.1.5) of *Skanda Purāṇa*, although there is no description of her or her vehicle (p. 226).

6. Śītalā, in other regions of north India, is a protector of children and a benevolent auspicious healing mother. Only in West Bengal, Bangladesh and Assam—to my knowledge—she is an angry goddess who causes disease and epidemics to punish those who refuse to worship her (whether human or divine).

the physicians of the gods (*Ṛg Veda* 1.34.9; 8.74.7),[7] they are known as impure and ominous beasts. Indra is summoned and asked to destroy the inauspicious ass (*Ṛg Veda* 1.29.5) while the she-ass is associated to witchcraft and thus compelled to leave by means of powerful spells (*Atharva Veda* 10.1.14). In both Vedic and post-Vedic literature, inauspicious goddesses ride (or are associated with) the ass:

1. Nirṛti ('Injustice', 'Disorder'): the Vedic goddess of death, decay and corruption. Early and late Vedic literature refers to her as a goddess to be kept away (*Ṛg Veda* 5.41.17, 6.74.2, 10.59.1-10). Nothing suggests Nirṛti was represented on a donkey although she has been later identified with ass-riding goddesses such as Jyeṣṭhā and Alakṣmī (Kinsley 1997: 178). According to the *Laws of Manu* (second century BCE), to placate Nirṛti one is supposed to sacrifice a one-eyed ass at a cross-road at night (*Mānavadharmaśāstra* 11.119, in Olivelle 2009a). In the *Parāskara-Gṛhyasūtra* (3.12.1-11), 'a Vedic student who has violated his vow of chastity should sacrifice an ass to Nirṛti. He has to dress himself in the skin of the ass and eat a piece of the sacrificial victim cut out of its penis' (Parpola 2004–2005: 33).[8]
2. Jyeṣṭhā ('The Elder [Wife]'): the goddess of misfortune and disease. She usually has no mount and is represented as an old woman with flaccid skin, pendulous breasts and an ugly face. Jyeṣṭhā's vehicle and symbol is the crow. Yet as Leslie informs us (1991: 118, cf. White 2003: 51) she rides an ass (*khararūḍha*) in *Suprabhedāgama* 3 and in *Śabdakalpadruma* 1.1 page 120, where she is called *gardhabharūḍha*.
3. Alakṣmī ('Misfortune'): often equated to Jyeṣṭhā. She has a 'dry shrivelled up body, sunken cheeks, thick lips, and beady eyes and she rides a donkey' (Pattanaik 2008: 51). Alakṣmī/Jyeṣṭhā is also known as Akīrti ('disgrace') and Atulā ('imbalance') (*Liṅga Purāṇa* 2.6.16).
4. Kālarātrī ('Black Night'), a Tantric goddess identified with the fearsome aspect of Kālī or Bhairavī. Kālarātrī is worshipped as the seventh *śakti* of Durgā and, as a goddess of destruction, is related to everything leading to death, including disease. She is often worshipped along with Śītalā and her images are found in many *śākta* temples.[9] The goddess is black or dark-blue complexioned with long dishevelled curly black hair. She wears a garland of *javā* flowers (or, alternatively, skulls) and, naked, rides an ass (*Pratiṣṭhā-lakṣaṇa-sāra-samuccaya*, an eleventh-twelfth century Tantric text, in Bühneman 2003: 40). Kālarātrī is also associated to the 'pestilence goddess' Mahākālī (*Devīmāhātmya* 12.35-38 in Coburn 1991) (Fig. 3).

7. On the Aśvinas and asses, see Parpola and Janhunen (2011: 88).
8. Wild asses are also sacrificed to Īśāna (Rudra or Mahādeva) in *Vājasaneyī Saṃhitā* 24.28.
9. See my ethnography of the Śrī Dakṣiṇī Ādi Śītalā (Buṛhiyā Māī) Mandir on Śītalā-ghāṭ, Varanasi, in Ferrari forthcoming.

5. Cāmuṇḍā (or Caṇḍamārī), the slayer of the demons Caṇḍa and Muṇḍa, is described in the *Vāmana Purāṇa* (29.70) in a way very similar to Śītalā, that is, naked and riding an ass. Cāmuṇḍā, among her many names, is also called Kālīkā and in this form she rides an ass (*Matsya Purāṇa* 261: 37–38).
6. Dhumāvatī ('Smokey'), the widow goddess. Described as an ugly crone, Dhumāvatī is normally accompanied by a crow. The presence of a donkey is probably related to her identification with Jyeṣṭhā. Despite her inauspicious nature, the goddess has become an object of popular devotion and her most important place of worship, a temple in Varanasi, attracts childless couples and mothers concerned for the health of their children.
7. The 64 *yoginis* (*causaṭṭī yoginī*), a class of Tantric semi-divine half-human half-animal female beings. Widely reputed to be sorceresses or witches, the *yoginīs* are considered powerful and accomplished ritual practitioners. Some *yoginīs* are represented as either standing on a donkey or as ass-faced beings (e.g. Gandhārī and Vaināyakī in the Hirapur temple, or Hārārāvā, Tālajanghā and Piśītāśā in, respectively, Hemadri's *Caturvarga Cintāmaṇi*, the *Matottara Tantra* and the *Pratiṣṭhā-lakṣaṇa-sāra-samuccaya*) (Dehejia 1986: 205–207).
8. Mātaṅgī ('the intoxicated One'): one of the ten *mahāvidyās*, she is represented as a richly adorned young women, with firm breasts, long black hair, three eyes, green (or blue) skin. She sits on a corpse and her companion is a green parrot. She is known as the outcaste goddess and is related to pollution and leftover food. 'Her name literally means "she whose limbs are intoxicated (with passion)"' (Kinsley 1997: 218). In Tantric Kaula circles, Mātaṅgī is equated to Vaināyakī, the *yoginī* with the elephant head who stands on a donkey.
9. Mūtēvī ('Elder Goddess'): a Southern variant of Jyeṣṭhā. She represents ill fortune, discord and disease and is worshipped along with her younger sister Śrīdevī (fortune and prosperity). The goddess rides an ass, is dark complexioned and holds a banner with the image of a crow (Sonnerat 1782: 160, Shulman 1989: 51).
10. Raktābatī ('Bloody'), Śītalā's servant (also worshipped as a companion goddess). To my knowledge her presence is limited to Bengal only (cf. *Birāṭ pālā* in Nityānanda Cakrabartī's *Śītalā maṅgal*) where she was also a synonym for the black pox (i.e. haemorrhagic smallpox). Raktābatī is represented as a beautiful lady who rides an ass or, alternatively (in lower Bengal), a tiger. According to folk stories and songs, her visit is an ominous sign. Hearing knocks, bumps (the donkey's hooves) or scratches (the tiger's claws) from rooftops at nighttime indicates her arrival.

Fig. 3 Śītalā (right) and Kālarātrī (left) – both ass-riding – in the *guphā* (cave) of the Śītalā Mandir, Dasashwamedh ghat, Varanasi (November 2010). Photo by Fabrizio M. Ferrari.

The ass is also present in other South Asian demonic narratives, or stories of disease deities:

1. Kali ('Discord'): the demon of the Dark Age. In the *Kalki Purāṇa*, Kali confronts Kalki, the tenth *avatāra* of Viṣṇu, and tries to destroy the world. He rides an ass while his divine opponent—as many other solar deities—has a white stallion.
2. Dhenuka, a ferocious anthropophagous ass-demon living in the Talavan forest, near Vṛndāvana. According to the *Dhenukavadha* myth (*Harivaṁśa* 57, *Bhāgavata Purāṇa* 10.15; *Viṣṇu Purāṇa* 5.8), Dhenuka, along with other ferocious ass-demons, was killed by the hand of Balarāma (Kṛṣṇa's brother) who went in the wine palm grove to pick up fruits.
3. Rāvaṇa, the lord of the *rākṣasas*. According to folk traditions, he was given the head of an ass on top of his ten heads to lessen his pride. In the *Rāmāyaṇa* he rides a chariot of donkeys (5.27.24-25) and is brother to Khara, the Ass-Demon.
4. Khara ('Ass'): a ferocious and anthropophagous *rakṣasa* chief, brother (or cousin) to Rāvaṇa. Khara is described in the third book of the *Rāmāyaṇa* (19–30; see also 1.1.47) in his attempt to vindicate his sister

Śūrpaṇakhā (the One with 'fingernails like winnowing fans'), whose nose was cut off by Rāma's brother Lakṣmaṇa.

5. Khaḍgarāvaṇa, a mantra-deity born out of Śiva's roar (*khaḍga*) to vanquish demons at the origin of negative possession (i.e. illness). The *Khaḍgarāvaṇa-mantra* is supposed to counter *jvālāgardabha*, a pustular condition of the skin imputed to worms, or insects (chapter 28 of the *Kriyākālaguṇottara Tantra*, c. ninth-tenth century CE).[10]
6. The Tibetan guardian goddess dPal-ldan Lha-mo (Palden Lhamo)—or Śrī Devī, in Sanskrit—is portrayed as riding a huge red ass (possibly a kiang) on whose back are two heavy bags made of ulcerated human skin full of the germs of virulent diseases (smallpox, cholera, leprosy, plagues, etc.).
7. The Chinese smallpox goddess Ch'uan Hsing Hua Chieh ('One who hands on fragrant flower') rides a large donkey, or a horse (Hopkins 1983: 136).

South Asian narratives portray the ass following four trends. First, the animal is believed to be demonic, impure and a disease carrier. *Piśācas* are believed to be asses (Filippi 2002: 105), just like *rakṣasas* (*Vājasaneyi Saṃhitā* 24.40). The word *khara* ('ass') indicates any *asura*, particularly the *daityas* (Bhattacharyya 2000: 110). Issues of purity have also contributed to enhancing the reputation of the ass as an inauspicious (*Mānavadharmaśāstra* 10.51, in Olivelle 2009a) or demonic animal (Visuvalingam 1989: 170). The *Rāmāyaṇa* too confirms the impurity of the ass: 'If in a dream, a person sees a man going in a chariot, yoked with donkeys, the smoke of a funeral pyre will soon be seen ascending him' (2.69.18). Parpola has found numerous references that mention the inauspiciousness of the ass:

> The sounds of dogs, asses, jackals, vultures and crows forebode evil (Atharvaveda-Pariśiṣṭa 61,1,8), and Vedic recitation is to be suspended when dogs are barking, asses (*gardabha-*) are braying or jackals are howling (cf. Āpastamba-Dharmasūtra 1,10,19; Gautama-Dharmasūtra 16,8). Dreaming of camels, pigs, asses etc. forebodes evil (cf. Mānava-Gṛhyasūtra 2,14,11). In Rāmāyaṇa 2,63,14-16, Bharata's dream of a man driving an ass-chariot is explicitly stated to portend death. In spite of its fecundating power, the ass is an animal connected with Nirṛti, the goddess of Destruction, the guardian deity of the inauspicous direction of southwest. It is to her, Nirṛti, or to Yama (the god of death) that the ass is to be sacrificed in breaches of chastity and this in the wilderness (*araṇye*) (cf. Vasiṣṭha-Dharmasūtra 23,1; Baudhāyana-Dharmasūtra 2,1,30-35). The main reason for the ass's connection with destruction and death is, I suspect, the habitat of the wild ass, the lifeless salt desert. Indeed, in the Dhenukavadha myth...the wild ass is compared to the god of death (Antaka).
>
> (Parpola and Janhunen 2011: 71)

10. Khaḍgarāvaṇa—as convincingly argued by Slouber (2005: 14–15)—is unlikely to be the epic Rāvaṇa, although the latter is associated to donkeys.

The ass is also socially impure. The *Śatapatha-Brāhmaṇa* explains that the ass is representative of the two lowest *varṇas*, *vaiśya* and *śūdra* (6.4.4.12), a feature derived by the fact that 'whilst being one, double impregnates' (i.e. the mare and the she-ass) (*Śatapatha-Brāhmaṇa* 6.3.1.22-23; cf. *Aitareya-Brāhmaṇa* 4.9). In *Baudhāyana-Śrauta-Sūtra* 27.8 and 28.10, the ass is associated to dogs, crows, *śūdras* and 'untouchables' as an impure animal (Smith 1994: 286). As per more recent reports, stories of asses used to parade women accused of witchcraft are fairly common in India, and are widely reported in national media.

Second, in Indic folklore the ass is the epitome of stupidity, stubbornness and sexual voraciousness. Tales like 'The ass in the leopard skin' (Olivelle 2009b: 112–13)[11] or 'The ass without ears or a heart' in the *Pañcatantra* (pp. 152–54) confirm that the animal is an example not to follow and add to the image of a beast driven by sexual impulses. Such low appetites have contributed to establishing a normative pattern for punishing illicit sex (a practice attested in *Mānavadharmaśāstra* 8.370). Parpola reports that asses were customarily sacrificed for illicit sexual behaviour:

> a student of the Veda who has broken his vow of chastity should offer an ass (gardabha-) (cf. Āpastamba-Dharmasūtra 1,26,8; Gautama-Dharmasūtra 23,17; Vasiṣṭha-Dharmasūtra 23,1) and in this sacrifice the cut-off portion to be eaten by the sacrificer should be taken from the penis of the ass (cf. Kātyāyana-Śrautasūtra 1,1,13 and 17; Baudhāyana-Dharmasūtra 2,1,30-35). The Manu-Smṛti (11,122-123) instead prescribes that the guilty student should for one year wear the skin of the ass and proclaim his lapse while begging for his food.
>
> (Parpola and Janhunen 2011: 70)

Erotic literature too identifies the ass with all possible degrading features. The *Anaṅga-raṅga* (fifteenth-sixteenth century) says: 'The Kharasatvastri, [the woman] who preserves the characteristics of the ass, is unclean in her person, and avoids bathing, washing, and pure raiment: she cannot give a direct answer, and she speaks awkwardly and without reason, because her mind is crooked. Therefore she pleases no one' (Burton and Arbuthnot 1885: 38).

Third, the ass as a beast of burden. Folk narratives across North India seem to confirm such interpretation. Yet while considering the worship of Śītalā in greater details (Ferrari forthcoming), I noticed that the Bengali *maṅgal-kābya* tradition begs to differ. The ass is needed by Śītalā by virtue of its strength (the animal carries the goddess and her heavy load of pulses, i.e. poxes).[12] However, the equid is not the sole beast of burden available. When Śītalā attacks her enemies, or even innocent villagers, with virulent diseases she: (1) sits on an ass while other beasts of burden carry the germs of disease (e.g.

11. An alternative version is found in *Hitopadeśa* (Haksar 2006: 140–42).
12. To my knowledge, only one *Śītalā-maṅgal-kābya* does not mention the ass. This is the *Bardhamān Pālā* of Kabi Jagannāth (eighteenth century) (cf. Nicholas 2003: 132–48).

in Kṛṣṇarām Dās' *Śītalā-maṅgal-kābya* the bags with the germs of diseases are carried by oxen, cf. Stewart 1995: 394); (2) sits on a ass and marches towards her enemies followed by an horde of diseases in the form of horrid ghouls or demons (e.g. Mānikrām Gāṅgulī's *maṅgal*, cf. Nicholas 2003: 155); and (3) holds herself the load of poxes in the crook of her arm (p. 155) before unleashing the pestilence (Mānikrām Gāṅgulī and Kabi Jagannāth' *maṅgals* in ibid, pp. 134 and 155). Only in this literature Śītalā is Rogeśbarī (Queen of Fevers) and Byadhipati (Master of Diseases).

Fourth, the ass is a symbol of fertility. The male donkey/ass is well-known for his sexual voracity. Besides impregnating other equines (cf. *Śatapatha-Brāhmaṇa* 6.3.1.23), *Atharva Veda* (6.72.3) reports a spell to make one's penis grow as that of the ass and in *Matrāyaṇī Saṃhitā* (3.1.6.7, 16) 'the ass [*gardhabo*] is the most virile animal of all' (Parpola 2004: 34). The she-ass, as provider of milk, an essential ingredient in indigenous folk medicine, is an animal praised for her fecundity. In the past, health seekers were treated with the milk of jennets to placate the burning heath of fevers and smallpox as an alternative to variolation (the cutaneous inoculation of infected dried pus extracted from human smallpox victims' scabs or pustules and aiming to result in a milder form of smallpox), although no ritual or devotional texts sanction this practice.[13] The *Aṣṭāṅgahṛdaya-saṃhitā* (*sūtrasthāna* 5.26) of Vāgbhaṭa (an Āyurvedic compendium composed between the sixth and seventh centuries CE) says that: 'The milk of single hoofed animals (like horse, donkey, etc.) [*ekaśapha kṣīra*] is very hot (in potency), cures vāta disorders localised in the śākhās, (blood and other tissues), is slightly sour and salt and causes lassitude (lazyness) [sic]'. The business of donkey's milk in the Subcontinent is still thriving as this ingredient continues to be used as a remedy for poxes and fevers (Nirmalānanda 1413BS: 80; Bang 1973: 86; Mukhopadhyay 1994: 25).[14] Tempting as it may be to argue that Śītalā mounts a jennet that provides the milk to heal patients/devotees, I am not in favour of this reading. Neither informants nor any textual source I am aware of confirm this. I thus suggest *kṣīra* is symbolic of a hot animal that is controlled (mounted) by a cold goddess. Further to that, it is worth noting that Śītalā, a goddess associated with cool waters and the refreshing seasonal rain, rides a wild-tempered desert beast who has a reputation for being a voracious drinker (*Ṛg Veda* 1.16.5; 8.74.7 but also the *Dhenukavadha* myth in *Harivaṃśa* 57.16). This structural feature depends on the urinary system of the ass and its capacity to drink enormous

13. Larry Brilliant (2009), a former medical officer of the WHO smallpox eradication campaign in India, informs us that the milk of 'wild assess' was believed to be the only cure against smallpox.

14. In 2001 the Department of Chemistry at the University of Lucknow was working on a project sponsored by the Uttar Pradesh Council of Science and Technology on the immunostimulant proprieties of donkey's milk. Clinical trials have been done in association with the Sanjay Gandhi Postgraduate Institute of Medical Science and the Central Drug Research Institute (Times of India, 2001).

quantities of water (even salty water) in a very short time (up to 100 litres in less than ten minutes) (Parpola and Janhunen 2011: 84). This is corroborated by the custom (an apotropaic ritual) to marry asses in rural temples to call for rain if the monsoon is late, or during droughts. (The fact that the mating season of the ass occurs during the rainy season seems relevant.)

THE CURSE IN THE NAME: ASSES AND SKIN DISEASES

The ass is attested in relation to impurity and inauspiciousness since Vedic times. As for Śītalā, the most popular ass-riding deity in pre-modern and contemporary South Asia, I have elsewhere argued that the label 'disease/smallpox goddess' is one resulting from colonial readings (Ferrari 2010 and, more extensively, Ferrari forthcoming). Functional explanations of Śītalā's *vāhana* as a beast of burden or a provider of milk are not convincing. I will thus try to explain the presence of the ass in relation to equine diseases and their symptoms so as to explore other long-forgotten and perhaps domesticated meanings.

During the last ten years (2001–2005 and 2007–2012), I have conducted extensive fieldwork in North India (especially in Uttar Pradesh and West Bengal). Yet only recently, after a series of visits to the main Śītalā *mandir* in Varanasi (at Dāsāśvamedh ghāṭ) and a site of pilgrimage in the nearby village of Adalpura, I grew increasingly intrigued by Śītalā's *vāhana*. In these two temples, like in many others, the goddess is represented both with and without the ass. Unfortunately none of my informants could explain this. Also, nobody knew—or was remotely interested in knowing—why Śītalā and goddesses who are related to life-threatening diseases and conditions resulting in social stigma (e.g. infertility) mount an allegedly 'stupid' animal. After reading and listening to several mythological narratives, observing countless *pūjās* and admiring all sort of visual representations (from statues to bass-reliefs, batiks, posters, postcards, stickers, calendars, votive medals, theatrical and *philmī* renderings), I came to the conclusion that to identify the kind of equine Śītalā mounts might be relevant for justifying her specialism.

Sanskrit and vernacular sources seem particularly concerned with the animal's inauspiciousness, stupidity, vulgarity, sexual appetite and loud unpleasant (scary) bray. Conversely, ethnographic research[15] proved extremely useful in answering many questions related to representations, visualizations or manifestations of the goddess.[16] Several images of Śītalā show a small grey-

15. I refer to my interviews with devotees and ritual specialists, analyses of regional narratives incorporated in 'texts' such as folk theatre, scroll-paints and songs, ritual formulae, observation of healing sessions (including therapeutic possession), *pūjās*, animal sacrifices (*balidān*) and elaborate celebrations involving hook-swinging and acts of self-harming.
16. Informants who experienced Śītalā's visitation vividly told me that the arrival (descent) of the goddess is preceded by an ominous pattering of hooves and the bray of the ass. Local physi-

coated animal identifiable with the domesticated donkey (*Equus asinus*). Alternative representations and oral narratives suggest that the goddess' *vāhana* is a big wild red, sandy or brown beast.[17] Professional storytellers, image-makers and ritual specialists from the most disparate castes associate the reddishness of the equid's coat with the hotness of its temper. Two animals correspond to such description; the Indian Wild Ass (*Equus hemionus khur*) or khur, an Anglicized form of the Sanskrit *khara*, and the Tibetan Wild Ass (*Equus Kiang*, formerly known as *Equus hemionus kiang*), or kiang.[18] Given the behavioural and morphological features of these equines, who famously stroke popular imagination for their fierce aspect (the kiang is the largest wild ass), their loud bray, their insatiable thirst, their long ears, their sexual voraciousness and their aggressiveness,[19] it is unsurprising that they may have been associated with Śītalā, a mother goddess who has power to cool, soothe and heal.

This seems to find confirmation in the way the ass is called in North India. The Bengali *maṅgal* poems and vernacular variants of the *Śītalā-cālīsā-saṁgraha*, the *Śītalā-ārtī*, the *Śītalāṣṭakaṣṭotraṁ* and the many *Śītalāvratkathās* refer to the ass as *khara*, *gardabha* and *rāsabha*. But the most popular word to indicate Śītalā's mount in Indic Northern languages (Urdu, Hindi, Bengali, Bhojpuri, Assamese, Nepali, Panjabi, etc.) is *gādhā* (or equivalent forms). This word, from the Sanskrit *gardabhaḥ*, seems to point at the loud nature of the ass (√*gard*, 'to roar'). Parpola, however, explains that *gardabha* is a loan from Proto-Dravidian **kaẓutay*, a word whose meaning is 'kicker of the salt desert' (from **kaẓ(i)*, 'saline soil', and **utay*, 'to kick') (Parpola and Janhunen 2011: 74).[20] From *gardabhaḥ*, a word that links the morphological and behavioural features of the ass, is derived the noun *gardabhaka*, 'a cutaneous disease (eruption of round, red, and painful spots)' (Monier-Williams 1997: 349). Such

cians interpreted this as paracusia (auditory hallucination) and suggested the 'noises' are a cultural response to a situation of stress. Alternatively, I learnt, paracusia may be imputed to a wide range of diseases, from mental disorders, to brain tumours, encephalitis, epilepsy, high fever and forms of otitis, the analysis of which goes beyond the purpose of this study.

17. In Mānikrām Gāṅgulī's *maṅgal*, the author glorifies the goddess who is seated on the ass, 'whose gait is like that of the Greatest among Elephants' (Nicholas 2003: 150). As for the colour, Parpola has convincingly explained that *gaura-khara* ('cow-coloured' ass) is in fact another name for the wild ass attested from at least the second century BCE (Parpola and Janhunen 2011: 80–84).
18. Today these feral equines, closely related to the onager (*Equus hemionus*), are an endangered species protected in sanctuaries. The former was extremely common in Iran, Afghanistan, Pakistan and North-Western India (particularly Rajasthan and Gujarat); the latter is indigenous of the Tibetan Plateau but is also found in Ladakh, Jammu and Kashmir and Nepal.
19. In Sanskrit, the ass is given names that qualify it for its loud and unpleasant bray (*rāsabha*, *upakroṣṭṛ*, *gardabha*, *rūkṣasvara*), ears (*karṇin*, *lambakarṇa*), dusty colour (*dhūsara*, *reṇurūṣita*), hooves (*nighṛṣva*), strength in carrying loads (*bhāraha*, *bhāravāhana*), sexual appetite (*ramaṇa*, *smarasmarya*), similarity to horses (*grāmya aśva*), capacity to urinate for a long time (*ciramehin*) or its mischievous and unpredictable temper (*daśeraka*).
20. Asses, introduced to South Asia from 2000 BCE, had been the only known equines to the local population and their habitat in the salty deserts of North-Western India.

term, attested in *Agni Purāṇa* 31.36 (*doṣā jvālāgardabhakādayaḥ*), indicates a failure (*doṣā*) caused by small worms or insects whose larvae are found in dung. These 'small asses'[21] are at the origin of the *jvālāgardabha* found in magic texts (such as the already mentioned *Kriyākālaguṇottara Tantra*). However, they were well known in early Āyurvedic compendia as the cause of (minor) ulcerative conditions of the skin. In *Suśruta Saṃhitā*, *jālagardabha* indicates a skin ailment (*-gardabha*) involving muscular, vascular, ligamentous and bony tissue (*jāla*). This affliction is listed with, amongst the others, *gardabhī* and *visphoṭaka* (later cumulative names to indicate smallpox) (SuS *cikitsāsthāna* 20.6–7).[22]

Sharing the same names with the ass must have contributed to associating this animal with ulcerative diseases of the skin such as, for instance, sarcoids, tumours involving epithelial, muscular and connective tissue which frequently appears on donkeys. Sarcoids, dry scaly masses, tend to ulcerate and bleed, like big smallpox pustules. Verrucous sarcoids, the most common on donkeys, often occur on the head, chest, shoulder and under-leg and, lacking hair, they are easy to spot. Their growth mostly appears in spring (*vasanta*, hence Śītalā's most come title in Bengal, Basanta Rāy—the Spring Queen), when smallpox used to burst in South Asia. Although changing factors must be considered (dietary change, increased ultraviolet light, fly strike, changing routine and stress levels), the symptoms of sarcoids—like poxes and cutaneous diseases in general—are traditionally believed in North Indian folklore to be caused by solar rays and the heat of the sun.

As for viral pustular afflictions, early Āyurvedic compendia are vague. Caraka (c. first-second centuries CE) and Suśruta (c. third-fourth centuries CE) mention diseases whose symptoms are skin eruptions. These, however, do not appear to be contagious in nature and do not seem life-threatening conditions (CaS, *sūtrasthāna*, 26.102; *cikitsāsthānam* 12.90, 93; SuS, *nidānasthāna*, 13.17.41-45). It may be therefore inferred that smallpox was not known in South Asia before the fifth century CE. Vāgbhaṭa, in his *Aṣṭāṅgahṛdaya-saṃhitā*, indicates *visphoṭa* and *masūrikā* as *kṣudra roga* (minor ailments). Conversely the eighth century *Nidāna* of Mādhavakara discusses the very same diseases as serious conditions which may cause death (53.11; 54.30-31). It seems thus likely that the strain of smallpox known in South Asian between the sixth and the eight centuries was not as deadly as the one that plagued the Subcontinent in the following centuries.[23] Amongst other minor diseases, the *Aṣṭāṅgahṛdaya-saṃhitā* men-

21. I would attempt an alternative etymology: *garda-* 'crying' but also 'voracious' + OIA animal name suffix *-bha* and the diminutive suffix *-ka*, that is 'tiny hungry animals'.
22. A description of *jālagardabha* is given in SuS *nidānasthāna* 13.13–17. Another pustular affliction of the *-gardabha* type is *pāṣāṇagardabha*, a hard swelling (*pāṣāṇa* means 'small stone') on the jaw which may suppurate but is still considered a *kṣudra roga* (SuS *nidānasthāna* 13.12 and *cikitsāsthāna* 20.5). SuS indicates as *kīṭagardabhaka* a class of dangerous insects that may cause serious illness (*kalpasthāna* 8.11).
23. The *Bhāvaprakāśa* mentions a disease similar to smallpox and calls it interchangeably *masūrikā* (lentil disease) or *vispoṭha(ka)* (*madyakhaṇḍa* 38.30 and *madyakhaṇḍa* 60). The fact that a goddess is invoked as sole protection may indicate that smallpox was known in all its

tions *gardabhī*, an affliction of the windy (*vāta*) and bilious (*pitta*) humours causing 'circular, wide, raised, slightly reddish patch studded with small eruptions' (AHS *uttarasthāna* 31.10b), and *jāla gardabha*, described as a 'śopha (swelling) caused by all the doṣās with the predominance of pitta, spreading from place to place slowly, not undergoing pāka (suppuration/ulceration) coppery in colour and producing fever...' (31.13b–14a). Śītalā and the donkey are not mentioned but the names of these two diseases point at the ass (*gardabha*) as a beast with a long history as a symbol of disease, disorder and impurity.

The so much feared 'spring fever' (*vasanta rog*) was, with all probability, a loose label for all kinds of seasonal ailments affecting humans and animals (cowpox, horsepox, camelpox and various strains of smallpox). Such ailments were believed to be caused by sun rays (and lack of water) and their most evident symptoms were skin ulcerations and high bodily temperature. In fact, most non-orthopox viral diseases are transmitted by insects such as hematophagous flies or worms. The latter, first attested in the *Atharva Veda* as *kṛmi* (Zysk 1993: 63–69), are known as voracious beings whose activity is more noticeable in the spring season, before the monsoon (i.e. *vasanta*). It is worth noting that in Apte's Sanskrit dictionary, the ass is called *kṛmi*. The animal, largely employed for heavy works in the heat of the sun (donkeys were expendable and used until their last breath—as it still happens in South Asia), is one of the main victims not just of 'worms' but of *Trypanosoma evansi*, a blood infection known as surra and transmitted via hematophagous flies. The symptoms of surra are high fevers, fatigue, respiratory deficiency, anaemia, emaciation and lethargy. If untreated, case fatality rate in equines is near 100 percent. Other symptoms of surra are very similar to poxes. They include petechial haemorrhages, hydrothorax, ascites and enlarged lymph nodes (OIE 2009).

To summarize, asses are prone to contracting a number of diseases—some nearly fatal—whose symptoms cause visible ulcerations and/or deformations of the epidermis (including depigmentation and loss of hair). The combination of this with the bellicose nature of the wild ass, its strength and its insatiable sexual appetite might have contributed to identifying this creature with some of the most dreaded diseases (smallpox), and to assigning it to a goddess capable of healing.[24] This interpretation provides a radically new aetiology of folk representations of illness, including the study of deities like Śītalā. Although she is widely known as the 'a disease goddess' or the 'goddess of smallpox', for devotees and ritual specialists, Śītalā is not disease *per se*. Rather she is an *adhiṣṭhātrī*, a controller. By riding—that is, controlling—the ass, Śītalā shows her cooling power over dreadful occurrences (from droughts to infertility and diseases) popularly interpreted as an unnatural state of hotness.

---

virulence from at least the sixteenth century. Bhāva Miśra continues to list *gardabhikā* and *jālagardabha* as *kṣudra roga* (BP *madyakhaṇḍa* 68.150–51).

24. A similar interpretation has been put forth by Dimock (1969: 219) who noted that in the case of the Bengali goddess Ṣaṣṭhī it is her vehicle, the cat, who steals children while the goddess returns them to their mothers.

THE ABSENT DONKEY AND THE FORGIVING MOTHER IN A NORTH INDIAN SHRINE

The Śītalā Dhām ('abode of Śītalā') is one of the most popular sites of worship of the goddess in Uttar Pradesh. Situated on a mound near a small market town called Adalpura, about 25 kilometres from Varanasi, the *baṛī Śītalā mandir* ('temple of the elder Śītalā')—as it is popularly known—is a recent small rectangular structure dating back to the 1970s. The site, however, is with all probability very ancient. The walls of an earlier structure can be dated back to the beginning of the eighteenth century although it seems plausible that the original place of worship might belong to the twelfth century (Singh and Rana 2006: 272). Local informants in Varanasi suggest an even more ancient origin and link the site to an *ādivāsī* (indigenous, 'tribal') settlement. Whatever the origin of Śītalā worship in Adalpura, the existence and resistance of peculiar ritual and iconographic patterns make this place a unique site.

To enter the temple one must pass through a huge gate where invocations to the goddess are displayed in big bold red characters (*jai mā Śītalā*) above a brass bell with two tigers by the sides.[25] Once past the portal, one enters the local bazaar. Mostly dealing in *pūjā* articles (medium and big posters, bandanas, flags, stickers, small figurines for car dashboards, CDs, Video-CDs, and activation codes to get mobile *Śītalā-bhakti-gān* ringtones), the market includes food, tea, *lassī* and juice stalls, toys kiosks, artisans' shops and repair businesses. The village, which is well connected to surrounding cities (Mirzapur, Allahabad, Varanasi) via bus services, has a post office and one bank branch. Villagers belong to different castes (15 or 16 *jātis*) but the Śītalā Dhām is administered exclusively by *mallāh*s (or *niṣādās*), that is, boatmen and fishermen.[26] The population in Adalpura is limited but it rises considerably with every full moon, on the occasion of the monthly celebration of Śītalā, while during the *Navarātri* of Caitra (March-April) and Aśvina (September-October) it may reach half a million (Singh and Rana 2006: 272).

In the premises of the Śītalā Dhām, the goddess is represented according to the traditional iconography, that is, as a pious maiden, fully dressed, holding a pitcher and a broom and riding a large ass. But such images disappear once inside the temple. The Śītalā of Adalpura does not conform to the standard myth. In fact, she is a riverine goddess. Local narratives and devotional songs in Bhojpuri do not mention her mount—a means of transportation she

25. The presence of tigers suggests the association of Śītalā with Durgā, a pan-Hindu goddess successfully established across all strata of South Asian Hindu populations. In the Adalpurā market, Śītalā is even more blatantly associated with *Durgā-pūjā* and her iconography merges with that of Durgā at the point that the 'pox-goddess' is represented as *mahiṣāsuramardiṇī* ('slayer of the buffalo-demon', one of the most popular attributes of Durgā).

26. Śītalā is often related to OBC ('Other Backward Castes') and *ādivāsīs*. In Kṛṣṇarām Dās' *Śītalā-maṅgal-kābya* she is explicitly called 'Lord of the Śūdras' (Stewart 1995: 397).

does not actually need. According to local folklore, the goddess revealed herself to a fisherman (the ancestor of all *mallāhs*) some 400 years ago. She gave indications through *svapna-darśan* (dream apparition) about how to retrieve an ancient *mūrti* lying on the bottom of the river Ganges. The next morning the fisherman threw his net and caught a small anthropomorphic stone image of the goddess. This was positioned in a humble shrine on the banks of the Ganges and there it stayed until the goddess decided it was not a sufficiently decorous place. Hence she appeared again in her devotee's dreams and ordered the building of a proper *mandir*. In exchange she promised protection, good health and fortune.

Although mythical narratives and popular songs do not indulge in detailed descriptions of the *baṛī Śītalā mūrti*, local *mallāh paṇḍits* confirmed to me—and I was able to observe—that the icon has no *vāhana* (Fig. 4). The lack of the ass here is justified by the aquatic nature of Śītalā. The goddess was born and lives in the Ganges and is often identified with the river itself. This is, however, somehow contradicted by one significant detail. Covered with a silver mask and entirely surrounded by marigold garlands, *nīm* (*Azadirachta indica*) branches and red drapes, the *mūrti* of the elder Śītalā is entirely hidden from the sight of devotees. Over the goddess' head hang two silver *chatra* (parasols) while on the background there is a huge silver panel with two columns on each side and carved floral motifs. Below the goddess, at the centre of the panel, is represented a small pot surmounted by a coconut and auspicious *harā pattā* (leaves of *nīm*) while on each side there is the bass-relief of an ass (Fig. 5). When I asked the reason for using images of the goddess that do not find a confirmation in local folklore (*laukik* or *āñcalik saṁskṛti*), I was given contrasting answers. Several informants never considered such issues and some let me clearly understand I was too much concerned with meaningless details, thus spoiling the devotion behind Śītalā worship. Some *mallāh* priests, however, gave me an alternative explanation. Much of the iconographic material reproduced and displayed in the temple and the surrounding bazaar is not a local product. It reflects a 'Hindustani custom'. Adalpura *mahimā* has no mount but, I was told: 'We know that this [indicating a postcard with the goddess on a donkey] is a very popular aspect of Śītalā. And we love it too'. (Fig. 6)

By reflecting on the conversations I had with local *pūjārī*s and *bhaktas*, I realized a profound awareness of and an appreciation for the multiform ways in which the goddess Śītalā is manifested.[27] The spread of a standard iconography is no doubt the result of commercialization and gentrification processes. After all, as I learnt from my informants, 'all good goddesses have a *vāhana*'.

27. The only exception is animal sacrifice (*balidān*). Devotees from most of the Northern Indian sites I visited do not condone *balidān* which is a dominant ritual pattern in the North-east only.

Fig. 4 Baṛī Śītalā, Śītalā Dhām, Adalpura (November 2010). Photo by Fabrizio M. Ferrari.

Fig. 5 Reproduction of the main altar of the Śītalā Dhām. Poster, purchased in Adalpura (November 2010).

Fig. 6 Śītalā riding the ass. Popular poster, purchased in Adalpura (February 2012).

Ass-riding goddesses in the past were scary and dangerous and Śītalā herself is still considered ambiguous. Remnants of these beliefs can still be found in the Bengali *maṅgal-kābya*, in short (Sanskrit) *ślokas* and images where the goddess is naked, prone to wrath and vengeful. However, in practice, Śītalā is a peaceful, caring and motherly figure. In Adalpura the goddess is visualized as a young, good-looking, fair-complexioned maiden. Unlike scriptures that portray her naked (*digambara*, lit. 'sky-clad'), she is decently dressed and beautifully adorned with jewels. In no way does her aspect suggest menace. In the temple there is not even the traditional ritual fan made of oxtail (or peacock feathers) to cool her wrath (a distinctive trait in several *mandirs*). The goddess is cold by nature.

A further particularity of Adalpura is that Śītalā is not principally worshipped as a healing goddess who can also cause illness. I did observe concerned mothers bringing feverish children in front of the goddess' altar for *darśan*. But for the local *mallāh* community, as well as pilgrims from the Varanasi region, Śītalā is most of all an auspicious deity who brings fertility, good luck and prosperity.[28] The worshipping pattern is also different from the extremely ritualized one I observed elsewhere, for instance in nearby Varanasi. *Mallāh pūjārīs* are neither Brahmans nor healers, and their intervention is minimally invasive. The approach to the goddess is personal and direct. In particular, emphasis is laid on forgiveness. Several songs and many narratives revolve around wrongdoing and ways to atone. Devotees present (vegetarian) offerings, make promises and ask the goddess to forgive them for acts that are reputed to attract blame:

> Eh Mother, forgive me!
> Rise again from the Ganges, Mother
> Eh Mother, forgive me!
> Please (*kṛpaya*) bless my family again, Mother
> Eh Mother, forgive me!
> Please come again to my house, Mother
> Eh Mother, forgive me!
> I am coming to beg you, my Mother
> Eh Mother, forgive me!
> I am coming to cleanse your feet, Mother
> Eh Mother, forgive me!
> I'll pay you my respects, my Mother
> Eh Mother, forgive me!
> Being your servant will make my life better
> Eh Mother, forgive me!
> Eh Mother, forgive me![29]

The worship of Śītalā in Adalpura proves an interesting case-study. As a riverine goddess of prosperity and fertility, she does not cause diseases. Indeed she heals—especially children—but this is believed to be part of a larger pattern where healing is a way to restore a disrupted order. Deprived of the ass, Śītalā does not inflict diseases and confirms herself a gentle presence, a benevolent goddess who helps the *mallāh* community of the Varanasi area in the turbulent waters of their difficult lives.

CONCLUSION

In Northern Indian culture, Śītalā and other, perhaps more ancient, 'disease goddesses' have been associated to the ass. Sanskrit and vernacular literary sources have portrayed the animal as impure, demonic and a disease carrier.

28. Her worship is very similar to that of Sarasvatī or Gaṅgā-mā. Conversely there are profound differences with the Bengali Śītalā. There the goddess is not only gentle, caring and motherly. She has also a terrifying and vindictive side. She can be threatening, merciless, violent, ugly and unjust.
29. *e maīyā māph karī*, recorded at Adalpura Śītalā Dhām on 21 November 2012.

The ass is not a talkative mount. It does not display feelings, intentions and dispositions. It is stubborn and abounds in sexual appetite.

Despite such features, the ass—a strong beast of burden and a well-known symbol of fertility—is widely acknowledged as part of Śītalā's standard iconography. Gentrification processes and the reproduction on industrial scale of selected themes have contributed to the domestication of many aspects of regional folklore. It is so that the wild ass tamed by Śītalā becomes a domesticated donkey, a *vāhana* that carries the ambiguous 'smallpox goddess'. This pattern fades when the goddess is worshipped in contexts free from the Durgā-fication that is homogenizing goddess worship across the Subcontinent and when Śītalā expresses community culture, as in Adalpura. Here the goddess is not a threatening, disease-inflicting deity. Worshipped as a gentle female who brings fertility and prosperity to the *mallāhs*, Śītalā is a riverine goddess who is carried by the Ganges, not by an ass. The traditional iconography is accepted as an established pattern, but this does not mean vernacular culture has been obliterated. In the *Baṛī Śītalā Dhām* different representations coexist, and they do not exclude each other.

In this chapter I intended to show that alternative interpretations of established narrative and iconographical patterns are possible. There are still many unexplored elements in Hindu iconography, especially those related to 'folk deities', which may offer new insights into important aspects of South Asian culture. Because of my interest in healing rituals, the goddess Śītalā has attracted my attention since I first met her almost 20 years ago. Although she is profusely mentioned in academic literature, there are elements of her worship that have been neglected. It is the case of the goddess' mount. Rather than being disease *per se*, as assumed by those who repeatedly call her 'smallpox goddess', Śītalā is a cold (healing) force that contrasts hotness, that is, disease and the agents that spread disease. This performance is symbolically rendered by riding the ass, a wild unpredictable thirsty animal associated with a number of dangerous and scarring ailments. If so examined, the goddess Śītalā becomes a far more complex—and strategic—figure in Hindu culture. Complex because she represents a form of control over injustice, unevenness and decay yet strategic because, eventually, she has the power to negotiate health and health-seeking, rather than to just unleash pain.

REFERENCES

Anonymous. 2001. 'Donkey Milk to Be Tried on Humans.' *Times of India. Lucknow*, 26 September 2001, from: http://articles.timesofindia.indiatimes.com/2001-09-26/lucknow/27233965_1_donkey-milk-human-body-trials (accessed 24 October 2011).

Apte, V. S. 1957–1959. *Revised and Enlarged Edition of Prin. V. S. Apte's The Practical Sanskrit-English Dictionary*, 3 vols. Poona: Prasad Prakashan.

Bandhu, Vishva (ed.). 1960–62. *Atharva Veda Saṁhitā*, 4 vols. Hoshiarpur: Vishveshwar-Anand Vedic Research Institute.

Bang, B. G. 1973. 'Current Concepts of the Smallpox Goddess Sitala of West Bengal.' *Man in India* 53(1): 79–104.

Berriedale Keith, A. (trans.). 1967. *Taittirīya Saṃhitā, or the Veda of the Black Yajus School*. Delhi: Motilal Banarsidass.

Bhattacharyya, N. N. 2000. *Indian Demonology: The Inverted Pantheon*. Delhi: Manohar.

Bimali, O. N., and K. L. Joshi (trans.). 2005. *Vāmana purāṇa*. Delhi: Parimal Publications.

Brilliant, L. 2009. 'Sitala and Cultural Concerns.' In L. Brilliant, *The History of Smallpox Eradication*. London: The Wellcome Trust Centre for the History for the History of Medicine at UCL. Podcast retrieved on from: https://itunes.apple.com/gb/itunes-u/history-smallpox-eradication/id390454919 (accessed 10 May 2013).

Bühneman, G. (ed.). 2003. *The Hindu Pantheon in Nepalese Line Drawings: Two Manuscripts of the Pratiṣṭhālakṣaṇasārasamuccaya*. Varanasi: Indica Books.

Burton, R. F., and F. F. Arbuthnot (trans.). 1885. *The Ananga Ranga*. London and Varanasi: Kama Shastra Society.

Cakrabartī, N. 1968. *Bṛat Śītalā maṅgal bā Śītalār jāgaraṇ pālā*. Kalikātā: Tārācānd Dās & Sons.

Caraka Saṁhitā (based on Cakrapāṇi Datta's Āyurveda Dīpikā), 6 vols. 2011. Edited and translated by R. K. Sharma and B. Dash. Varanasi: Chowkhamba Sanskrit Series Office.

Coburn, T. B. 1991. *Encountering the Goddess. A Translation of the Devī-Māhātmiya and a Study of Its Interpretation*. Albany: SUNY Press.

Dehejia, V. 1986. *Yoginī Cult and Temples: A Tantric Tradition*. New Delhi: National Museum.

Dimock, E. C Jr. 1969. 'Manasā, Goddess of Snakes: The Ṣaṣṭhī Myth.' In J. M. Kitagawa and C. H. Long (eds), *Myth and Symbols: Studies in Honor of Mircea Eliade*: 217–26. Chicago: The University of Chicago Press.

Ferrari, F. M. 2010. 'Old Rituals for New Threats: The Post-Smallpox Career of Sitala, the Cold Mother of Bengal.' In C. Brosius and U. Hüsken (eds), *Ritual Matters*: 144–71. London and New York: Routledge.

— Forthcoming. *Religion, Devotion and Medicine in North India: The Healing Power of Śītalā*. London and New York: Bloomsbury.

Filippi, G. G. 2002. 'Il movimento della Devī: un'epidemia di possessione collettiva.' *Annali di Ca' Foscari* 41(3): 191–210.

Goldman, R. P., and S. Sutherland Goldman (trans.). 2006. *Rāmāyaṇa V: Sundara*. New York: New York University Press.

Griffith, R. T. H. (trans.). 1987. *Vājasaneyi Saṃhitā, or the Texts of the White Yajurveda*. Delhi: Munshiram Manoharlal.

Haksar, A. N. D. (trans.). 2006. *Hitopadeśa*. New York: Penguin Books.

Hopkins, D. R. 1983. *The Greatest Killer: Smallpox in History*. Chicago and London: The University of Chicago Press.

Kinsley, D. 1997. *Tantric Visions of the Divine Feminine: The Ten Mahāvidyās*. Berkeley: University of California Press.

Leslie, J. 1991. 'Śrī and Jyeṣṭhā: Ambivalent Role Models for Women.' In J. Leslie (ed.), *Roles and Rituals for Hindu Women*: 107–27. London: Pinter Publishers.

Miśra, B. 1958. *Bhāvaprakāśah*. Translated by Pandit Lalacandraji Vaidya. Delhi: Motilal Banarsidas.

Mitra, R. (ed.). 1870–1879. *Agni-Purāṇa*, 3 vols. Calcutta: Asiatic Society of Bengal.

Monier-Williams, M. 1997. *Sanskrit-English Dictionary*. Delhi: Motilal Banarsidass.

Mukhopadhyay, S. K. 1994. *Cult of Goddess Śītalā in Bengal: An Enquiry into Folk Culture*. Calcutta: Firma KLM.

Müller, M. (trans.). 1966 (1890). *Ṛg Veda Saṁhitā*, 4 vols. Varanasi: Chowkamba Sanskrit Series Office.

Nicholas, R. 2003. *Fruits of Worship: Practical Religion in Bengal*. New Delhi: Chronicle Books.

OIE: Office International des Epizooties. 2009. *Trypanosoma evansi* infections (including surra). *World Organization for Animal Health*, http://www.oie.int/fileadmin/Home/eng/Animal_Health_in_the_World/docs/pdf/TRYPANO_EVANSI_FINAL.pdf (accessed 9 May 2012).

Olivelle, P. (trans.). 2009a. *The Law Code of Manu*. Oxford: Oxford University Press.

Olivelle, P. (trans.). 2009b. *The Pañcatantra: The Book of India's Folk Wisdom*. Oxford: Oxford University Press.

Parpola, A. 2004–2005. 'The Nāsatyas, the Chariot and the Proto-Aryan Religion.' *Journal of Indological Studies* 16/17: 1–63.

Parpola, A., and J. Janhunen. 2011. 'On the Asiatic Wild Asses and their Vernacular Names.' In T. Osada and H. Endo (eds), *Linguistics, Archaeology and the Human Past. Occasional Paper 12*: 59–124. Kyoto: Indus Project—Research Institute for Humanity and Nature.

Pattanaik, D. 2008. *Lakshmi: The Goddess of Wealth and Fortune: An Introduction*. Mumbai: Vakils, Feffer & Simons.

Pollock, S. L. (trans.). 2009. *Rāmāyaṇa II: Ayodhya*. New York: New York University Press.

Sbami Nirmalānanda. (1413BS). *Debadebī o tānder bāhan*, 7th edition. Kolkātā: Bhārat Sevāśram Saṅgha.

Shastri, J. L. (trans.). 1973. *Liṅga Purāṅa*, 5 vols Delhi: Motilal Banarsidass.

Shastri, J. L., and G. V. Tagare (trans.). 1976. *Bhagavata Purana*. 5 vols. Delhi: Motilal Banarsidass.

Shulman, D. D. 1989. 'Outcaste, Guardian, and Trickster: Notes on the Myth of Kāttavarāyan.' In A. Hiltebeitel (ed.), *Criminal Gods and Demon Devotees: Essays on the Guardians of Popular Hinduism*: 35–67. Albany: SUNY Press.

Singh, R. P. B., and P. S. Rana. 2006. *Banaras Region: A Spiritual and Cultural Guide*. Varanasi: Indica Books.

Sonnerat, P. 1782. *Voyage aux Indes orientales et à la Chine*, http://archive.org/stream/voyageauxindeso03sonngoog#page/n4/mode/2up (accessed 9 May 2012).

Slouber, M. J. 2005. 'The Cult of Khaḍgarāvaṇa.' Unpublished MA dissertation, Department of South and Southeast Asian Studies. Berkeley: University of California.

Smith, B. K. 1994. *Classifying the Universe: The Ancient Indian Varṇa System and the Origin of Caste*. Oxford: Oxford University Press.

Stewart, T. K. 1995. 'Encountering the Smallpox Goddess: The Auspicious Song of Śītalā.' In D. S. Lopez, Jr (ed.), *Religions of India in Practice*: 389–97. Princeton, NJ: Princeton University Press.

Suśruta Saṁhitā, 3 vols. 2003. Translated by Kaviraj Kunjalal Bhishagratna and edited by Laxmidhar Dwivedi. Varanasi: Cowkhamba Sanskrit Series Office.

Taluqdar of Oudh. (trans.). 1980. *Matsya Purāṇam*. Delhi: Oriental Reprint.

Tiwari, M. N. 1996. 'Śītalā in Indian Art and Tradition.' *Berliner Indologische Studies* 9/10: 451–62.

Vāgbhaṭa's Aṣṭāṅga Hṛdayam, 3 vols. 2011. Translated by K. R. Shrikantha Murthy. Varanasi: Chowkhamba Sanskrit Series Office.

Visuvalingam, E. 1989. 'Bhairava's Royal Brahmanicide: The Problem of the Mahābrāhmaṇa.' In A. Hiltebeitel (ed.), *Criminal Gods and Demon Devotees: Essays on the Guardians of Popular Hinduism*: 157–229. Albany: SUNY Press.

White, D. G. 2003. *Kiss of the Yogini: 'Tantric Sex' in its South Asian Contexts*. Chicago and London: The University of Chicago Press. http://dx.doi.org/10.7208/chicago/9780226027838.001.0001

Wilson, H. H. (trans.). 2006. *The Vishnu Purana: A System of Hindu Mythology and Tradition*, 6 vols. Cambridge: Read Country Books.

Zysk, K. G. 1993. *Religious Medicine: The History and Evolution of Indian Medicine*. London: Transaction.

Index

Lightning Source UK Ltd.
Milton Keynes UK
UKOW04f1412270414

230688UK00001B/8/P

9 781908 049599